The Railroad Question.

Wᵐ Larrabee

THE

RAILROAD QUESTION

A HISTORICAL AND PRACTICAL TREATISE ON
RAILROADS, AND REMEDIES FOR THEIR ABUSES.

BY
WILLIAM LARRABEE,
LATE GOVERNOR OF IOWA.

———

Salus populi suprema lex.

———
THIRD EDITION.
———

BOOKS FOR LIBRARIES PRESS
FREEPORT, NEW YORK

385.0973
L333

HE
1071
, L332
1971

First Published 1893
Reprinted 1971

INTERNATIONAL STANDARD BOOK NUMBER:
0-8369-5703-2

LIBRARY OF CONGRESS CATALOG CARD NUMBER:
76-150190

PRINTED IN THE UNITED STATES OF AMERICA

88886

Dedication

To the Members of
the Twenty Second
General Assembly
of the State of Iowa,
to whom our
people are indebted
for their wise & efficient
railroad laws, this
book is respectfully
dedicated

PREFACE.

THE people of the United States are engaged in the solution of the railroad problem. The main question to be determined is: Shall the railroads be owned and operated as public or as private property ? Shall these great arteries of commerce be owned and controlled by a few persons for their own private use and gain, or shall they be made highways to be kept under strict government control and to be open for the use of all for a fixed, equal and reasonable compensation?

In a new and sparsely settled country which is rich in natural resources there may be no great danger in pursuing a *laissez-faire* policy in governmental affairs, but as the population of a commonwealth becomes denser, the quickened strife for property and the growing complexity of social and industrial interests make an extension of the functions of the state absolutely necessary to secure protection to property and freedom to the individual.

The American people have shown themselves capable of solving any political question yet presented to them, and the author has no doubt that with full information upon the subject they will find the proper solution of the railroad problem. The masses have an honest purpose and a keen sense of right and wrong. With them a question is not settled until it is settled right.

It must be conceded that of all the great inventions of modern times none has contributed as much to the prosperity and happiness of mankind as the railroad.

Our age is under lasting obligations to Watt and Stephenson and many other heroes of industry who have aided in bringing the railroad to its present state of perfection. Their genius is the product of our civilization, and their legacies should be shared by all the people to the greatest extent possible. An earnest desire to aid in attaining this end has prompted this contribution to the literature on the subject.

The author is not an entire novice in railroad affairs. He has had experience as a shipper and as a railroad promoter, owner and stockholder, and has even had thrust upon him for a short time the responsibility of a director, president and manager of a railroad company. He has, moreover, had every opportunity to familiarize himself with the various phases of the subject during his more than twenty years' connection with active legislation.

He came to the young State of Iowa before any railroad had reached the Mississippi. Engaging early in manufacturing, he suffered all the inconveniences of pioneer transportation, and his experience instilled into him liberal opinions concerning railroads and their promoters. He extended to them from the beginning all the assistance in his power, making not only private donations to new roads, but advocating also public aid upon the ground that railroads are public roads.

As a member of the Iowa Senate he introduced and fathered the bill for the act enabling townships, incorporated towns and cities to vote a five per cent. tax in aid of railroad construction. He favored always such legislation as would most encourage the building of railroads, believing that with an increase of competitive lines the common law and competition could be relied upon to correct abuses and solve the rate problem. He has since become convinced of the falsity of this doctrine, and now realizes the truth of Stephenson's saying that where combination is possible competition is impossible.

It is the object of this work to show that as long as the railroads are permitted to be managed as private property and are used by their managers for speculative purposes or other personal gain, or as long even as they are used with regard only for the interest of stockholders, they are not performing their proper functions; and that they will not serve their real purpose until they become in fact what they are in theory, highways to be controlled by the government as thoroughly and effectually as the common road, the turnpike and the ferry, or the post-office and the custom-house.

This book has been written at such odd hours as the author could snatch from his time, which is largely occupied with other business. He is under obligations to many of our ministers and consuls abroad for statistics and other valuable information concerning foreign railroads, as well as to a number of personal friends for other assistance, consisting chiefly in rendering the railroad literature of Europe accessible to him.

WILLIAM LARRABEE.

Clermont, Iowa, May, 1893.

CONTENTS.

LIST OF AUTHORS AND WORKS CONSULTED AND QUOTED

ACKWORTH, W. M. - - The Railways of England
ADAMS, C. F., Jr. - Railroads, Their Origin and Problems
ADAMS, H. C. - - · - - Public Debts
ADAMS, HENRY - - History of the United States
ATKINSON, EDWARD - - The Distribution of Products
BAGEHOT, WALTER - - The English Constitution
BAKER, C. W. - - Monopolies and the People
BEACH, CHARLES F., JR. - On Private Corporations
BLACKSTONE, W. - Commentaries on Laws of England
BOISTED, C. A. - The Interference Theory of Government
BOLLES, ALBERT S. - - Bankers' Magazine
BONHAM, JOHN M. - Railway Secrecy and Trusts
BRYCE, JAMES - - The American Commonwealth
BUCKLE, H. T. - History of Civilization of England
CAREY, H. C. - - Principles of Social Science
"   "   -   -   -   -   Unity of Law
CARY, M. View of System of Pennsylvania Internal Improvements.
CLOUD, D. C. - - Monopolies and the People
CLEWS, HENRY - Twenty-eight Years in Wall Street
COOLEY, THOMAS M. - Constitutional Limitations
CONGRESSIONAL RECORD.
COMPILATION OF ENGLISH LAWS UPON RAILWAYS.
DABNEY, W. D. - The Public Regulation of Railways
DILLON, SIDNEY - - North American Review
DORN, ALEXANDER - Aufgaben der Eisenbahnpolitik
DRAPER, J. W. - Intellectual Development of Europe
ENCYCLOPEDIA, AMERICAN.
ENCYCLOPEDIA BRITANNICA.
ENCYCLOPÄDIE (ROLL'S) DES EISENBAHNWESENS, 1892.
FINDLAY, GEORGE. Working and Management of English Railways.
FINK, ALBERT - Cost of Railroad Transportation, etc.
FISHER, G. P. - - Outlines of Universal History

13

FISK, JOHN   -   -   -   American Political Ideas
"   "   -   Critical Period of American History
FOREIGN COMMERCE OF AMERICAN REPUBLICS AND COLONIES.
GRAHAM, WM.   -   -   -   Socialism Old and New
GIBBON, EDWARD   -   Decline and Fall of the Roman Empire
GREEN, JOHN K.   -   -   History of English People
GILPIN, WM.   -   -   The Cosmopolitan Railway
GRINNELL, J. B.   -   Men and Events of Forty Years
GUNTON, GEORGE   -   .   Wealth and Progress
GUIZOT, M.   -   -   -   -   History of Civilization
HABOUR, THEODOR   -   Geschichte des Eisenbahnwesens
HADLEY, A. T.   -   -   Railway Transportation
HALL'S LIFE OF PRINCE BISMARCK.
HUDSON, J. T.   -   -   The Railways and the Republic
JEANS, J. S.   -   -   -   -   -   Railway Problems
JERVIS, JOHN B.   -   -   -   -   -   Railway Property
JEVONS, W. S.   -   -   -   Methods of Social Reform
KENT, JAMES   -   -   Commentaries on American Law
KIRKMAN, M. M.   Railway Rates and Government Control
                    and other works.
LECKEY, W. E. H.   -   England in Eighteenth Century
LIEBER, FRANCIS   -   -   -   -   -   Political Ethics
"   "   Civil Liberty and Self-Government
"   "   -   -   -   -   Miscellaneous Essays
LODGE, H. C.   -   -   -   Life of General Washington
MARTINEAU, HARRIET   -   -   -   History of England
MCMASTER, J. B.   -   History of People of United States
MACAULAY, T. B.   -   -   -   History of England
MOTLEY, J. L.   -   -   -   -   The Dutch Republic
"   "   -   -   -   The United Netherlands
PAINE, CHARLES   - ·   The Elements of Railroading
PATTEN, J. H.   -   Natural Resources of the United States
PEFFER, W. A.   -   -   -   The Farmer's Side
POOR'S RAILWAY MANUAL.
PORTER, HORACE   -   -   -   North American Review
RAWLINSON, GEORGE   -   -   Seven Great Monarchies
REDFIELD   -   -   -   -   On Law of Railways
RECORDS OF CENTRAL IOWA TRAFFIC ASSOCIATION, 1886-1887.
RECORDS OF ASSOCIATION OF GENERAL FREIGHT AGENTS OF
   THE WEST.

RECORDS OF JOINT WESTERN CLASSIFICATION COMMITTEES.
REPORTS OF STATE BOARDS OF COMMISSIONERS.
REPORT OF HEPBURN COMMITTEE.
REPORTS OF UNITED STATES CENSUS.
REPORT OF WINDOM COMMITTEE.
REPORT OF BANKERS' ASSOCIATION, 1892.
REPORT OF CULLOM COMMITTEE.
ROEMER, JEAN - - Origin of English People, etc.
REUBEAUX, F. - - Der Weltverkehr und seine Mittel
RICHARDSON, D. N. - - A Girdle Round the Earth
ROGERS, JAMES E. THOROLD. Economic Interpretation of
        History.
ROSCHER, WM. - - - Political Economy
SCHREIBER - - - Die Preussischen Eisenbahnen
SCHURZ, CARL - - - Life of Henry Clay
SMITH, ADAM - - - - Wealth of Nations
SPELLING, T. CARL - - - On Private Corporations
SPENCER, HERBERT - - - Synthetic Philosophy
STERN, SIMON. Constitutional History and Political Devel-
        opment of the United States.
STICKNEY, A. B. - - - The Railroad Problem
STATISTIQUES DES CHEMINS DE FER DE L' EUROPE, 1882.
TAYLOR, HANNIS. Origin and Growth of the English Con-
        stitution.
THE AMERICAN RAILWAY. Published by Charles Scribner's
        Sons.
VERSCHOYLE, REV. J. - History of Ancient Civilization
VON WEBER, M. M. - Privat-, Staats- und Reichs-Bahnen
   "   "   "   " - Nationalität und Eisenbahn Politik
VON DER LEGEN, ALFRED. Die Nordamerikanischen Eisen-
        bahnen.
WALKER, ALDACE F. - - - - - The Forum
WEEDEN, W. B. Economic and Social History of New
        England.

THE RAILROAD QUESTION.

CHAPTER I.

WHILE the prosperity of a country depends largely upon its productiveness, the importance of proper facilities for the expeditious transportation and ready exchange of its various products can scarcely be overrated. The free circulation of commercial commodities is as essential to the welfare of a people as is the unimpaired circulation of the blood to the human organism.

The interest taken by man in the improvement of the roads over which he must travel is one of the chief indications of civilization, and it might even be said that the condition of the roads of a country shows the degree of enlightenment which its people have reached. The trackless though very fertile regions of Central Africa have for thousands of years remained the seat of savages; but no nation that established a system of public thoroughfares through its dominion ever failed to make a distinguished figure in the theater of the world. There are some authors who go even so far as to call the high roads of commerce the pioneers of enlightenment and political eminence. It is true that as roads and canals developed the commerce of Eastern Asia and Europe, the attention of their people was turned to those objects which distinguish cultured nations and lead to political consequence among the powers of the world. The systems of roads

and canals which we find among those ancients who
achieved an advanced state of civilization might well put
to shame the roads which disgraced not a few of the
European states as late as the eighteenth century.

Among the early nations of Asia of whose internal
affairs we have any historic knowledge are the Hindoos,
the Assyrians and Babylonians, the Phœnicians, the Per-
sians and the Chinese.

The wealth of India was proverbial long before the
Christian era. She supplied Nineveh and Babylon, and
later Greece and Rome, with steel, zinc, pearls, precious
stones, cotton, silk, sugar-cane, ivory, indigo, pepper,
cinnamon, incense and other commodities. If we accept
the testimony of the Vedas, the religious books of the
ancient Hindoos, a high degree of culture must have prevailed on the shores of the Ganges more than three thousand years ago. Highways were constructed by the state
and connected the interior of the realm with the sea and
the countries to the northeast and northwest. For this
purpose forests were cleared, hills leveled, bridges built
and tunnels dug. But the broad statesmanship of the
Hindoo did not pause here. To administer to the convenience and comfort of the wayfaring public, and thus still
more encourage travel and the exchange of commodities,
the state proceeded to line these public roads with shade
trees, to set out mile-stones, and to establish stations
provided with shady seats of repose, and wells at which
humane priests watered the thirsty beasts.

At intervals along these routes were also found commodious and cleanly-kept inns to give shelter to the
traveler at night. Buddha, the great religious reformer
of the Hindoos, commended the roads and mountain
passes of the country to the care of the pious, and the

Greek geographers speak with high praise of the excellence of the public highways of Hindostan.

Among the Babylonians and Assyrians agriculture, trade and commerce flourished at an almost equally remote period. The ancient inhabitants of Mesopotamia cultivated the soil with the aid of dikes and canals, and were experts in the manufacture of delicate fabrics, as linen, muslin and silk. To them is attributed the invention, or at least the perfection, of the cart, and the first use of domestic animals as beasts of burden. Their cities had well-built and commodious streets, and the roads which connected them with their dependencies aided to make them the busy marts of Southeastern Asia.

During the later Babylonian Empire immense lakes were dug for retaining the water of the Euphrates, whence a net-work of canals distributed it over the plains to irrigate the land; and quays and breakwaters were constructed along the Persian Gulf for the encouragement of commerce. While highways among the Babylonians served the development of agriculture and the exchange of industrial commodities, they were constructed chiefly for strategic purposes by the more war-like Assyrians, whose many wars made a system of good roads a necessity. The Greek geographer Pausanias was shown a well-kept military road upon which Memnon was said to have marched with an Assyrian army from Susa to Troy to rescue King Priam. Traces of this road, called by the natives "Itaki Atabeck," may be seen to this day.

The Phœnicians, who were the first of the great historic maritime nations of antiquity, occupied the narrow strip of territory between the mountains of Northern Palestine and the Mediterranean Sea. From their situation they learned to rely upon the sea as their principal highway.

They transported to the islands of the Mediterranean as
well as the coast of Northern Africa and Southern Europe
heavy cargoes consisting of the product of their own skill
and industry as well as of the manifold exports of the east.
They sailed even beyond the "Pillars of Hercules" into
the Atlantic Ocean and the North Sea. Through their hands
"passed the gold and pearls of the east and the purple
of Tyre, slaves, ivory, lion and panther skins from the
interior of Africa, frankincense from Arabia, the linen of
Egypt, the pottery and fine wares of Greece, the copper
of Cyprus, the silver of Spain, tin from England, and iron
from Elba."

But while the Phœnicians for their commercial intercourse with other nations relied chiefly upon the sea, the
great highway of nature, they neglected by no means road-
building at home. They connected their great cities, Sidon
and Tyre, by a coast road, which they extended in time as
far as the Isthmus of Suez. They also established great
commercial routes by which their merchants penetrated
the interior of Europe and Asia. Caravan roads extended
south to Arabia and east to Mesopotamia and Armenia,
penetrating the whole Orient as far as India, and even
the frontiers of China. The Phœnicians thus became the
traders of antiquity, Tyre being the link between the east
and the west.

The Persian Empire, which under Darius stretched
from east to west for a distance of 3,000 miles and comprised no less than two million square miles, with a population of seventy or eighty millions, had, with the exception of the Romans, perhaps the best system of roads
known to ancient history. Indeed, it is doubtful whether
without it such a vast empire, more than half as large as
modern Europe, could have been held together. Each

satrap, or prefect of a province, was obliged to make regular reports to the king, who was also kept informed by spies of what was taking place in every part of the empire. To aid the administration of the government, postal communication for the exclusive use of the king and his trusted servants connected the capital with the distant provinces. This postal service was, four or five centuries later, patterned after by the Romans. From Susa to Sardes led a royal road along which were erected caravansaries at certain intervals. Over this road, 1,700 miles long, the couriers of the king rode in six or seven days. Under Darius the roads of the empire were surveyed and distances marked by means of mile-stones, many of which are still found on the road which led from Ecbatana to Babylon. These roads crossed the wildest regions of that great monarchy. They connected the cities of Ionia with Sardes in Lydia, with Babylon and with the royal city of Susa; they led from Syria into Mesopotamia, from Ecbatana to Persepolis, from Armenia into Southern Persia, and thence to Bactria and India.

The Chinese commenced road-building long before the Christian era. They graded the roadway and then covered the whole with hewn blocks of stone, carefully jointed and cemented together so that the entire surface presented a perfectly smooth plane. Such roads, although very costly to build, are almost indestructible by time. In China, as well as in several other countries of Asia, the executive power has always charged itself with both the construction and maintenance of roads and navigable canals. In the instructions which are given to the governors of the various provinces these objects, it is said, are constantly commended to them, and the judgment which the court forms of the conduct of each is very much regulated by the attention which he appears to have paid to this part of his instructions. This solicitude of the sovereign for the internal thoroughfares is easily accounted for when it is considered that his revenue arises almost entirely from a land-tax, or rent, which rises and falls with the increase and decrease of the annual produce of the land. The greatest interest of the sovereign, his revenue, is therefore directly connected with the cultivation of the land, with the extent of its produce and its value. But in order to render that produce as great and as valuable as possible, it is necessary to procure for it as extensive a market as possible, and, consequently, to establish the freest, the easiest and the least expensive communication between all the different parts of the country, which can be done only by means of the best roads and the best navigable canals.

In Africa the Egyptians and Carthaginians are the only nations of antiquity of which we have much historic knowledge. The former kept up a very active commerce not only with the south, but also with the tribes of Lydia on the west and with Palestine and the adjoining countries on the east. To facilitate commerce, they constructed and maintained a number of excellent highways leading in all directions. One of the most important among these was the old royal road on the coast of the Mediterranean Sea, or the "Road of the Philistines" of the Scriptures. This road crossed the Isthmus of Suez and led through the land of the Philistines and Samaria to Tyre and Sidon. Another road led, in a northwesterly direction, from Rameses to Pelusium. This, however, crossed marshes, lagoons and a whole system of canals, and was used only by travelers without baggage, while the Pharaohs, accompanied by their horses, chariots and troops, preferred the former road. A third road led from Coptos, on the Nile, to Berenice, on the Red Sea. There were between these two cities ten stations, about twenty-five miles apart from each other, where travelers might rest with their camels each day, after traveling all night, to avoid the heat. Still another road led from the town of Babylon, opposite Memphis, along the east bank of the Nile, into Nubia. Much of the commerce of Egypt in ancient times, as in our day, was conducted on the Nile and its canals. The boatman and the husbandman were, in fact, the founders of the gentle manners of the people who flourished four thousand years ago in the blessed valley of the Nile. There is one canal among the many which deserves special mention. It flowed from the Bitter Lakes into the Red Sea near the city of Arsinoe. It was first cut by Sesostris before the Trojan times, or, according to other writers, by the son of Psammitichus, who only began the work and then died. Darius I. set about to complete it, but gave up the undertaking when it was nearly finished, influenced by the erroneous opinion that the level of the Red Sea was higher than Egypt, and that if the whole of the intervening isthmus were cut through, the country would be overflowed by the sea. The Ptolemaic kings, however, did cut it through and placed locks upon the canal.

Carthage was a Phœnician colony. The city was remarkable for its situation. It was surrounded by a very fertile territory and had a harbor deep enough for the anchorage of the largest vessels. Two long piers reached out into the sea, forming a double harbor, the outer for merchant ships and the inner for the navy. This ·city early became the head of a North African empire, and her fleets plied in all navigable waters known

to antiquity, Her navy was the largest in the world, and
in the sea-fight with Regulus comprised three hundred
and fifty vessels, carrying one hundred and fifty thousand
men. Though we have but meager accounts of the
internal affairs of Carthage, there can be no doubt that
much attention was given, both at home and in the colonies, to the construction of highways, which were
distinguished for their solidity. It is said that the
Romans learned from the Carthaginians the art of paving
roads.

European history began in Greece, the civilization of
whose people passed to the Romans and from them to the
other Aryan nations which have played an important role in
the great historical drama of modern times. The physical
features of the Balkan Peninsula were an important factor
in the formation of the character of its inhabitants. The
coast has a large number of well-protected bays, most of
which form good harbors. Navigation and commerce
were greatly stimulated in a country thus favored by
Nature. Nearly all the principal cities of Hellas could be
reached by ships, and the need of internal thoroughfares
was but little felt. Nevertheless, public highways connected all of the larger towns with the national sanctuaries
and oracles, as Olympia, the Isthmus, Delphi and Dodona.
Athens, after the Persian wars the metropolis of Greece,
was by the so-called Long Walls connected with the
Piræus, its harbor. This highway, protected by high
walls built two hundred yards apart, was over four miles
long, and enabled the Athenians, as long as they held
the command of the sea, to bring supplies to their city,
even when it was surrounded by an enemy on the land.

Rome is the connecting link between antiquity and
mediævalism. The great empire sprang from a single

city, whose power and dominion grew until it comprised
every civilized nation living upon the three continents then
known. Under the emperors, the Roman empire extended
from the Atlantic to the Euphrates, a distance of more
than three thousand miles, and from the Danube
and the English Channel to the cataracts of the Nile
and the Desert of Sahara. Its population was from
eighty to one hundred and twenty millions. The empire
was covered with a net-work of excellent roads, which
stimulated, together with the safety and peace which
followed the civil wars, traffic and intercourse between the
different regions united under the imperial government.
More than 50,000 miles of solidly constructed highways
connected the various provinces of this vast realm. There
was one great chain of communication of 4,080 Roman miles
in length from the Wall of Antoninus in the northwest to
Rome, and thence to Jerusalen, a southeastern point of
the empire. There were several thousand miles of road
in Italy alone. Rome's highways were constructed for the
purpose of facilitating military movements, but the benefits
which commerce derived from them cannot easily be
overestimated. These military roads were usually laid
out in straight lines from one station to another. Natural
obstacles were frequently passed by means of very extensive works, as excavations, bridges, and, in some instances, long tunnels. The resources of the Roman Empire were
almost inexhaustible, and no public expenditures were larger than those made on account of the construction of new
roads. The fact that many of these roads have borne the
traffic of almost two thousand years without material injury
is abundant proof of the unsurpassed solidity of their construction. The Roman engineers always secured a firm
bottom, which was done, when necessary, by ram-

ming the ground with small stones, or fragments of
brick. Upon this foundation was placed a pavement
of large stones, which were firmly set in cement. These
stones were sometimes square, but more frequently irregular. They were, however, always accurately fitted to
each other. Many varieties of stone were used, but the
preference was given to basalt. Where large blocks could
not be conveniently obtained, small stones of hard
quality were sometimes cemented together with lime,
forming a kind of concrete, of which masses extending
to a depth of several feet are still in existence. The
strength of the pavements is illustrated by the fact that
the substrata of some have been so completely washed
away by water, without disturbing the surface, that a
man may creep under the road from side to side while
carriages pass over the pavement as over a bridge. The
roads were generally raised above the ordinary surface of
the ground. They frequently had two wagon-tracks,
which were separated by a raised foot-path in the center,
and blocks of stone at intervals, to enable travelers to
mount on horseback. Furthermore, each mile was marked
by a numbered post, the distance being counted from
the gate of the wall of Servius. The mile-post was at
first a roughly hewn stone, which in time was exchanged
for a monument, especially in the vicinity of Rome and
other large cities. The most celebrated road of Italy,
which has always excited the admiration of the student of
antiquity, was the Via Appia, the remains of which are
still an object of wonder. It was first built from Rome to
Capua by Appius Claudius Cæcus in the fourth century
before Christ, and was afterwards continued as far as
Brundusium. It was broad enough for two carriages to
pass each other, and was built of solid stone. The stones

were hewn sharp and smooth, and their corners fitted into one another without the aid af any connecting material, so that, according to Procopius, the whole appeared to be one natural stone. Each side of the street had a high border for foot-passengers, on which were also placed alternately seats and mile-stones. In spite if its age and heavy traffic parts of this road are still in a good state of preservation. After the completion of the Via Appia similar roads were constructed, so that under the emperors seven great highways started from Rome, viz. : the Via Appia and Latina to the south; two, Valeria and Salaria, to the Adriatic; two, Cassia and Aurelia, to the north-west; and the Via Æmilia, serving for both banks of the Po.

Nor were the provinces by any means neglected. During the last Punic war a paved road was constructed from Spain through Gaul to the Alps, and similar roads were afterwards built in every part of Spain and Gaul, through Illyricum, Macedonia and Thrace, to Constantinople, and along the Danube to its mouths on the Black Sea. So, likewise, were the islands of Sardinia, Corsica, Sicily and Great Britain crossed by them. It has justly been said that the roads of the Roman Empire, whose strong network enlaced the known world, were the architectural glory of its people. These military roads caused in the various parts of the empire a wonderful social and commercial revolution. They made it possible for civilization to penetrate into the most remote retreats and to conquer their inhabitants more completely than could Cæsar at the ·head of his legions.

The Romans also had an efficient postal service, which was first instituted by Augustus and greatly improved by Hadrian. The former, as Gibbon states in his ''Decline and Fall of the Roman Empire," placed upon all roads leading away from the golden milestone of the Forum, at short distances, relays of young men to serve as couriers, and later provided vehicles to hurry information from the provinces. These posts facilitated communication through all parts of the empire, and while they were originally established in the interest of the government, they proved serviceable to individuals as well, for there is no doubt that, together with the official dispatches, every courier carried private letters also.

The expenses of the post were largely defrayed by the cities through which it passed, these cities being obliged to provide the stations established within their territories with the necessary stores. At the principal stations were found inns, where the proprietors were held responsible for injuries suffered by travelers while in their houses.

The communication of the Roman Empire was scarcely less free and open by sea than it was by land. Italy has by nature few safe harbors, but the energy and industry of the Romans corrected the deficiencies of nature by the construction of several artificial ports.

After the downfall of the Roman Empire its roads were either destroyed by the people through whose territories they led or by the conquerors, to render more difficult the approach of an enemy.

Civilization and commerce greatly suffered through the downfall of Rome, and did not again revive until after the struggles of the Northern Christian races with the Southern and Eastern nations, which had become Mohammedan. The sixth and seventh centuries were the darkest in the history of Europe. Charlemagne, toward the close of the eighth century, caused many of the old Roman roads to be repaired and new ones to be constructed. He, as well as several of his immediate successors, made use of mounted messengers to send imperial mandates from one part of the realm to the other. The rulers of the succeeding centuries did not profit, however, by this example, and the roads of the empire again fell into decay. Moreover, the public safety was greatly impaired by robbers and feudal knights, whose depredations were so heavy a tax upon commerce as to greatly discourage it. Trade under these circumstances would have been entirely destroyed, had it not been for the merchants' unions which were formed by the larger cities for the protection of their interests. These organizations maintained the most important thoroughfares, and even furnished armed escorts to wayfaring merchants. Commerce thus flourished in, and commercial relations were kept up among, the cities immediate between Venice and Genoa, as well as the cities on the Rhine and Danube. Florence, Verona, Milan, Strasburg, Mayence, Augsburg, Ulm, Ratisbon, Vienna and Nuremberg were flourishing marts, and through them flowed the currents of trade between the north and the south. Out of these commercial unions grew in time the Hanseatic League, which from the thirteenth to the fifteenth century controlled the commerce of the northern part of Europe on both the water and the land. The object of this league, which at the height of its power included eighty-five cities, was to protect its members against the feudal lords on the land and against pirates on the sea. Its power extended from Norway to Belgium and from England to Russia. In all the principal towns on the highways of commerce the flag of the Hansa floated over its counting houses. Wherever its influence reached, its members controlled roads, mines, agriculture and manufactures. It often dictated terms to kings, and almost succeeded in monopolizing the trade of Europe north of Italy.

It is characteristic of the social and political condition of this time that the postal service was not carried on by the state, but was in the hands of the various municipalities, convents and universities. During the fifteenth and sixteenth centuries national power and national life made themselves felt, and with a change in the political system the system of communication and transportation changed also. Louis XI. of France took the first step toward making a nation of the French when he transferred the postal service from the cities and other feudal authorities to the state. Two or three centuries later, France obtained a national system of roads and canals. The idea was largely due to Colbert, the minister of Louis XIV. It was, however, not executed in detail until the middle of the last century. Many abuses grew up in connection with it, but on the whole it was probably the soundest and most efficient part of the French administration. A system of lines of communication, radiating from Paris, was constructed by skilled engineers, and placed under the supervision of men of talent, especially trained for the purpose at the Ecôle des Ponts et Chaussées. The whole system was further improved by Napoleon, and has served as a basis for the present system of railroad supervision.

The first artificial waterway constructed in France was the Languedoc Canal, connecting the Bay of Biscay with the Mediterranean. This gigantic work, designed by Riquet, was commenced in 1666, and completed in 1681. The canal is 148 miles long and its summit level is 600 feet above the sea, the works along its line embracing over one hundred locks and fifty aqueducts. A large number of canals have since been constructed, and France has at present over 4,000 miles of artificial waterways, or more than any other country of Europe. Nowhere else was the same completeness of organization possible. The regular mail service of Germany dates back to the year of 1516, when Emperor Maximilian established a postal route between Brussels and Vienna and made Francis Count of Taxis Imperial Postmaster-General. The postal service of the empire greatly improved up to the time of the Thirty Years' War, which completely demoralized it. After the war the individual states and free cities, usurping imperial prerogatives, established postal routes of their own and thereby crippled the national service. The same war also did great damage to the public thoroughfares, and the commercial and manufacturing interests of the German empire were until the end of the eighteenth century in a deplorable condition. Frederick the Great, recognizing the fact that the industrial paralysis of Germany was owing chiefly to its defective means of communication, commenced to construct turnpikes and canals in Prussia, and the minor German princes one by one imitated his example, until the Napoleonic wars again put an end to internal improvements. The good work was resumed, however, after the downfall of Napoleon, and in 1830 Germany was intercrossed by from three to four thousand miles of turnpike.

In the Netherlands canals were constructed as early as the twelfth century. Being particularly well adapted to the flat country of Holland, they were rapidly extended until they connected all the cities, towns and villages of the country, and to a large extent took the place of roads. The largest canal of Holland is the one which connects the city of Amsterdam with the North Sea. It

was constructed between the years of 1819 and 1825 at
an expense of more than four million dollars. The city
of Amsterdam owes to this canal its present commercial
prosperity.

Public roads and the state postal service are of comparatively recent origin in Great Britain. The first public postal route was established in 1635, during the reign
of Charles I. In 1678 a public stage-coach route was
established between Edinburgh and Glasgow. The distance is only forty-four miles, but the roads were so bad
that, though the coach was drawn by six able horses, the
journey took three days. It was considered a great
improvement when in 1750 it could be completed in half
the time originally required. In 1763 a mail-coach made
only monthly trips between London and Edinburgh, eight
long days being required for the journey, which to-day is
made in less than twelve hours. The number of stage
passengers between these two capitals averaged about
twenty-five a month, and rose to fifty on extraordinary
occasions. In those days coaches were very heavy and
without springs, and travelers not unfrequently cut short
their journeys for want of conveniences.

Turnpikes in Great Britain do not even date as far
back as stage-coaches. It is true the first turnpike act
was passed as early as 1653, but the system was not
extensively adopted until a century later. Previous to
that time the roads of England, such as they were,
were maintained by parish and statute labor. In the latter half of the last century, under improved methods of
construction, turnpike roads multiplied rapidly. Both
roads and vehicles attained, previous to the advent of the
railroads, such a degree of perfection that the stage-coach
made the journey between London and Manchester, 178

miles, in 19 hours; between London and Liverpool, 203 miles, in less than 21 hours; and between London and Holyhead, 261 miles, in less than 27 hours.

In spite of these improved facilities, the transportation of merchandise continued to be very expensive. Goods had to be conveyed from town to town by heavy wagons, and the cost of land-carriage between Manchester and Liverpool, a distance of thirty miles, was at times as high as forty shillings per ton.

The various disadvantages of land transportation directed, toward the middle of the last century, the attention of the British people to the importance of a system of canals. They realized that these water highways would open an easier and cheaper communication between distant parts of the country, thus enabling manufacturers to collect their materials and fuel from remote districts with less labor and expense, and to convey their goods to a more distant and more profitable market. It would also facilitate the conveyance of farm produce to a greater distance and would thereby benefit both the producer and consumer. The canal era was formally inaugurated in 1761, when the Duke of Bridgewater presented to Parliament a petition for a bill to construct the canal which has since borne his name. The canal was commenced in 1767 and was completed in 1772. The next forty years were a period of great activity in canal building, but it was left to private enterprise, with very little aid from the government. Over a hundred canal acts were passed by Parliament before the year 1800. The largest canal of the British Isles is the Caledonian, extending from Inverness to Fort William, a distance of sixty-three miles. It was commenced in 1803 and completed in 1847, and cost £1,256,000. Other canals of importance are the Great Canal, which connects the North

Sea with the Atlantic Ocean, and the Grand Function Canal, which is over one hundred miles long and connects most of the water-ways of central England with the Thames River. It is estimated that there were over 2,200 miles of navigable canals in Great Britain before the introduction of railroads.

Canal-building in Spain dates back to the beginning of the sixteenth century, when Charles V. built the Imperial Canal of Aragon, which is over sixty miles long. The political and commercial decline of the country during the seventeenth and eighteenth centuries, however, brought the development of her highways to a standstill, and, with the exception of Turkey, probably no European country has at the present time more deficient transportation facilities than Spain.

The comparatively high state of civilization which existed in the Italian cities during the middle ages, their commercial and industrial thrift and the importance of Rome as the metropolis of the Catholic Church combined to maintain many of the excellent ancient highways of Italy. A number of canals were built in Northern Italy as early as the fifteenth century, and it is claimed by some writers that locks were first used on the Milanese canals in 1497. But while public thoroughfares have always been well maintained in Northern Italy and even as far south as Naples, they were during the past two or three centuries permitted to greatly deteriorate in the southern part of the peninsula, to the great detriment of both agriculture and commerce. The condition of the large Italian islands is still more lamentable, Sicily and Sardinia being almost entirely devoid of roads. She that was the granary of ancient Rome to-day scarcely produces enough grain to supply her own people.

Denmark and the Scandinavian peninsula had a good system of highways long before the railroad era. Among the many excellent canals of Sweden may be mentioned the Göta Canal, which was commenced by Charles XII. in the early part of the last century, but was not entirely completed until 1832. It is, inclusive of the lakes, 118 miles long, and its construction cost \$3,750,000, three-fifths of which was contributed by the state. This canal connects the Baltic Sea with Lake Wener, as well as, through the Göta-Elf, with the North Sea.

Next to Turkey and Spain, no country of Europe has been as slow to appreciate the advantages of a system of highways as Russia. At the beginning of the nineteenth century the vast empire of the Czar had but a few roads connecting its principal cities, and these were almost impassable in the spring and fall. Much progress has, however, been made since then, and at present Russia has over 75,000 miles of wagon-road and artificial water-way, and 19,000 miles of railroad. A road has been built through Siberia, extending from the Ural Mountains to the city of Jakutsk on the Lena and sending out many branch roads north and south. The development of Russia's resources has kept pace with that of her system of highways, and the agricultural and mineral products of that country are in the markets of the world constantly gaining ground in their competition with the products of Western Europe and America.

Passing now to the Western Hemisphere, we find that in ancient Peru the Incas built great roads, the remains of which still attest their magnificence. Probably the most remarkable were the two which extended from Quito to Cuzco, and thence on toward Chile, one passing over the great Plateau, the other following the coast.

Humboldt, in his "Aspects of Nature," says of this mountain road : "But what above all things relieves the severe aspect of the deserts of the Cordilleras are the remains, as marvelous as unexpected, of a gigantic road, the work of the Incas. In the pass of the Andes between Mausi and Loja we found on the plain of Puttal much difficulty in making a way for the mules over a marshy piece of ground, while for more than a German mile our sight continually rested on the superb remains of a paved road of the Incas, twenty feet wide, which we marked resting on its deep foundations, and paved with well-cut, dark porphyritic stone. This road was wonderful and does not fall behind the most imposing Roman ways which I have seen in France, Spain and Italy. By barometrical observation I found that this colossal work was at an elevation of 12,440 feet." The length of this road, of which only parts remain, is variously estimated at from 1,500 to 2,000 miles. It was built of stone and was, in some parts at least, covered with a bituminous cement, which time had made harder than the stone itself. All the difficulties which a mountainous country presents to the construction of roads were here overcome. Suspension bridges led over mountain torrents, stairways cut in the rock made possible the climbing of steep precipices, and mounds of solid masonry facilitated the crossing of ravines. Under the rule of the Spaniards the roads of the Incas went to ruin. In fact, throughout South America but little, if anything, was done by the mother country to aid transportation.

North America, or at least that part of it which was settled by the Anglo-Saxon race, fared much better in this respect. The great utility of good roads was universally recognized even in the colonial times, but the scarcity of capital, the great extent of territory as compared with the population, and the want of harmonious action among the various colonies, delayed extensive road and canal building until after the establishment of the Union. Mistaken local interests but too often wrecked well-advanced plans, and what road-building was done during the colonial times was almost entirely left to individual exertion, without any direct aid from the government. The first American turnpike was built in Pennsylvania in 1790. From there the system extended into New York and Southern New England. Up to 1822 more than six million dollars had been expended in Pennsylvania for turnpikes, one-third of which sum, or over $1,000 a mile, had been contributed by the commonwealth.

In 1800 three wagon-roads connected the Atlantic coast with the country west of the Alleghanies, one leading from Philadelphia to Pittsburg, one from the Potomac to the Monongahela, and a third passed through Virginia to Knoxville, in Tennessee. Much as was done during this period for the improvement of the roads, stage-coach travel remained for years comparatively slow. In 1792 Mr. Jefferson, then Secretary of State, wrote to the Postmaster-General to know if the post, which was then carried at the rate of fifty miles a day, could not be expedited to one hundred. Even this latter rate was considered slow on the great post-roads forty years later. In the year 1800 one general mail-route was extended from Maine to Georgia, the trip being made in twenty days. From Philadelphia a line went to Lexington in sixteen and to Nashville in twenty-two days. The government of the United States, appreciating the importance, for military purposes, of good roads leading to the frontiers, commenced the construction of national, or military, roads. A road was thus built from Baltimore through Cincinnati to St. Louis, and another from Bangor to Houlton, in Maine. In 1807 Albert Gallatin, Secretary of the Treasury, advocated the extensive construction of public roads and canals by the general government. Mr. Gallatin took the ground that the inconveniences, complaints, and perhaps dangers, resulting from a vast extent of territory cannot otherwise be radically removed than by opening speedy and easy communications through all its parts; that good roads and canals would shorten distances, facilitate commercial and personal intercourse, and unite by a still more intimate community of interests the most remote quarters of the United States, and that no other single operation within the power of the government could more effectually tend to strengthen and perpetuate that union which secured external independence, domestic peace and internal liberty. The principal improvements recommended by Mr. Gallatin were the following:

1. Canals opening an inland navigation from Massachusetts to North Carolina.

2. Improvement of the navigation of the four great Atlantic rivers, including canals parallel to them.

3. Great inland navigation by canals from the North River to Lake Ontario.

4. Inland navigation from the North River to Lake Champlain.

5. Canal around the Falls and Rapids of Niagara.

6. A great turnpike road from Maine to Georgia, along the whole extent of the Atlantic sea-coast.

7. Four turnpike roads from the four great Atlantic rivers across the mountains to the four corresponding Western rivers.

8. Improvement of the roads to Detroit, St. Louis and New Orleans.

Mr. Gallatin also recommended that a sufficient number of local improvements, consisting either of roads or canals, be undertaken so as to do substantial justice to all parts of the country. The expenditure necessary for these improvements was estimated at twenty million dollars. Local jealousy and State rights prejudice practically defeated this movement, the Cumberland road, or National Pike, being the only result of any importance. The failure of the government to provide the country with adequate roads left the construction of turnpike roads to private enterprise, and these roads, before the general introduction of railroads, often yielded much profit to capitalists. Great as were the conveniences afforded by the turnpike, they were entirely inadequate for the development of the resources of the interior of the country. The products of a forest or a mine could not be transported upon them to any great extent. The crossing of a single water-shed, owing to the necessity for largely increased motive power, would often materially decrease the value of the goods to be transported.

These drawbacks of land transportation directed, toward the close of the last century, the attention of the people of the United States to the necessity of providing for a system of canals that should bind together the various parts of their extended country in the interest of commerce. General Washington was among the first to urge upon his countrymen the introduction of this great highway of inter-state traffic, although but little was done in this direction until after the War of 1812. The people of New York had from an early period of the settlement of their State been impressed with the importance of con-

necting the Hudson with the Western lakes. In 1768 the
provincial legislature discussed this subject, but the
political agitations of the times and the following
revolutionary struggle arrested further proceedings.
After the war the project was frequently brought
before the legislature, but nothing was done until 1808,
when the assembly appointed a committee to investigate
the subject and to solicit the coöperation of the general
government, if the project should be found practicable.
The report of the committee concerning the practicability
of the undertaking was in every respect favorable, and
in 1810 the legislature provided for a survey of the entire
route from the Hudson River to Lake Erie. The survey
was made, but, the expected aid from the national government not being forthcoming, the matter rested until
after the war with England. In 1816 a new board of
commissioners was appointed, and the following year an
act was passed providing for a system of internal
improvements in the State. On the 4th day of July next
the excavation of the Erie Canal was commenced, and on
the 26th of October, 1825, the first boat passed from
Lake Erie to the Hudson. The canal was 378 miles long
and four feet deep. It had a width of 40 feet at the
surface and 28 feet on the bottom, and carried boats of
76 tons burden. Owing to the rapid increase of trade, the
capacity of the canal was found inadequate within ten
years after its opening, and in 1835 measures were taken
to enlarge it to a width of 70 and 56 feet by a depth of
seven feet, thus allowing the passage of boats of 240 tons.
The total length of the canal was, however, subsequently
shortened 12½ miles, making its present length 365½
miles. This enlargement was completed in 1862, and
cost the State over $7,000,000, making the total cost

of the canal about $50,000,000. New York has, inclusive of branches, some ten other canals in operation, among them the Champlain Canal, extending from the head of Lake Champlain to its junction with the Erie Canal at Waterford; the Oswego Canal, from Lake Ontario at the city of Oswego to the Erie Canal at Syracuse; the Black River Canal, from Rome to Lyon Falls; the Cayuga and Seneca canals, extending from the Erie Canal to the Seneca and Cayuga lakes. The State has expended for the construction of canals not less than $70,000,000.

Canal-building in the State of Pennsylvania commenced about the time that the original Erie Canal was completed in New York. In 1824 the legislature authorized the appointment of commissioners to explore canal routes from Philadelphia to Pittsburgh and the West. A year later surveys were authorized to be made from Philadelphia to Pittsburgh, from Allegheny to Erie, from Philadelphia to the northern boundary of the State, and also south to the Potomac River. The construction of the main lines of communication between the east and the west and the coal fields in the north was soon commenced. Large loans were repeatedly made, and the work was vigorously prosecuted. In 1834 Pennsylvania had 589 miles of State canals, among them the Central Division Canal, 172 miles long, and the Western Division Canal, 104 miles long. Public opinion strongly favored an extended system of internal improvements, and it was believed that these water-ways would soon become a source of revenue to the State. These expectations might have been realized had the State carried on enterprises on a less extensive and more economical basis. In 1840 the financial condition of the State had become such that canal-building had to be abandoned. The amount expended by the State of Pennsylvania for canals, including the Columbia Railroad, was about $40,000,000, while the difference between net earnings and interest paid by the State up to that time is estimated at $30,000,000. In 1857 and 1858 these works were sold to the Pennsylvania Railroad Company and the Sunbury and Erie Railway Company for $11,375,000, or about one-sixth of their cost to the State.

In Ohio the legislature authorized the survey of a canal from Lake Erie to the Ohio River. In 1825 an act was passed providing for the construction of the Ohio Canal and a number of feeders. In 1831 the canal was in operation from Cleveland to Newark, a distance of 176 miles, and the whole system was finished in 1833.

The State of Illinois completed in 1848 the Illinois and Michigan Canal, connecting Chicago with La Salle on the Illinois River. This canal is 102 miles long, 60 feet wide and six feet deep. The construction by the general government of the Hennepin Ship Canal, connecting the Mississippi with Lake Michigan, has long been agitated in the Northwest. Such a canal would be one of the most important channels of commerce in the country, and it is to be hoped that this great project will be completed at no distant day.

We have besides in the United States a large number of canals that were constructed, and are still operated, by private companies, as the Delaware and Hudson in New York and Pennsylvania, the Schuylkill, Lehigh and Union canals in Pennsylvania, the Morris Canal in New Jersey, the Chesapeake and Ohio and Maryland, etc. A large number of canals, some public and others private property, have since the construction of railroads been abandoned. Thus in New York 356 miles of canals,

costing $10,235,000; in Pennsylvania 477 miles, costing
$12,745,000; in Ohio 205 miles, costing $3,000,000; in
Indiana 379 miles, costing $6,325,000, are no longer in
use. All the canals that were ever built in New England
have likewise been abandoned for commercial purposes.
Nor was Canada slow in realizing the advantages which
a system of canals connecting the great lakes with the
Atlantic Ocean promised to give her. The construction
of the Welland and St. Lawrence canals made it possible
for vessels to clear from Chicago direct for Liverpool, and
this has to a considerable extent diverted grain shipments
to Montreal, giving the Canadian dealers a decided advantage in this traffic.

It is a strange fact that, at least in this country, the
zenith of the canal-building era is found in the decade
following the invention of the steam railroad. For many
years it was not believed that under ordinary circumstances the iron horse could ever compete with the canal
boat in rates. The most sagacious business men had
unlimited faith in the destiny of the canal as a prime commercial factor and invested largely in canal stocks. To many
these investments proved a disappointment. The marvelous improvements in locomotives and other rolling
stock, the unprecedented reductions in the prices of iron
and steel, and above all the fact that in our climate
canal carriage is unavailable during five months of the year,
gave the railroads a decided advantage in their competition
with canal transportation. There can be no doubt, however, that the presence of this competition was one of
the chief causes of the great reduction of railroad rates
on through routes. In this respect alone the canals have
accomplished a very important mission. In the transportation of many of the raw products of the soil and the

mine canals still compete successfully with the railroads, and it is still an open question whether future inventions may not enable them to regain lost ground in the carriage of other goods. It would certainly be a short-sighted policy for our people to discourage the construction of new canals.

For the improvement of navigable rivers, appropriations have been made by Congress ever since the establishment of our national government, and these appropriations now amount to millions of dollars annually. Since the introduction of railroads the usefulness of these national highways of commerce has ceased to depend upon the tonnage carried upon them, but the influence which they exert upon the cost of transportation is so great that it is not likely that the policy of making annual appropriations for the improvement of these water ways will be abandoned by the American people for many years to come.

There has recently been a strong agitation in some portions of the United States in favor of extending government aid to the Nicaragua Ship Canal, and there seem to be indeed many arguments in favor of such a policy. President Harrison said in his annual message to Congress in December, 1891:

"The annual report of the Maritime Canal Company of Nicaragua shows that much costly and necessary preparatory work has been done during the past year in the construction of shops, railroad tracks and harbor piers and breakwaters, and that the work of canal construction has made some progress. I deem it to be a matter of the highest concern to the United States that this canal, connecting the waters of the Atlantic and Pacific oceans, and giving to us a short water communication between our ports upon those two great seas, should be speedily constructed, and at the smallest practical limit of cost. The gain in freights to the people and the direct saving to the government of the United States in the use of its naval vessels would pay the entire cost of the work within a short series of years. The report of the Secretary of the Navy shows the saving in our naval expenditures which would result. The Senator from Alabama, Mr. Morgan, in his argument upon this subject before the Senate of the last session, did not overestimate the importance of the work when he said that 'The canal is the most important subject now connected with the commercial growth and progress of the United States.'"

And in his message of 1892 that:

"It is impossible to overestimate the value from every standpoint of this great enterprise, and I hope that there will be time, even in this Congress, to give it an impetus that will insure the early completion of the canal and secure to the United States its proper relation to it when completed."

It is sincerely to be hoped that the people of the United States can be convinced of the advisability of extending government aid to this enterprise. It must be admitted that the experience of our government with the Pacific railroads has created a strong prejudice among the masses against such subsides as were granted to those corporations, but it is probable, with the people on the alert, that Congress would not again permit great impositions to be practiced against the government. When the great advantages to be derived by the people of the United States from the use of this canal and the small outlay required are considered, it would seem to be a wise policy for our government at once to take such steps as are necessary to secure the early completion and the future control of this great international highway.

CHAPTER II.

IN making inquiry into those inventions and improvements which were the precursors of the modern railroad, we meet early the desire to render the movement of wagons easier by a smooth roadway. Traces of this may be found even in ancient times. The Romans constructed tracks consisting of two lines of cut stones, and in the older Italian cities stone tracks may still be seen in the streets, corresponding to wagon tracks, and evidently designed for the purpose of rendering the movement of the wheels easier.

The first rail tracks of which we have any knowledge were constructed at the end of the sixteenth century. These rails, which were made of wood, appear to have been an invention of miners in the Hartz Mountains. They were the result of pressing necessity, for, as mines were usually so situated that roads could only with great difficulty and expense have been built to them, some cheaper sort of communication with the high road had to be contrived.

After various experiments the wooden railway was adopted, and the product of the mine was carried upon them to the place of shipment by means of small cars. Queen Elizabeth had miners brought into England, to develop the English mines, and through them the rail track was introduced into Great Britain. Later the wooden rail was covered with an iron strap to prevent the rapid wear of the wood, and about the year 1768 cast-iron rails commenced to be used. At the end of the last century

46

wheels were constructed with flanges, to prevent derailing. More attention was also paid to the substructure, wood, iron and stone being used for this purpose. Wrought-iron rails were patented in 1820.

The first authentic account of heat or steam engines is found in the "Pneumatica" of Hero of Alexandria, who lived in the second century before Christ. Hero describes a number of contrivances by which steam was utilized as a source of power. Although these contrivances were at the time of very little practical value, they are interesting as the prototypes of the modern steam engine. The attempts to move wheels by steam date back to the seventeenth century, when a number of experiments were made, but their exact nature is not known, because they were all soon abandoned, either on account of unsuccessful results or lack of means. At the beginning of the eighteenth century Denis Papin constructed a small steamboat, upon which he sailed in 1707 on the Fulda River from Cassel to Munden, a distance of about fifteen miles.

The construction of locomotives engaged the attention of ingenious minds a century and a half ago. It is claimed that Newton experimented with a steam motor in 1680. Dr. Robinson described in 1759, in his "Mechanical Philosophy," a steam vehicle. The Glasgow engineer James Watt devoted himself from 1769 to 1785, with great energy, to the development of the steam engine, and succeeded in inventing the system which became the parent of the modern engine. An American, Oliver Evans, constructed at the beginning of the present century a carriage propelled by steam, and exhibited it, in 1804, in the streets of Philadelphia, before twenty thousand spectators. While Evans' invention was never put to any practical use, he prophesied that the time would come when steam cars would be considered the most perfect means of transportation.   On Christmas eve, 1801, Richard Trevithick exhibited at Camborne, England, a steam coach, and soon afterwards he and his cousin, A. Vivian, obtained an English patent on a "steam engine for propelling carriages." Seven years later a Mr. Blinkensop, of Middleton Colliery, near Leeds, constructed another locomotive engine, upon which he obtained a patent in 1811. These and a number of other inventors of steam engines vainly expended great ingenuity in attempting to overcome a purely imaginary difficulty. They believed that the adhesion between the face of the wheel and the surface of the road was so slight that a considerable portion of the propelling power would be lost by the slipping of the wheels. It was not until about the year 1813 that the important fact was ascertained that the friction of the wheels with the rails was sufficient to propel the locomotive and even drag after it a load of considerable weight. On the other hand these inventors failed to provide in their engines adequate heating-power for the production of steam.   In 1814 George Stephenson commenced to apply himself to the construction of an improved locomotive. When, owing to his invention of the tubular boiler, he saw, after fifteen years of arduous toil, his labors crowned with success, the civilized world entered upon a new era of social, industrial and commercial life.   The first line upon which Stephenson's invention was used was the Liverpool and Manchester Railway.   In the year 1821, a number of Liverpool merchants formulated a plan for the construction of a tramway between their city and Manchester.   The question of motive power was left open as between horses and the steam engine, with which Mr. Stephenson was then experimenting. After much opposition on the part of Parliament and the public a charter was obtained in 1826. When the construction of the road was nearly completed, the directors of the company, after having determined upon the use of steam engines, offered a prize of £500 for the best locomotive engine to run at a public trial on the Liverpool and Manchester Railway. This proposal was announced in the spring of 1829, and the trial took place at Rainhill on the 6th of October of that year. The competing engines were the Rocket, constructed by Mr. Stephenson; the Sanspareil, by Hackworth; the Perseverance, by Burstall, and the Novelty, by Messrs. Braithwaite and Ericsson. Both Braithwaite and Ericsson became subsequently residents of the United States, and the latter achieved immortal fame as the inventor of the screw propeller and the builder of the Monitor. The Rocket was the only engine that performed the complete journey proposed, and obtained the prize. It is claimed by the biographers of John Ericsson that he had really built a much faster locomotive than Stephenson, and that, although it had to be constructed very hastily and therefore broke down during the trial, the superiority of the principle involved in it was universally recognized by the engineers of that time. The Stephenson engines became the motive power of the Liverpool and Manchester road, which was opened for public traffic on the 16th of September, 1830. This line was, however, neither the first public railway nor even the first steam railway. The first railway or tramway act was passed in England in 1758, and in 1824 no less than thirty-three private railway or tramway companies had been chartered. In 1824 a charter was granted by Parliament authorizing the construction of the Darlington and Stockton Railway, to be worked with "men and horses, or otherwise." By a subsequent act the company was empowered to work its railway with locomotive engines. The road was opened in September, 1825, and was practically the first public carrier of goods and passengers. The Monklands Railway in Scotland, opened in 1826, and several other small lines soon followed the example of the Darlington and Stockton line and adopted steam traction, but the Liverpool and Manchester Railway was the first to convince the world that a revolution in traveling had taken place.

The road was from the very first successful, its traffic and income greatly exceeding the expectations of its managers. It should also be noted here that the cost of construction fell largely below the elaborate estimates made by several distinguished engineers. The company had expected to earn about £10,000 a year from passenger traffic, and the very first year the receipts from that source were £101,829. The gross annual receipts from freight had been estimated at £50,000, but were £80,000 in 1833. From the first the stockholders obtained a dividend of eight per cent., which soon rose to nine and to ten per cent. It has since been demonstrated that the revenues of new roads almost always exceed expectations.

The success of this railway stimulated railway enter prise throughout Europe and America. But while railroad projects created much enthusiasm on one side, they also met with bitter opposition on the other. The prejudice of the short-sighted and the avarice of those whose interests were threatened by a change in the mode of transportation used every weapon in their power against the proposed innovation. The arguments used were often most absurd. It was said that the smoke of the engine was injurious to both man and beast, and that the sparks escaping from it would set fire to the buildings along the

line of road, the cows would be scared and would cease
to give their milk, that horses would depreciate in value,
and that their race would finally become extinct. Nor
did many of the European governments favor the new
system of transportation. Some openly opposed it as
revolutionary and productive of infinitely more evil than
good. The Austrian court and statesmen especially
looked upon the new contrivance with undisguised distrust; and from their point of view this distrust was
perhaps well founded. The rapid movement of the iron
horse seemed to savor of dangerous radicalism, not to say
revolution. When the Emperor finally, in 1836, concluded
to sign a railroad charter, he based his action upon the
dubious ground that "the thing cannot maintain itself,
anyhow." It may be said that the history of the railroad
is a conspicuous illustration of human short-sightedness.
The Prussian Postmaster-General Von Nagler opposed
the construction of a railroad between Berlin and
Potsdam upon the ground that the passenger business
between those two cities was not sufficient to keep even
the stage-coach always full. It never occurred to the
Postmaster-General, as it does not occur to many railroad
men of to-day, that new and cheaper means of transportation increase the traffic. Even so wise a statesman
as Thiers said when railroad construction was first agitated
in France: "I do not see how railroads can compete with
our stage-coaches." M. Thiers also opposed for years
the building of a railroad between Paris and Versailles,
declaring that on account of a railroad not one passenger
more would make the journey between these two places.

But railroads came whether monarchical governments
liked them or not. The success of the Liverpool and
Manchester Railroad stimulated railroad building in Eng-

land to a marvelous extent.   Between 1830 and 1843 no
less than seventy-one different companies were organized,
representing about 2,100 miles.   During the next four
years 637 more roads, with an authorized length of 9,400
miles, were chartered.   The construction of each new road
required a special act of Parliament.   These early roads averaged only fifteen to thirty miles in length.   The competition
which ensued soon led to the consolidation of roads, which
continued until now the 14,000 miles of railway in England and Wales are practically owned by only a dozen
companies.   The total number of miles of railroad in
Great Britain and Ireland is at present over 20,000.

The news of the opening of the first steam railway in
England spread through Europe comparatively slowly.
There were in those days but few newspapers printed on
the continent, and these were read very sparingly.   Railroad discussions were confined to merchants and manufacturers.   Even after the success of the railroad was
assured in England, a large number of people would not
believe that, except between the largest cities, railroads
on the continent could ever be profitable.   But few railroads have ever been built which with honest, efficient
and economical management would not pay a fair rate of
interest on actual cost of construction.   But in spite of
this we have to this day a large number of otherwise
well-informed people who question the financial success
of every new railroad that is proposed.

In those days it occurred only to the most sagacious
minds that with increased facilities commerce would
expand.   The missionaries of railroad enterprise found it
therefore a difficult matter to interest capital in their
projects.   Railroad committees were in time formed in all
cities of any importance, but, with capital cowardly, as

usual, and governments distrustful, their task was often a thankless one. Railroad projects matured very slowly, and, when matured, were often wrecked by jealous and short-sighted governments. After the formation of a company five and even ten years would often pass away before a charter could be secured and the work of construction commenced. It is true, there were some laudable exceptions to this rule. Thus the governments of France and Belgium led the people in railroad construction; but upon the whole it can be said that the railroad forced itself by its intrinsic merit upon monarchical governments. It soon became evident even to the most stupid of autocratic ministries that it was a choice between the new mode of transportation and national atrophy.

The first German line was built between the cities of Nuremberg and Furth in 1835. It was only about four miles long, but the success of the experiment gave an impetus to railroad building in other parts of Germany. The Leipzig and Dresden line followed in 1837, and the Berlin-Potsdam and Brunswick-Wolfenbuttel lines in 1838. At the end of 1840 Germany had 360 miles of railroad. In that year Frederick William IV. succeeded to the throne of Prussia and inaugurated a new and exceedingly liberal railroad policy in his realm. In 1843 the Prussian government concluded to guarantee certain railroad companies a dividend of $3\frac{1}{2}$ per cent. on the capital actually invested. The state also secured considerable influence in the administration of the roads as well as in the right to assume the management of the various lines under certain conditions. The governments of the states of Southern Germany now commenced to build state roads, and their example was, chiefly for strategic reasons, soon imitated by Prussia. The system has since grown to over 26,000 miles, and no less than eighty-seven per cent. of the mileage is under state control. In all the states and provinces of the empire, except Bavaria, the rates for transportation of passengers and freight on all lines are controlled absolutely by the government.

In Austria, as has already been indicated, the building of railways was greatly discouraged by the government until 1836. In that year the Emperor rather reluctantly granted Baron Rothschild a charter for a railway from Vienna into the province of Galicia. Another charter was granted to a Baron Sina for a line from Vienna to Raab and Gloggnitz. The policy then adopted in Austria guaranteed to each railroad company a monopoly in its own district during the period for which the charter was granted. Soon after the state also commenced building lines, but the growth of the Austrian system was slow until after the war of 1866. An era of railroad speculation was then inaugurated, which ended with the crisis of 1873. The total length of the railroads of Austria-Hungary was 10,790 miles in 1875. At present that monarchy has nearly 16,400 miles of railway, 8,600 of which are owned by private companies.

It has been the policy of Austria to reduce rates, and several roads, especially those built in mountainous districts, have a certain revenue guaranteed to them by the government.

The zone system recently adopted in Hungary reduced both the passenger and freight rates of the government roads at least one-third, and this reduction has, contrary to expectation, greatly increased their net revenues.

In France railroad agitation commenced in 1832. A few short lines were opened, as those from Paris to St. Germain and to Versailles; but, owing to the conservatism of French capitalists, but little more was done until the state took the matter in hand. Thiers proposed a scheme by which the state was to furnish about half the cost while private companies were to build the lines and operate them. The Western Railroad, the first line of any great extent, was opened in 1837 between Paris and Rouen, and the Eastern Railroad was opened two years later. There were in 1859 six large companies operating their lines with profit, but, to induce them to build additional lines that were needed, the state guaranteed the interest on the capital required to make their improvements. In 1884 there were about 17,000 miles of railroad in operation. To bring about the construction of another 7,000 miles of road, and to thus complete the railroad system of the country, the government now guaranteed each company a dividend equal to the average of recent years, but not to exceed seven per cent. It is doubtful whether this system of monopoly has in all respects been favorable to the encouragement of enterprise in the railroad circles of France. In granting charters the state has, however, reserved valuable rights which at a future period it will have an opportunity to assert for the public benefit. The railroad companies have generally a lease for ninety-nine years, and their lines become the property of the state after the expiration of that period. To extinguish the bonded debt and stock, a sinking fund has been created, from which a certain portion of the shares and outstanding bonds is annually paid off and canceled. The government requires of the companies the free carriage of the mails and the transportation of military and other employes at very low rates. Besides this the state levies upon the traffic of the railroads a duty of ten per cent. of their gross earnings from passengers|

and from all goods carried by fast trains. These facts
are usually overlooked by our railroad men when they
indulge in making comparisons between the railroad rates
of this country and those of France. The French Republic had 13,400 miles of road in 1875, and 22,600 in 1890.
When all of the proposed lines are completed, the total
mileage of that country will be over 25,000.

Belgium has the best-developed track system on the
continent. The state commenced the construction of railroads as early as 1834, and the first line (Brussels Malines)
was opened May 5th, 1835. Four great state lines were
constructed in different directions, and between these
lines private roads were permitted to be built. Between
1850 and 1870 the private lines increased from 200 to
1,400 miles, and competition between them and the state
lines became so active as to reduce rates to the lowest
possible point. In 1870 the government decided to buy a
large number of competing lines. In 1874 it had acquired
more than half, and at present, with a few exceptions, they
are all owned and controlled by the state. The exceptions
to this are a few short lines that were built in the early days
of railroad construction. The total mileage is now 3,210.
Rates have, however, not been increased since this consolidation, and they are still lower than any other country
in Europe. The transportation of mails is free, and
troops, military materials and prison vans are carried at
reduced rates.

Railroads were originally built in Switzerland merely
for the accommodation of tourists and the local traffic.
The first line, between Zurich and Aarau, was completed
in 1847, but general railroad enterprise did not develop
until after 1860. The St. Gothard route was then projected, which opened a direct through line between Italy

and Germany. The roads are all owned by private companies, but are under strict government control. Great publicity of their affairs is required. The total mileage of Switzerland was 2,043 in 1891.

In Italy railroad enterprises have received attention since 1853. The first roads were those of Lombardy, being commenced while that province was still under Austrian rule. The treaties of Zurich in 1859 and of Vienna in 1866 delivered these roads and the Venetian lines to the kingdom of Italy. Between 1860 and 1870 the systematic construction of a railroad net was commenced which connected the various lines with each other and with Rome. Nearly all the railroads of Italy fell into the hands of the government, but in 1885 they were leased for a term of sixty years to three companies, terminable at the end of twenty or forty years by either party upon two years' notice. Under the lease the state received two per cent. of the gross receipts. The tariffs are fixed by the state, are uniform and can be reduced by the state. A Council of Tariffs, composed of delegates for the government, for agriculture, commerce and industry, and for the railroad companies, all elected by their own boards, has been instituted to study the wants and best interests of the country. The total number of miles of railroad in Italy was 8,110 in 1889.

The first road in Spain was opened in 1848 between Barcelona and Mataro. The government greatly encouraged railroad construction by subsidies, and during the decade following 1855 the development of the railway system of the country was rapid. More than thirty companies have been formed, which have built about twenty main lines, aggregating 6,200 miles.

In Portugal very little railroad building was done previous to 1863, when a little over three hundred miles of road was constructed. The government owns nearly half of the roads of the country, the remaining lines being the property of private companies. The total number of miles operated in the kingdom in 1889 was 1,280. The service and the financial condition of the roads of Portugal are far from being satisfactory.

In Denmark the first railroad was built on the island of Seeland in 1847. Previous to 1880 the larger part of the roads of the kingdom was owned by private companies. Since then several of the most important private roads have been purchased by the state, which in 1889 owned 963 miles, while only 251 miles remained in private control. Only about thirty miles more have since been constructed. The roads are well managed, but their net earnings are less than two per cent. of the capital invested.

On the Scandinavian Peninsula the railroad system has developed rather slowly. Norway built the first line from Christiana to Eidsvold in 1854, and Sweden commenced railroad building two years later. The narrow-gauge system is fully developed here. While in Norway the greater part of the lines is owned by the state, the roads of Sweden are chiefly in the hands of private companies which on an average control but little more than twenty-five miles each. The total mileage of Sweden is 5,970, and that of Norway 970.

The first line of railroad in the Russian Empire was constructed from St. Petersburg, sixteen miles, to Tsarskoji-Sielo, in 1842. The St. Petersburg and Moscow line was opened in 1851. Railroad building then stagnated until after the Crimean War, when a large number of lines were constructed at once. The roads were surveyed by the government, but constructed and operated by private companies. State aid was, however, freely given. During the past ten years the Russian government has directed its attention to the development of the railroad system in its Asiatic possessions. A railway between the Black and Caspian seas was completed in 1883, and the Siberian railroad is extended as fast as the financial condition of the empire permits. There are now about 20,000 miles of road in the Russian Empire operated by private companies. The construction of a large number of the Russian railways was dictated by military rather than commercial considerations. Maximum rates are specified in charter, and every change of rates must be approved by the Minister of Finance.

In the Balkan Peninsula railroad facilities are still ill provided for. A few lines have been built, but these are, as a rule, badly managed. Trains are slow, and rates often so high as to be prohibitory. Roumania has undoubtedly the best railroad system of any of the Balkan states, the government controlling 1,000 miles of road. Greece is also making some progress and has at the present time 610 miles of railway. There is reason to believe that through communication will soon be established in these countries on a larger scale.

The introduction of the railway into Asia has been, except in the Russian and English possessions, a very difficult task. The conservatism or ignorance of the governments and the superstition of the people combined to throw numberless obstacles before those who proposed to pave the way for the iron horse. British India opened her first railway for public traffic between Bombay and

Tannah on November 18, 1852. In 1855 she had 841 miles of road, which increased to 6,515 miles in 1875 and to 15,828 miles in 1889, of which 8,423 miles were owned and operated by the state. The total cost of these roads was $880,000,000.

In Asiatic Turkey the first line was opened between Smyrna and Trianda on the 24th day of December, 1860. This line was in 1866 extended to Aiden, and in 1882 to Sarakio. There are at present five lines with a total extent of 446 miles, all owned by English companies. New lines, covering in all 3,952 miles, have recently been projected.

The first line in Persia, only seven miles long, and extending from Teheran to Schah-Abdal-Azzim, was opened on the 25th day of June, 1888. Another line, from the Caspian Sea to Amol, is now in process of construction. A line was opened last September between Joppa and Jerusalem. It is 53 miles in length.

Japan may be said to be already thoroughly familiar with the European system. The first and principal line was opened on the island of Napon, between Tokio and Yokohama, on the 14th of October, 1872. Two other short lines followed in 1874 and 1876, when the total extent of the Japanese roads was about 135 miles. In 1883 the construction of the Grand Trunk Railroad, from Tokio to Kioto, was commenced, which line has been in operation for the past five years. Other lines, aggregating over 400 miles, will soon be opened for traffic. The total extent of road in operation in 1888 was 580 miles, 310 of which were controlled by the state, and the remainder by private companies. In 1890 the total number of miles exceeded 900. The total average cost per mile was $58,000.

No nation has probably opposed the introduction of the railway as stubbornly as the Chinese. The first railroad, scarcely seven miles long, was built by an English company near Kaiping to facilitate the transportation of coal from the mines in that vicinity. In 1886 a Chinese company purchased this line and has since extended it to Tientsin, making its present length about eighty-four miles. The Chinese government has recently authorized the further extension of this line to Yangchou, a place but a few miles distant from Pekin.

Of the Asiatic islands Java has the largest and oldest railroad system. On the 10th of August, 1867, the first line was opened between Samarang and Tangveng. Other coast lines have since been constructed, but communication is still sadly neglected in the interior. In 1889 there were operated on the island nearly 800 miles of road, the greater part being the property of private companies.

A road was opened upon the island of Ceylon between Colombo and Kandy in 1867, to which several branch lines and extensions have since been added. The total system comprises at present about 180 miles.

Short lines have also been built in Burmah (1889); in the Malay Peninsula (1885), in Sumatra (1876), and in Cochin China (1885). A line from Bangkok to Bianghsen, in Siam, is being projected at the present time.

In Africa, if we except its northern coast, the construction of railroads has only kept pace with the slow development of the resources of that continent. Its European colonies are still but thinly inhabited, and their industrial and commercial life still resembles much that of the American colonies of the seventeenth century. There can be little doubt, however, that with the increas-

ing immigration the growing demand for better transportation facilities will speedily be met by European
capital.

The first railroad upon African soil was built by the
Egyptian government from Alexandria to Cairo, and from
there through the desert to Suez. A part of this line,
130 miles long, was opened to traffic in 1856, and the
remaining ninety miles the year following. Nothing
further was done until after Ismail Pasha ascended the
throne, in 1863. The railroad system of Lower Egypt,
between Alexandria in the west, Cairo in the south, and
Ismaila in the east, was then greatly extended and the
service materially improved.

After the opening of the Suez Canal the line through
the desert to Suez was abandoned. The railroad system
of Egypt comprises at present about 1,250 miles, all of
which belongs to the government except two short lines
which are private property.

The beginning of the railroad system of Algiers dates
back to 1860, when the French government gave a charter
to the Companie des Chemins de Fer Algériens, authorizing it to build a number of lines connecting the principal
cities of the province with the Mediterranean. The line
from Algiers to Blidah, thirty-two miles long, was opened
on September 8, 1862. Further construction was then
delayed until 1863, when the charter of the original
company was transferred to the Paris, Lyons and Mediterranean Railroad Company. The original plans were then
in the main carried out, until the disturbances caused by
the Franco-Prussian war again put an end to railroad enterprises. In 1874 three new companies were chartered and
railroad building was resumed. In 1888 the Algerian
railroad system comprised 1,350 miles.

The first road in Tunis was built in 1872 from the city of Tunis to Bardo and Gouletta by English capitalists. It was, in 1880, sold to an Italian company to which the Italian government for political reasons had seen fit to guarantee certain dividends. Other small lines have since been constructed, and more important ones have been prospected. The number of miles at present in operation is 153.

The French colony on the Senegal River has a number of short lines, of which the first was opened in July, 1883. These lines aggregate at present about 200 miles. It is now contemplated to extend this system to the upper Niger. This would necessitate the construction of 240 additional miles of road.

The Cape Colony has the largest mileage of any of the European colonies in Africa, the absence of navigable rivers rendering railroads here more necessary than elsewhere. The first line was opened on the 13th of February, 1862. It then extended from Cape Town to Earste River, but was extended to Wellington the following year. The number of miles of road in operation in 1875 was 906, and in 1891 it had increased to 2,067. All the roads of the colony, excepting a line of 93 miles belonging to the Cape Copper Mining Company, are operated by the colonial government. Their net revenue in 1886 was 2.84 per cent. of the capital actually invested.

Port Natal built her first railroad in 1860. It was only two miles long and extended from the city of Durban to its harbor. Since then several inland lines, aggregating over four hundred miles, have been constructed at a cost of twenty-two million dollars. The roads are operated by the colonial government and yielded in 1891 a net revenue of 4.4 per cent on the capital expended.

Short lines have also been built on Mauritius and Reunion, and there is now every indication that Portuguese Africa and the Congo State will be provided with railroad facilities in the near future.

The introduction of railroads into Australia dates back to the sixth decade of the present century. The total number of miles of road reported in 1889 by the several colonies was 8,883. If we estimate the population of the continent at 3,000,000 for that year it will be seen that Australia has more miles of road per capita than any other grand division of the globe, save North America.

New South Wales, the mother colony of the Australian continent, opened its first road on September 26, 1855, between Sydney and Paramalta. This road was built by a private company, but was soon after its completion purchased by the colonial government, and was in 1869 extended to Goulbourn. In 1875 the colony had only 436 miles of road in operation. The mountains, however, which separated the wide plains of the interior from the coast had been surmounted, and the government commenced to push the construction of new roads with great vigor. At the end of the year 1886 New South Wales had no less than 1,888 miles of road in operation, for which the colony had expended $113,000,000. The net revenue during that year was 2.9 per cent. on the capital invested. The total number of miles of railroad in this colony was 2,247 in 1889.

Victoria, the smallest of the colonies, has made by far the greatest progress in railroad building. The first road in the colony, and, in fact, the first road upon the Australian continent, was built in 1854 between the city of Melbourne and its port, a distance of two and one-half miles. Within the next five years four other lines were constructed, connecting Melbourne with Williamston, St. Kilda, Brighton and Echuca, respectively. In 1870 there were in the colony 275 miles of railroad, which had increased to 1,198 miles in 1880, and to 2,283 miles in 1889. Several of the roads were originally owned by private companies, but all of them were in time acquired by the colonial government, the last one in 1878. The total capital invested in 1887 was $125,000,000, which yielded a net revenue of $5,800,000. All lines are under the control of a board so constituted as to be entirely removed from political influence.

In South Australia a short line was built in 1856 from the city of Adelaide to Port Adelaide. Another line was constructed in 1857 from Adelaide to Salisbury, which three years later was extended to Kapunda. The colony had then forty miles of road. The increase during the next decade was only ninety-three miles. Since then the development has been much more rapid, the whole system of railroads comprising 1,752 miles in 1889. All the roads save a few suburban lines are owned and operated by the colony. Their total cost is not far from $60,000,-000, and their net annual revenue is about two and one-half per cent. of the capital invested.

The colony of Queensland has only a system of narrow-gauge roads, with the construction of which it commenced in 1865. Up to September, 1887, the colonial government had constructed 1,641 miles of road at a total cost of $47,700,000. The total number of miles has since been increased to 2,058. The net revenue of the roads was a little over one million dollars in 1886.

The transportation facilities of West Australia are still far behind those of her sister colonies. The first line was opened in 1873, and the total number of miles of road operated in the colony in 1889 was only 496. The government controls nearly all the railroads of tne colony.

Of the islands of Australasia, Tasmania and New Zealand are as yet the only ones that have railroad communication. The former built its first road in 1870 and had at the end of the year 1890 about 1,900 miles in operation. New Zealand opened its first railroad between Christchurch and Lyttleton on December 1, 1863. The development of the system was slow at first, there being but 25 miles of road in operation in 1870. In 1891 the number of miles of road had increased to 1,916, all but 92 miles being operated by the colonial government. The total amount expended by the government for railroads is $55,000,000. The net revenue in 1887 was about 2½ per cent of the amount invested.

In South America railroad building is of comparatively recent date. The first road was built in 1851, but the line was short and remained the only one for several years. With thirty million people the South American states have at present but little more than 16,000 miles of railroad, a condition which must at least in part be ascribed to the peculiar conservatism of the Latin race.

The United States of Colombia possesses less than 250 miles of road. Its first line was the Panama Railroad, from Colon to Aspinwall. It connects the Pacific with the Atlantic ocean, is 48 miles long and was constructed in 1855. This, as well as the several other roads of Colombia, is the property of private companies. A number of new roads have recently been surveyed.

Venezuela opened in 1866 a road, 56 miles long, from Puerto Caballo to Palito, which in 1870 was extended to Aroa. A number of other short roads, aggregating about 350 miles, have since been constructed. The total extent of railroad in Venezuela was 432 miles in 1889, of which the greater part was operated by private companies. Several important lines are in the process of construction, and will connect Caracas with Carabobo, San Carlos and the port of La Guayra.

The Republic of Ecuador constructed in 1876 a road from Jaguachi to Puente de Chimbo, a distance of 43 miles. This line was recently extended to Siambe, and has now a total length of 94 miles. In 1886 a charter was granted to a North American company, authorizing the construction of a road from San Lorenzo to Esmeraldas and guaranteeing certain dividends on the investment. At the close of the year 1889 Ecuador had 167 miles of road.

The first railroad in Peru was built in 1851, connecting the seaport Callao with the capital, Lima. After this but little was done for more than twenty years. At the beginning of the seventies an extensive railroad system was projected at the instigation of President Don Manuel Pardo, and the construction of the principal road of the system from Mollendo on the Pacific Ocean to Santa Rosa was at once entered upon. This road ascends the Western Cordillera, crosses a number of prodigious mountain passes, reaches Lake Titicaca, and then proceeds in a northwesterly direction to Santa Rosa. It is over 300 miles long, and reaches near Puna an altitude of 14,700 feet. An extension of this line from Santa Rosa to the old Inca city Cuzco was opened in 1875, but was subsequently destroyed in the war with Chile, and has not been reopened. Another road, extending from Callao to San Mateo, was opened in 1876. It is eighty-seven miles long, and reaches with its enormous grades a height of over 13,000 feet. It belongs, with the Santa Rosa road, to the boldest creations of railroad engineering. Since the war with Chile railroad enterprise has been checked. The number of miles of road in operation rose from 962 in 1875 to 1,615 in 1880, but was, owing to the abandonment of certain lines, diminished to 813 in 1884. Since that time about 400 miles of new road have been opened.

In the Republic of Bolivia the first railroad was built about twenty years ago from Antofogasta to Solar. After the cession of the province of Antofogasta to Chile there remained but thirty-five miles of road in Bolivia. More than 200 miles have since been added by the construction of several short roads, chiefly the property of mining companies.

The Republic of Chile was the first of the South American states to initiate the construction of railways. The building of a line from the seaport Caldera to Copiapo was commenced in May, 1850, and was completed on January 2, 1852. This line was constructed and operated by a private company. The first state road, extending from Valparaiso to Santiago, was opened on the 15th of September, 1865. To this road has since been added an extension to Talcahuana, as well as several branch lines. The total amount that has been expended by the Chilean government for the construction of railroads is $43,000,000. The total number of miles of road operated in Chile in 1887 was 1,674, of which 992 were the property of private companies and 682 miles were owned by the state. Two hundred and fifty miles of road have since been constructed, and the construction of 700 additional miles of railroad has been authorized by the government.

The Argentine Republic opened its first road, extending from Buenos Ayres to Belgrano, in December, 1862.

Several other lines soon followed, and in 1870 over 600 miles of road had been constructed. This number had increased to 1,440 in 1880 and to 5,100 in 1889. Since then several new lines have been completed, aggregating over 600 miles. Among the principal lines of the Argentine Republic is the transcontinental road which connects the Atlantic with the Pacific Ocean. The whole line is 880 miles long, of which 665 miles are in the Argentine Republic and the remaining 115 miles in Chile. Of the 3,705 miles of road which were in operation at the beginning of the year 1887 the republic owned 1,148, the province of Buenos Ayres 572, the province of Santa Fe 102, and private companies 1,888 miles. The total amount invested in railroads was $154,000,000 in 1887, which yielded an average dividend of 3.9 per cent.

The oldest railroad in Brazil is the Petropolis road. It was built by a private company and opened on December 16, 1856. In 1881 the total number of miles in operation was 2,422, and in 1889 it had increased to 5,766. Furthermore charters had been granted for the additional construction of 2,271 miles of road. Of the lines in operation about 1,200 miles are the property of the state, yielding a revenue of nearly 3 per cent. on the capital invested. The state gives aid, besides, to several private roads. The most important road of Brazil is the state road Dom Pedro I., which connects the three richest provinces of the country, Rio de Janeiro, Minas Gerals and Sao Paolo, with the national capital. It was opened in 1883, and has a total extent of 544 miles.

The principal roads of Uruguay were built between 1865 and 1875. In the latter year the total number of miles in operation in Uruguay was 190, which in 1880 had increased to 230, and in 1889 to 469 miles.

In the remaining political divisions of South America the railroad extended its dominion still more slowly. Paraguay opened as early as 1863 a line 45 miles long from Asuncion to Itangua, and in 1892 her railroad system had increased to 159 miles in extent. British Guiana completed in 1866 a line from Georgetown to New Amsterdam, but not one mile of railroad has been built in that colony since. Of the islands of South America Trinidad is the only one into which the railroad has been introduced. The island has at present 50 miles of road, to 16 in 1878.

Central America has less than 600 miles of railway. The causes which have retarded the development of the railroad system in South America are also operative here. Of the five republics of Central America Costa Rica has the largest number of miles of railroad, viz.: 161. It has three different lines, of which the Limon and Carillo line, seventy miles long, is the most important. This road, which connects with a New York line of steamers at Limon, has greatly furthered the cultivation of bananas in the Santa Clara valley.

Nicaragua completed its first road in 1880 between Corinto and Chinandega, and has at present about 100 miles of railway in operation. The Nicaragua Canal Company is constructing a road from Juan del Norte to Ochoa, a distance of thirty-two miles, to be used in the construction of the canal.

Honduras opened in 1871 its only line, thirty-seven miles long, between Puerto Cabello and San Jago. In recent years an extension of nine miles has been added to it.

San Salvador has, besides a street-car line between the cities of San Salvador and Santa Tecla, only one line of railroad between Acajutla and Armea, which was constructed with public funds and opened for traffic on July 15, 1882.

Guatemala was the last of the Central American States to introduce the railroad. Its first road, seventy-four miles long, and extending from San Jose on the Pacific Ocean to the capital, Guatemala, was built by a San Francisco company and opened on August 20, 1884. The state has at the present time about 100 miles of road, with several short but quite important lines under construction.

The West Indies have between 1,200 and 1,400 miles of railway, of which more than 1,000 are in Cuba. The first road upon this island, 179 miles long and extending from Habana to Guanajay, was opened as early as 1837. The next ten years developed almost the whole of the railroad system of the western half of Cuba. A number of important roads have since been opened in the central and eastern portions of the island, whose railroad mileage is at present larger per capita than that of any other political division of the Western Hemisphere save that of Canada and the United States. The second of the West India islands to construct a railroad was Jamaica. A line connecting Kingston and Spanishtown was opened on the 21st of November, 1845. Two branch lines have since been added, making the total number of miles of road on this island seventy-six at the present time. About twenty-five miles more are now in the process of construction. San Domingo and Hayti have also recently commenced to build railroads. In the former republic a line from Sanchez to LaVega, sixty-two and one-half miles long, is now open to traffic, and Hayti is constructing a line from Gonaives, on the western coast, to Porte de Paix, on the eastern coast of the island. The Spanish government in 1888 also granted a charter for the construction of a railroad on the island of Porto Rica.

Of our neighbors on the North American continent, Mexico and Canada, the former has been by far the slower to avail herself of the advantages of railroad communication. The slow growth of the railroad system of Mexico must be ascribed chiefly to the frequent political disturbances of the country as well as to the many topographical obstacles which presented themselves to the railroad engineer. The first Mexican railway, excepting tramways, was the one which connects the capital with the city of Vera Cruz. It was constructed by an English company and was opened on the first day of January, 1873. In 1875 the total number of miles of road in Mexico was 327, and five years later somewhat less than 700. Since then the development of the system has been much more rapid. In 1880 several companies were formed for the purpose of building a system of roads which would connect the Mexican capital with the United States as well as with the most important harbors of the gulfs of Mexico and California. The projectors of these lines, who were citizens of the United States, received the hearty coöperation of the Mexican government, and the work was at once pushed very vigorously. At the end of the year 1885 more than 2,500 miles of new road were open for traffic, and a thousand miles more at the end of the following year. In 1889 Mexico had 5,332 miles of road. The principal one of the newly constructed roads is the Mexican Central, which connects Paso del Norte with the City of Mexico. This line will also, when its branches are completed, form a through route between the Gulf of Mexico and the Pacific Ocean. Another scarcely less important through line north and south is the National Mexican Railway, which is 722 miles long and connects Laredo, on the Rio Grande, with the capital and the southern states. Another line has recently been opened from Torreon to Durango. The number of miles of road at present in operation in the Republic of Mexico is about 6,800, with a number of new lines rapidly nearing completion. The development of Mexico's resources has, during the past decade, kept pace with the rapid expansion of its railroad system.

In the Dominion of Canada about fifteen miles of railroad line were built as early as 1837, but only forty-three miles was added during the next ten years. In 1852 there was still only 212 miles of railroad in all of the British possessions in North America. At that time the construction of the Grand Trunk system was commenced, the first section of the system, Portland-Montreal, being opened in 1853. After this railroads increased very rapidly in Canada, reaching an extent of 2,087 miles in 1860, 4,826 miles in 1875, 6,891 miles in 1880, and 10,150 miles in 1890. The majority of Canadian railroads are in the hands of private companies, some of which have been very materially aided by the government. One of the conditions upon which the union of the several British provinces, except Newfoundland and Prince Edward Island, was effected in 1867, was the construction of a railroad by the Dominion government connecting the provinces of Ontario, Quebec, Nova Scotia and New Brunswick. This road, the main line of which extends from Point Levis, opposite Quebec, to Halifax, was accordingly built, and is still operated by the Canadian government. Its cost was about 46,000,000.

But the most important enterprise in which the government is interested is the Canadian Pacific Railway. Like the intercolonial railway, this line was a result of the political union of the colonies. Its construction was commenced by the government, but was . subsequently assigned to a private corporation, the Canadian Pacific Railway Company, all that had been done by the government being turned over to the company as a gift. It is estimated that the direct gifts of money, the land grant and other privileges conferred by the Dominion government upon the Pacific Railway Company exceed $100,-000,000 in value, and that, with the amount of bonds and stock guaranteed by the government, the par value of its various aids amounts to $215,000,000, or $48,000,-000 more than the cost of the road, as will be shown by the following table, taken from the report of the Interstate Commerce Committee of the Senate of the Fifty-first Congress:

Subsidy granted by the act of Parliament of
    February 13, 1881.......................... $25,000,000
Seven hundred and fourteen miles of railroad constructed by the Dominion Government, original cost and interest 36,760,785
Capital stock guaranteed.................... 65,000,000
Loan to the company authorized by Parliament of
    1884, in part......................... 29,880,912
Balance of above loan........................ 15,000 000
Bonds, interest guaranteed by the Dominion for
    50 years at 3½ per cent................. 15,000,000
Land grant bonds........................... 25,000,000
Subsidy of $186,000 a year, for 20 years......... 3,720,000

    Total......................................$215,361,697
Total cost of road, according to the company's
    balance sheet of December, 1888............$131,350,019

The Dominion Government owns and operates four railways, the cost of which up to June 30, 1890, was $52,-

800,000. It has also granted to railroad companies cash subsidies which to June 30, 1889, amounted to over $46,000,000. The total number of miles of railroad in Canada was 14,004 in 1890. The people of Canada have, since the political union of the colonies, pursued an exceedingly liberal policy toward their railroads, but it appears that the great indulgence of the government only bred license in railroad circles. The evil increased from year to year, until the many complaints on the part of the public against railroad management caused Parliament in 1886 to appoint a commission to examine into the alleged abuses and to report as to the advisability of the adoption of a general railroad law, and the appointment of a Board of Railroad Commissioners. The committee reported to the Governor-General of Canada on the 14th of January, 1888, and, acting upon its recommendation, Parliament passed the Railway Act of May 22, 1888. This act, containing 309 paragraphs, provides for the complete regulation of railroad affairs, and for this purpose creates a Board of Railroad Commissioners, consisting of the Minister for Railroads and Canals, the Minister of Justice and two or more members of the Privy Council. The act also repeals all former railroad laws. Though it has been in force less than five years, its beneficial effects are already extensively felt by the Canadian public.

CHAPTER III.

IN no country in the world has the growth of railroads been so rapid as in the United States. With a population less than one-fifth as large as that of Europe this country has a larger number of miles of railroad than that continent. While European countries generally opposed the introduction of the new system of transportation, our people extended to it a hearty welcome. This difference of sentiment can easily be accounted for. At the time of the invention of railroads Europe had a system of turnpikes and canals which, at least for the time being, answered every purpose. It became necessary for the railroads to enter into competition with these well-established agencies of transportation, which had the test of time, popular prejudice and governmental sanction in their favor. Moreover, the railroad as a new and unknown quantity caused a feeling of uneasiness in all conservative circles. It seemed to make war against time-honored principles of statecraft and society, and threatened to bring about a revolution the outcome of which no one could foresee.

The condition of things was entirely different in the United States. There were but few good roads and still fewer turnpikes and canals. A vast territory in the interior awaited cultivation. Excepting the coast and a few cities situated on the large navigable rivers, the East and the West and the North and the South were practically without commercial relations, and were only held together by a community of political traditions and the artificial cement of a common constitution. Even had the country had a system of turnpikes and canals, the Mississippi River would still have been a forty days', and the extreme Northwest a three months' journey distant from New York. It seems extremely doubtful whether the different sections of so large a realm, having so little community of commercial interests, could long be kept together under a republican system of government. The settlement of the central portion of the country and the development of its resources seemed to be the task of future centuries. The railroad under these circumstances made its appearance at a most opportune time for America, and the American people were not slow to make the best of the opportunities presented to them.

In the United States, as in England, the railroad was preceded by the tram-road. The first tram-road in this country was opened in 1826. It connected the granite quarries of Quincy with the Neponset River, and was operated by horse-power. The second road of this kind was the Mauch Chunk tramway, in Pennsylvania, opened in 1826, for the transportation of coal. The trains were drawn up an inclined plane by stationary engines and were moved down by their own weight. During the same year the Delaware and Hudson Canal Company opened the Carbondale and Homesdale tramway, connecting their mines with the Delaware and Hudson Canal. It appears that an English locomotive was imported for use on this line in 1828, but that it did not answer its purpose.

During the same year was commenced the construction of the first line of importance in this country, the Baltimore and Ohio. The line was opened for traffic in 1830, having then an extent of fourteen miles. In 1831 it was extended sixty-one miles, and the year following sixty-seven miles. For a year the road was operated by horse-power, but in 1831 the company purchased for its road an American locomotive.

The first road upon which a locomotive engine of American manufacture was used was the South Carolina Railroad, which was commenced in 1830. The engine was manufactured at West Point and was placed upon the road in December of the same year. The line had then an extent of ten miles. In 1832 it had increased to sixty-two miles, and in 1833 to 136 miles. The construction of the Mohawk and Hudson was commenced in August, 1830, and the road was opened in September of the following year. Its first locomotive engine was also imported from England, but, being found too heavy, was soon replaced by an American engine of half its weight. In 1831 two other New York roads were commenced, the Saratoga and the New York and Harlem. A small portion of the latter was opened during the same year, and the former in July, 1832. The Camden and Amboy Railroad in New Jersey was likewise commenced in 1831, but its completion was not reached till 1834. The New Castle and Frenchtown Railroad was completed in 1832, the Philadelphia and Trenton in 1833, and the New Jersey in 1834. In 1835 the Washington branch of the Baltimore and Ohio was opened, and the entire line had at the end of that year attained an extent of 115 miles. During the same year three Massachusetts roads, connecting Boston with Providence, Worcester and Lowell respectively, were opened. In 1836 the New York Central route was opened to Utica. In 1837 the Richmond, Fredericksburg and Potomac Railroad was completed from Richmond to Fredericksburg. In 1838 the Richmond and Petersburg and the Philadelphia, Wilmington and Baltimore railroads were opened. The

Wilmington and Weldon Railroad was completed in 1840, and the Petersburg and Roanoke three years later. There was now a continuous line of railway from the Potomac to Wilmington, North Carolina. In 1842 the whole line of the Boston and Albany road was completed, which thus became the first important through route in America.

The construction of railroads in the United States was from the first carried on without a system. Railroads in an early day were purely local affairs. Each locality operated its own road in its own interest and without any supervision from the State which had granted its charter. Acts of incorporation or charters were granted as a matter of course. Railroads were looked upon as the natural feeders of canals, and their future importance was foreseen by very few men. The early roads were a heavy burden on the capital of the country. A number of small roads were built that proved unprofitable and had to be abandoned. After the financial panic of 1837 there was, except in New England, a very perceptible stagnation in railroad enterprise, which lasted until the discovery of gold in California, in 1848. The average number of miles of road constructed per annum during the ten years preceding 1848 was 380, while it was nearly 1,800 per annum during the seven years following.

It may be said that with the discovery of gold in the West ends the first or formative period of railroad construction. From the first opening of the Baltimore and Ohio to the beginning of the year 1848, a period of eighteen years, there were constructed in the United States 5,205 miles of railroad, or an average of 289 miles per annum. The discovery of gold on the Pacific gave a new impetus to railroad construction throughout the country. Railroads now ceased to be local works and became inter-

state or national thoroughfares. Extensive new lines were
built and through routes were formed by the coalition of
local roads. It was during this period that railroad companies first became conscious of the importance of their
mission and that they commenced to compete with river
and canal carriers. In 1848 a through route was completed between Cincinnati and Lake Erie. A more direct
line, the Cleveland, Columbus and Cincinnati road, was
opened in 1851. During the same year the Erie Railroad
reached Lake Erie and connected the lake with the Hudson, and a year later Chicago received railroad connection
with the East by the completion of the Michigan Central
and Michigan Southern. In 1854 the Chicago and Rock
Island reached the Mississippi River, and in 1855 the
Chicago and Galena was opened. One year later the
Illinois Central reached the Mississippi at Cairo, and the
Chicago, Burlington and Quincy Railroad was opened to
Quincy. The Ohio and Mississippi, between Cincinnati and
St. Louis, was completed at about the same time. The
Pittsburgh, Fort Wayne and Chicago, an extension of the
Pennsylvania road, was completed to Chicago in 1858.
At the beginning of 1859 the Hannibal and St. Joseph Rail-
road reached the Missouri River, and eight years later the
Cedar Rapids and Missouri was completed to the Missouri
at Council Bluffs.

To encourage the extension of railroads into new and
thinly settled territories, and to thus hasten their settlement and the development of their resources, the people
of the United States began at the commencement of this
period to favor the policy of land grants. Such grants
had repeatedly been made to roads and canals prior to the
crisis of 1837. The first railroad that received a land
grant was the Illinois Central. The scheme was proposed

as early as 1836, but the act making the grant was not passed until September 20, 1850. Other grants followed in 1852 in Missouri, in 1853 in Arkansas, in 1856 in Michigan, Wisconsin, Iowa, Florida and Louisiana. As a rule these lands were granted by the National Government to the States, and by them to the railroads. The land grants made during President Fillmore's administration amounted to eight million, and those made during Pierce's administration to nineteen million acres. The financial crisis of 1857 and the War of the Rebellion again checked railroad building, but this period developed a new phase of railroad enterprise as well as of the land grant policy. In those times of national trial a railroad to the Pacific Coast seemed a political necessity. The project of connecting the Atlantic and Pacific oceans by a line of railroads was first brought prominently before the American people by Asa Whitney of New York. At a meeting held under his auspices in Philadelphia on the 23d day of December, 1846, a movement was inaugurated for the purpose of interesting the people in this enterprise and securing the aid of the government for its accomplishment. Various plans were urged, and earnest discussions followed, in which the ablest minds of the nation participated. The continual agitation of the subject finally led, on the 1st of July, 1862, to the passage by Congress of an act incorporating the Union Pacific Railway Company and the adoption of the central route. The Union and the Central Pacific companies received a virtual money subsidy of $30,000,000 and a land grant aggregating nearly twenty-three million acres, a domain almost equal to the State of Indiana. Other direct grants of territorial lands soon followed. The Northern Pacific received, just before the close of the war, a grant of forty-seven million acres of land. In the Southwest public lands were also freely given to new Pacific lines. The various grants made to railroads comprise no less than 300,000 square miles, equal to four and a half times the area of New England, or six times that of the State of New York, or equal to the total area of Iowa, Wisconsin, Illinois, Indiana, Michigan and Ohio. Where these grants were not deemed sufficient inducement for the construction of roads, counties, cities and towns freely voted subsidies, while private citizens made donations to or subscribed for the securities of the new railroads.

As has already been stated, the consolidation of connecting lines and their transformation into a few large through routes was one of the characteristic features of this period. As through traffic, and particularly through freight, grew in importance, it became more and more apparent that frequent transhipment was an expense to the railroads as well as a burden to the public. The system of railroad ownership and management soon adapted itself to the necessities of business. The change seems to have been inevitable, for it occurred in all parts of the world at about the same time. Sagacious men early recognized the importance of railroads as national lines of communication. This idea no doubt controlled the projectors of the Baltimore and Ohio, of the Erie, and of the Boston and Albany roads. The first consolidation of any importance took place in 1853, when eleven different roads between Albany and Buffalo were united to form the New York Central. Five branch roads were added to the system between 1855 and 1858. In 1864 Cornelius Vanderbilt secured control of the Hudson River road, and in 1867 of the New York Central, which lines he consolidated in 1869. By gaining soon afterward control of the Lake Shore and Michigan Central and Southern Canadian roads, he united under one management over 4,000 miles of railroad between New York and Chicago, and thus created the first through line between the East and the West.

As has already been stated, the Pennsylvania road gained control of the Pittsburgh, Fort Wayne and Chicago in 1858 and thus extended its system as far as Chicago. Through the absorption of other lines it reached an extent of over 7,000 miles. The creation of this through route was chiefly the work of Thomas A. Scott, at that time vice-president, and later president, of the Pennsylvania railroad.

In 1874 the Baltimore and Ohio, under the management of John W. Garrett, extended its system to Chicago, and became a competitor of the two older lines in the transportation of through freight. At about the same time two other parallel trunk lines were developed, the Grand Trunk on the north, and the Erie, between the Lake Shore and Pennsylvania lines. There were, therefore, in 1874 five rival trunk lines competing for the business between the West and the seaboard.

During the same period large rival lines developed west of Chicago and St. Louis. From the former city radiate the St. Paul and Northwestern systems, each with from 6,000 to 8,000 miles; the Atchison, Topeka and Santa Fe with over 9,000 miles; then the Rock Island, the Chicago, Burlington and Quincy, the Illinois Central, the Chicago Great-Western, and the Chicago and Alton, their systems ranging from 1,000 to 6,000 miles in extent. From St. Louis radiate the various branches of the Missouri Pacific and the closely allied Wabash system, controlling together some 10,000 miles of road.

This process of consolidation also went on in the Southern States, though to a less extent. Their systems do not run parallel, like the trunk lines, nor do they radiate from a common center, like the roads of the Northwest, but they radiate from the principal ports of the Atlantic and the Gulf of Mexico toward the interior.

We now enter upon the third period of the history of American railroads, the period of combinations. During the time of great activity in railroad construction following the War of the Rebellion many abuses in railroad management had been developed, which caused general complaint and led to what is known as the Granger movement. Laws were demanded, especially in the agricultural States of the West, which should regulate the rates, methods of operation, and the political relations of the railroads. The friends of this movement were successful in the political contests that followed, and Granger legislatures were elected in the States of Illinois, Wisconsin, Iowa and Minnesota. Laws were passed fixing the rates on different classes of roads and providing penalties for their violation. The companies contested these acts in the courts, but were defeated at every step, until in 1877 the Supreme Court of the United States sustained the constitutionality of the Granger laws. In the meantime railroad managers tried their utmost to render, by shrewd manipulation, these laws obnoxious, and they finally succeeded in having them repealed or so amended as to render them largely ineffectual.

It was the principal object of the Granger movement to do away with the many discriminating tariffs which so injuriously affected local points. It is true, discriminations between individuals were practiced at business centers, but rates upon the whole were low at such points as compared with those which obtained at local stations. While the Granger contest was still going on in the West, a new evil developed in the East, which became characteristic of the period and finally grew into one of the most intolerable abuses of railroad management. Railroad men had gradually learned that it was in their power to maintain high rates at competitive as well as at non-competitive points, provided all the roads centering at such points could be induced to coöperate, or rather to conspire for that purpose. The final solution of the problem was, after some experimentation, found in the device to control the prices of transportation generally known as the pool. It is doubtful whether any contrivance connected with railroad management ever threatened to subvert long-established principles of the common law more completely than this. Within a few years it extended its dominion over the whole country, exacting a heavy tribute from its commerce, until the people's patience finally became exhausted and their determined demand for railroad reform led to the enactment of the Interstate Commerce Act in 1887.

When this act passed, dire results were predicted by nearly every railroad man in the country Prophecies were freely made that it would ruin half of the roads and seriously cripple and sadly interfere with the usefulness of the other half, that it would derange the business of the country, greatly depreciate all railroad securities and put an end to railroad construction. Nearly seven years have passed since the adoption of the law, but not one of these prophecies has come to pass. There are at present probably less bankrupt roads in the United States than there have been at any time for twenty years, our business interests have been improved, the securities of honestly managed roads are in better repute than they were previous to the passage of the law, and the railroad mileage of the country is increasing at the rate of about 6,000 miles a year. If any branch of business has suffered in consequence of the enactment of the law, it is the branch monopolized by Wall Street. Since 1885, the time when the Interstate Commerce Bill was first seriously agitated, the aggregate of railroad securities has increased nearly $2,500,000,000, or about one-third. This certainly does not look as if capital had been seriously frightened by the Interstate Commerce Act. There are other proofs of railroad prosperity. In 1885 the gross earnings of the railroads of the United States were $772,568,833, or 9.9 per cent. on their reported capital. In 1886 their gross earnings were $829,940,836, or 10.2 per cent. on the reported railroad capital. In 1890 the gross earnings had increased to $1,097,847,428, and equaled 10.8 per cent. on the reported capital. This includes even the capitalization of new lines and others not reporting operations. Mr. Poor gives the reported cost of the lines actually operated as $8,519,670,421, against $10,122,635,900 reported cost of all the railroads built. Omitting from the computation the lines not reporting operations, the gross earnings of the roads actually operated equaled 12.7 per cent. and their net earnings 4 per cent. on the actual cost of the lines which reported. The gross earnings for 1891 were $1,138,024,459, and for the year ending June 30, 1892, $1,222,711,698.

The gross earnings per mile have increased from $6,265 in 1885, and $6,570 in 1886, to $6,946 in 1890, and $7,409 in 1892. In 1885 the capitalization per mile of road was $55,059 and the net earnings per mile were $2,185. In 1890 the capitalization per mile had decreased to $53,783, while the net earnings per mile increased to $2,195. The railroad mileage of the country has grown from 128,361 in 1885 to 166,817 in 1890, to 170,601 in 1891, and to 175,000 in 1892.

The railroad system of the United States has had a phenomenal growth, especially since 1870, since which time nearly 120,000 miles of road, or more than two-thirds of the total mileage, have been constructed. The table below shows the number of miles of railroad constructed and in operation, by quinquennial periods from 1830 to the close of 1890, inclusive:

YEAR.	MILES IN OPERATION.	INCREASE.
1830	23	
1835	1,098	1,075
1840	2,818	1,720
1845	4,633	1,815
1850	9,021	4,388
1855	18,374	9,353
1860	30,626	12,252
1865	35,085	4,459
1870	52,922	17,837
1875	74,096	21,174
1880	93,296	19,200
1885	128,361	35,065
1890	166,817	38,456

It will be noticed that in the sixty years covered by the above table there are but two quinquennial periods which show a falling-off in the rate of growth, viz.: 1860–65 and 1875–80. During the former period railroad construction was partially checked by the War of the Rebellion, during the latter by the general financial depression following the panic of 1873.

The length of railroads in the world has grown from 206 miles in 1830 to about 400,000 miles in 1892. The following table shows the growth of railroad mileage by quinquennial periods:

YEAR.	MILES.	YEAR.	MILES.
1830	206	1865	90,280
1835	1,502	1870	131,638
1840	5,335	1875	182,927
1845	10,825	1880	231,190
1850	23,625	1885	303,172
1855	42,340	1890	385,000
1860	66,413		

From this table it is seen that the railroad mileage of the world has doubled during the past fifteen years, and that its average annual increase is at present not far from 17,000 miles. There is no doubt that the extent of railroad construction has everywhere exceeded all anticipations. So fast has the railroad system expanded in the most highly civilized countries that it soon outgrew in nearly all of them the laws originally adopted for railroad control. In time an almost universal demand arose for reform, and the most progressive governments were not slow in heeding it. For the past fifteen years there has been a decided drift on the European continent toward state ownership of railroads, or to such strict control of the transportation business as virtually deprives the operating companies of the power to do injustice to the public.

The railroad is assuming more and more the character of an international highway. A movement is on foot to connect the railroad systems of the United States with those of South America by an intercontinental or "Pan-American" railroad. Appropriations have been made by the United States and several of the South American republics for a preliminary survey of the proposed line. Three different surveying parties are in the field, one in Central America and the other two in the United States of Colombia and Ecuador. The progress so far reported by them is encouraging, and there is now some hope that before the close of the nineteenth century one may be able to travel by railroad from New York to Valparaiso without even a change of cars.

It has also been proposed to span Behring Strait and connect North America with Asia and Europe by an international railway. This line, if constructed, would be simply an extension of the proposed Pan-American railroad and would follow the western coast of the United States as far as Behring Strait, then cross over into Asia, traverse Siberia and finally reach London via St. Petersburg, Berlin and Paris. It is very questionable whether such a line is at present feasible either from a technical or financial point of view, but the time will probably come when the railroad track will connect New York and London.

CHAPTER IV.

MONOPOLY IN TRANSPORTATION.

FROM time immemorial efforts have been made by designing men to control either commerce or its avenues, the highways on the land and on the sea, by a power which law, custom, ingenuity, artifice or some other agency had placed into their hands.

The ancient Phœnicians early aimed at and finally obtained the empire of the sea by making themselves masters of the most commodious harbors of the Mediterranean Sea and the Arabian Gulf. They established a regular intercourse with the countries bordering on the Mediterranean as well as with India and the eastern coast of Africa. From these latter countries they imported many valuable commodities which were not known to the people of other parts of the world, and during a long period they held this lucrative branch of commerce without a rival. The character and the situation of the Phœnicians aided them greatly in acquiring this mastery of commerce. Neither their manners and customs nor their institutions showed any marked national peculiarity; they had no unsocial prejudices and they mingled with the people of other countries without the least scruple or repugnance. As their native country was small and quite barren, they early learned to rely upon commerce as the best source of riches and power. Like the other Semitic tribes, the Phœnicians were noted for their energy and acumen, and while they were not a literary people in the strict sense of the word, ancient civilization received probably a more powerful impetus through their commercial supremacy than through any other agency.

During the reign of King Solomon the Jews made an attempt to wrest from the Phœnicians at least a part of the world's trade. Solomon built ships and imported Phœnician sailors for his fleet. For a time it seemed as if the Israelites might become the rivals of their teachers in the art of navigation and in the mysteries of trade; but their peculiar religious customs in that early day proved a serious impediment to commercial ascendancy, as it rendered them incapable of that unreserved intercourse with strangers so essential in commerce.

The monopoly of the sea, at least of the Mediterranean, passed to the Carthaginians, their descendants. The latter extended their navigation toward the west and north. They planted colonies and opened new harbors, and up to the time of the Punic wars kept almost the entire trade of the countries bordering on the Mediterranean in their hands.

After the downfall of Carthage the control of the commerce of Southern Europe and Northern Africa descended to the Romans. When Rome became the capital of the world, it gathered the wealth and valuable productions of all its provinces. Under the consuls and the earlier emperors the vigilance of the Roman magistrates and the spirit of the Roman government gave every possible security to commerce and prevented for a time the rise of monopoly. Nowhere was national union so complete or commercial intercourse so perfect as in the Roman empire. The intelligence and the power of Rome stimulated and regulated the industry of her people and permitted them to enjoy the fruits of their efforts without public or private restrictions.

We have seen that the intercourse of Rome and her provinces was facilitated by the construction of roads and

the establishment of imperial posts.   During the decline
of the empire the maintenance of these posts led, however, to a grave abuse.   We are informed by Gibbon in
his "Decline and Fall of the Roman Empire":

"But these beneficial establishments were accidentally
connected with a pernicious and intolerable abuse.   Two
or three hundred agents or messengers were employed,
under the jurisdiction of the master of the offices, to
announce the names of the annual consuls and the edicts
or victories of the emperors.   They insensibly assumed
the license of reporting whatever they could observe of the
conduct either of the magistrates or private citizens, and
were soon considered as the eyes of the monarch and the
scourge of the people.   Under the warm influence of a
feeble reign they multiplied to the incredible number of
ten thousand, disdained the mild though frequent admo-
nitions of the laws, and exercised in the profitable management of the posts a rapacious and insolent oppression.
These official spies, who regularly corresponded with the
palace, were encouraged by favor and reward anxiously to
watch the progress of every treasonable design, from the
faint and latent symptoms of disaffection to the actual
preparation of an open revolt.   Their careless or criminal
violation of truth was covered by the consecrated mask of
zeal; and they might securely aim their poisoned arrows
at the breast either of the guilty or the innocent, who had
provoked their resentment."

After the downfall of the Romans, commerce remained
paralyzed during the period of Gothic ignorance and bar-
barism.   The crusades for the recovery of the Holy Land
from the Saracens, in the eleventh and following centuries, opened again communication between the east and
the west by leading multitudes from every European
country into Asia; and though the object of these expe-
ditions was conquest, and not commerce, their commercial
effects were both beneficial and permanent.   The crusades
were especially favorable to the commercial pursuits of

the Italian states. The vast armies which marched from
all parts of Europe toward Asia gave encouragement to
the shipping of Venice, Genoa, and Pisa, which sometimes transported them, and always supplied them with
provisions and military stores. Besides the immense
sums which these states received on this account, they
obtained commercial privileges of great consequence in
the settlements which the crusaders made in the East.
All the commodities which they imported or exported
were exempted from every imposition, the property of
entire suburbs in some of the maritime towns, and of
large streets in others, was vested in them, and all questions arising among persons residing within their precincts,
or who traded under their protection, were decided by
their own laws and by judges of their own appointment.
When the crusaders took Constantinople, the Venetians
did not neglect to secure to themselves many advantages
from that event. Nearly all the branches of commerce
were in time transferred from Constantinople to their city.
At the end of the crusade period Venice had monopolized
nearly all the foreign trade of Europe. She supplied the
people of Italy, France and Germany with those commodities with which the crusaders by their intercourse with more
refined nations had become acquainted. The possession
of many Eastern ports and the maintenance of a powerful
navy made it possible for the Venetians to retain their
monopoly for several centuries.

The growth of commerce in Central Europe was but
slow, owing to the dangers to which it was exposed in
those days of feudalism. The mountain fastnesses of
robber knights, which controlled every road and navigable
river, were so many toll-gates at which the wayfaring
merchant was stopped to pay tribute. In time this sys-

tem of plunder grew to such an extent that hundreds of feudal lords relied upon it for their support. Such a tax upon commerce greatly enhanced the value of all commodities, and this deplorable state of things lasted until the cities made their power felt by forming alliances for mutual protection. One of these alliances, the Rhenish League, comprised in time seventy towns, and the ruins of the strong castles destroyed by its forces still exist along the Rhine, picturesque memorials of these lawless times.

Perhaps the most powerful commercial union of the middle ages was the Hanseatic League. To protect their commerce, the cities of Hamburg and Lubeck formed about the middle of the thirteenth century an alliance for mutual defense. The advantages derived from this union attracted other towns to the confederacy. In a short time about eighty of the largest cities lying between the Baltic and the Rhine joined this famous league, which in time became so formidable that its alliance was courted and its enmity was dreaded by the greatest monarchs. The League divided its territory into several districts. Its members, like railway associations of the present day, made their own laws, and met for this purpose at regular intervals in the city of Lubeck. The original object of the League, mutual assistance against outside attacks, was soon lost sight of, and its constantly growing power was used to obtain still greater commercial privileges in the adjoining countries, and even to force their rulers to concede to its members a commercial monopoly. In 1361 a controversy arose between the League and the King of Denmark, which led to a long and bitter war between them. This war was participated in by no less than seventy-seven cities on the part of the League. It terminated in 1370, leaving the Hansa master of the situation. For many years after this the League exerted its power in Denmark, Sweden and Norway, and the rulers of these countries were compelled to respect the wishes and even submit to the orders of these proud merchants. The countries bordering on the Baltic Sea remained the domain of the League for several centuries. They gathered there immense quantities of raw material, which they sold in the various ports of Europe. The influence of the League even reached as far as Novgorod in the east and London in the west. In both cities the League had its quarters, and within them it virtually exercised the right of sovereignty. Its main market was at Bruges in Flanders, which was then a bee-hive of industry and thrift. There the Italian traders came with the products of the east, such as spices, perfumes, oil, sugar, cotton and silk, to exchange them for the raw materials of the north. While taxes and imposts everywhere else harassed merchants, commerce was free in the cities of Flanders, owing to the liberality, or rather shrewdness, of her rulers. In Bruges the members of the Hansa met the merchants of Venice on equal terms, and the exchange of the products of the north for those of the east and south could be effected there to the greatest advantage of both.

While it must be admitted that the Hanseatic League developed the resources of Northern Europe, and that, even at the time of its greatest power, there was always competition among its own members, the fact remains that it abused its power by the suppression of all outside competition, and that it usurped rights which belong only to the state, thus often producing abuses as great as those which it was organized to remedy. Its final downfall was caused by the development of national power in the northern kingdoms and the growth of commerce and navigation in Great Britain. A stubborn assertion of antiquated privileges on the part of the Hansa involved it in a feud with the illustrious and lion-hearted Queen Elizabeth of England. In 1589 the Queen caused sixty of their vessels to be captured on the Tagus, and later even took possession of their hall and wharves in London. After this the League's decline was very rapid, though its organization was kept up till 1669, when its delegates held their last session.

Contemporary with the decline of the Hanseatic commerce in the north was that of the Italian cities, especially Venice, in the south. They had prospered by their commerce with the Levant until Vasco de Gama discovered the sea route to East India in 1497. His countrymen, the Portuguese, soon utilized this discovery. They took possession of the coast of India and of the islands to the south of it. They also succeeded in excluding the Arabs from the commerce with that country, of which up to that time they had had exclusive control. For this purpose they built fortresses and factories on the west coast of Hindostan, took possession of the island of Socotra in the Arabian, and of Ormus in the Persian Gulf, and forced the Indian princes to grant them the exclusive privilege of trading with their subjects. They also captured the city of Malacca, where the trade between China, Japan, the Philippine Islands, the Moluccas and India had concentrated itself. In this way they got in a comparatively short time control of the commerce of India, Arabia, and even Egypt. By forcing the Venetians and their commercial allies out of those markets, they secured for themselves a monopoly of the commerce between Europe and the east. The political ascendancy of the Turks in the islands situated in, and in the countries bordering on, the Eastern Mediterranean, caused the loss of Cyprus, Crete (Candia) and Morea to the Venetians and greatly aided the Portuguese in establishing their commercial supremacy. Less profitable for the latter was the possession of their American colonies. They, as well as the Spaniards, adopted here a policy which ultimately brought commercial and industrial ruin upon both. Entirely neglecting agriculture and relying on the mineral resources of their transatlantic colonies, which were believed to be inexhaustible, they strove to amass riches by reserving for themselves the exclusive privilege of supplying them with the manufactures of Europe in exchange for American gold. Neglecting home industries, they bought their supplies as well as those of their colonies in France, Holland and England. A spirit of speculation and adventure enervated their people, and led in time to commercial bankruptcy and political disaster.

Spain also drained her treasury by her wars with her Dutch dependencies, and the loss of her northern provinces was a serious blow to her commerce. Antwerp, which had become the successor of Bruges as the commercial emporium of the north, began to decline, and Amsterdam, the metropolis of the new Dutch republic, became heir to its glory and its riches. The young republic at once commenced to compete in the carrying trade with Spain and Portugal, and to make inroads into the eastern commerce of the latter.

The Dutch East India Company, which was organized in 1602, sent a fleet of fourteen vessels into the Indian Archipelago to found colonies in Java, Sumatra and the Moluccas. In a short time they had monopolized the entire spice trade, which immediately became a source of great wealth. A cargo of five vessels, which returned to Amsterdam in 1603, consisted of over two million pounds of spices. This cargo was purchased for 588,874 florins and was sold for 2,000,000 florins. It is under these circumstances not surprising that the dividends of the company's stockholders often amounted to 75 per cent., and never went below 12½ per cent. previous to 1720. Holland's colonial trade made Amsterdam the commercial metropolis of Europe. It became the grain market from which Spain, Italy and other countries drew their supplies. All the products of the world found purchasers here, and a well-developed banking system greatly facilitated the exchange. The rapid accumulation of fortunes by the Dutch merchants and bankers was without precedent in Europe. Besides this, the progress which Holland made in ship-building and navigation and the advantages which she derived from her colonial trade placed her in a position to outstrip all other nations in the carrying trade of Europe. During the first half of the seventeenth century the Dutch were justly called the freighters of Europe. But the injury which their policy did to the commercial and manufacturing interests of other European nations led both England and France to adopt measures well calculated to accomplish, in a short time, their commercial emancipation. Louis XIV., in order to build up French shipping, collected a tonnage from every foreign ship which entered a French harbor. England went still further. In 1651 Oliver Cromwell promulgated the Navigation Act, by which foreign ships were prohibited from importing into England any goods except such as were produced or manufactured in their own countries. This was a heavy blow at the Dutch, who were thus deprived of the privilege of effecting the exchange of commercial commodities between England and her colonies as well as the continent. The war which the Dutch Republic waged against England, to force her to revoke this act, resulted in favor of the latter and ended the commercial supremacy of the Dutch in Europe.

England, which before this time had played but a secondary role as a commercial power, rose fast to promi nence after her successful struggle with the Dutch. She commenced to strengthen her industries by the adoption of a high tariff policy, and her merchants were encouraged to enter into commercial relations with colonists and foreigners. The privileges which had been given to foreign tradesmen were revoked, while ship-building and navigation were greatly favored by the government. As England gained greater strength as a naval power, her foreign policy became more aggressive.

In 1600 the "Company of Merchants of London Trading to the East Indies" obtained a charter, and, in spite of Dutch and Portuguese opposition, soon gained a foothold on the Moluccas and the coast of Malabar, whence it extended in time its dominion to Surat, Bombay, Madras and Calcutta. Here they built forts and established their commerce. From these places the company pushed into the interior, until finally, after repeated struggles with the natives and European rivals, the whole of Hindostan came under English dominion. As its power increased, the company commenced to abuse shamefully the monopoly which it had been granted, by inaugurating a system of plunder and oppression which is perhaps without its equal in the annals of history. These growing abuses led to frequent revolts and seriously imperiled England's dominion in these territories.

To remedy these evils, Parliament at the close of the

seventeenth century annulled the charter of the company
and declared the commerce with the East Indies open to
all of the King's subjects. A number of small companies
were formed, but in 1702 they all combined and organized
the East India Company. Monopoly was again established, but the patience of the natives was exhausted, and
England's interests in Hindostan were in a critical condition. At this juncture the East India Company
adopted a policy of moderation, and this, together with
the aid which the government gave to the company,
enabled it to strengthen again its weakened commercial
relations and to further enlarge its territory. But the
temptation to abuse its power was too great for this
strong corporation to be long resisted. Abuses again
crept into its management and continued to grow until its
charter was finally repealed.

The policy adopted by Great Britain for the government of her American colonies during the eighteenth
century was less rapacious, but scarcely more just than
that pursued in her eastern possessions. To retain those
colonies as commercial no less than as political dependencies, Parliament enacted laws compelling their people
to trade with the mother country exclusively and laying
restraint on their manufactures. But the American pioneers felt that they had brought with them across the
ocean the rights of Englishmen; they objected to taxation
without representation, and the men who for opinion's
sake had left comfortable homes to brave upon a distant
shore the dangers of frontier life were prepared, if necessary, to emphasize their objection by armed resistance.
England, intent upon maintaining her barbaric system of
discriminative duties and commercial monopolies, blindly
attempted coercion, but the war which resulted wrested

from the English crown its brightest jewel, and the War
of 1812 established upon American soil the principle of
industrial and commercial liberty.

It must not be supposed, however, that America and
the United States in particular have been free from monopolies growing out of the transportation business. Nothing
would be farther from the truth. There is no law so
stringent but that it will be violated; there is no government so vigilant but that it will at times be imposed upon.
It is true, our government sanctions no monopoly, but the
very liberty of action which exists here among corporations as well as individuals offers to organized wealth and
power a wide field for abuses.

We have seen in the foregoing that almost from time
immemorial efforts have been made to monopolize transportation and trade, and that these efforts were successful
whenever either from ignorance or weakness the masses
fell into political apathy. There is a natural tendency
among men to utilize commercial advantages to the detriment of others. In modern times the opportunities for
building up large monopolies have greatly increased and
have been turned to the most profitable account by designing men. Great and even unbearable abuses have always
followed where the greed and ambition of such men have
not been checked by governmental agencies. In this
respect the people of the United States have had about
the same experience as the rest of mankind. Ever since
the introduction of railroads into this country there has
been a well-marked drift toward monopolizing the transportation business.

As long as the dangers of monopoly remained unknown
to the American people, legislation for the control of railroads and other public carriers was both scarce and crude,

and shrewd railroad men were not slow in taking advantage of the situation. It is foreign to the design of this treatise to give a complete history of railroad monopoly in the United States. The author will therefore confine himself to showing that transportation companies will, like the great commercial organizations of the past, when left to follow their instincts, invariably use their power to oppress the public by exacting excessive charges for their services, or to discriminate against the many by extending special privileges to the few. Hundreds of cases might be given to illustrate the above rule, but a history of two of these corporations will suffice to show to what extent corporate abuses can be carried, and to serve as a warning against the adoption of any *" laissez faire "* policy in the railroad legislation of the future. The corporations selected for this purpose are the Camden and Amboy Railroad and the Standard Oil Companies, both typical representatives of the Rob Roy policy which organized wealth has pursued since the dawn of civilization, when not prevented by the wisdom and strength of a good government.

THE CAMDEN AND AMBOY RAILROAD COMPANY.

For almost forty years the Camden and Amboy Railroad was the only direct route between the cities of New York and Philadelphia. It is doubtful whether previous to the war a more important or a more remunerative road existed in the United States, for, besides connecting the two largest cities in the Union, it formed part of the direct land route from the East to the South.

The efforts to open a direct through route between New York and Philadelphia date back to the year 1812, when the construction of a canal between the Hudson and the

Delaware was proposed, but an ill-advised jealousy of the State of Pennsylvania delayed for many years the realization of the project. When this obstacle was finally overcome, a change of sentiment had taken place in New Jersey. Railroads had just made their appearance in the United States, and a large number of the people of New Jersey preferred a railroad to a canal.

The matter was finally compromised in the legislature of New Jersey, which on the 4th of February, 1830, simultaneously granted charters to the Delaware and Raritan Canal Company and the Camden and Amboy Transportation Company, fixing the capital stock of each company at $1,000,000, with the right to increase it to $1,500,000. The charter further stipulated what taxes should be paid to the State, and also contained the provision that within five miles of the starting-point and within three miles of the terminus of each line no other railroad or canal should be built. It was believed the existence of both a water and a land route would be sufficient to maintain competition on this important thoroughfare of interstate traffic. The construction of the railroad, which had been surveyed in almost a straight line between its termini, was at once commenced. A number of well-to-do and practical men took hold of the enterprise, among them one John Stevens, who together with his three sons took one-half of the capital stock. The canal project did not do so well at first. At the middle of the year 1830 only about one-twelfth of its capital stock had been sold, and there was great danger that the company might forfeit its charter, as the time allowed for the subscription of its stock was nearing its end. At this juncture Robert Field Stockton, a young man of ability, enthusiasm and wealth, came to the rescue of the canal company. He not only bought for himself a goodly share of the canal stock, but also prevailed on his rich father-in-law, Mr. John Porter, to invest $400,000 in the enterprise. The financial difficulties of the company were thus removed. At the next session of the legislature Mr. Stockton secured an amendment to their charter which apparently only authorized the enlargement of the canal, but in reality empowered the canal company to construct a second railway.

It was from the beginning Mr. Stockton's object to share with the railroad company the advantages which their line promised to give them. The enlargement of his company's franchise placed him in a position to dictate terms to the Camden and Amboy Transportation Company. The latter was given the choice, to prepare for competition with a rival railroad line, or to consolidate with the Delaware and Raritan Canal Company. It chose the latter alternative, and on the 15th day of February, 1831, the two companies became one. The consolidation still required the sanction of the legislature. This was obtained in consideration of the transfer of 2,000 shares of the capital stock of the company to the State. It was further stipulated that the new company should pay to the State a tax of 10 cents for each passenger and of 15 cents for each ton of freight carried over its line through the State, as well as an annual tax of $30,000, and that the State in return should protect the company against any and all competition in the direct passenger and freight traffic between the cities of New York and Philadelphia. Serious doubts were at the time entertained by many, whether the State of New Jersey under the Federal Constitution possessed the right to thus create a monopoly in transportation facilities, and to regulate arbitrarily the commerce between sister States.

Five days after it had granted this charter to the Camden and Amboy Company, the legislature granted another charter authorizing the construction of a railroad from Jersey City to New Brunswick on the Raritan River. On the 23d of February of the same year a charter had been granted by the legislature of the State of Pennsylvania to a company which had been formed for the purpose of constructing a railroad from Philadelphia to Trenton. This company had likewise been authorized by its charter to buy the right of way for a railroad from Trenton to New York, which it proceeded at once to do. It was evident that as soon as the two new roads would meet at New Brunswick, an understanding would be reached between them, by which another through line would be created between New York and Philadelphia, which would have the advantage over the Camden and Amboy road that it touched the capital of New Jersey and could thus make itself serviceable to members of the legislature, officers of State and influential politicians.

The Camden and Amboy Freight Company soon arrived at the conclusion that it could not permit such rivalry. It appealed to the legislature for protection. Resolutions were passed in its favor, but the Philadelphia and Trenton Railroad Company paid no attention to those resolutions, but quietly continued to lay its track. Mr. Stockton and his friends did not dare to invoke the aid of the courts, because a judicial investigation might have resulted in the destruction of their own charter. The situation was critical, but Mr. Stockton was equal to the occasion. He bought quietly a sufficient number of shares to control the management of the Philadelphia and Trenton road, and, in April, 1836, secured the consolidation of the Philadelphia and Trenton and the Camden and Amboy railroad companies.

The canal of the company was not completed until 1838. It had consumed a sum of money largely in excess of the original estimate. To connect the two lines of the consolidated company, a branch road was constructed from Trenton to Bordentown. Later the road from Trenton to Brunswick was completed and an agreement entered into with the Jersey City company for a division of the traffic of the two roads. The large cost of these improvements suggested to the company the advisability of increasing its revenues and of decreasing its expenditures. Its charter provided for a payment to the State of 10 cents for each through passenger. By an artifice the company avoided the payment of this tax. It compelled its through passengers to walk over the bridge at Trenton and then continue their journey by rail via Bordentown to Jersey City.

The company's charter also stipulated that the fare between New York and Philadelphia should not exceed $3 per passenger. Its officers interpreted this stipulation to apply only to the intermediate traffic and proceeded to collect $2.50 for the trip from New York to Trenton, and $1.50 from there to Philadelphia, thus increasing the fare for the entire journey to $4.00, one dollar above the maximum allowed by law. One Jacob Ridgway, who was the owner of a ferry-boat at Camden, saw here an opportunity for starting a lucrative business. He bought a steamer and carried passengers from Philadelphia to Trenton for one-third of the fare demanded by the railroad. After the Camden and Amboy Company had made several unsuccessful attempts to intimidate Mr. Ridgway and his force, one of which even brought Mr. Stockton in contact with the criminal courts, it purchased the boat with all terminal facilities at Philadelphia and Trenton. The attention of the legislature of New Jersey was repeatedly called to the company's failure to comply with the provisions of its charter, but these appeals were on the whole of no avail. In 1842, after a long discussion, a resolution was carried declaring the charge of $4 for the through journey illegal, but the company entirely ignored this legislative reminder and continued its old tariff.

The company's charter also reserved for the State the right to acquire the Camden and Amboy road under certain conditions upon the payment of a reasonable compensation. In 1844, through Mr. Stockton's engineering, the constitution of New Jersey was so amended as to practically deprive the State of the power to acquire the company's property.

During the first few years of the existence of the Camden and Amboy Transportation Company its business was managed in the interest of its owners, but soon a few of its leading stockholders managed to turn its enormous profits into their own pockets. The Stevens and Stockton families, together with two other directors of the Camden and Amboy Company, had come into possession of a line of steamers that plied on the Raritan, between New Brunswick and New York. The enterprise, in spite of its largely watered capital, had been made to pay dividends ranging from 30 to 40 per cent. Its owners saw an opportunity for a larger field of usefulness and larger dividends. In 1834 a majority of the board of directors of the Camden and Amboy Company proposed that the company rid itself of the responsibility connected with the transportation business and lease its railroad and canal. Mr. Stevens, as representative of the Camden and Amboy Company, then negotiated with Mr. Stevens, the representative of the Napoleon Steamer Company, and the negotiations soon resulted in an agreement between the two companies by which the latter leased the railroad and canal lines of the former and agreed to pay it a fixed toll of $7.64 per ton upon all freights carried by rail, and one-quarter of all its revenues derived from the canal. Soon afterward the Napoleon Company entered into a similar contract with the Camden Ferry Company and now had a complete monopoly of the transportation business between New York and Philadelphia. It at once commenced to develop a system of organized plunder. Instead of the maximum charter tariff of 8 cents per ton per mile, it charged 10, 12, and even 15 cents. The through rates charged were several times as high as those fixed by the charter. Canal rates were raised to such an extent as to make them prohibitory and to compel the public to ship by rail. It is difficult even to estimate the total annual profits of the directorial syndicate. Their accounts, if any were kept, were not accessible, and surmises can only be based upon such data as occasionally found their way to the public. In 1845 the share of the canal tolls paid to the company's stockholders was $359,000. The directors' share under the terms of their lease is thus found not to have been less than $1,077,000. Another item of $170,000, tolls collected for the transportation of 27,000 tons of freight, was so divided that the Camden Ferry Company, or its other self, the directorial syndicate, received $32,000 for one mile, while the Camden and Amboy Railroad Company received $63,000, or less than twice as much, for ninety-two miles. The directors under their lease were entitled to the remaining $75,000.

The service of the company was as bad as it was expensive; its trains were slow and irregular, and its employes arrogant. The syndicate which controlled the company defied its stockholders, the public and the courts alike. When one of the stockholders, a Trenton merchant by the name of Hagar, applied to the courts for an order to compel the directors to produce their books and render an account, the syndicate bought Mr. Hagar's shares, for which he had paid $125 a share, at the price of $1,456 a share. The suit was then withdrawn and the matter hushed up.

In 1848 a number of articles appeared in a paper published at Burlington, Pa., which were signed by "A Citizen of Burlington" and contained much surprising information concerning the Camden and Amboy Transportation Company. It was charged that the directors had defrauded both the State and the company's stockholders of large sums of money, that they had grossly violated their charter by charging illegal and extortionate rates, oppressive to both commerce and travel. It was shown that while the average rate per ton per mile of thirty-five neighboring roads was 2.85 cents, that of the Camden and Amboy Company was 4.54 cents. It was also shown that neither the stockholders nor the State had received the share of the company's revenues to which they were entitled. These articles were extensively reprinted and caused a great commotion wherever they appeared. After the first storm had subsided the directors issued an address to the people of New Jersey, in which they bitterly complained of the people's loss of confidence in their integrity, and declared that the charges preferred against them were founded on falsehoods.

The "Citizen of Burlington" replied by accusing the directors of defalcation and falsifying their books. He charged that from 1840 to 1847 no account had been rendered of the receipt of no less than $5,266,431, on which $493,066 was due to the State.   As soon as the legislature convened, a resolution was introduced that a commission be appointed to investigate the charges preferred against the Camden and Amboy Transportation Company. The resolution was adopted, but it was virtually left to the accused to select the members of the commission. That the directors had a guilty conscience appeared from the fact that the last annual report of the company, which had just been printed, was withdrawn and destroyed. To silence their unknown accuser, they threatened him with criminal prosecution. He now gave his name. It was Henry C. Carey, the noted writer and authority on political economy. Mr. Carey did not give up the contest. He proceeded to show how the policy of the managers of the Camden and Amboy Transportation Company depressed commerce, manufactures and agriculture alike. He showed how the company as a public carrier discriminated in favor of industries which they carried on as private individuals. He claimed that the company had forfeited its charter, and that it was the duty of the State to authorize the construction of another road. In the meantime, early in 1849, the legislative investigation committee submitted its report. It was perhaps as shameless a document as was ever placed before a legislative assembly. It lauded the directors, to whose influence the members of the commission owed their selection, and whitewashed their past management of the company's affairs.

But the people of New Jersey were far from being satisfied with this report and demanded the appointment of another committee. Another investigation was ordered, and this time the company, or rather its directors, found it impossible to control the selection of its members. Soon after their appointment the committee asked Mr. Carey to lend them his assistance in their labors, and he readily consented. During the summer of 1849 the members of the committee had occasion to go to Bordentown, to inspect the company's books. From that time on a wonderful change seemed to have come over the committee. They found they could dispense with Mr. Carey's further services. What had previously appeared to them a ring of rapacious monopolists seemed now an association of worthy philanthropical gentlemen. In their report to the legislature they completely exonerated the company's managers. They admitted that the State had not been paid all that was due to it, but they asserted that this difference in the company's accounts was due solely to clerical errors, for which the management were in no wise responsible. The report was accepted, although not even the annexed testimony supported it, and thus the matter was dropped.

This was a great victory for Mr. Stockton and his friends. It demonstrated the success of their methods of dealing with public servants. Mr. Carey repeated his charges, but the directors failed to prosecute him for libel as they had threatened. He asked that he be permitted to inspect the company's books, but was met with a peremptory refusal. Public opinion was defied, and the old methods were continued.

The extortionate and discriminating tariff of the only through route of New Jersey affected seriously the agricultural as well as the commercial interests of that State. The Camden and Amboy monopoly kept the State of New Jersey for many years far behind the New England States in railroad facilities. In 1860 New Jersey had only one

mile of railroad for every 17.6 square miles of territory,
while the proportion of miles of railroad to square miles
of territory for the same year was 1 to 7.9 in Connecticut,
1 to 7.6 in Rhode Island, and 1 to 6 in Massachusetts.
At present New Jersey has one mile of railroad to every
3.79 square miles, and therefore leads all the States in
the Union in density of railroad track.

The question may be asked how the Camden and Amboy Transportation Company, or rather the syndicate
which controlled it, contrived to maintain its power for so
many years, to the great detriment of industry and commerce. The only answer that can be given is that the
men for whom the maintenance of the monopoly was a
source of great wealth were constantly using a part of
this wealth for the corruption of those who were in a position to influence public opinion or to direct the policy of
the State. Prominent politicians were favored with
passes, attorneys were retained by the company as local
solicitors, corrupt and servile legislators were bribed by
money or the promise of lucrative positions, and newspapers were given large subsidies. In addition to this
public men were constantly made to realize the political
power of the company, whose many employes had always
been trained to do the bidding of their masters. If the
opposition, in spite of this, was ever successful at legislative elections, the company's managers found it less
expensive to gain the good will of a few members of the
legislature after election than it would have been to gain
the good will of their constituents before election. Dis-
satisfied stockholders who threatened with judicial investigation were quietly bought out or impressed with the
danger of inviting public discussion in regard to the validity of the company's charter, as it might lead to its

annihilation. The good people of New Jersey made several attempts to rid the State of the despotism of the company by making the question a political issue, but they were each time defeated through the lavish and scandalous expenditure of the company's money.

The original charter of the Camden and Amboy Railroad Company was granted for a period of twenty years, and should have expired in 1853, but its managers succeeded in having it extended to January 1, 1859. In 1854 another extension was asked for, and after a long and bitter debate the company was again triumphant. An act was passed on the 16th of March, 1854, making it illegal to build previous to the first day of January, 1869, without the consent of the Camden and Amboy Transportation Company, a railroad in the State of New Jersey for the transportation of passengers and freight between New York and Philadelphia. At the end of this period even a third extension was granted, and the company, though after January 1, 1867, under a new name, maintained its monopoly until it consolidated, in 1871, with the Pennsylvania Railroad Company.

That the spirit of the past is still at work was shown by the recent act of the legislature of New Jersey legalizing the consolidation of the coal roads. The coal barons found the legislature as servile as the managers of the Camden and Amboy Railroad Company had found them of yore, and their well-planned scheme would probably have been successful had it not been for Governor Abbot's courageous veto of the disgraceful act, and it is more than probable that they will yet succeed. They have, in fact, during the last year advanced the price of coal about one dollar per ton.

THE STANDARD OIL MONOPOLY.

The Standard Oil monopoly may be said to be the crowning monument of corporation conspiracy. It is, indeed, doubtful whether the combined brotherhoods of mediæval knights ever were guilty of such acts of plunder and oppression as the Standard Oil Company and its railroad allies stand convicted of before the American people. The facts that have been unearthed by official investigations show a frightful prevalence of corporate lawlessness and official corruption, and there can be no doubt that, could certain high railroad dignitaries have been compelled to testify, and could the truth have been fathomed, it would have been found that not only the public, but railroad stockholders as well, were victimized by those transactions.

The founder of the Standard Oil monopoly was some twenty years ago part owner of a petroleum refinery at Cleveland, Ohio. His fertile brain conceived the thought that with the coöperation of the railroad companies a few men of means could control the petroleum business of the United States. With this end in view he approached the managers of the New York Central, the Erie and the Pennsylvania Central railroad companies, and on January 18, 1872, entered with them into a secret compact by which they agreed to coöperate with the South Improvement Company (an organization formed by that gentleman to aid in the accomplishment of his designs) to grant to said companies certain rebates and to secure it against loss or injury by competition. The South Improvement Company, in consideration of these favors, guaranteed to the railroad companies a fair division of its freights. The existence of this contract soon became known and caused a violent protest among the oil-producers. An indignation meeting was held and a committee was appointed to wait on the railroad managers and demand fair treatment for all.

The railroad companies yielded and promised to give equal rates to all shippers and to grant to no person either rebates or any other advantage whatever. New rates were fixed for the transportation of both crude and refined oil, and it was agreed on the part of the railroad companies that at least ninety days' notice should be given of any change that might be made in the rates. Steps were also taken to have the charter of the South Improvement Company canceled because it had been found that it was neither the owner of a refinery nor of an oil well, and could therefore not comply with the legal requirements concerning the organization of stock companies. While the South Improvement Company thus came to a sudden and rather inglorious end, its founders soon contrived other means to carry out their ingenious plans. They bought a refinery, reorganized by taking the prepossessing title of Standard Oil Company, and were now prepared to resume their operations under the guise of legal authority.

The railroad companies seemed to have relished their novel business connections, for, without paying the least attention to the agreement into which they had entered with the other producers and refiners of oil, they extended the privileges of the defunct South Improvement Company to its successors. The new company received secret rebates ranging from 50 cents to $1.32 per barrel. The agreement also contained the stipulation that if lower rates should ever be granted to their competitors, an additional rebate should be given to the Standard Oil Company. Endowed with these privileges, the favored company proceeded to unite under its banner, by consolidation, purchase or lease, the leading refineries of Cleveland.

The effect of the discriminations practiced against independent refineries soon became apparent. In less than two years there were closed in Pittsburgh twenty-one refineries, that represented an aggregate capital of $2,000,000 and had given employment to over 3,000 people. A large number of the remaining refineries were forced to consolidate with the Standard Oil Company.

The next step toward the entire suppression of competition was an attack planned against the independent pipe lines. The Standard had early secured control of the United Pipe Line. To exterminate competing lines, they again appealed to the railroad companies, and on the 9th day of September, 1874, J. H. Rutter, general freight agent of the New York Central, issued a new oil tariff which discriminated greatly in favor of the oil brought by the United Pipe Line to the refineries. Up to that time this company had done from 25 to 30 per cent. of the total business of the various pipe lines. Within one year after the adoption of the new tariff it did fully 80 per cent. of the entire business. This forced the independent lines either to sell out to the Standard or to suspend business, for the latter's rebate was larger than their toll. The oil tariff of the Pennsylvania Central compelled the independent Pittsburgh refiners to ship their refined oil over that company's line, if they would avail themselves of the rebate which it granted on the rates for the transportation of crude oil to Pittsburgh. The evident purpose and the effect of such a tariff was to prohibit oil shipments over the Baltimore and Ohio. Had this road made ever so reasonable a tariff, the combined charges for the transportation of the crude petroleum from the oil regions to Pittsburgh by the Pennsylvania Central, and for that of the refined oil to the sea coast by the Baltimore and Ohio, would still have been prohibitive in competition with the special transit rates granted to the Standard Oil Company. As a remedy it was proposed to organize a new pipe line, it being believed that the crude oil could be brought to Pittsburgh by that line, refined there, shipped to the seaboard by the Baltimore and Ohio, and sold there at as good or even a better profit than the product of the Standard, notwithstanding the favors received by the latter from the allied trunk lines. This movement resulted in the creation of the Columbia Conduit Company, which at once proceeded to lay its pipes from the oil wells to Pittsburgh. Under the laws of the State of Pennsylvania it became necessary for this company to obtain the permission of property-holders to lay the pipes through their lands. Consent was everywhere readily given, and the pipes were laid without hindrance until the track of the Pennsylvania Railroad was reached, within a few miles of the Pittsburgh refineries. This company peremptorily refused to let the pipes be laid under its track. The pipe line company after some delay contrived a way to obviate the difficulty. It laid its pipes on each side of the road as close to the track as it could without trespassing against the legal rights of the Pennsylvania Central, and then conveyed the oil from one side of the track to the other by means of large oil tanks on wheels, which could not be prevented from passing over the railroad track at the public crossing. After several months the railroad company allowed the pipes to be laid under its track, but it soon appeared that another combination had been effected to destroy the value of this concession. A railroad war had given the three trunk lines an opportunity to force the Baltimore and Ohio into the pool. A uniform rate of $1.15 was established for shipments of refined petroleum from any point to the seaboard. While this was in itself an unjust discrimination against Pittsburgh, which is 250 miles nearer tidewater than Cleveland, the railroads in addition granted the Standard secret rebates which enabled it to sell its oil on the coast for less than the sum of its first cost at the refineries and the open rate of transportation to the points of export. The independent refiners of Pittsburgh found themselves again cut off from the market, but necessity soon made them discover another outlet. Shipping their oil down the Ohio River to Huntington, W. Va., they had it taken by the Chesapeake and Ohio Railroad to Richmond. In spite of the fact that this route was more than twice as long as the direct line from Pittsburgh to the seaboard, and in spite of the further fact that it necessitated an expensive transfer, a rate equal to about two-thirds of the trunk line rate for the direct shipment proved remunerative to the Chesapeake and Ohio. The independent refiners kept up their competition for some time, but the great disadvantage of river travel and the insufficient export facilities of Richmond finally forced them to give up the contest.

Until the year 1877 the Standard Oil Company had worked hand in hand with the railroads. It had obtained all its privileges by asking for them and by holding out inducements to railroad managers to grant them. It now commenced to dictate terms to refractory railroad companies.

The Pennsylvania road ventured to carry oil not the property of the Standard on terms which that company did not approve. The latter ordered the road to refuse to carry the product of their competitors. This the railroad company declined to do, and the Standard at once withdrew its custom. The Pennsylvania retaliated by carrying the oil of the independent refineries at merely nominal rates and even went so far as to make its rates dependent upon the profits realized by the shippers. A fierce freight war was thus precipitated, in which the Erie and New York Central supported the Standard Company. The Pennsylvania road was soon forced to surrender and sign an ignominious treaty.

The Baltimore and Ohio, which had again commenced to carry the product of those Pittsburgh refineries which received their crude oil through the Columbia Conduit Company, was in a similar manner forced to reject their freights. The pipe line, whose value was thus almost entirely destroyed, was soon after sold to the Standard Oil Company. This company had now an almost complete monopoly of the oil business of the United States, and still it was not satisfied. It appears that some of the producers of crude oil had been in the habit of shipping a part of their product in spite of the advantages which the Standard had through its rebates. To prevent even these shipments, or rather to exact another tribute from railroad stockholders, the American Transfer Company, one of the auxiliaries of the Standard Oil Trust, in 1878, demanded and received from the Pennsylvania road a "commission" of 20 cents a barrel on all shipments of petroleum *made by any* shipper. It had been shown to the satisfaction of the Pennsylvania Railroad Company that similar commissions, ranging from 20 to 35 cents a barrel, were being paid by the New York Central and Erie roads.

When, in 1879, an effort was made to establish a pipe

line from the oil regions to the seaboard, nothing was
left undone by the trunk lines to thwart the enterprise.
The new company finally succeeded in making connection
with a railway which had no part in the pool, and there
was some hope that under this arrangement competition
might at least be maintained at some points. The Standard Company again appealed to the trunk lines to protect it against injury by competition and obtained from
them a special rate of 20 cents per barrel, which rate was
even reduced to 15 cents per barrel two months later.
Against such a rate it was impossible to compete, and
after a short struggle the new line found itself compelled
to sell its works to the Standard.

To crown its monopoly, the Standard Oil Company
finally bought of the New York Central and Erie roads
their terminal facilities for the transportation of oil, and
thereby made it virtually impossible for them to transport
oil for any of its few remaining competitors. Mr. Josiah
Lombard, part owner of the New York refinery, stated in
1879 before the investigating committee of the legislature
of New York that in 1878 he had requested the Erie
Company to transport for him 100 cars of crude oil from
Carrollton to New York; that he had called upon Mr.
Vilas, the general freight agent of the company, in person,
but had never been able to obtain the cars, though the oil
had been held in Carrollton three or four months ready to
be loaded. This gentleman also testified that he had found
it impossible to obtain cars from the New York Central,
and that the company's general freight agent had informed
him that the road did not own and could not furnish any
oil cars.

After the Standard Oil Company had secured control
of the various pipe lines of the oil regions, it frequently

lowered the price of crude oil to such an extent as to make its production unprofitable. It even refused to buy oil, basing its refusal upon the ground that the railroad companies failed to furnish cars for its transportation. When the well-owners had their tanks filled, they had the choice to let the oil run away or to be at the expense of closing up their wells. In one instance, however, when their ruse threatened to cause a riot, several hundred cars were brought to the wells within a few hours.

The Standard Oil Trust, not satisfied with the monopoly of the wholesale trade, even tried in places to control the retail trade by peddling oil at private houses. This method of destroying competition was chiefly resorted to where independent dealers obtained their supply by a water route.

That many of the deeds of the Standard are dark is evident from the fact that its members, when summoned by the Hepburn committee, declined to testify, lest their testimony be used to convict them of crime. Officials of the trust have bribed or attempted to bribe employes of rival firms, for the purpose of ruining their business. By its peculiar methods the company has been successful in courts of justice and legislative halls, and has enjoyed an impunity for its conspiracy against the public that is without precedent in America. It has accumulated a capital of more than $100,000,000, and it is even claimed that for years its annual dividends have exceeded in amount the capital actually invested. This is not at all strange when it is considered that they have levied upon the producers, consumers and transporters alike. Mr. Cassat testified before the New York investigating committee that in eighteen months the railroads had paid the Standard in rebates no less than $10,000,000. And the

very payment of these enormous rebates enabled the
Standard to decrease the price of oil to the producer and
to increase it to the consumer.

It is claimed by the defenders of the Standard monopoly that under the trust the price of petroleum has been
constantly decreased to the consumer. That the price of
kerosene is lower now than it was fifteen years ago is
undoubtedly true, but the reductions were brought about
not by the trust, but in spite of the trust. The price now
maintained is an unnatural one. The Standard Oil Company never lowered the price of its oil except when compelled to do so by competition. The largely increased
output of crude oil, the improved methods of refining, the
greatly lowered cost of transportation would have lowered
the price of coal oil without the philanthropy of the
Standard Oil Company. Iron, steel, calico, woolen goods
and a thousand other commodities have within almost the
same period suffered much larger reductions than coal
oil. But even if the Standard monopoly had voluntarily
lowered the price of its products, the American people
could never approve of its methods. They can never be
made to believe that the end sanctifies the means,
especially when those means are railroad favors, secret
combinations, bribery, intimidation and lawless arrogance.

Many other interesting cases might be given. The
Southern Pacific Railway Company, for instance, owns
nearly all of the railways of California, and enjoys at the
present time almost a complete monopoly of the transportation business of that State and much more of the Pacific
Coast. Perhaps no set of managers would be more considerate of the people's rights in the absence of legal
restraint than those in charge of this company, yet there
is not a business man on the Pacific Coast who comes in

contact with this company who does not realize and feel the power of its iron hand, unless it be those who for various reasons are recipients of its special favors. It has become notorious that the legislature, Board of Railroad Commissioners and some of the judges of the courts of that State are as servile to the demands of this railway company as are its own employes.

The railway company is a closely organized body of shrewd, active men, while those who furnish business for it are not organized, and they will never be able to properly protect their own interests until they control the machinery of their State government.

CHAPTER V.

A S has already been shown, railroad enterprise met with comparatively little opposition in the United States, for, as compared with the interests certain to be benefited by the introduction of the new mode of transportation, those likely to be injured by it were insignificant. It is true, the innate conservatism of man even here recorded its objections to the innovation. It viewed with distrust the new power which threatened to revolutionize well-established systems of transportation and time-honored customs and to force upon the people economic factors the exact nature and value of which could only be ascertained by practical tests. But the progressive portion of the community was so decidedly predominant that these protests were soon drowned in the general demand for improved facilities of transportation. The farmer who had to haul his produce a great distance to reach a market appreciated the advantages to be derived from the location of a railroad station nearer home. The manufacturer who heretofore had, had a very limited territory for the sale of his products well realized that he could with the aid of a railroad enlarge his territory and increase his output, and with it his profits. The pioneer merchant found that he could no longer compete with former rivals in adjoining towns, since the iron horse had reached them and lowered their freights, and he also became a convert to the new order of things and clamored loud for railroad facilities. Railroads seemed the panacea for industrial and commercial ills, and every inducement was held out and every sacrifice made by communities to become participants of their blessings. So great was the estimate of the conveniences afforded by them and so strongly was public opinion prejudiced in their favor that it is no exaggeration to say that railroad companies as a rule were permitted to prepare their own charters, and that these charters almost invariably received legislative sanction.

To such an extent was the public mind prepossessed in favor of railroads that any legislator who would have been instrumental in delaying the granting of a railroad charter for the purpose of perfecting it, to protect the people against possible abuses, would have been denounced as a short-sighted stickler and obstructor of public improvements. Anxious for railroad facilities, the people were deaf to the warnings of history. Their liberality knew no bounds. National, State and county aid was freely extended to new railroad enterprises. Communities taxed themselves heavily for their benefit, and municipalities and individuals vied with each other in donating money, rights of way and station buildings. This was especially true of the West, whose undeveloped resources had most to gain by railroad extension. So large were the public and private donations in several of the Western States that their value was equal to one-fifth of the total cost of all the roads constructed. To still more encourage promoters of railroad enterprises, general incorporation laws were passed which permitted companies to be formed and roads to be built practically without State supervision. In their admiration for the bright side of the picture, the people entirely overlooked the shady side.

Besides this, there was virtually an absence of all law regulating the operation of railroads. It was, under these circumstances, not strange that abuses early crept into railroad management which, long tolerated by the people and unchecked and even encouraged by public officers, finally assumed such proportions as to threaten the very foundation of free government. Great discoveries that add rapidly to the wealth of a country tend to overthrow a settled condition of things, and organized capital and power, if not restrained by wholesome laws and public watchfulness, will ever take advantage of the unorganized masses. The people of those regions which the railroad stimulus had caused to be settled thrived for years so well upon a virgin soil that they gladly divided their surplus with the railroad companies. They looked upon the railroads as the source of their prosperity and upon railroad managers as high-minded philanthropists and public benefactors, with whom to quarrel would be an act of sordid ingratitude, and they paid but little attention to the means employed by them to exact an undue share of their earnings. Railroad men did whatever they could to foster through their emissaries this misplaced adoration. They posed before the public as the rightful heirs of the laurels of Watt and Stephenson, insisting that their genius, capital and enterprise had built up vast cities and opened for settlement and civilization the boundless prairies of the West. These claims have been persistently repeated by railroad men, though they are so preposterous that they scarcely deserve refutation. The railroad, gradually developed by active minds of the past, and greatly improved by the inventions of hundreds of men in the humbler walks of life, is the common inheritance of all mankind, though no class of people have derived greater benefits from it than railroad constructors, managers and manipulators. Railroad managers are no more entitled to the special gratitude of the public for dispensing railroad transportation at much more than remunerative rates than is the Western Union monopoly for maintaining among us an expensive and inefficient telegraph service. No one believes that the disbanding of the Western Union would leave us long without telegraphic communication. In like manner railroads will be built whenever and wherever they promise to be profitable. If one company does not take advantage of the opportunities offered, another will. That large cities have been built up by the railroads is true, but it is equally true that these cities by their commerce and manufactures administer to the prosperity of the railroads as much as the railroads administer to theirs. Commercial centers in days gone by existed without railroads, but railroads could not long exist without the stimulating influence of these busy marts of trade. The same argument applies with still greater force to the agricultural sections of our country, especially the great Northwest. The dry-goods merchant might as well boast of having clad the public as the railroad manager of having built up farming communities by selling to them transportation.

And yet the American people have never ceased to be mindful of the conveniences afforded to them by this modern mode of transportation. On the contrary, they have been but too prone to credit railroad men with being benefactors, when they were but beneficiaries, and this liberality of spirit made them overlook, or at least tolerate, the abuses which grew proportionately with the wealth and power of the companies.

The first railroad acts of England had contemplated to make the roads highways, like turnpikes and canals. These roads were established by the power of eminent domain. Companies were empowered to build and main-

tain them and to reimburse themselves by the collection
of fixed tolls. Had the owners of the roads from the
beginning been deprived of the privilege of becoming carriers over their own lines, the system might have so
adjusted itself as to become entirely practicable; but as
they were allowed to compete with other carriers in the
transportation of passengers and merchandise, they were
soon able to demonstrate, at least to the satisfaction of
Parliament, that the use of the track by different carriers
was impracticable and unsafe. A number of circumstances combined to aid the railroad companies in their
efforts to monopolize the trade on their lines. In the first
place, when the early railroad charters were granted, but
few persons had any conception of the enormous growth
of commerce which was destined to follow everywhere the
introduction of railways. The tolls as fixed in the charters
soon yielded an income out of proportion to the cost of
the construction and maintenance of the roads. Their
large margins of profit enabled the owners of the roads to
transport goods at lower rates than other carriers and to
thus compel the latter to abandon their business. Another
defect of the original charters worked greatly to the disadvantage of independent carriers. They contained no
provision as to the use of terminal facilities. The railroad
companies claimed that these facilities were not affected
by the public franchise and were therefore their personal
property. This placed independent carriers at a great
disadvantage and made in itself competition on a large
scale impossible. These carriers were thus at the mercy
of the railroad companies for the transportation of their
cars, and the companies never permitted their business to
become lucrative enough to induce many to engage in it.
It soon became apparent that under the charters granted

to the railroad companies such competition as existed on turnpikes and canals was out of the question on their roads. In England the great abundance of water-ways exercised for many years a wholesome control over the rates of railway companies, until these companies, greatly annoyed by such restraint, absorbed many of the larger canals by purchase and made them tributary to their systems. These companies have also acquired complete control over many important harbors.

In the United States the people depended from the beginning of the railroad era on free competition for the regulation of railroad charges. This desire to maintain free competition led to the adoption of general incorporation acts, it being quite generally believed that such competition as obtains between merchants, manufacturers and mechanics was possible among railroads and would, when allowed to be operative, regulate prices and prevent abuses. The remedy was applied freely throughout the country, but for once it did not prove successful. Stephenson's saying, that where combination was possible competition was impossible, was here fully verified. The great ingenuity of the class of men usually engaged in railroad enterprises succeeded in thwarting this policy of commercial freedom. The opportunities for those in control of railroads to operate them in their own interest, regardless of the interests of their patrons or stockholders, were so great that men of a speculative turn of mind were attracted to this business, which indeed soon proved a most productive field for them. One road after another fell into the control of men who had learned rapidly the methods employed to make large fortunes in a short time.

As the roads multiplied, transportation abuses increased. A considerable number of people early favored State control of railroads as the best means of regulating transportation, but a majority looked upon the existing abuses as being merely incidental to the formative period, and hoped that with a greater expansion of the railroad system they would correct themselves. And this doctrine was industriously disseminated by railroad managers and their allies. They lost no opportunity to impress upon the people that State regulation was an undue interference with private business and that such a policy would soon react against those who hoped to profit by it, inasmuch as it would prevent the building of new roads and would thus hinder, rather than aid, in bringing about the right solution of the railway question, viz., regulation by competition. They contended, in short, that State regulation would be destructive to railroads as well as to every other class of property.

Railroad sophistry for many years succeeded in preventing the masses from realizing that an increased supply of transportation does not necessarily lower its price, or, in other words, that railroad abuses do not necessarily correct themselves through the influence of competition. A large capital is required to build and maintain a railroad, which must necessarily be managed by a few persons. Besides this, the construction of a railroad practically banishes at once from its field all other means of land transportation. The railroad has thus a practical monopoly within its territory, and its managers, if left to follow their instinct, will despotically control all the business tributary to it, with unlimited power to build up and tear down, to punish its enemies and to reward its friends.

It is not true that State control checks railroad building. While it may prevent the construction of useless lines and discourage speculation, it will encourage the building of roads for which there is a legitimate demand. Stockholders as a whole do not participate in the management of the roads and do not profit by railroad abuses, the origin of which may almost invariably be traced to selfish designs on the part of a few entrusted with the management of the property. Where through wise legislation these abuses are prevented, the roads are managed in the interest of all the stockholders, develop business and enjoy lasting prosperity.

It may be laid down as a general rule that the policy which best subserves the interests of the patrons of a road is always the best policy for its owners. Injustice to a railroad will interfere with its usefulness; injustice to shippers depresses production and consumption; and in either case both the road and its patrons will suffer. State control is therefore as much needed in the interest of the owners of railroads as in the interest of their patrons. What should be the nature of such control will be discussed hereafter. A full understanding of the question at issue, however, makes necessary an inquiry into the various abuses which unrestrained railroad management of the past has developed. Perhaps no better presentation of the evils and abuses of railroads and their consequences can be found than that contained in the report of the Senate Committee on Interstate Commerce, submitted by Senator Cullom, in 1886. This report charges:

1. That local rates are unreasonably high, as compared with through rates.

2. That local and through rates are unreasonably high at non-competing points, either from the absence of competition or in consequence of pooling agreements that restrict its operation.

3. That rates are established without apparent regard to the actual cost of the service performed, and are based largely on "what the traffic will bear."

4. That unjustifiable discriminations are constantly made between individuals in the rates charged for like service under similar circumstances.

5. That improper discriminations are constantly made between articles of freight and branches of business of a like character, and between different quantities of the same class of freight.

6. That unreasonable discriminations are made between localities similarly situated.

7. That the effect of the prevailing policy of railroad management is, by an elaborate system of secret special rates, rebates, drawbacks and concessions, to foster monopoly, to enrich favored shippers, and to prevent free competition in many lines of trade in which the item of transportation is an important factor.

8. That such favoritism and secrecy introduce an element of uncertainty into legitimate business that greatly retards the development of our industries and commerce.

9. That the secret cutting of rates and the sudden fluctuations that constantly take place are demoralizing to all business except that of a purely speculative character, and frequently occasion great injustice and heavy losses.

10. That, in the absence of national and uniform legislation, the railroads are able by various devices to avoid their responsibility as carriers, especially on shipments over more than one road, or from one State to another, and that shippers find great difficulty in recovering damages for the loss of property or for injury therefor.

11. That railroads refuse to be bound by their own contracts, and arbitrarily collect large sums in the shape

of overcharges in addition to the rates agreed upon at the time of shipment.

12. That railroads often refuse to recognize or to be responsible for the acts of dishonest agents acting under their authority.

13. That the common law fails to afford a remedy for such grievances, and that in cases of dispute the shipper is compelled to submit to the decision of the railroad manager or pool commissioner, or run the risk of incurring further losses by greater discriminations.

14. That the differences, in the classifications in use in various parts of the country, and sometimes for shipments over the same roads in different directions, are a fruitful source of misunderstandings, and are often made a means of extortion.

15. That a privileged class is created by the granting of passes, and that the cost of the passenger service is largely increased by the extent of this abuse.

16. That the capitalization and bonded indebtedness of the roads largely exceed the actual cost of their construction or their present value, and that unreasonable rates are charged in the effort to pay dividends on watered stock and interest on bonds improperly issued.

17. That railroad corporations have improperly engaged in lines of business entirely distinct from that of transportation, and that undue advantages have been afforded to business enterprises where railroad officials were interested.

18. That the management of the railroad business is extravagant and wasteful, and that a needless tax is imposed upon the shipping and traveling public by the necessary expenditure of large sums in the maintenance of a costly force of agents engaged in a reckless strife for competitive business.

Under the operation of the Interstate Commerce Law some of these evils have, so far at least as interstate commerce is concerned, disappeared, and others have been considerably mitigated. It cannot be expected, however, that a bad system of railroad management, to the development of which the ingenuity of railroad managers has contributed for two generations, could be entirely reformed in a few years. It is a comparatively easy task for shrewd and unscrupulous men, assisted by able counsel and unlimited wealth, to evade the spirit of the law and to obey its letter, or to violate even both its letter and spirit, and escape punishment by making it impossible for the State to obtain proof of their guilt.

It is a humiliating spectacle to see the self-debased railroad officials confessing their own guilt by refusing to testify before the Interstate Commerce Commission on the ground that they would thereby criminate themselves. Congress should have sufficient respect for this commission and for itself to provide a way to punish such recusant witnesses who are willing to degrade themselves in so base a manner. Whether the law will eventually be respected by all depends upon the vigilance and courage of the people.

That our railroad legislation is not yet perfect even its friends will admit; and as under a free government the demand of an enlightened public opinion is the first step toward the enactment of a law, it behooves the intelligent citizen to study the various railroad problems and to then exert his influence toward bringing about such a solution of them as justice and wisdom demand.

In discussing the various evils of railroad management, the author will commence with and dwell more particularly upon those abuses which maybe said to be the cardinal ones, viz., discrimination, extortion, combinations and stock and bond inflation. When these are once effectually eradicated, other abuses of railroad management which have been the subject of public complaint will not long survive them.

One of the strongest arguments that could be adduced by the founders of the American Constitution in favor of the establishment of a more perfect union was that the inequality of taxes placed upon commerce by the various States was a serious obstacle to its free development. Much as the individual States dislike to give up a part of their sovereignty to a central or national power, the demand for a common and uniform system of commercial taxation was so great that they were forced to yield and ratify the new Constitution. Our forefathers thus considered it a dangerous policy to permit a single State to lay any imposts upon the commercial commodities which passed over its borders. They were rightly of the opinion that industrial and commercial liberty was as essential to the welfare of the nation as political freedom and that therefore interstate commerce should not be hemmed in or controlled within State lines, but that the power to regulate it should be lodged in the supreme legislative authority of the nation, the Congress of the United States. For over half a century Congress alone exercised the power thus conferred upon it by the people. After the introduction of railroads, however, their managers gradually assumed the right to regulate the commerce of the country in their own interest through the adoption of arbitrary freight tariffs. Freight charges are practically a tax which follows the commodity from the producer to the consumer. An arbitrary and unjust charge is therefore an arbitrary and unjust tax imposed upon the public without its consent. It is a well-established rule of society that laws should be equitable and just to all citizens. Congress never assumed the role of Providence by attempting to equalize those differences among individuals which superior intellect, greater industry and a thousand other uncontrollable forces have ever created and will ever create. It has been reserved to railroad managers to demonstrate to the public that a power has been allowed to grow up which has assumed the right to counteract the dispensations of Providence, to enrich the slothful, to impoverish the industrious, to curtail the profits of remunerative industries and revive by bounties those languishing for want of vitality, to humble proud and self-reliant marts of trade and to build up cities in the desert. It will scarcely be claimed even by railroad managers that their policy of thus arbitrarily regulating commerce originated in philanthropic motives. They are forced to admit that it grew out of an attempt to increase the income of railroads by the extension of favors to naturally weak enterprises and to recoup by overtaxing stronger ones.

The practical operation of this system soon showed to railroad managers their power and to the patrons of railroads their dependence upon those who dispensed railroad favors. The former soon discovered that their power might be used to further their private interests as well as those of the roads, and unscrupulous patrons were not slow to offer considerations for favors which they coveted. When such favors were once granted by the officials of one road, rival roads would grant similar ones in self-protection. Thus this vicious system grew until the payment of a regular tariff rate was rather the exception than the rule, and special rates became an indispensable condition of success in business.

We may distinguish three classes of railroad discriminations, viz. :

1. Those which affect certain individuals.
2. Those which affect certain localities.
3. Those which affect certain branches of business.

Discrimination between individuals is the most objectionable, because it is the most demoralizing of all. Where
such discrimination obtains, every shipper is in the power
of the railroad corporation. It makes of independent
citizens of a free country fawning parasites and obsequious
sycophants who accept favors from railroad managers
and in return do their bidding, however humiliating this
may be. The shipper, realizing that the manager's displeasure or good will toward him finds practical expression
in his daily freight bills, finally loses, like the serf, all
self-esteem in his efforts to propitiate an overbearing
master. He is intimidated to such an extent that he
never speaks openly of existing abuses, lest he lose the
special rates which have been given him, or, if he is not a
participant of such privileges, lest additional favors be
given to his rivals and they be thus enabled to crush him.
Intimidation of shippers prevailed to such an extent previous to the enactment of the Interstate Commerce Law
that when, in 1879, the special committee on railroads
appointed by the legislature of New York invited all persons having grievances against railroads to come before
them to testify, not one shipper testified voluntarily. On
the contrary, they all insisted upon being subpœnaed,
hoping that the railroad managers would not hold them
responsible for any statement which they might be compelled to make under such circumstances. The report of
that committee stated that the number of special contracts
in force within the period of one year on the New York

Central and Hudson River Railroad alone was estimated by the railroad people at 6,000. Mr. Depew, when he made the statement: "In territories comparatively new, and with little responsibility on the part of the managers to distant owners, they became in many cases very arbitrary and exercised favoritism and discriminations, which led to popular indignation and legislation," had probably not heard of this. The committee's report further stated that these special rates conformed to no system and varied without rule, that every application for a special rate was judged by itself and with reference to its own peculiar circumstances, and that it depended upon the judgment, or rather caprice, of the officer to whom the application was made, whether and to what extent a special rate should be granted. The reductions made to privileged merchants often amounted to more than what would be a fair profit to the dealer on the commodities shipped. The privileged dealer was thus enabled to undersell his rivals and eventually force them out of business or into bankruptcy. It was not at all uncommon for railroad companies to allow discounts amounting to 50, 60, 70 and even 80 per cent. of the regular rates. The New York Central gave a Utica dry-goods merchant a special rate of 9 cents while the regular rate was 33 cents on first-class freights. The lowest special rate granted at Syracuse was as low as 20 per cent. of the regular tariff rate on first-class goods. David Dows & Company and Jesse Hoyt & Company, by means of a grain rate from $2\frac{1}{2}$ to 5 cents lower than those given to other firms, were enabled to control in the winter of 1877 the grain trade of New York. The railroad even extended its fostering aid to A. T. Stewart & Co., giving them a special rate "to build up and develop their business." The testimony given by Mr. Goodman, assistant general freight agent of the New York Central, in reference to the principle by which he was guided in granting special rates, is of sufficient interest to be given a place here:

Question. You made the rate for A. T. Stewart & Company? Answer. Yes, sir.

Q. Was that to build up and develop their business? A. Yes, sir.

Q. That was the object? A. That was one of the objects.

Q. January 11th, 1879? A. Yes, sir.

Q. You thought that business was not yet sufficiently built up and developed? A. No, sir; not the manufacturing part of it.

Q. How long had the factories of A. T. Stewart & Company been in existence? A. The one at Duchess Junction about three years, I think; it isn't completed yet.

Q. And they were languishing and suffering? A. To a great extent; yes, sir.

Q. And you acted as a fostering mother to A. T. Stewart & Company to build it up? A. Yes, sir; I added my mite to develop their traffic; we wanted to carry the freight; boats might have carried it in the summer.

Q. Do you know anything of G. C. Buell & Company? A. Yes, sir.

Q. You wanted to develop their business? A. Yes, sir; they are at Rochester—wholesale dealers.

Q. Do you know H. S. Ballou, of Rochester? A. I do not.

Q. He seems to be a grocer there? A. A small concern, perhaps.

Q. Small concerns are not worth developing, according to your opinion? A. Our tariff rates are low enough for them at Rochester.

Q. That is to say, a small concern ought to pay 40, 30, 25 and 20, as against a large concern, 13; that is your rule? A. Well, if he is a grocer, most of his business is fourth-class freight.

Q. And he ought to pay 20, as against 13? **A.** Yes, sir.

Q. That small man has no right to develop? **A.** He has the same chance that the other man has.

Q. At 20 against 13? **A.** Oh, yes.

Q. Do you call that the same chance? **A.** About the same chance, yes, sir.

Q. You consider it the same chance? **A.** Yes, sir.

Many reasons were assigned by railroad men in justification of their practices. It was claimed that special rates were given to regular shippers, but it has been proved that not all regular shippers had special rates, and that persons who made only single shipments were often fortunate enough to obtain special favors. It was further claimed that special rates were given to those who, starting out new in business or developing new enterprises, needed aid and encouragement. But it was shown on the other hand that the aid and encouragement thus given to some bankrupted others, and in the end deprived the companies of more business than their policy of discrimination brought them. Railroad managers also argued that they could afford to make lower rates on large shipments than on small ones for the same reasons that the wholesale merchant can sell his goods for less than the retailer. But while this may be a good reason why rates on car-load shipments should be lower than rates on shipments in less than car-load lots, it is certainly no good reason why five car-loads belonging to one shipper should be transported the same distance for less than five car-loads belonging to five shippers. In the case of local shipments the car is scarcely ever loaded to its full capacity; one shipment after another is taken from it as the train moves along, and the car perhaps reaches its final destination nearly, if not entirely, empty. The terminal charges are here also largely increased, and it is but just that the shipper should pay the additional cost of carrying and handling the goods. The case is entirely different when the railroad company carries five full carloads from one station of its line to another. Whether they have been loaded by one or five persons, whether they are consigned to one or five persons, matters little to the railroad company. It merely transports the cars, and in either case its responsibility and its services are the same. The car-load must therefore be accepted and is now generally accepted by the best railroad men as the unit of wholesale shipments, and any discrimination made in favor of large wholesale shippers is arbitrary and unjust. In the shipment of some commodities, such as wheat, flour and coal, a small advantage in rates is sufficient to enable the favored shipper to "freeze out" all competitors. It is certainly not to the interest of any railroad company to pursue such a policy; for by driving small establishments out of the business it encourages monopoly, which almost invariably enhances prices and decreases consumption. The railroad thus suffers in common with the public the consequences of its short-sighted policy. That even railroad managers realize that these practices cannot be defended upon any principle of justice or equity is apparent from the fact that one of the never-varying conditions of special rates is that they be kept secret. A specimen of a special rate agreement which was placed before the New York investigating committee is here presented to the reader:

"This agreement, made and entered into this eighteenth day of March, 1878, by and between the New York Central and Hudson River Railroad Company, party of the first part, and Schoellkopf & Mathews, of the city of Buffalo, N. Y., party of the second part:

"Witnesseth, That said party of the first part hath promised and agreed, and by these presents does promise and agree to transport wheat from the elevator in Buffalo, reached directly by said first party's tracks, except at such mills as time said tracks may be obstructed by snow or ice, to the which said second party may erect or operate at Niagara Falls, N. Y., at and for the rate of one and a quarter cents per bushel.

" And further, that said first party shall and will at all times give, grant and allow to said second parties as low rate of transportation on all property shipped by them from their said mills at Niagara Falls, and as favorable facilities and accommodation in all respects as are afforded by the party of the first part to the millers of Buffalo and Black Rock. And also that the said party of the first part will transport for said second party all of their eastbound New York freight at and for the price or rate of forty-seven per cent. of the current all-rail through rates, via the route of party of the first part, from Chicago to New York, at the times of shipment, adding thereto three cents per barrel for flour and one and one-half cents per hundred pounds for mill feed or grain, as a terminal charge, to provide for the incidental expenses attending local transportation.

" And will transport their freight to Boston and all points in New England, taking Boston rates at the same rate as to New York, with ten cents per barrel added for flour and five cents per hundred pounds added for mill feed or grain.

· " Provided, however, and this agreement is made upon the express understanding and consideration, that said second party shall regard and treat this agreement as confidential, and will use all reasonable precaution to keep the same secret.

" And upon condition also that said second party shall ship by the first party's road all the product from their mill at Niagara Falls destined to all points in New York, Pennsylvania and New England, reached by said first party, directly or by connections with other routes.

" And this agreement shall be and remain in force for

the term of five years from and following the first day of
September, 1878, after which period it may be terminated
by sixty days' written notice from either party.

" In witness whereof, the parties hereto have signed
these presents the day and year first above written.

"N. Y. C. & H. R. R. R. Co.,"

By J. H. RUTLER,

"General Traffic Manager.

"SCHOELLKOPF & MATHEWS."

It will be noticed that this agreement was based upon
the expressed condition that Schoellkopf & Mathews
treat it as "confidential," and use all reasonable precaution to keep it secret. It is difficult to account for this
strong injunction of secrecy except upon the assumption
that the managers of the road, conscious of the great wrong
which they inflicted upon the body of the people by their
discriminations, hoped to escape public criticismby adopting a policy of secret dealing. Much as special rates
were sought after, but few shippers to whom they had been
granted were contented with their lot, for none was confid-
ent that his rivals did not have better rates than himself.

Discriminations between localities had their origin in
the natural desire of competing roads to increase their
business at the expense of their rivals. When two or
more railroads touched the same point each would attempt
to secure the largest possible share of the through business by holding out every possible inducement in rates to
the shippers of that place. Indeed, the freight rates at
competitive points were often so low that railroad managers found themselves placed in a rather unpleasant
dilemma. They either had to admit that the rates charged
by them at non-competitive places were exorbitant or
that they were carrying the freights of competitive points
at a loss and were thus squandering the money of their

stockholders. They preferred as a rule to admit that they were doing competitive business at a loss, but asserted that, inasmuch as they were compelled to run their trains, they could better afford to do competitive business temporarily at a loss than not to do it at all. The same logic might with equal propriety be employed by the grocer. To draw to him distant customers, he might offer to sell to them at cost or even at a loss; and then, to recuperate, he might advance the prices of his goods for his regular customers. If there is any difference between the grocer and the railroad company, it lies in the fact that the former's old customers would soon find relief at a rival store, while the patrons of the railroad at non-competitive points are like the traveler in the hands of a highwayman, without immediate redress. The railway company which discriminates between competitive and non-competitive points forgets that its line is a common highway for all points tributary to it; that all have equal rights, and that the only differences in tariff which the principles of the common law permit are those which arise from a difference of service and cost. All other differences that railroad companies may make are unjust discriminations in violation of their charter and expose them to a forfeiture of the franchises conferred upon them.

The nature and extent of the discrimination practiced between different places are often such that no interest of the company can possibly be subserved by them, and the conclusion is forced upon us that the advantages granted by railroad managers to certain places are designed to serve chiefly personal and selfish interests. The great fortunes amassed in a brief period of time by railroad managers can in almost every case be traced to stock, real estate, commercial and other speculations directly or indirectly connected with railroad construction or management. And where other than personal interest cannot be shown, this is the only basis upon which the many apparent absurdities of railroad discrimination can be harmonized.

It is claimed by railroad men that transportation by water is a regulator of railway rates which they must respect. It is contended, for instance, that, although the cities situated on our large lakes enjoy superior commercial advantages which are mainly due to their having at their disposal water communication with the Atlantic Ocean, inland towns have no cause to complain against the railroads for not equalizing those differences which nature has largely created. It might be more difficult to meet this argument if, owing to peculiar combinations, these water rates were not made to extend their influence to almost every inland city north, east and south in the Union, and if those cities were not given much lower rates than hundreds of places much nearer the lakes. The teamster who, half a century ago, found it impossible to compete with the canal, river or lake boats, simply surrendered the field to them and confined his operations to such a territory as could give him assurance of a profitable business. Let the railroads do likewise. No company has a right to destroy a rival route, water or rail, by adopting special tariffs for competing points. There are at points accessible to water transportation certain freights requiring speedy carriage which will go to the railroads at profitable rates, but the heavier freights, as coal, lumber and even certain kinds of grain, should go to the carrier by water if he can afford to transport them at lower cost.

There have been but few legislative investigations of railroad abuses in this country, but the disclosures which they have made to the public are astounding. The most noteworthy of these were made by the Hepburn committee, of New York, to which reference has already been made. It is difficult to understand how a free and enlightened community could so long and so patiently bear railroad despotism. Individual discrimination might, under the veil of secrecy, long escape notice, but that a system of open and widespread discrimination affecting every non-competitive and even many a competitive point in the State, doing visible and irreparable injury to thousands of shippers, and infringing upon the rights of millions, should long be borne by a free and enlightened people, is a strange phenomenon of democratic endurance.

It would lead us too far from our subject to review in detail the many and glaring instances of local discrimination which the report enumerates. A few will suffice to show their scope and nature.

William W. Mack, of Rochester, a manufacturer of edged tools, testified that, in order to save fourteen cents per hundredweight on his freights to Cincinnati, he shipped his goods to New York and had them shipped from there to their destination, via Rochester; and that he availed himself of the same roundabout route for his St. Louis shipments, and saved thereby eighteen cents per hundredweight. In both of these cases the railroad company carried the goods 700 miles farther than the direct distance for a less charge.

Port Jervis millers had their grain shipped from the West to Newburgh, a point fifty miles to the east of them, and then had it returned to Port Jervis on the same line, at a less rate than that charged for a direct shipment.

The grain rates from Chicago to Pittsburgh were 25 cents per hundred in March, 1878, and only 15 cents from Chicago to New York.

Flour was carried from Milwaukee to New York for 20 cents, while the rate from Rochester to New York was 30 cents at the same time. It was also carried from East St. Louis to Troy at the same rate as from Rochester to Troy. The rate on butter from St. Lawrence County, N. Y., to Boston, over the Ogdensburg and Lake Champlain and Vermont Central, was 60 cents per hundred; from the nearer county of Franklin, 70 cents; it then continued to increase as the distance decreased, until it reached 90 cents at St. Albans, Vermont.

Soap shipped by Babbit & Co., of New York, to Crouse & Co., of Syracuse, paid 8 cents per box when the freight was paid in Syracuse, but 12 cents per box when paid by the shipper in New York.

It cannot even be said that New York fared worse than any of her sister States. There is hardly a business man in any community in the United States who cannot cite many cases of similar discrimination. Hundreds of well authenticated cases have been reported from every part of the country. A few striking ones may be given space here:

The Illinois Central Company hauled cotton from Memphis to New Orleans, a distance of 450 miles, at $1.00 a bale, while the rate from Winona, Miss., to New Orleans, about two-thirds of the distance, was $3.25 a bale. The same company charged for fourth-class freight from Chicago to Kankakee, a distance of 56 miles, 16 cents per hundred, and only 10 cents to Mattoon, 116 miles farther. The rate from New York to Ogden was $4.65 per hundred, and only $2.25 per hundred from New York to San Francisco. The car-load rate on the Northern Pacific was $200 from New York to Portland and just twice as much to a number of points from 100 to 125 miles east of Portland. The Chicago, Burlington and Quincy hauled stock from points beyond the Missouri River to Chicago for $30 per car-load, while it exacted $70 per car in Southwestern Iowa for a much shorter haul.

To what extent local discrimination has been carried by railroad companies is well illustrated by the following incident: A nurseryman residing at Atlantic, Iowa, a station on the Chicago, Rock Island and Pacific Railroad, 60 miles east of Council Bluffs, bought a car-load of grape-vines at Fredonia, New York. Finding that the through rate from Fredonia to Council Bluffs, plus the local rate from the latter place to Atlantic, was less than the rate for the direct shipment from Fredonia to Atlantic, he caused the car to be consigned to Council Bluffs, intending to have it thence hauled back to Atlantic. Being short of stock at the time the train containing his car passed through his town on its way to Council Bluffs, the consignee prevailed upon the station agent to set out his car. In due time he received a request from the general office of the railroad to pay an amount equal to the rate per car-load from Council Bluffs to Atlantic. The request was promptly complied with by the appreciative nurseryman, who after all had been saved an annoying delay by the courtesy of the company's agent.

An infinite number of similar discriminations might be cited. They all show the same violation of the fundamental principles of justice and equity, the same despotical assertion of the power of the railroads to regulate the commerce of the country as the caprice or selfish interests of their managers might direct.

Discriminations between commodities, or, as they might also be called, discriminations in classification, are probably the most common of unjust railroad practices. For the purpose of establishing as near as may be uniform rules in all matters pertaining to rates, the various roads operating in a certain territory usually form traffic associations. The general freight agents of the roads that are members of the association in turn form a select body known as the rate committee. These committees of freight agents have for more than twenty years constituted the supreme authority in all matters pertaining to freight classification. The trunk line classification recognizes six regular and two special classes, and every article known to commerce is placed in one of these classes.

One whom Providence has not favored with the mysterious wisdom of a general freight agent might suppose that considerations of bulk, weight, insurance and similar factors formed a basis of railroad classification. Nothing, however, is farther from the truth. Freight charges, when permitted to be fixed by railroad companies, are invariably such as the traffic will bear, and freight classifications are arranged on this principle, provided competition by water, rail or other land transportation does not demand a modification. It is, as a rule, not to the advantage of a railroad to entirely starve out any commercial or industrial concern along its line. Hence tariffs are scarcely ever made entirely prohibitory. Railroads proceed here upon the principle of the robber knight of mediæval times, who simply plundered the wayfaring trader to such an extent as to reduce his profits to a minimum. He never stripped him, for by doing so he would have prevented his return and would have destroyed his own source of revenue. In like manner a railroad will never annihilate any weak branch of business along its line, nor will it, if it is in its power, permit any business to prosper without paying to it heavy tributes out of its profits. Every commodity is therefore made to pay a transportation tax based chiefly on its value and the profit which it yields, and all classifications are prepared with this object in view.

The protection which, through exceptionally low rates, is extended by the railroad companies to certain industries, may not be objectionable *per se*, but the question arises whether the railroad companies or the people should exercise the right to determine when and where such protection is necessary. Moreover, to tax one branch of commerce for the benefits bestowed upon another is a practice of extremely doubtful propriety, and the power to do so should certainly never be conferred upon a private corporation. When customs laws are proposed in Congress ample opportunity is given to the representatives of the various industries of the country to be heard upon the subject. No hasty step is taken. Members of Congress have every opportunity to ascertain the sentiment of their constituents, through the public press, petitions and private correspondence. The subject is discussed in all its phases, both in the committee-rooms and upon the floors of both houses of Congress. Every detail is fully considered, and many compromises are often necessary to secure for a bill the support of the majority. When it finally passes it represents the will of the people, or at least the will of their legal representatives, who may be expected to know their wants and are accountable to them for their acts. Freight classifications, however, while they are fully as far-reaching as customs laws, are made by a few freight agents meeting in secret session, listening to no advice and acknowledging no higher authority.

It is claimed by the railroad men that it is to the interest of railroad companies to do justice to all, and that the best classification for the largest number of people is also the best for the roads. If this be true, it is difficult to see why railroads should fail to consult their patrons in the arrangement of their freight classifications. Intelligent shippers may certainly be supposed to know as well as the railroad companies what classification is to their common interest. Railroad managers are naturally despotical. They do not wish and do not tolerate any outside interference with what they obstinately term their private business. Even if the general policy of the companies designed the greatest good to the greatest number, the opportunities and temptations of their agents to pursue selfish ends or take advantage of individuals in the preparation or application of their tariffs are such that in the practical execution the evil will always outweigh the good.

It is not within the scope of the present inquiry to review in detail the various classifications in force, or to point out the unjust features. The author will confine himself to showing by a few characteristic examples that the power now in the hands of the railroad companies to classify the various commodities of commerce for the purpose of rating is greatly abused and is a potent means of railroad extortion. And that it may not be charged that abuses have been cited which are a thing of the past, the examples will chiefly be taken from cases which have come before the Interstate Commission for adjudication.

A complaint was filed with the commission in 1887 by T. J. Reynolds against the Western New York and Pennsylvania Railroad Company, from which it appeared that that company charged a greater price for the transportation of railroad ties from points in the State of Pennsylvania to points in the State of New York than was charged at the same time for the transportation of lumber between the same points. The commission held that this was a case of unjustifiable discrimination and ordered the company to place railroad ties in the same class with other rough lumber. Many Western roads for years have been guilty of the same discrimination. The reasons for such a policy are obvious. A high tariff on railroad ties prevents their being shipped, depreciates their market price at home, to the sole benefit of the discriminating company, which is thus enabled to buy ties at a low price. Prohibitory rates on ties and rails are also often maintained by railroad companies to either delay or render more costly the construction of new lines which threaten to become their competitors. The Union Pacific Railroad Company several years ago even went so far as to make prohibitory rates on steel rails intended for the construction of a road which promised to become a competitor of one of its connecting lines.

From another case decided by the Interstate Commerce Commission it appeared that the Lake Shore and Michigan Southern Railway Company charged for blocks intended for wagon-hubs, and upon which only so much labor had been expended as was necessary to put them in condition, a higher rate than for lumber, claiming that such blocks were unfinished wagon material and were therefore, as articles of manufacture, subject to higher charges than raw material. The commission justly held that these blocks were as much to be regarded as raw material as the boards from which wagon-boxes are made.

In the classification of the Southern Railway and Steam-ship Association pearline was placed in the fourth class, with a rate of 73 cents per hundred pounds, and common soap in the sixth class, with a rate of 49 cents per hundred pounds.

This latter article, when shipped by large manufacturers, enjoyed besides a special rate of 33 cents per hundred-weight. Pearline and scap are competitive; there is no appreciable difference between them as regards the cost of transportation; but one commands a higher price in the market than the other, and upon this fact solely did the railroad company base its alleged right to levy upon pearline a transportation tax 120 per cent. in excess of that levied upon soap, though the service rendered by the company was the same in either case. The commission held that the discrimination made by the "special rate" of the Southern Railway and Steamship Association between pearline and common soap was unjust, and ordered that it be discontinued and that, with common soap in the sixth class, pearline be placed in the fifth.

For years the rate from Indianapolis to New York was the same for corn as for its direct products, such as ground corn, cracked corn, corn meal, hominy and corn feed. Such a tariff made it possible for Western mills to compete with similar mills that had been established in the East, since a discrimination of 5 per cent. was sufficient to absorb three or four times the profits of any Western mill. It was shown by the evidence produced that the actual cost of transportation was substantially the same for direct corn products as for the raw corn. The only defense which the railroad company could make for this discrimination was that in the carriage of raw corn they had to meet lake competition. The weakness of this argument will be perceived when it is remembered that Indianapolis is 154 miles from the nearest lake-shipping point. There is but little doubt that this discrimination was made by the railroad company because it was to its interest to haul the raw corn from the West to the

East and to return it in altered form.   Railroads care, as
a rule, little for a waste of force, if such waste is to their
own advantage.

In another case brought before the commission in 1889
it was shown that the "Official Classification" placed
common soap in carload lots in Class V, while such articles as coffee, pickles, salted and smoked fish in boxes
or packages, rice, starch in barrels or boxes, sugar, cere-
a line and cracked wheat are placed in Class VI.   The
chief reply of the railroad companies to this complaint
was that soap was justly placed in Class V because the
components from which it is in part made stood in
Class V.

In another case it was shown that one kind of soap
was burdened with a higher transportation tax than
another, irrespective even of cost, because one had been
advertised as toilet and the other as laundry soap.

The principle of charging what the traffic will bear is
well illustrated by the relative rates on patent medicines
and ale and beer, as maintained by the Official Classification.

In a complaint made by a prominent manufacturer of
proprietary medicines against the New York Central and
other roads, it was shown that the complainant's products
were shipped at owner's risk, and that they were in bulk
and intrinsic value similar to ale and beer, but that in
spite of these analogies the former were rated as first-
class and the latter as third-class goods, simply because
they retailed at a higher price.

Another unwarrantable discrimination is that in favor
of live stock and against dressed beef.   While Mr. Fink,
the commissioner of the Trunk Line Pool, himself admit
ted that the cost of carrying dressed beef from Chicago to

New York was only 6¼ cents per 100 pounds in excess of the cost of hauling live stock, the trunk lines maintained on dressed beef a rate 75 per cent. higher than that on live cattle. The railroad companies asserted that this was due to those people in the East whose living depended on the live-stock interest. The railroads have in this assumed a paternalism which would not be tolerated even in the Government. To protect the East, railroads will not permit the West to engage in new industries.

The position which the Interstate Commerce Commission has assumed in interpreting the rights of shippers under the law which railroad companies are bound to respect in the preparation of their tariff sheets and classifications cannot but be most gratifying to the people. In a decision relating to the classification and rates for carloads and less than car-loads, filed March 14, 1890, the commission laid down the following rules for the guidance of railroad companies:

"1. Classification of freight for transportation purposes is in terms recognized by the act to regulate commerce, and is therefore lawful. It is also a valuable convenience both to shippers and carriers.

"2. A classification of freight designating different classes for car-load quantities and for less than car-load quantities for transportation at a lower rate in car-loads than in less than car-loads is not in contravention of the act to regulate commerce. The circumstances and conditions of the transportation in respect to the work done by the carrier and the revenue earned are dissimilar, and may justify a reasonable difference in rate. The public interests are subserved by car-load classification of property that, on account of the volume transported to reach markets or supply the demands of trade throughout the country, legitimately or usually moves in such quantities.

"3. Carriers are not at liberty to classify property as a basis of transportation rates and impose charges for its carriage with exclusive regard to their own interests, but they must respect the interests of those who may have occasion to employ their services, and conform their charges to the rules of relative equality and justice which the act prescribes.

"4. Cost of service is an important element in fixing transportation charges and entitled to fair consideration, but is not alone controlling nor so applied in practice by carriers, and the value of the service to the property carried is an essential factor to be recognized in connection with other considerations. The public interests are not to be subordinated to those of carriers, and require proper regard for the value of the service in the apportionment of all charges upon traffic.

"5. A difference in rates upon car-loads and less than car-loads of the same merchandise, between the same points of carriage, so wide as to be destructive to competition between large and small dealers, especially upon articles of general and necessary use, and which, under existing conditions of trade furnish a large volume of business to carriers, is unjust and violates the provisions and principles of the act.

"6. A difference in rate for a solid car-load of one kind of freight from one consignor to one consignee, and a car-load quantity from the same point of shipment to the same destination, consisting of like freight or freight of like character, from more than one consignor to one consignee or from one consignor to more than one consignee, is not justified by the difference in cost of handling.

"7. Under the official classification the articles known in trade as grocery articles are so classified as to discriminate unjustly in rates between car-loads and less than car-loads upon many articles, and a revision of the classification and rates to correct unjust differences and give these respective modes of shipment more relatively reasonable rates is necessary and is so ordered."

The efforts which the commission has made to bring about a uniform classification throughout the country are in the right direction, while the results of its labor are not yet satisfactory.

In their fifth annual report, the Commissioners, after giving an account of their efforts and the shuffling and double-dealing of the railroad companies with them upon this matter of uniform classification, said:

"Its conviction remains unchanged that the necessities of commerce require that the existing classifications be consolidated, and that this result should be accomplished as speedily as may be found practicable; and it does not feel justified in asking for the further efforts of the carriers the same measure of indulgence which from time to time it has heretofore suggested should be extended to them, and which was thought to be required in the public interest.

"The commission can not but think that if legislation to that end be enacted by Congress the carriers will speedily consummate the reform already begun in this direction. It is therefore recommended that an act be passed requiring the adoption within one year from the date of its passage of a uniform classification of freight by all the carriers, subject to the act to regulate commerce, and providing that if the same be not adopted within the time limited, either this commission or some other public authority be required to adopt and enforce a uniform classification."

The present confusion which exists in the classification and rates of the seventeen hundred railroad organizations of the country makes it difficult for the commission to do justice to all interests and localities. With the adoption of a uniform classification it is to be hoped that in time many of the present inequalities will be adjusted, especially if an intelligent public sentiment upon the subject of railroad regulation is maintained. A prominent railroad manager in the East, whose devotion to corporate interest is only equaled by his political ambition, has recently made repeated efforts to convince the people that railroad abuses are things of the past and that, if any such abuses still linger in isolated districts,

they are simply unavoidable exceptions to the rule which
will soon have to yield to the general spirit of fairness
and amity for which, in his opinion, the railroads have
of late been distinguished. He reasons that the law has
fulfilled its mission, that the railroads have reformed, and
that it now behooves the people to relent and to extend
to the much persecuted corporations the hand of friendship and good will. The postprandial eloquence of this
gentleman has often suavely intimated that the repeal of
the Interstate Commerce Act would be the most opportune recognition of restored confidence.

Still bolder champions of the railroad cause do not hesitate to demand the repeal of the law. It is not likely
that the sophistry of railroad hirelings will triumph over
the practical logic of an intelligent public. No law, be it
ever so wise, can in the space of a few years correct all
the abuses which half a century of unbridled railroad
domination has developed. Yet, since both the friends
and the enemies of the law agree that it has been partially successful in its operation, it should be continued
and improved to keep it in harmony with new conditions and a progressive public sentiment. It is claimed
by railroad managers that the adoption of a uniform
classification will remove the only vestige of discrimination still left. This is not true, for by far the largest
number of complaints that have recently been brought
before the Interstate Commerce Commission charged personal and local discrimination independent of any question of classification.

It is shown by the reports of the commission that discriminations are still practiced by various companies, that
annual passes are still illegally issued to bribe or appease
men of influence, that discounts are still given to favor

shippers under various pretexts, that some large railroad centers still enjoy more favorable rates than smaller towns, and that the long and short haul clause of the Interstate Commerce Act is still violated by railroad companies. There are besides these scores of other devices in vogue among railroad managers to subvert the principles of the common law. No doubt discriminations are now much less frequent, and are possibly the exception where but a few years ago they were the rule, but the fact that such abuses still exist is a strong argument for the retention of the law as well as for the necessity of continued vigilance on the part of the people and those especially charged with the execution of the laws. The railroad acts of Congress and the various States ask nothing of common carriers but just and equitable treatment for all their patrons. If this is freely accorded, these laws are no burden to the railroads. If, on the other hand, there is a tendency on the part of the railroads to resort to subterfuges and evasions, the wholesome restraint of the statute is absolutely necessary for the protection of the shipper.

The repeal of the Interstate Commerce Law, or the adoption of such amendments as are demanded by railroad men, would be interpreted by them as an abandonment of all its principles and would inaugurate an era of unprecedented railroad oppression. History ever repeats itself. Unchecked license will always lead to arrogance and despotism, and any power which is long permitted to defy the state will in time control it. It is not likely that the people of the United States can be induced to demonstrate to the world that democratic government is incapable of profiting in the dear school of experience.

Our railroad legislation contains no principle that is not found in the common law. Its maxims are our birthright and will be the birthright of our children and children's children, and while railroad companies may be able in the future, as they have been in the past, to violate the law temporarily with impunity, they will never be able to prevail upon the American people to abandon the policy of railroad reform which the passage of the Interstate Commerce Law inaugurated.

The Interstate Commerce Commissioners say in their sixth annual report:

"Whoever will read the report of the special committee of the United States Senate, commonly called the 'Cullom Committee,' will be astounded at the magnitude and extent of railroad abuses brought to light by their investigation. Those unfamiliar with the facts made public at that time can hardly believe the outrages which were proven to exist and the manifold devices by which the most flagrant injustice was perpetrated. A single illustration will furnish a better reminder than extended comment.

"It appears from that report that the Standard Oil Company, in one instance at least, boldly demanded from a certain railroad that its shipments should be carried for 10 cents a barrel; that all other shippers should be charged 35 cents a barrel on the same article, and that 25 cents of the 35 paid by such other shippers should be handed over by the railroad to the Standard Oil Company, and the penalty threatened for non-compliance with this impudent extortion was a withdrawal of its entire business.

"The foregoing statements but imperfectly describe the situation which existed when the Interstate Commerce Law was enacted. In any reasonable view of the case it was too much to expect that the common and long continued abuses of railroad management could be corrected in less than half a dozen years, or that the first scheme of legislative regulation would prove adequate to that end. It would be contrary to all experience if so great and radical a reform could be thus speedily accomplished, or if the initial statute should be found sufficient to bring it about. The law was the outgrowth of an aroused and determined public sentiment, which, while united in demanding Government interference, was divided and uncertain as to the best methods of affording relief. Like all attempts in a new field of legislation, the statute was a compromise between divergent theories and conflicting interests. It was scarcely possible that it should be so complete and comprehensive at the outset as to require no alteration or amendment. Those who are familiar with the practices which obtained prior to the passage of this law and contrast them with the methods and conditions now existing will accord to the present statute great influence in the direction of necessary reforms and a high degree of usefulness in promoting the public interest.

" Whoever will candidly examine the reports of the commission from year to year, and thus become acquainted with the work which has been done and is now going on, will have no doubt of the potential value of this enactment in correcting public sentiment, restraining injustice and enforcing the principle of reasonable charges and equal treatment. Imperfections and weaknesses which could not be anticipated at the time of its passage have since been disclosed by the effort to give it effective administration. The test of experience, so far from condemning the policy of public regulation, has established its importance and intensified its necessity. The very respects in which the existing law has failed to meet public expectation point out the advantages and demonstrate the utility of Government supervision.

" Moreover, it may be fairly claimed that much greater benefits would have been realized had the statute as enacted expressed the evident purpose of those who framed it, and received a construction according to its apparent import. It is not too much to say that judicial interpretation has limited its scope and ascribed to it an intent not contemplated when it was passed. If its supposed meaning, as understood at the time of its passage, had been upheld by the courts, it is believed that its operation would have been much more effective and its

usefulness greatly increased. So far as failure has
attended the efforts to give it proper administration, that failure can be mainly attributed to differences between its apparent meaning and the judicial
interpretation which some of its provisions have received;
and the commission is of the opinion that if the present law could be so altered as to express clearly and beyond doubt what it was evidently intended to express at
the time of its enactment, it would prove, even without
other amendment, an instrumentality of the highest value
in removing the evils against which it is aimed.

" The specific instances in which the statute has received judicial construction, and the limitations upon its
scope and meaning which the courts have imposed, will be
alluded to at greater length in another part of this report.

" It seems proper, however, to observe in this connection that the effect of these decisions in weakening the
law and preventing its enforcement has been greatly exaggerated. The impression has been created in many directions that judicial construction has invalidated the essential feature of the statute and condemned the general
principle which lies at its foundation. That impression
cannot be too speedily corrected, for nothing has been
decided which permits such an inference. On the contrary, neither the power of the national legislature to regulate the transportation of interstate commerce nor the
general policy of the existing law has been questioned by
any tribunal."

Probably no law in the United States has ever before
been so fiercely attacked at all of its vital points as has
this law. It is not strange that among the great number
of National and State courts the railroad companies
have found occasionally a judge ready and willing to assist
them in breaking it down, but upon the whole the
judiciary has been disposed to co-operate with other
departments of the Government in their efforts to secure
effective regulation of the transportation business.

CHAPTER VI.

THE complaint is frequently heard from railroad men that our freight rates are too low, and in support of it the statement is usually made that the greater part of the railroad stocks of the United States pays dividends considerably smaller than the average interest realized by capitalists on money loaned or invested in other enterprises.

This statement may be true, and yet it is valueless as an argument for higher rates. It may be admitted that the dividends declared upon the face values of railroad stocks are quite moderate, but it is a fact too well authenticated to be contradicted that railroad securities represent to a considerable extent only fictitious capital. The public concedes that liberal returns should be allowed to railroad companies on money actually invested, but it naturally objects to being taxed for the purpose of making dividends on watered stock. The evil referred to is a serious one, and has contributed much to the general demand for railroad reform. Most of the early roads of this country were built for the accommodation of local traffic. They were constructed and managed by business men upon business principles. The stock issued by the companies was in most cases paid for in full and was not unfrequently sufficient for the completion of the entire road, and no incumbrance was permitted by the owners to be placed upon the property. These enterprises as a rule proved very profitable. One of the first roads running west of Chicago will serve as an illustration. The Galena and Chicago Union Railroad Company paid a 10 per cent. dividend within a year after being opened to traffic, and gradually increased its dividends to 15, 20 and 22 per cent. During the first two years of the road's operation its expenses were only 38½ per cent. of its earnings. During the second year the company, after paying a 15 per cent. dividend, diminished its debt nearly $60,000 and increased its surplus $11,700. In 1856 the road had a length of 232 miles, on which the gross earnings amounted to $2,315,787. This revenue exceeded the estimate made by the company's officers the year previous by $300,000. In his annual report for 1856 the president of the company said: "This result shows an *increased surplus* of $65,000, after paying 22 per cent. in dividends and all expenses and interests chargeable to income account." The report also shows that expensive improvements, such as large permanent bridges and stone culverts, displacing as a rule wooden ones, were charged to current expenses.

The financial success of railroads soon attracted the cupidity of financial adventurers—men of great energy, but small means—whose aim was to secure the greatest possible returns with the least possible outlay of money. With the introduction of these elements into railroad cir- cles the era of speculation commenced. Take the line just referred to. In 1852 the average number of miles operated was 62, and the year following, 90. But while the number of miles operated increased less than 50 per cent., the capital stock of the company grew from $444,193 to $1,362,559, and its debt from $60,145 to $542,287. The capitalization of the road was thereby increased from $8,000 to $21,000 per mile, and this was done for the purpose of making the capital appear adequate to its earnings. Nearly all railroads became in time the foot-balls of shrewd manipulators. They were bonded before they were constructed, and often for more than the value of the completed road. Stocks at the best only represented nominal values and were given as premiums to the bondholders or promoters of the road.

But the science of stock-watering did not reach its fullest development until during the period of railroad consolidation. Fictitious values were now created as often as a new consolidation took place. Watered stocks and bonds were watered again and again, until they represented little more than a purely imaginary capital upon the basis of which dividends might be declared. Take the case of the New York Central and Hudson River Railroad companies, which consolidated in 1869 with a capital of $103,110,137.31. The former of these roads was organized in 1853 by the consolidation of ten smaller roads connecting the cities of Albany and Buffalo. The capital stock of these companies amounted to $20,799,800, of which $16,852,870 was claimed to have been paid in. Their funded debt was $2,497,526. It is impossible at this day to ascertain the original cost of all these roads, but it is certain that the above sums represent about three times the amount actually expended for their construction.

One of the roads entering into the consolidation was the Utica and Schenectady. It was 78 miles long and formed about one-fourth of the consolidated line. It had the heaviest grading and rock-cutting, was the best-equipped and undoubtedly the most expensive, in proportion to its extent, of the ten roads out of which the New York Central was created. The original cost of this line was $2,000,000. Bonds were never issued by the company. The line was profitable from the very beginning, paid regularly ten per cent. dividends,—the limit to which railroad companies were then restricted,—and had a large surplus, which it expended mainly for improvements. No assessment was ever made on the stock beyond the $1,500,000 which was originally paid in by the shareholders and upon which they had drawn regular and liberal dividends. Taking the original cost of this line as a basis, it is but fair to presume that the entire line from Albany to Buffalo, covering a distance of 297 miles, did not cost to exceed $6,000,000. These roads, however, entered into the consolidation with a capital stock of $15,274,800 and a bonded indebtedness of $1,696,326.

Estimating the cost of the branches upon the same basis upon which we have estimated that of the main line, we shall find that the total original cost of the consolidated lines cannot have exceeded $8,000,000. The Mohawk Valley road was put in at $2,000,000 and the Syracuse and Utica direct at $600,000, though the roads only existed on paper and did not represent any value whatever. The Schenectady and Troy road, which went into the consolidation with $650,000 stock and $90,000 bonds, had been bought for less than $100,000 two months previous to the consolidation.

It will thus be seen that already nearly one-third of the stocks and bonds of the consolidated companies was water. The consolidation agreement fixed the capital stock of the New York Central at $23,085,600 and its funded debt at $11,564,033.62, increasing the stock over $2,000,000, and the bonded debt over $9,000,000. The latter was more than quadrupled, and $8,000,000 worth of bonds were, under the name of consolidation certificates, given as a present to the stockholders of the new road. The capital stock of the New York Central grew steadily up to the time of its consolidation with the Hudson River road, when it was $28,795,000. All improvements made during this time were paid for out of its surplus earnings, with the single exception of the Athens branch, for which the company issued $2,000,000 of its stock.

The gross earnings of the New York Central in 1854 were $5,000,000, and its net earnings $2,830,000. In 1863 its gross earnings were in round numbers $10,000,-000, and in 1869 they reached $15,000,000. The dividends paid during that year amounted to $4,300,000, and the interest to $894,000. In view of the fact that the bonded indebtedness of the road was from two to three million dollars more than the original cost, this dividend of 15 per cent. upon a wholly fictitious capital must be regarded as an unwarranted tribute levied upon the commerce of the country. But we shall soon see that in railroad hydraulics, as well as in other branches of human industry, success stimulates to still greater energy.

The Hudson River Railroad Company was organized in 1847. It extended from New York City to East Albany and was 144 miles long. There are no data extant upon which could be based a reliable estimate of its original cost. Estimating it upon the basis of that of the Utica and Schenectady, we should have to place it somewhat below $3,000,000. While such an estimate may be too low, the amount of its funded indebtedness in 1851, which was $5,640,000, probably more than covers the amount actually expended in the construction of the road. In 1851 the capital stock of the Hudson River road was $4,000,000. In 1853 the funded debt had increased to $7,000,000, and in 1862 to $9,000,000. In 1869 the

bonded indebtedness had decreased to $4,309,000, but
the capital stock had grown to over $16,000,000. Between
1853 and 1869 the company increased its stock and
bonded indebtedness nearly $11,000,000, while the
assessments paid by its stock and bondholders during
this time did not exceed $1,000,000. Improvements
were made, but these were chiefly paid for out of the surplus earnings of the road. It has been shown by experts
that $6,640,000 is a high estimate of the actual original
cost of the Hudson River road to its stock-and bondholders, and that securities to the amount of more than $13,-
000,000 represented surplus earnings and water. At the
time of the consolidation of the Hudson River and New York
Central railroads the capital stock of the two roads had
grown to $44,800,000. Under the consolidation agree-
ment the stock was fixed at $45,000,000. The new com-
pany also assumed all the bonded and other indebtedness
of both roads. If the consolidation manipulators had
paused here, the capital of the new company would have
been somewhat less than $60,000,000, or more than three
times the cost of the property. But the road was, under
existing rates, capable of earning dividends on a much
larger capital, and this emergency was met by the
issuance of consolidation certificates to the amount of
$45,000,000. The total capital of the road was thus
increased to and made to pay dividends on over $103,-
000,000, while the total cost of the road and its equipment, as claimed by the company in 1870, was less than
$60,000,000, their estimate being based upon assumed
consolidation values and the expenditures made from
surplus earnings. During the same year the gross earnings of the company were $22,363,320, and their net
earnings $8,295,240. In 1880 the gross earnings had

increased to $33,175,913, and the net earnings to $15,326,019. The company was able to declare in that year 11.82 per cent. dividend on its $89,500,000 of fictitious stock. In 1890 its gross earnings were $37,-008,403, or $26,050 per mile, while its total net earnings were $12,516,273. The gross earnings have largely increased during the years 1891 and 1892. It is safe to say that $2,000,000 per annum would pay very liberal interest and dividends on the amount of money expended upon the construction of the New York Central and Hudson River Railroad from the proceeds of its bonds and stocks. By the creation of fictitious values the managers of the company have attempted to impose an exorbitant tax upon the commerce and travel of the country for all time to come. The Government guarantees an inventor a monopoly only for a limited space of time, upon the expiration of which his invention becomes the common property of the people; but railroad managers endeavor to collect, under the protection of our laws, an exorbitant royalty from our people forever.

The case of the New York Central and Hudson River Railroad Company is only one of the innumerable instances of stock watering in the history of American railroads. Indeed, it can be shown that stock-watering reached a still higher degree of development in the case of the Erie road. It has been demonstrated that the actual original cost to the stock- and bondholders of the New York Central Railroad Company, which was, with its branch lines, 593 miles long, did not, including the Athens branch, exceed $10,000,000. Its cost to its owners, in 1869, including the bonuses, premiums, commissions and fictitious equalization values of several transfers, was reported by them to be only $37,600,000, or about $63,400 per mile.

At about the same time the main stem of the Erie
Railway, extending from New York to Dunkirk, a distance of 459 miles, was represented by a capital of $108,-
807,687, or $237,000 per mile. Considering the infe-
riority of this road to the New York Central, we are forced
to the conclusion that nearly 85 per cent. of the capital
of the road represented water, or, in other words, that the
commerce of the United States was taxed to pay dividends on about $90,000,000 of watered securities. In
1863 the Erie Railroad had outstanding $11,437,500 of
common stock. In 1864 this had been increased to $15,-
693,000, in 1868 to $37,765,000, and in 1869 to $70,-
000,000. Not one-tenth of this enormous increase of
capital was ever expended on the property of the road.
The stock was sold at from 20 to 40 cents on the dollar,
and the proceeds disappeared in the hands of its managers. To what extent this freebootery was carried will
probably never be known. An idea of the rottenness of
the Erie management may be had from the fact that the
courts at one time ordered its president to restore to the
company $9,000,000 of diverted securities, which order
was complied with. Vast private fortunes were amassed
by nearly all the men who directed the affairs of the road,
and the mismanagement became in time so notorious
that the legislature of the State of New York was appealed to, to remove the directors of the road for the
protection of its stockholders, and to reduce the capital
stock of the company to the amount actually paid for it.
This movement failed, however, because it was opposed
by the very stockholders whose interests were supposed to
have suffered by directorial mismanagement. They preferred to continue to draw dividends on the face value of
stocks which they had purchased at 20 cents on the dollar.

The capitalization of the company has since been increased to $163,679,825, and it is by no means a secret among those familiar with railroad values that the bonded indebtedness of the Erie road represents alone many millions more than the total amount that was ever invested in the property.

The principal competitor for through traffic of the two companies whose financial operations we have just reviewed is the Pennsylvania Central Company. It has often been asserted by the managers and friends of this company that its capital is free from water; but this is not true. In 1864 a dividend of $4,130,760 was made out of the surplus earnings of the road. This dividend was payable in capital stock and was equal to 30 per cent. of the then outstanding capital. Similar surplus dividends, each equal to 5 per cent. of the company's outstanding stock, were declared in 1867 and 1868. The people were thus taxed to pay dividends on a capitalized surplus which had been derived from excessive charges previously imposed on them. I shall not attempt here to determine whether the capital represented by the Pennsylvania Railroad Company has been honestly invested. A committee of Congress has expressed the opinion that the capitalization of its main line exceeds the amount of the actual cost of the property by more than eleven million dollars. There is, however, a system of inflation practiced by the Pennsylvania Railroad Company which is simply a new form of bond and stock watering. More than one-half of the capital of this company has been invested in the stocks and bonds of other corporations. In 1891 the amount so invested was $154,319,240, and the income derived from it $4,852,181. This does not only cause the stocks and bonds of certain companies to be counted twice, but exacts a double tax from the commerce of the country, interests and dividends upon the same capital being paid both to the bond- and stockholders of the Pennsylvania Central and to the bond- and stockholders of the roads in whose securities it has made investments. The income of the company is thus swelled far beyond the amount which the traffic reports indicate. It will be seen that, to perpetuate extortionate rates, this process of manifolding securities might be continued indefinitely.

The cost to its stock- and bondholders of the Baltimore and Chicago line of the Baltimore and Ohio Railroad, which has a length of 795 miles, was estimated by the company's officers at about $57,000,000. The actual cost of this road, owing to its expensive mountain grades, was probably greater than that of any of the other through lines between the sea-coast and Chicago, but there can be no doubt that the capitalization of this road represents from one-half to one-third pure water. At the time of the completion of this road to Chicago the surplus earnings of the company, after the payment of interest and dividends, amounted to over $29,000,000. This had been charged to "profit and loss" and used in the construction of branch lines. Thus an amount equal to more than half of the reported cost of this line had at the time of its completion been returned to its owners in other railroad values.

The Select Senate Committee on Transportation Routes to the Seaboard in 1874 estimated the excess of the capital over actual cost of the Erie road, from New York to Dunkirk, at $68,807,000; that of the New York, Lake Shore and Michigan Southern line to Chicago at $115,188,137, and that of the Pennsylvania and Fort Wayne line to Chicago at $11,290,374. If this estimate was correct

the entire over-capitalization of these lines, on which the
commerce between the West and the East was forced to
pay a dividend of 8 and 10 per cent. per annum, was no
less than $195,000,000. The committee assumed the act-
ual cost of these roads to be $182,000,000, or about $78,-
000 per mile. They based their estimate upon the cost of
the main branch of the Baltimore and Ohio, as reported by
their officers, supposing it to represent the actual outlay
made by its stock- and bondholders. Various revela-
tions which have since been made to the public, as
to the real cost of railway construction, justify the belief
that the estimated cost of $78,000 per mile for those roads
is far too high. Mr. Henry Poor, several years ago, estimated the average cost of the roads of the United States
at $30,000 a mile. Making allowance on one hand for
Mr. Poor's tendency to favor the railroad side of the
question, and on the other hand for the more expensive
grades, double tracks and better terminal facilities of
these trunk lines, $50,000 per mile may be considered a
fair estimate of their average cost. Upon this basis the
total cost of the three lines in question would amount to
$116,450,000, and the excess of their capital over actual
cost would be the enormous sum of $261,000,000, or 325
per cent. of their actual cost, and probably not less than
400 per cent. of the original cost to their stock- and
bondholders. The capital of these companies has since
been considerably increased, to enable their managers to
increase their dividends, and with it the tax levied upon
the commerce of the country.

These are only a few of the many instances of stock
watering that might be mentioned. In fact, there are
to-day very few railroads in the United States that are
entirely free from it. It is a notorious fact that the

stock of a large number of railroad companies represents
little or no value, having either been sold at a mere nominal price or been donated as a premium or bonus to those
who purchased a large amount of the company's bonds.
In recommending, in his December, 1891, annual message,
Government aid for the Nicaragua Canal, President Harrison said : " But if its bonds are to be marketed at heavy
discounts and every bond sold is to be accompanied by a
gift of stock, as has come to be expected by investors in
such enterprises, the traffic will be seriously burdened to
pay interest and dividends." It is not difficult to surmise
to what enterprises the President referred. It has for
many years been a well-settled principle among railroad
incorporators that no larger assessments should be made
upon the stockholders than is necessary to float the company's bonds. A company, for instance, is organized with
a capital stock of, say, $1,000,000. Five per cent. of this
sum, or $50,000, is paid in to defray preliminary expenses.
The road is then bonded for perhaps $2,000,000,
but as the bonds are sold for only 80 per cent. of their
face value and as the incorporators allow themselves 5 per
cent. for the negotiation of the bonds, only $1,500,000 is
realized for the construction of the road. The incorporators now vote to themselves a contract to construct the
road for $1,500,000 and at once sublet it to a contractor
who is ready and anxious to build the road for $1,200,000.
The incorporators thus realize $1,000,000 worth of stock,
a portion of which is unloaded upon unsophisticated investors, and $300,000 in cash, at an outlay of $50,000;
and the road, which cost $1,200,000, is made to pay inter-
est and dividends on a total capital of $3,000,000, and
this is subsequently watered indefinitely if the road proves
profitable or a consolidation with some other road justifies

the belief that its earning capacity might be increased. Nor is this an overdrawn picture. On the contrary, instances might be cited where only one-half of one per cent. of the company's stock was paid in by the shareholders.

In the days of inflation such transactions did not seem to seriously affect railroad securities. Even when they were no longer a secret to the public, stocks and bonds sold readily, because, owing to the large earnings of the roads, this class of investments was unusually productive.

In 1868 the earnings of the railroads of Massachusetts averaged $15,400 a mile, and were equal to 38 per cent. of the total reported cost of all the lines of the State. The Chicago, Burlington and Quincy earned $15,386 per mile in 1867, and paid a 15 per cent. dividend. Its stocks were quoted 100 per cent. above par. In 1867 the Lake Shore Railroad earned more than 50 per cent., and the Terre Haute and Indianapolis even as much as 57.2 per cent. of the amount of its cost. Previous to the war the inflation of railroad securities was, as a rule, confined to the stock. Where roads were bonded for more than the cost of construction it was, with but very few exceptions, done to make their capital to correspond with their earning capacity, or rather to divert public attention from the fact that the rates in force had outlived their reasonableness. It was reserved to the Union Pacific and the Central Pacific companies to bond their roads from the beginning to an amount equal to twice their actual cost, or, in other words, to virtually receive them as a present from the Federal Government, bond them for all they were worth, and, in addition, issue stock to an amount largely in excess of the cost of construction, and then try to earn interest and dividends on the whole amount of securities issued. The history of these companies forms so interesting and instructive a chapter in the railroad annals of America that a short synopsis of it may not seem out of place here.

The charter of the Union Pacific Railroad Company was granted by Congress on the first day of July, 1862. Shortly after the beginning of the War of the Rebellion it was made to appear to the country that a transcontinental road was a national necessity; that without it we could not hope to retain long the Pacific Coast. It was also very plausibly argued that the political benefits to be derived by the country from the construction of such a road, as well as its great length and extraordinary cost, made it the duty of the nation to aid liberally its enterprising and patriotic promoters in the prosecution of their gigantic task. In those stirring times few people were inclined to question the motives of those who advocated what appeared to be patriotic measures, or to be penurious in the expenditure of public funds when the public weal seemed to demand such expenditure.

The Union Pacific Railroad charter, which in substance was passed by Congress as it had been drafted by the promoters of the enterprise, gave to the new company the right of way through the public lands, and authorized it to take, from the lands adjacent to the line of its road, earth, stone, timber and other materials for its construction. It further granted to the company every alternate section of land to the amount of five alternate sections per mile on each side of its line, excepting only those lands to which preëmption or homestead claims attached at the time when the line of the road should be definitely fixed. In addition to these donations the United States issued to the company subsidy bonds in an amount equal to $16,000 per mile for the distance from the Missouri River to the eastern line of the Rocky Mountains, $48,000 per mile for a distance of 150 miles through the Rocky Mountains, and $32,000 per mile from the western base of the Rocky Mountains to the terminus of the road. Similar franchises were at the same time given to the Central Pacific Railroad Company, a corporation which had previously been chartered by the State of California. Besides its grant of right of way, land, timber, etc., this company received subsidy bonds at the rate of $16,000 a mile for a distance of 7.18 miles east of Sacramento, of $48,000 a mile for 150 miles through the Sierra Nevada, and of $32,000 a mile for the distance from the eastern base of that mountain range to its junction with the Union Pacific. The charters of the two companies provided that, to secure the repayment to the United States of the amount of those bonds, they should *ipso facto* constitute a first mortgage on the entire lines of the road, together with their rolling stock, fixtures and other property. The franchises and donations thus granted by Congress were most valuable; in fact, the latter were alone sufficient to build and equip the roads. In spite, however, of the liberal grants and in spite of the urgent necessity of the roads in those years of national trial, both of these enterprises made very slow progress. Their promoters were men of small means, and the capitalists to whom they appealed for help failed to realize the value of the franchises. No doubt when these men first engaged in their cause they expected to encounter serious obstacles in Congress, supposing that that august body would consider the proposed measure with much deliberation and to act upon it with still more circumspection. Their success greatly surprised them. They made the discovery that members of Congress could be imposed upon as easily as private citizens, and when they fully realized how readily their demands had been granted, they were greatly provoked at themselves because they had not asked for more.

According to a story told by my old friend Mr. J. O. Crosby, an experienced member of the brotherhood of tramps late one afternoon chanced to stroll into the city of Alton. Having no visible means of support, he was picked up by the police and brought before the Mayor to give an account of himself and to be dealt with as that dignitary might see fit. The tramp, a printer by profession, and by no means a tyro in meeting such emergencies, so managed to impress the Mayor with his superior accomplishments that the latter concluded it would be a good investment, both for himself and the city over which he presided, to offer the genial stranger a contribution to his traveling fund, upon the condition that he would no longer than absolutely necessary molest the city with his presence. He accordingly told the intercepted tourist that while it had been for years the policy of the city and its officials to entertain all tramps found within the limits of Alton for thirty days at the city jail in exchange for a fair amount of labor, he would, in consideration of the apparent fact that he was of better metal than the average tramp, make an exception in his case, and would, even at the risk of being censured for it by his constituents, hand over to him five dollars from the municipal funds if he would agree to leave the city early next morning. The tramp gladly accepted the proposition, replenished his empty purse with the proffered bounty and withdrew from the City Hall, to take a stroll through Main Street. The city seemed to him as prosperous as the Mayor had shown himself liberal. It occurred to the itinerant typographer that its treasury would not have been the worse off for a ten-dollar levy, and he hastily returned to the Mayor's office to plead for a larger donation. The Mayor, not disposed to argue the question, handed him another five-dollar bill and improved the opportunity to remind him of his previous promise and to give expression to the hope that as a gentleman of honor he would now discharge his obligation. The tramp fairly overwhelmed His Honor with assurances of good faith and bade him an affectionate good-by. The next rising sun found him on his onward journey. His route led through Alton on the Hill, a portion of the city which he had not seen before. He viewed with surprise the many fine residences and other evidences of opulence which this part of the city contained. He passed on in a pensive mood until he reached the summit of the hill, which commanded a fine view of the entire city. Here he turned to cast a farewell glance over the town ruled over by the most generous mayor that it had ever been his privilege to meet. As he beheld before him the fine homes and beautiful yards, and below in the valley the lofty church-steeples, the many school-houses, the massive business blocks, the long and well-paved streets and the spacious and shady parks, an expression of mingled surprise and disappointment stole over his face. He thrice slapped his wrinkled brow and then hurriedly retraced his steps down the hill. When the chief magistrate of Alton came to his office that morning, he met the irrepressible tramp anxiously waiting for him at the door. "Mr. Mayor," said the wily extortioner, "I acted very hastily yesterday when I accepted your second proposition. You have here a much larger town than I ever supposed. I have been constrained to take our last agreement into reconsideration, and I shall not leave this point until you add another five dollars to your consideration. You can certainly better afford to do that than to throw away thirty days' board and the ten dollars which you have already paid me besides."

The diplomacy of the Union Pacific and Central Pacific railway companies was the same as that of the Alton tramp. They had found Congress as generous as the tramp had found the Mayor of Alton, and now reproached themselves for their modesty and resolved to bring the pliability of Congress to a severer test. They again appeared before that body in 1864 and asked that their charter be so amended as to grant to them ten alternate sections instead of five on each side of the road, and also all the iron and coal found within ten miles of their track, which had previously been reserved by Congress. And in addition to this they asked that they be authorized to issue their own mortgage bonds on their respective roads to an amount equal to the bonds of the United States, and that the lien of the United States bonds be made subordinate to the lien created by the companies' bonds. By the act of Congress, July 2, 1864, all these demands were granted, and the two companies were thus virtually presented with their roads and were at the same time given permission to mortgage this gift of the people and divide the proceeds among their shareholders, many of whom had received their stock chiefly in consideration of their influence in and out of Congress. The contribution of the United States to these companies on account of their main lines has not been far from $80,000,000, of which over $52,000,000 was paid in bonds, and the remainder in lands, which aggregated about 23,000,000 acres. The whole line from Council Bluffs to Sacramento is 1,780 miles long. It will thus be seen that the national contribution was about $45,000 per mile, besides the right of way and all timber, iron and coal found within ten miles of the road. There is no doubt that this contribution was equal to, if it did not exceed, the actual cost of the road. There has been an erroneous impression abroad which has likened the Pacific road to those wonderful and very expensive lines which cross the Andes and the Alps. Those who have not crossed the continent can hardly believe that the construction of this line was neither more difficult nor more expensive than that of any of the numerous railroads crossing the mountain ranges of the East, but such is the fact.

Starting from Omaha, the Union Pacific follows for nearly 500 miles, or almost half of its entire length, the valley of the Platte River. A better route for a railroad cannot be found upon the western continent. There are between Omaha and Cheyenne but three bridges worthy of the name. The Platte Valley is almost straight, rising toward the west at a nearly uniform rate of about 10 feet to the mile. Grading was practically unnecessary, and the work of construction consisted of little more than the laying of the ties and track. From the base of the mountains at Cheyenne to their summit is a distance of about thirty-two miles, the difference in altitude between the two points being less than 2,200 feet. The average grade is therefore about 68 feet to the mile, and nowhere are the grades heavier than 80 feet to the mile. There are heavier grades than these in the prairie State of Iowa, and the mountain grades of a number of Eastern roads exceed those of the Union Pacific by from 30 to 40 feet to the mile. The rise is, if not uniform, at least gradual, and the construction of even this portion of the road required, therefore, neither great engineering skill nor any unusual expenditure of money. The road now crosses a plateau which extends almost to the terminus of the Union Pacific at Ogden, and a very large portion of this is as favorable for a road-bed as the average railroad territory of the country.

The route of the Central Pacific presented to the engineer no great obstacles between Ogden and the State line of California, the only elevation of any note to be surmounted being the Humboldt Mountains in Nevada. Their highest point, Humboldt Wells, is 221 miles west of Ogden, and has an elevation of 5,650 feet above the level of the sea, while that of Ogden is 4,320 feet. Upon an average the grades of this portion of the road do not differ from those found in the Mississippi Valley. The portion of the Central Pacific Railroad which traverses the Sierra Nevada is the most expensive of the whole line, but the cost of construction did not, even on this division, exceed the amount contributed for it by the Federal Government; for the statement is made upon good authority that a few of the leading promoters of the road built the first western section of twenty miles with their own capital, of less than $200,000, and a loan from the city of Sacramento and Placer County, amounting to $550,000, and then drew $848,000 Government subsidy, or more than enough to build the second section and draw another installment of the subsidy; and that they repeated the operation until the whole line was completed. These men were in such haste to realize the profits which their undertaking promised them that they did not even take sufficient time to make a proper survey of their line. Had they done so, a great saving, both in the construction and in the subsequent operation of the road, might have been effected. It is now well known that a route could have been found through the Sierra Nevada Mountains, not far distant from the route chosen, which would have saved 800 feet in elevation and at least 25 per cent. in the expense of grading.

It is certainly safe to say that if less than forty thousand dollars a mile was sufficient to construct the road through the Sierra Nevadas the Federal contribution of $50,000,000 for the entire line, from Omaha to San Francisco, left, after the completion, a respectable surplus, either to the companies or those of their members who had the construction contract, and that the $75,000,000 of capital stock and the $55,000,000 of first mortgage bonds which the two companies issued were a gigantic dividend to the stockholders, for which, practically, no consideration was given.

The companies might well have been satisfied with the Government's generosity, but their success in imposing upon Congress stimulated their greed. The act of 1864 provided that the charge for Government transportation over these roads should be applied to the liquidation of its bonds, and that after the completion of the lines five per cent. of their net earnings should likewise be so applied. When the Secretary of the Treasury, under the law, refused to pay them the amount earned by Government transportation, and in addition to this demanded the five per cent. of their net earnings in liquidation of their debt, the companies applied to Congress to again amend their charters so as to relieve them for the time being from any direct payment of either principal or interest of the Government bonds, and to make it the duty of the Secretary of the Treasury to pay to the companies in money one-half of the compensation allowed to them by law for services performed for the Government. And again Congress responded to their demands, grant-

ing them, by a rider to the army appropriation bill, passed
March 3, 1871, all the relief asked for. Owing to the
policy of the managers of the Pacific line to pay as little
of the interest on the Government subsidy debt as is absolutely necessary to prevent foreclosure proceedings, the
unpaid interest has accumulated until it now almost equals
the amount of the original indebtedness. The last report
of the Commissioner of Railroads shows that the total
indebtedness, principal and interest, to the United States
of the Pacific railroad companies, was $114,490,000 on
July 1, 1892. The Commissioner seems to be of the opin
ion that the Union Pacific Company will not be able to
pay the subsidy bonds at maturity, and he urges that
some step be taken in the matter by Congress, whether it
be to extend the loan, which will mature within the next
six years, or to sell the road. The managers of the
Pacific roads and their friends ask an extension of the
Government subsidy bonds for fifty years, and a reduction
of interest from 6 to 2 per cent. If Congress continues to
be servile to these interests, the Pacific railroad lobby will
secure just such legislation as they demand.

At the time the Pacific roads were built the people of
the United States had no adequate knowledge of the topography of the Territories, and the promoters of the road
for a while found it a difficult task to convince capitalists
that the investment would be a safe one. That they
knew the value of the projected road was shown by the
contest between the Central Pacific and the Union Pacific
for mileage. For a distance of over 200 miles the two
companies graded roads side by side in contest for the
Government subsidy.

The promoters were even disappointed in the cost of
the roads, as Mr. Sidney Dillon states in an article pub-

lished in the August number of *Scribner's Magazine*, 1892, in which he says:

" At the end of 1867 the road was completed to the top of the mountains and nearly half way to Salt Lake City. The cost of building over the mountains was so much less than we had expected that the construction company found itself with a surplus from the proceeds of the subsidy bonds. This was imprudently distributed in dividends."

The United States Government could parallel to-day the line of either road for less than the amount of its first mortgage bonds, and its subsidy bonds are therefore nearly worthless.

Mr. Clews, in his "Twenty-Eight Years in Wall Street," says:

"After the Thurman bill had been sustained by the Supreme Court Mr. Gould had a plan to build a road from Omaha to Ogden, just outside the right of way of the Union Pacific, and give that road back to the Government. It would give others 'a chance to walk.' The Government tried to squeeze more out of the turnip than was in it. For $15,000,000 a road could be built where it had cost the Union Pacific $75,000,000."

It may be admitted that the Pacific roads, even at an extravagant cost, have proved a good investment for the country, yet their history reflects severely on the statesmanship of those members of Congress whose duty it was to properly protect the interests of the nation at that time. They were unequal to their task.

The Great Northern Railway Company has just completed its road to the Pacific Coast. Its line is very direct, and it has unusually light curvature and low grades, which will enable it to be operated more cheaply than any Pacific line yet constructed. Much of its route is through a rich and productive country, insuring to it a heavy local business.

The following statistics concerning it are given in the *Railway Age :*

    Total mileage, December 18, 1890...... ..   2,850
    Average bonded debt per mile.............$18,636 75
    Average stock per mile.................... 7,015 67
    Total 25,652 42
    Interest charges per mile................. 1,005 76
    Dividend charges per mile.................   420 94

A comparison of these figures with those corresponding of other transcontinental lines is instructive, and is commended to Congressmen who have to deal with the Union Pacific and Central Pacific questions.

Stock and bond inflation, it may confidently be asserted, has created from five to six thousand millions of dollars of fictitious railroad capital. In 1890 the average liabilities of the railroads in the United States, including the capital stock and the funded and unfunded debt, were $63,600 per mile. According to Mr. Poor's estimate of the average cost of American railroads per mile, more than 50 per cent. of this vast sum is pure water. But, as has, been stated before, Mr. Poor is partial to the railroad interest, and his estimate of $30,000 a mile is too high for the time at which it was made. Furthermore, railroad building has since then been materially cheapened. Tens of thousands of miles of road have been built in recent years that did not cost to exceed $10,000 a mile. Very recently the Union Pacific Railroad Company proved, before the Board of Equalization at Salt Lake City, by the testimony of engineers, that the average cost per mile of the Utah Central line was only $7,298.20, itemized as follows :

    Engineering ....$ 300 00
    Grading 5-ft. fill, 18,480 yds............... 2,310 00
    Ties, 2,640, at 30 cts......................   792 00
    Rails, 82 tons............................... 1,845 00

Splices......	12	00
Bolts	24	00
Spikes....... ....-.....	142	20
Track-laying.....	600	00
Bridges.....	200	00
Station-building...........................	100	00
Fences...........	150	00
Right of way..............................	720	00

$7,298 20

In a recent article Mr. C. Wood Davis states that "many auxiliary lines have been built at costs ranging from $8,000 to $15,000 per mile, and capitalized at two, three, four, and even five times their cost, as in the case of the 107 miles of the Kansas Midland, costing, including a small equipment, but $10,200 per mile, of which 30 per cent. was furnished by the municipalities along its line. Yet, with construction profits and other devices, this road shows a capitalization of $53,000 per mile."

And that "the Missouri Pacific line from Eldora to McPherson, Kansas, a comparatively expensive prairie road, being located across the line of drainage, cost much less than $10,000 per mile, as have thousands of miles of other prairie roads."

It is safe to say that $25,000 is a liberal estimate of the average cost per mile of American roads to the stock- and bondholders, and that their capitalization represents $38,000 of water per mile. The total net earnings of the railroads of the country were $341,666,639 in 1890, and $356,227,883 in 1891, upon an actual investment of only about $4,250,000,000. This is a return of about 8½ per cent. and shows the force of Mr. Poor's statement that, if the water were squeezed out of railroad securities, no better-paying investment could be found in the country.

We often see references to the fact that no dividends

are paid upon a large portion of railroad stocks, but there
is no reason why dividends should be paid upon many of
them, as they represent no capital whatever that has gone
into the road.   It is probable that not to exceed ten cents
on the dollar upon an average was originally paid for these
stocks, and the $80,000,000 distributed annually as divi-
dends upon them does not vary much from fifteen to
twenty-five per cent. upon the amount actually invested
in them.

CHAPTER VII.

COMBINATIONS.

IT is the favorite argument of railroad men, and the writer must confess that he himself formerly believed, that if all legal restraints were removed from railroad business, the laws of trade would regulate it more successfully and more satisfactorily, both to the railroad companies and their patrons, than the wisest statutes could ever regulate it. To give force to their argument, they cite the old Democratic maxim that that State is governed best which is ruled the least. They also assert that it is the province of the State to guarantee to each of its citizens industrial freedom; to permit him to transact any legitimate business according to his best judgment; to buy and to sell where and at what price he pleases; in short, to earn without restriction the reward of his intelligence and his industry. They further contend that under a free government the law of supply and demand should be allowed free sway, and that he who buys or sells transportation should not be hampered in his transactions any more than the grocer and his customer.

The reply to this is that, while the grocer is a natural person, the railroad company is an artificial person, and that, while the business of the former is purely private, that of the latter is quasi-public. The grocer must rely solely upon his personal rights and private resources, but the railroad company accepts from the State the franchises which enable it to do business. And yet, if the public had any assurance that the laws of trade would regulate both kinds of business alike, it is not likely that the State would distinguish between the two. They claim that their business is like other private business, and therefore they should be let alone; that competition can be relied upon to correct abuses; and where competition does actually exist they forget, and then claim that their business is not like other private business, and they should be allowed to make pools and combinations, because in their business competition is ruinous. Experience has certainly demonstrated that competition is only possible where combination is impossible. Where the same commodity is supplied by a large number of individuals, there is but little danger for the public from those who supply it, for an agreement among many cannot easily be effected; and even if an understanding could be reached, it would not long be satisfactory to all parties. Disagreements would arise which would end in the dissolution of the combination. Where, however, the number of competitors is small, agreements can be easily effected and successfully maintained.

It is doubtful whether there is at present any interest in the commercial world which has a greater tendency to monopoly and combination than the railroad interest. There are in the United States some 40,000 railroad stations. Not more than 4,000 of these are junctions of two or more roads. At 90 per cent. of these stations shippers are therefore confined to one line of railroad, and are, in absence of State regulation, compelled to pay for transportation whatever price the companies may be disposed to charge, subject only to such restrictions as the proximity of competing points may impose. If competition obtained at all points where two or more roads meet, many railroad companies could not afford to charge excessive rates at non-competitive points along their lines of road, for such a policy would slowly but surely drive a large volume of their legitimate business to rival roads, to whose interest it would be to encourage by every means in their power such diversion of traffic. Railroads early recognized this fact and took steps to enable each line to control its local business. The first combinations among railroad companies to control prices at competitive points were rather crude; in fact, much cruder than the first Granger legislation. They were simple agreements among the various roads touching a common point to maintain certain fixed rates. But while each road was anxious to have the rates agreed upon maintained by all of its rivals, it cared but little about maintaining its own good faith, and it improved every opportunity to get business at reduced rates so long as it could reasonably hope to escape detection. As soon as any of the competing roads, through the falling-off of its business, became convinced that it was the victim of overreaching rivals, it retaliated by offering still lower rates to close-tongued shippers. This tricky rivalry would be continued until the animosity engendered by it would lead to an open rupture, and what railroad men are pleased to term a rate war would follow. As the schedule rates had before been unreasonably high, so they became now unreasonably low. Hostilities would be continued until all belligerents became exhausted and manifested a disposition to negotiate a treaty of peace. The former high rates would then be restored; the compact was carried out for a short time, to be again violated and finally annulled. These rate agreements were in vogue in New England before the War of the Rebellion and gradually found their way to the Middle States and the West. Wherever they were tried they were violated, until even among the most unsophisticated of freight agents a rate agreement was looked upon as a farce.

The statement is often made by railroad managers that excesses in railroad competition are the result of the peculiar conditions of their business, which has heavy fixed charges on one hand and a fickle patronage on the other; that the uncertainty of through business compels them to rely upon the local business for such revenue as is necessary to meet these fixed charges; and that, inasmuch as their trains *must* run, and any through freight hauled by them is so much business taken from the enemy, they can better afford to take it at any price than to have one of their competitors take it.

It is difficult to see why this reasoning should not be applied to other branches of business; for instance, to milling. The mill-owner, like the railroad company, has heavy fixed charges. He has to earn the interest on his capital, he has to keep his mill in repair, he now and then has to meet the demands of the times and purchase improved appliances, and he has to keep a certain number of employes, whether business is brisk or slack. He might, therefore, if he saw fit to employ the logic of railroad managers, earn revenue enough to meet his fixed charges from the business which his regular customers give him, and then do any business coming from beyond this circle at any price rather than surrender it to a rival.

It will readily be conceded that any enterprise conducted on such principles could, at the best, flourish only temporarily, for it would soon encounter difficulties from two sources. Its local customers, thus discriminated against, would withdraw their patronage, while its competitors, finding their territory encroached upon, would, in self-defense, offer still better terms to the public to regain their lost customers. Such ruinous competition, if long persisted in, must necessarily cripple, if it does not bankrupt, a majority of those who engage in it. It is fortunately as rare in industrial and commercial circles as it is common among public carriers.

This difference can easily be accounted for. Where there are a large number of competitors the prices of the commodities supplied by them are leveled down until they reach a point where they will afford only a reasonable margin of profit, and beyond which they will cease to be profitable, and will therefore cease to be supplied until the equilibrium is again established. Where, however, the number of competitors is small, the price of the commodities supplied by them will, by agreement, for a time at least, be maintained at a point where it affords considerable more than a reasonable profit. Here the large gain presents to the various competitors such a temptation to outstrip their rivals and increase their business at the expense of good faith, that but few, if any, of them will, in the long run, resist it. The tendency to underbid rivals will always be strong where profits are large, and it may safely be asserted that efforts to maintain, through combinations, excessive rates are the most fruitful source of ruinous competition.

In time railroad managers became convinced that, unless it was possible to radically reform railroad ethics, rate agreements could never be relied upon for the maintenance of excessive rates at competing points. The combined roads found it an easy matter to agree upon excessive rates, but were powerless to enforce them. Experience convinced their managers that to make their tariffs effective it was necessary to deprive individual roads of the power or the inducement to cut below the agreed rates. Their ingenuity in time developed a system which promised to remove from individual roads every temptation to take business at less than schedule prices. This device consists in a division of railroad business and is commonly called a pool. There are various ways in which such a division is made. Either the traffic is divided among the various companies meeting at a common point, or each road is allowed to carry all freights that it may receive, and then the earnings of the different roads are divided, each road being paid the actual cost of such service as it has performed. There is still a third pooling arrangement, consisting in a division of territory, but this has been found less satisfactory and is now but rarely resorted to.

It is said that the first regular pool organized in the United States was the Chicago-Omaha pool, formed in 1870 by the Chicago, Burlington and Quincy, the Chicago, Rock Island and Pacific, and the Chicago and Northwestern railroad companies, then the only three lines connecting the cities of Chicago and Omaha. This pool, which was subsequently joined by other lines, made an equal division of the traffic, and was so well organized that it lasted fourteen years "without a break." The abuses practiced by the companies belonging to this pool were one of the chief causes of the Granger movement in Iowa. It is indeed doubtful whether any other railroad combination ever maintained itself longer or pursued its ends with greater pertinacity than this pool. Another pool of national notoriety was the Southern Railway and Steamship Association, which was organized, though at first under a different name, in the State of Georgia, in 1875. It was probably the first money pool formed in the United States. Each member was awarded a certain percentage of the total business between the various competitive points along its line. If a company carried more than its share, it was compelled to turn over the receipts from such additional traffic to its rivals, which paid it a nominal price for carriage. This allowance was always made so low that there was no inducement for any company to seek to carry more than its allotment. The pool had its own executive, legislative and judicial departments, and it enforced its decrees with an iron hand. It maintained a strong centralized government, and rebellious members had but little mercy to expect from it. It provided that if any officer or representative of any company should authorize or promise, directly or indirectly, any variation from established tariffs, he should be discharged from the service, with the reason stated. The strong sentiment which we to-day find in the South in favor of State control of railways is the direct result of the many evils which this powerful pool introduced into the railway business of that section of the country.

Other pools followed, as the Southwestern Association, organized in 1876, to control the traffic between Chicago and St. Louis, and the Minnesota and the Colorado pools. Within a few years railroad pools covered the whole country. All pursued the same object, viz., the control of rates at competitive points, which enabled the companies to maintain excessive schedule rates at local points.

Between 1875 and 1880 the pooling system rapidly spread all over the Union. Wherever competition promised to regulate rates by the application of the law of supply and demand, the pool was resorted to as the never-failing remedy to preserve dividends on watered stock. As long as lake and canal navigation controlled the

carriage of heavy freights between Chicago and New York
by means of rates so low that railroads found it, or at
least thought it, impossible to compete with them in the
transportation of agricultural products during the greater
part of the year, railroad pools between Chicago and New
York could not be successfully maintained.   In 1873 the
railroads transported only about 30 per cent. of this kind
of freight from the West to Eastern ports.

Owing, however, to the rapid decrease of the cost of
transportation, railroad companies from this time on were
enabled to encroach rapidly upon the business of water
routes, so that in 1876 they carried over 52 per cent. of
the entire volume of agricultural products that were moved
from the West to the East.   As long as these products
were carried almost entirely by water from lake ports to
the East, New York, as the terminus of this route, enjoyed
decided advantages over the other Atlantic ports.   When,
however, the railroads commenced to successfully compete
with the water routes in the transportation of these commodities, a considerable share of this business was diverted
to Boston, Philadelphia and Baltimore, and it soon became
apparent that these ports, in some respects, enjoyed advantages for the export trade not possessed by New York.
It was, therefore, not surprising that the business men of
these cities, together with the railroads terminating in
them, made every effort to come in for their share of the
traffic which was drifting away from New York.

Competition between the New York Central and the
Pennsylvania Railroad for the Western through traffic
dated back as far as 1869, the year in which both systems
secured, through consolidation with connecting roads,
through lines to Chicago.   Rates fell in one year from
$1.80 to 25 cents per hundred pounds.   After a time the

managers of the two companies met, and schedule rates were restored. Rates were, at least outwardly, maintained until the Baltimore and Ohio and the Erie system entered Chicago, and the Grand Trunk made connections with Milwaukee and other lake points, and thus disturbed through rates. All efforts to maintain the level of the old tariffs, through agreements, proved now fruitless, for both the Baltimore and Ohio and the Grand Trunk found it to their interest to pursue independent policies, and refused to have their hands tied by an agreement with roads that were interested in continuing, if possible, the commercial supremacy of New York.

Rate skirmishing finally developed into open war in 1876, when fourth-class rates between Chicago and the Atlantic fell as low as 16 cents per hundred. This rate, however, was eclipsed in July, 1878, when wheat was carried from Chicago to New York for 10 cents per hundred. The existing conditions left no doubt in the minds of those familiar with railroad tactics that this war was simply the precursor of a gigantic combination between the trunk lines. An unsuccessful attempt to effect such a combination had been made before. In 1874 the managers of the Erie, Pennsylvania and New York Central met at Saratoga for the purpose of devising means for the suppression of competition in the trunk line traffic. This meeting, however, known in railroad history as the Saratoga Conference, was the first step toward the organization of a trunk line pool, although the conference did not lead to any immediate results, the Grand Trunk and the Baltimore and Ohio refusing to be bound by its decision. It was certainly no easy task to devise means to bring about an effective and permanent combination among five large through lines with greatly conflicting interests.

So far pools had never failed to suppress competition wherever they were organized. But in the past pools had, almost without exception, only attempted to control rates between common points. They accomplished their object by a division of the entire traffic or earnings from the traffic between common points. The schedule rates remained the same for all. But the traffic of the trunk lines brought a new factor into the problem. Here the rival routes did not terminate at the same points. It was contended by the Baltimore and Ohio that, whatever might be the facilities of Baltimore for exporting agricultural products, that port was at a disadvantage as compared with the more northern ports on account of the longer voyage and higher ocean rates to Liverpool, and that it could therefore not enter into a combination with the roads leading directly to New York and Philadelphia upon equal terms, since this would divert its legitimate share of the through business to those ports. The Grand Trunk, on the other hand, refused to enter the combination because, not having any direct Chicago connection, it feared that the enforcement of pool rates would materially diminish the volume of its business. As yet the railroad wiseacres did not seem to be equal to the emergency, and matters drifted along in the old channel. The rate war of 1876 gradually brought about an understanding among the belligerents. The competing roads accepted the terms offered, and with this a new principle entered into the science of pooling. Rates between Chicago and Baltimore were fixed somewhat lower than those between Chicago and Philadelphia, and in turn Philadelphia was allowed a small advantage over New York. This concession was made to equalize the difference in the ocean rates of the competing ports. These equalizing or

—to use railroad nomenclature—differential rates were subsequently granted by pools to such roads as, on account of some disadvantage, could not compete with other members of the pool on equal terms. Thus the longest route was usually permitted to charge the lowest, and the shortest route the highest rate. This practice is in conformity with the principle of charging whatever the traffic will bear, but it is certainly devoid of every consideration of justice and equity. If the longer line can afford to carry freight at rates lower than schedule prices, no further proof is needed under ordinary circumstances that the regular schedule rates of the shorter line are exorbitant.

The concession of differential rates settled, at least temporarily, the difficulties that had arisen out of the east-bound traffic of the trunk lines. This arrangement did not, however, in any way affect the traffic moving in the opposite direction. The volume of west-bound freight is very much larger at New York than at any other of the Atlantic ports. In order to get its share of the business, each trunk line maintained an office in New York. These offices eagerly solicited business for their respective roads, and the freights which they received for transportation to the West would be forwarded either directly or by a circuitous route; but, the longer the route, the lower as a rule was the compensation asked for the service. Under these circumstances competition was brisk, and the profits realized were far from satisfying the cupidity of the competing lines. It was apparent to their managers that the competition in the west-bound traffic was similar to that formerly existing between Chicago and Mississippi and Missouri River points, which had promptly yielded to pools. The temporary adjustment of the more perplexing

questions which had arisen out of the east-bound traffic
now paved the way for a pooling arrangement for the
west-bound freight. The Southern Pool, under the management of Albert Fink, had long attracted the attention
of the trunk line managers. Its system of dividing the
traffic, of reporting to a central office and of hearing and
deciding complaints had enabled it to exert an almost
absolute control over its members, to compel them to
make honest returns and to prevent rupture and rebellion.
It was believed that a pool of the trunk lines could not
be effective or permanent unless organized upon the
Southern basis and presided over by a trunk expert.
Accordingly, when in 1877 an agreement for the pooling
of the west-bound traffic was reached by the trunk lines,
Mr. Fink was tendered the position of pool commissioner.
Under the agreement reached the total tonnage of the
west-bound business was divided in such a way that the
Erie and New York Central roads each received 33 per
cent., the Pennsylvania 25 per cent., and the Baltimore
and Ohio 9 per cent. of it. If any road received more
freight than was allotted to it by the pool, it delivered
such surplus to the pool, or rather to such a road as the
pool commissioner designated as not having received its
allotment. The success of this pool from a railroad point
of view made the trunk lines anxious to organize a similar
pool for the whole east-bound traffic. It was proposed to
control by such a combination the rates on all the east-
bound traffic of the Northwest, by making Chicago the
pooling center, fixing for it a schedule of rates and making the rates of all the railroad centers in the West and
Northwest dependent upon it. The combination was to
comprise more than forty companies, controlling over
25,000 miles of road. The scheme was tried for three

months in 1878, but proved a failure, owing to the fact that nearly all of the many diverging interests sought their own advantage. The Eastern and Western trunk line pools were, through the efforts of their commissioner, successfully maintained, though even their harmony was occasionally marred by a short war precipitated by such members as would think themselves entitled to larger shares of the spoils. But a readjustment would invariably follow, and the expenditures of the war would be taxed up to the public.

After the failure of the gigantic Western pool which had been organized under the protectorate of the trunk lines, the companies which had composed it formed such local combinations as their individual interests dictated. It is doubtful whether during the five years immediately preceding the passage of the Interstate Commerce Law there was any junction of two or more roads in the United States which, except during the period of an occasional railroad war, had any competition in the transportation business. As has been shown before, discriminations without number were practiced between places and persons; goods were not unfrequently carried at a loss; but the general public was, as a rule, compelled to pay what the traffic would bear, or rather what the pooling roads thought it could bear.

It is claimed by railroad managers that pools are the only effective contrivances for checking ruinous competition among railroad carriers, and that they are therefore justifiable as a means of self-protection. This might perhaps be a valid argument if any attack were made upon the railroads which encroached upon their rights or endangered their existence, but if railroad companies are disposed to cut each other's throats, the public should not be made to pay the penalty of their depravity. As long as schedule rates are unreasonably high, railroads will be tempted to offer to certain shippers low secret rates; but as soon as all rates have been leveled down to a point where they will yield only a fair profit with good management, the inducement to cut below them is largely taken away. Pools, far from being a remedy for the evils of excessive competition, will in the end only aggravate the disease which they attempt to cure. The high rates which they maintain attract the attention of speculative men and lead to the construction of rival roads. While the traffic remains the same, the proceeds must then be divided among a larger number of carriers. Thus the construction of unnecessary roads, which has often been the subject of bitter complaint on the part of the older roads, is chargeable directly to their wrong policies.

One of the principal objections to industrial and commercial combinations is that they paralyze trade. Competition stimulates every competitor to offer the best at the lowest possible price. This increases the demand for the commodity, and both the producer and the consumer are in the end benefited by the operation of this law. On the other hand, combinations, or, what is the same, monopolies, increase the price, remove the stimulus to excellence, and reduce the demand, and thereby affect injuriously the producer and consumer alike. Competition in the railway service would mean an improved service and lower rates and would speedily be followed by a large increase of business.

Another serious objection to pooling is that it invariably leads to periodic wars, which unsettle all business, and but too often introduce into legitimate trade the element of chance. These wars give, moreover, to designing railroad managers an opportunity to enrich themselves by stock speculations at the expense of the stockholders, whose interests they use as a football for the accomplishment of their selfish ends. When rates are reduced to a right level, and are properly adjusted, and are equal to all, even railroad men will find no necessity for pools. The desire for such a combination is a desire to impose upon somebody, or some locality, or the public at large. The proposition to give legal sanction to pools, made by railroad managers, is preposterous; and even a pool to be approved by the Interstate Commerce Commission is out of the question, as it would cause the railroads to increase their efforts to control the appointment of the commission. However honest it may look on its face, however plausible may be the arguments produced in its favor, it should not be permitted.

There is no doubt but under the proposed pooling arrangement railroad interests, watered stocks and all, would be cared for, but there is every reason to believe that public interests would not be properly protected.

So long as servility by a member of the Interstate Commerce Commission to railroad influences serves as a stepping-stone to a high position in the employ of railroad combinations, with a salary of three or four times that of an Interstate Commerce Commissioner, so long will it be unsafe to permit such powers to be vested in that commission.

Pooling by railroads should not be permitted, if permitted at all, so long as representatives of speculative interests have a voice in their management, and not until all fictitious valuations are altogether banished from the equation, and until the roads are brought under complete Government control. There is no more necessity for pools among railroads than there is among merchants and manufacturers.   The capital actually invested in railroads is now receiving larger returns than investments in other lines of business, and their incomes are increasing from year to year.

Every pooling combination of railroad companies for the maintenance of rates is a violation of common law. From time immemorial the law has stamped as a conspiracy any agreement between individuals to support each other in an undertaking to injure public trade.   The Interstate Commerce Act reasserts this principle, and provides penalties for the maintenance of such combinations among railroad companies.   If, in spite of this act, the evil still exists, it is no argument against the merits of the law, but it does prove that the machinery provided for its enforcement is insufficient.   That railroad companies can be made to respect the law there can be no doubt; but much cannot be accomplished unless the people fully realize the magnitude of the undertaking and vest the Government with sufficient power to cope with an organized force whose total annual revenue is nearly three times as large as that of the United States.   The discussion of the question how this may be done will be reserved for a subsequent chapter.

CHAPTER VIII.

RAILROADS IN POLITICS.

THE question might be asked how the railroad companies for many years in succession have been able to prevent State control and pursue a policy so detrimental to the best interests of the public. One might think that in a republic where the people are the source of all power, and where all officers are directly or indirectly selected by the people to carry out their wishes and to administer the government in their interest, a coterie of men bent on pecuniary gain would not be permitted to subvert those principles of the common law and public economy which from time immemorial have been the recognized anchors of the liberty of the Anglo-Saxon race.

The statement that under a free government it is possible for a few to suppress the many might almost sound absurd to a monarchist, and yet is it true that for the past twenty-five years the public affairs of this country have been unduly controlled by a few hundred railroad managers.

To perpetuate without molestation their unjust practices and prevent any approach to an assertion of the principle of State control of railroad transportation, railroad managers have secured, wherever possible, the co-operation of public officials, and, in fact, of every semi-public and private agency capable of affecting public opinion. Their great wealth and power has made it possible for them to influence to a greater or less extent every department of the National and State governments. Their influence extends from the township assessor's office to the national capital, from the publisher of the small cross-roads paper to the editorial staff of the metropolitan daily. It is felt in every caucus, in every nominating convention and at every election. Typical railroad men draw no party lines, advocate no principles, and take little interest in any but their own cause; they are, as Mr. Gould expressed it, Democrats in Democratic and Republicans in Republican districts. The large means at the command of railroad companies, their favors, their vast armies of employes and attorneys and their almost equally large force of special retainers are freely employed to carry into execution their political designs, and the standard of ethics recognized by railroad managers in these exploits is an exceedingly low one.

It is a settled principle of these men that, if they can prevent it, no person not known to be friendly to their cause must be placed into any public office where he might have an opportunity to aid or injure their interests. The records of the various candidates of the principal parties for city, county, State, and national offices are therefore carefully canvassed previous to the primaries, the most acceptable among the candidates of each party are selected as the railroad candidates, and the local representatives of the railroad interest in each party are instructed to use all means in their power to secure their nomination.

· If none but candidates who are servile to the railroad interest are nominated by the principal parties, the election is permitted to take its own course, for, whichever side is successful, the railroad interest is safe. If, however, there is reason to believe that a nominee is not as devoted to their interests as the nominee of an opposing party, the latter is sure to receive at the polls whatever support railroad influence can give him. That a public official elected by the grace of a railroad manager is but too apt to become a tool in his hands needs no proof. Both gratitude and fear tie the average politician to the powerful forces which can control his political destiny.

The railroad manager, on the other hand, always kindly remembers his officeholding friends as long as they are loyal and in a position to serve him. Before the enactment of the Interstate Commerce Act there was every year a wholesale distribution of railroad passes among public officeholders and other prominent politicians. The pass was the token of the continued good will of the railroad dignitaries as the withholding of the "courtesy" was a certain indication of their displeasure. If the officeholder had personal or political friends whom he desired to have recognized, an intimation of this desire was generally sufficient to have the pass privilege even extended to them. And yet these favors were not bestowed indiscriminately. Thus the pass credit of a county official was more limited than that of an officer of the State, and the latter class were again rated according to their influence and rank. Furthermore, while annual passes were thus freely distributed among one class of officials, others could obtain them only by making special application for them. Members of the legislature would not unfrequently receive their supply of railroad passes before their certificates of election were issued, but legislative committee clerks and employes in the various departments of the State government were required to satisfy the railroad authorities that they were in a position to aid or to injure the railroad cause before their names were placed on the list of persons "entitled to the courtesy.

Of course the judiciary, as a coördinate branch of the government, could not well be slighted. Indeed, previous to the enactment of the Interstate Commerce Law, a judge would have regarded it an affront if he had not been furnished with passes by the various companies operating railroads in his district. It appears that the law has not entirely corrected this abuse, for only about two years ago the Chicago *News* made the discovery that nearly every judge in the city of Chicago traveled on passes. It is strange to what extent the pass often debased the judiciary. It was not unfrequent for judges to solicit passes for family and friends, and instances might be named where they demanded them in a wholesale way.

The impudent demands were usually honored by the railroad authorities, who reasoned that they could better afford to bear the shameless effrontery of the ermined extortioner than the damage which might result to them from adverse decisions.

A railroad pass, when presented by a public official or even by any public man, is now, in nine cases out of ten, a certificate of dishonor and a token of servility, and is so recognized by railroad officials. What equivalent railroad companies expect for the pass "courtesy" is well illustrated by the experience of an Iowa judge. This gentleman, who had been on the bench for years and always had been favored with passes by the various companies operating lines in his district, at the beginning of a new year failed to receive the customary pass from a leading road. Meeting its chief attorney, he took occasion to call his attention to what he supposed to have been an oversight on the part of the officer charged with the distribution of the passes. The attorney seemed to take in the situation at once. "Judge," said he, "did you not recently decide an important case against our company ? " "And was my decision," replied the Judge, " not in accordance with law as well as with justice ? " The attorney did not answer this question, but in the course of a few days the Judge received the desired pass.   A few months later it again became the Judge's unpleasant duty to render a decision adverse to the same company.   This second act of judicial independence was not forgiven, and the next time he presented his pass it was unceremoniously taken up by the conductor in the presence of a large number of passengers, and he was required to pay his fare.

Employes, while engaged in the legitimate business of their companies, should, of course, be transported free, but a great many persons receive passes and are classed as employes who never render any legitimate service for the company giving the pass, and by far the greater portion of passes are not granted from pure motives, but are given for the purpose of corrupting their holders.   It arouses antagonism, because as a rule passes are given to people who are fully able to pay their fare and are denied to those who are least able to pay it.   The passenger who pays his fare and then finds that a large number of his fellow-passengers travel on passes realizes that he is compelled to pay a higher fare that others may be carried free.   He feels that he is unjustly discriminated against, and wonders why such discrimination is tolerated in a country whose institutions are founded upon the very principle of equal rights to all.   A good anecdote is related which well illustrates this feeling.   A farmer and a lawyer occupied the same seat in a railroad car.   When the conductor came the farmer presented his ticket, and the lawyer a pass.   The farmer's features did not conceal his disgust when he discovered that his seat-mate was a deadhead. The lawyer, trying to assuage the indignation of the observing granger, said to him: " My friend, you travel very cheaply on this road. "   " I think so myself," replied the farmer, " considering the fact that I have to pay fare for both of us. "

But what must be a passenger's surprise when he finds that the judge who to-morrow is to preside at the trial of a case in which the railroad company is a party to-day accepts free transportation at its hands.   A judge may scorn the charge that he is influenced by a railroad pass, but his fellow-passenger who has paid his fare cannot understand why the railroad company should give passes to one class of people and refuse them to others, if it does not consider one more than others to be in a position to reciprocate its favors.

In their endeavor to win over the courts, however, the railroads do by no means confine their attention to the judges.   They are well aware that a biased jury is often more useful to them than a biased judge, and efforts are made by them to contaminate juries, or at least prejudice them in their favor.   A prominent Iowa attorney, the legal and political factotum of a large railroad corporation, for years made it a practice to supply jurors with passes. In one instance, when it was shown in court by the opposing counsel that all jurors in the case on trial had accepted passes from the railroad company which was the defendant in the case, the judge found himself compelled to discharge the whole jury.   The argument made by this counsel, in support of his motion that the jury be discharged, was certainly to the point.   He showed that in order to have an equal chance for justice it would be necessary for his client to give each juror at least fifty dollars to offset the bribes given to them by the railroad company.

That it has always been the policy of railroad managers to propitiate the judiciary is a fact too generally known among public men to admit of contradiction. If a judge owes his nomination or election to railroad influences, railroad managers feel that they have in this a guarantee of loyalty. If, however, he acquires the ermine in spite of railroad opposition, every effort is made to conciliate the new dispenser of the laws. The bestowal of unusual favors, flattery, simulated friendship and a thousand other strategies are brought into requisition to capture the wayward jurist. If he proves docile, if his decisions improve with time and show a gradual appreciation of the particular sacredness of corporate rights, the railroad manager will even forgive him his former heresy and rally to his support in the future. But if he asserts his convictions, if he attempts to discharge the duties of his responsible office without fear or favor, if he can neither be corrupted nor intimidated, all available railroad forces will be marshaled against him in the future.

It cannot be surprising that, under such circumstances, there always has been a tendency among judges to be conservative and to give the railroads the benefit of the doubt in their decisions. Judges well know that railroad companies appeal almost invariably when the decision of a lower court is adverse to them, but private citizens only in exceptional cases. They also know that railroads never forgive adverse decisions, whether right or wrong, while private citizens, as a rule, accept the decision of the court as justice, and do not hold the judge responsible for its being adverse to them. Our judiciary is, and probably always has been, as incorruptible as the judiciary of any country in the world; but our judges are made of no better material than our legislative or executive officers. Weak men, in all stations, are influenced by wealth and power, and weak judges can always be found who will be led or forced from the path of duty so long as corrupt men are permitted to manage railroads and to remain in possession of a power only inferior to that of an autocratic ruler.

The influence which railroads exert extends from the lowest to the highest court of the land. Federal courts have more than once been successfully appealed to to give legal sanction to the perpetuation of gigantic frauds, or to frustrate attempts made by the individual States to place restrictions upon roads operated within their respective borders. Twenty years ago a Federal judge aided Mr. Gould in his notorious Erie transactions, and in more recent years a Federal circuit judge in the West threw the property of the Wabash Railroad Company, upon the application of its own directors, into the hands of receivers selected by its former managers without the knowledge or notice of its creditors, and issued orders for the management of the property which greatly discriminated in favor of certain bondholders and were so manifestly unjust that Judge Gresham, before whom the case was subsequently brought, did not hesitate to say to them that "the boldness of this scheme to aid the purchasing committee, by denying equal right to all bondholders secured by the same mortgages, is equaled only by its injustice." At the same time one of the counsel for the dissenting bondholders characterized these strange orders as "the highwayman's clutch on our throat, the robber's demand, 'Your money or your life.'"

The decision which the Supreme Court of the United States rendered in the Granger cases in 1876, affirming the right of a State to control railroad charges for the transportation of passengers and freight wholly within the

State, was a serious disappointment to railroad men, for it was the first step toward wresting from them the power to arbitrarily control the commerce of the country. Ever since that time it has been their determined purpose to bring about, if possible, a reconstruction of the Federal Supreme Court, in order to secure a reversal or modification of the Granger decision. In the case of Peik vs. Chicago, 94th U. S., 176, the Supreme Court laid down the following broad principle of law: "Where property has been clothed with the public interest, the legislature may fix a limit to that which shall in law be reasonable for its use. This limit binds the courts as well as the people. If it has been improperly fixed, the legislature, not the courts, must be appealed to for a change." In one of the Granger cases the same court used the following language: "We know that this is a power which may be abused, but that is no argument against its existence. For protection against abuses by legislatures, the people must resort to the polls."

Fourteen years later, in the case of C. M. & St. P. R. Co. vs. Minn., decided in October, 1890, the same court rendered a decision so indefinite that the lawyers differed much in their opinions as to its meaning, and it appears that the members of the court who made the decision also differed in their opinions as to the meaning of the decision; for Justice Bradley said in his dissenting opinion, in which Justice Gray and Justice Lamar concurred, that the decision practically overruled Munn vs. Illinois; but the same court, in a case entitled Budd vs. New York, submitted in October, 1891, and decision rendered February 29, 1892, and opinion delivered by Justice Blatchford, in referring to the Minnesota case, after quoting the above statement from Justice Bradley, said: "But the

opinion of the court did not say so, nor did it refer to
Munn vs. Illinois, and we are of opinion that the decision
in that case is, as will be hereafter shown, quite distin-
guishable from the present case."

It is thus apparent that this court has adhered to the
decision in Munn vs. Illinois, and to the doctrines
announced in the opinion of the court in that case, and
those doctrines have since been repeatedly enforced in the
decisions of the courts of the States.

Judge Brewer, whose zeal for the defense of corporate
interests seems to amount almost to a craze, dissented.
He said: "I dissent from the opinion and judgment in
these cases. The main proposition upon which they rest
is, in my judgment, radically unsound. It is the doctrine
of Munn vs. Illinois reaffirmed. The paternal theory of
government is to me odious. Justice Field and Justice
Brown concur with me in this dissent."

It should be remembered that Justices Brewer and
Brown were both appointed to the Supreme bench by
President Harrison.

We have every reason to believe that, unless the people
of the United States are on the alert, as railroad managers
always are, there is, with further changes in the personnel
of the court, danger of its deviating from the sound principles of law laid down in its decision in the Granger
cases. Railroad attorneys have repeatedly been raised to
seats in the highest tribunal in the land. So great is the
power of the railroad interests, and so persistent are they
in their demands, that, unless a strong public sentiment
records its protest, their candidates for appointive offices
are but too apt to be successful. Representatives of the
railroads sit in the Congress of the United States, others
are members of the national campaign committees of both

of the great political parties, others control the politics of the States, and their influence reaches to the White House, whether its occupant is aware of it or not. Other interests in the past have succeeded in securing the appointment of biased men as judges of the Supreme Court who afterwards could always be relied upon to render decisions in their favor. Will the people profit by their experience, or will they be indifferent to the danger which surrounds them, until nothing short of a political upheaval can restore to them these rights of sovereignty, of which they have so insidiously been deprived?

Human gratitude is such that even high-minded men who, through the influence of the railroad interest, have been placed upon the Federal bench, find it impossible to divest themselves of all bias when called upon to decide a case in which their benefactors are interested. Such is the human mind that, when clouded by prejudiee, it will forever be blind to its own fault. Even the members of so high a tribunal as the Electoral Commission which decided the presidential contest between Hayes and Tilden could not divest themselves of their prejudices; each one, Republican or Democrat, voted for the candidate of the party with which he had cast his political fortune.

Last January, in an address delivered before the New York State Bar Association at Albany, Mr. Justice Brewer reminded his hearers that the rights of the railroads "stand as secure in the eye and in the custody of the law as the purposes of justice in the thought of God." And further on they were told that "there are to-day $11,000,-000,000 invested in railroad property, whose owners in this country number less than two million persons. Can it be that whether that immense sum shall earn a dollar or bring the slightest recompense to those who have invested perhaps their all in that business, and are thus aiding in the development of the country, depends wholly upon the whim and greed of that great majority of sixty millions who do not own a dollar? It may be said that that majority will not be so foolish, selfish and cruel as to strip that property of its earning capacity. I say that so long as constitutional guarantees lift on American soil their buttresses and bulwarks against wrong, and so long as the American judiciary breathes the free air of courage, it cannot."

Unfortunately judicial buttresses and bulwarks have not always been lifted against wrong. Judge Taney, like Brewer, supposed that it was left at his time for his court to preserve the peace and provide for the safety of the nation; but history has shown that we cannot depend upon that high tribunal for safety when it is controlled by weak or inefficient men.

When we consider what "that great majority" has done for this country in the past, and is doing for it at the present time, and especially when we contrast its sense of justice and right with the weakness and inability of some of its public servants, does it not seem to be a little presumptuous for them to assume that "the danger is from the multitudes—the majority, with whom is the power," and that, were it not for their superior wisdom and patriotic action, this great government of the people, by the people and for the people would be a failure?

Mr. Lincoln never feared "the whim and greed" of "that great majority," but he had at all times implicit confidence in the great mass of the people, and they in return had full confidence that no temptation of wealth or power was sufficient to seduce his integrity.

We cannot dismiss this subject without referring to a

stratagem which railroads have in the past repeatedly resorted to for the purpose of removing from the bench judges of independent minds whom they found it impossible to control. This stratagem consists of a well-disguised bribe, by which a Federal judge is changed into a railroad attorney with a princely salary. The railroad thus gets rid of an undesirable judge and gains a desirable solicitor at a price at which they could well have afforded to pension the judge.

The following is a copy of a broker's circular letter sent to prominent bankers of Iowa, and shows that even the Clerk of the United States Court is not overlooked:

" ...., June 30th, 1892.
"Mr. ....,
" We offer, subject to sale at par and interest, note $2,500. Date, July 5th, 1892. Time, six months; rate, 6 per cent. Payable where desired. Maker, ...
Endorser, Judge................ Mr. ....,
the maker, is clerk of the United States Circuit Court at .... Judge..........the well known attorney of the................and .... Railway Co., of............, stated to us to be worth $150,-000 to $200,000. Can you use it ? "

While railroad managers rely upon servile courts as a last resort to defeat the will of the sovereign people, they are far from losing sight of the importance of controlling the legislative branch of the government. By preventing what they are pleased to call unfriendly legislation they are more likely to prevent friction with public opinion, and they avoid at the same time the risk of permanently prejudicing their cause by an adverse opinion upon a constitutional question which they may find it necessary to raise in order to nullify a legislative act. There are three distinct means employed by them to control legislative action. First, the election to legislative offices of men who are, for some personal reason, adherents to the railroad cause. Second, the delusion, or even corruption, of weak or unscrupulous members of legislative bodies. Third, the employment of professional and incidental lobbyists and the subsidizing of newspapers, or their representatives, for the purpose of influencing members of legislative bodies and their constituencies.

There are probably in every legislative body a number of members who are in some way or other connected with railroad corporations. No doubt, a majority of these are personally irreproachable and even so high-minded as to always postpone private for public interest; yet there are also those whose political advancement was brought about by railroad managers for the very purpose of having in the legislative body servile members who could always be relied upon to serve their corporate masters. Nevertheless, were railroad interests restricted to the votes of these men for their support, the public would probably have no cause for alarm on account of the presence of railroad representatives in legislative bodies, but, as many other interests seek favorable legislation, railroad men are often enabled to gain support for their cause by a corrupt bargain for votes, and it is thus possible for them to double, triple, and even quadruple, their original strength, by a policy of reciprocity.

As in Congress and State legislatures, so these representatives of the railroads may be found in our city councils. The leaders of the railroads in Congress and in the legislatures of the various States usually rely upon discretion for obtaining their end, but railroad aldermen with but few exceptions seek to demonstrate their loyalty to the cause to which they are committed by a zealous advocacy of extreme measures, and will not unfrequently even gain their end through the most unscrupulous combinations. If their votes, together with such support as they obtain by making trades, are not sufficient to carry out or defeat a measure which the railroad interests may favor or oppose, even more questionable means are employed to gain a sufficient number of votes to command a majority.

Outright bribery is probably the means least often employed by corporations to carry their measures. While it may be true that the vote of every weak and unscrupulous legislator is a subject of barter, money is not often the compensation for which it is obtained. It is the policy of the political corruption committees of corporations to ascertain the weakness and wants of every man whose services they are likely to need, and to attack him, if his surrender should be essential to their victory, at his weakest point. Men with political ambition are encouraged to aspire to preferment and are assured of corporate support to bring it about. Briefless lawyers are promised corporate business or salaried attorneyships. Those in financial straits are accommodated with loans. Vain men are flattered and given newspaper notoriety. Others are given passes for their families and their friends. Shippers are given advantages in rates over their competitors; in fact, every legislator disposed to barter his vote away receives for it compensation which combines the maximum of desirability with the minimum of violence to his self-respect.

Those who attempt to influence or control legislative bodies in behalf of interested parties are collectively called the lobby. As a rule, the lobby consists of prominent politicians likely to have influence with members of their own party ; of men of good address and easy conscience, familiar alike with the subject under consideration and legislative procedure, and last, but not least, of confidential agents authorized and prepared to enter into secret negotiations with venal members. The lobby which represents the railroad companies at legislative sessions is usually the largest, the most sagacious and the most unscrupulous of all. Its work is systematic and thorough, its methods are unscrupulous and its resources great. Yet all the members of a legislative body cannot be bribed, either by money, or position, or favors. Some of them will not vote for any proposed measure unless they can be convinced that it is for the public welfare. These legislators, if their votes are needed, are turned over to the persuasive eloquence of those members of the lobby who, apparently, have come to the capital moved by a patriotic impulse to set erring legislators right on public questions. Their familiarity with public matters, their success in public life, their high standing in political circles, their apparent disinterestedness and their plausible arguments all combine to give them great influence over new and inexperienced members. In extreme cases influential constituents of doubtful members are sent for at the last moment to labor with their representatives, and to assure them that the sentiment of their districts is in favor of the measure advocated by the railroads. Telegrams pour in upon the unsuspecting members. Petitions in favor of the proposed measure are also hastily circulated among the more unsophisticated constituents of members sensitive to public opinion, and are then presented to them as an unmistakable indication of the popular will, although the total number of signers forms a very small percentage of the total number of voters of the districts in which these petitions were circulated. A common method employed

by the railroad lobby in Iowa has been to arouse, by ingenious arguments, the prejudices of the people of one
part of the State against those of another, or of one class
against those of another class ; for instance, the East
against the West, or that portion of the State the least
supplied with railroad facilities against that which is best
supplied ; or the river cities against the interior cities ; or
the country people against the city people ; or the farmer
against the merchant, and always artfully keeping in view
the opportunity to utilize one side or the other in their
own interest.

Another powerful reinforcement of the railroad lobby is
not unfrequently a subsidized press and its correspondents.
The party organs at the capital are especially selected to
defend as sound measures, either from a partisan or non-
partisan standpoint, legislation of questionable propriety
desired by the railroads.   When such measures are advocated by party organs, partisan members, either from fear
or prejudice, are apt to '' fall into line,'' and then to rely
upon these organs to defend their action.   Editors, re-
porters and correspondents are even retained as active
lobbyists and give the railroad managers' cause the benefit
of their prestige.   To such an extent has the abuse of the
press been carried that a considerable number of its unworthy representatives look upon railroad subsidies as
legitimate perquisites which they will exact through
blackmailing and other means of compulsion if they are
not offered.   A case may be cited here to illustrate their
mode of operation, as well as the ethics of railroad lobbies.   During one of the sessions of the Iowa legislature a
newspaper correspondent came in possession of some information which reflected severely on the railroad lobby.
He made his information the subject of a spicy article and

showed it to a friend who stood close to the gentleman chiefly implicated, with the remark that nothing but a hundred dollar bill would prevent the transmission of the article by the evening mail to the paper which he represented. Before sundown the stipulated price for the correspondent's silence was paid, and an enemy was turned into a friend.

Professor Bryce says of the American lobby system: "All legislative bodies which control important pecuniary interests are as sure to have a lobby as an army to have its camp followers. Where the body is, there will the vultures be gathered together." To such an extent is the lobby abuse carried that some large corporations select their regular solicitors more for their qualifications as lobbyists than for their legal lore. It is a common remark among lawyers that a great company in Chicago pays a third-class lawyer, who has the reputation of being a first-class lobbyist, an extravagant salary and calls him general solicitor, while it relies upon other lawyers to attend to its important legal business. The readiness of members of the bar to serve wealthy corporations is fast bringing the legal profession of America into disrepute abroad. The author just quoted, in speaking of its moral standard, says: "But I am bound to add that some judicious American observers hold that the last thirty years have witnessed a certain decadence in the bar of the great cities. They say that the growth of enormously rich and powerful corporations, willing to pay vast sums for questionable services, has seduced the virtue of some counsel whose eminence makes their example important, and that in a few States the degradation of the bench has led to secret understandings between judges and counsel for the perversion of justice."

There are, of course, able and honorable attorneys employed by railroad companies, but often railroad lawyers are selected more for their political influence, tact and ingenuity than for legal ability, and, as a rule, the political lawyer receives much better compensation for his services than does the lawyer who attends strictly to legitimate legal work.

The danger from railroad corporations lies in their great wealth, controlled by so few persons, and the want of publicity in their business. Were they required to render accounts of their expenditures to the public, legislative corruption funds would soon be numbered with the defunct abuses of railroad corporations, and, with bribes wanting in the balance of legislative equivalents, the representatives of the people could be trusted to enact laws just alike to the corporations and the public, while asserting the right of the people to control the public highway and to make it subservient to the welfare of the many instead of the enrichment of the few. .A wise law regulating lobbies exists in Massachusetts. Every lobbyist is required to register, as soon as he appears at the Capitol, to state in whose interest and in what capacity he attends the legislative session, to keep a faithful account of his expenses and to file a copy of the same with the Secretary of State. Were a similar law enacted and enforced by every State legislature, as well as by Congress, the power of railroad lobbies would be curtailed.

Railroad managers never do things by halves. Well realizing that it is in the power of a fearless executive, by his veto, to render futile the achievements of a costly lobby and to injure or benefit their interests by pursuing an aggressive or conservative policy in the enforcement of the laws, they never fail to make their influence felt in the selection of a chief magistrate, either of the Nation or of an individual State. No delegate, with their permission, ever attends a national convention, Republican or Democratic, if he is not known to favor the selection of a man as the presidential candidate of his party whose conservatism in all matters pertaining to railroad interests is well established. At these conventions the railroad companies are always represented, and their representatives do not hesitate to inform the delegates that this or that candidate is not acceptable to their corporations and cannot receive their support at the polls. During the Chicago convention of 1888 the statement was openly made that two of the Western candidates lost Eastern support because they were not acceptable to a prominent New York delegate who had come to Chicago in a threefold capacity—that of a delegate, a presidential possibility, and special representative of one of the most powerful railroad interests in the country. This same man appeared again last year at the Minneapolis convention as chief organizer of the forces of a leading candidate. His counterpart was in attendance at the Chicago convention looking after the same interests there.

It is the boast of prominent railroad men that their influence elected President Garfield, and the statement has been made upon good authority that "not until a few days before the election did the Garfield managers feel secure," and that "when the secret history of that campaign comes to be written it will be seen that Jay Gould had more influence upon the election than Grant and Conkling." It cannot be said that railroad managers, as a class, have often openly supported a presidential candidate. This may be due to the fact that with the uncertainty which has for years attended national politics they deem it the part of discretion to pretend friendship for either party and then shout with the victor. In conformity with this policy, a well-known New York railroad millionaire has for years made large and secret contributions to the campaign funds of both political parties. He thereby places both parties under political obligations, and believes his interests safe, whichever turn the political wheel may take. After the contest he is usually the first to congratulate the successful candidate. In the national campaign of 1884 this railroad king completely outwitted a prominent Western politician and member of the Republican national campaign committee who has always prided himself on his political sagacity. This gentleman had taken it upon himself to enlist the rich and powerful New Yorker in the Republican cause, and to obtain from him, as a token of his sincerity, a large contribution to the Blaine campaign fund. He succeeded, at least so far as the contribution was concerned ; but when the struggle was over and the opposition, in the exuberance of joy over their victory, told tales out of school, he was not a little chagrined to find that the managers of the Cleveland campaign had received from the astute railroad millionaire a campaign contribution twice as large as that which he had obtained from him. The diatribes which for weeks after the election filled the columns of his paper reflected in every line the injured pride of the outwitted general.

Judging from the laxity with which the railroad laws have been enforced in a considerable number of States, their executive departments are as much under the influence of railroad managers as are the legislative departments of others. This cannot be surprising to those who know how often governors of States are nominated and elected through railroad influences, and what efforts are made by corporations to humor servile and to propitiate independent executives. The time is not far remote when nearly every delegate to a State convention had free transportation for the round trip. This transportation was furnished to delegates by railroad managers through their local attorneys, or through favored candidates and their confidants. It was only offered to those who were supposed to be friendly to candidates approved by the railroad managers ; and as free passage was looked upon as the legitimate perquisite of a delegate, but few persons could be induced to attend a State convention and pay their fare. As a consequence, the railroad managers found it too often an easy matter to dictate the nomination of candidates.

Since the adoption of the Interstate Commerce Law convention passes, as such, have largely disappeared ; but many a prominent politician in going to and returning from political conventions travels as a railroad employe, though the only service which he renders to the railroad companies consists in manipulating conventions in their favor. If all the railroad candidates—and the companies usually take the precaution to support more than one candidate—are defeated in the convention of one party, and a railroad candidate is nominated by the other party, the latter is certain to receive at the polls every vote which railroad and allied corporate influence can command.

One might suppose that an attempt would at least be made to hide from the general public the interference of such a power with the politics of a State ; but railroad managers seem to rely for success as much upon intimidating political parties as upon gaining the good will of individual citizens. To influence party action, the boast has in recent years repeatedly and boldly been made in

Iowa that 30,000 railroad employes would vote as a unit against any party or individual daring to legislate or otherwise take official action against their demands, and forgetting that, with the same means used in opposition to them, a few hundred thousand farmers and business men could be easily organized to oppose them. Unscrupulous employers often endeavor to control the votes of their employes. This is particularly true of railroad companies, and they use many ingenious plans to accomplish it. In the Northwest, and especially in Iowa, they have for several years organized their employes as a political force for the purpose of defeating such candidates for State offices as were known to favor State control of the transportation business. They have even paid the expenses of the organization, although they have made every effort to make it appear as if the movement was a voluntary one on the part of their employes. They are employing this method in Texas and other States at the present time, in opposition to the effort that is being made by the people to secure just and reasonable treatment from the railroads.

That the chief executive of a State should be influenced in the discharge of his official duties by such favors as passes, the freedom of the dining- and sleeping-car, by the free use of a special car, or even a special train, one is loath to believe ; yet it is a fact, and especially during political campaigns, that such favors are frequently offered to, and accepted by, the highest executive officers, and it is equally true that many of these officers often connive at the continued and defiant violations of law by railroad officials. While the men who manage large railroad interests do not always possess that wisdom which popular reverence attributes to them, they certainly possess great cunning,

and expend much of their artfulness in efforts to win over
scrupulous, and to render still more servile unscrupulous
executives. The general railroad diplomate never omits to
pay homage to the man in power, to flatter him, to impress him with the political influence of his company, to
intimate plainly that, as it has been in the past, so it will
be in the future its determined policy to reward its friends
and to punish its enemies. If the executive proves in-
tractable, if he can neither be flattered, nor coaxed, nor
bribed into submission, he does not hesitate to resort to
intimidation to accomplish his purpose. This is by no
means a rare occurrence. There are few public men who,
if determined to do their duty, have not been subjected to
railroad insult and intimidation. The author may be permitted to give an instance from his personal experience.
Soon after his inauguration as Governor of Iowa a general
officer of one of the oldest and strongest Western railroads
called at his office and importuned him with unreasonable
requests. When he found that he had utterly failed to
impress the author with his arguments, he left abruptly,
with the curt remark that these matters could be settled
on election day, and he emphasized his statement by
slamming the door behind him.

A servile railroad press has always been ready to misrepresent and malign executive officers who have refused
to acknowledge any higher authority than the law, the
expressed public will and their own conception of duty.
This abuse has even been carried so far that the editorial
columns of leading dailies have been prostituted by the
insertion of malicious tirades written by railroad managers and railroad attorneys; and the fact that public
opinion has not been more seriously influenced by these
venal sheets must be solely attributed to the good judgment and safe instinct of the masses of the people.

However persistently railway organs deny it, it is a matter of general notoriety that railway officials take an active part in political campaigns. Hundreds of communications might be produced to show their work in Iowa, but the following two letters, written by a prominent railroad manager to an associate, will suffice for the purpose. It will be noticed that one was written before and the other after election. Comments upon their contents are unnecessary:

"........, Iowa, Nov. 2nd, 1888.

"DEAR SIR: I have just discovered this P. M. that the Central Committee have sent electrotypes to all the printing offices in the State of the State ticket, with the names of the Railway Commissioners and Supreme Judge in so small a space as to make it very difficult, if not impossible, to write in the names. I am having slips made with Commissioners' names and Judge written on them, and they will be sent to all agents, not later than to-morrow, to paste over the printed names on the ticket, and thus beat this scheme. Have you seen any tickets yet? And what do you think of this plan?

"Yours truly,

"................."

"........, Iowa, Nov. 11, 1888.

"DEAR SIR: Repeating the old and time-honored saying: 'We have met the enemy and we are theirs.' The Democratic Granger and the largely increased Republican vote was too much for us. Many friends voted with the railway men, but to no purpose. The comparison between Granger and Smyth will tell more than anything else the strength of the railway vote. But we are badly used up, and may as well take our dose.

"Yours truly,

"................."

While the result of this election was indeed a bad dose for speculating railway managers, it is the opinion of the

masses and of railway stockholders, who are more interested in the general welfare of the roads than in speculation in their stocks, that the dose was well administered,
and should be repeated whenever the necessity for it may
again arise.

It is probably true that railroad managers have lost
much of their former influence in politics. As their means
of corruption have become generally known they have become less effective.   The public is more on the alert, and
corrupt politicians often find themselves unable to carry
out their discreditable compacts.

But it is unreasonable to expect the evil to cease until
the cause is removed.   The trouble is inherent in the system, and the fault is there more than in the men who
manage the business, and not till the great power exercised by them is restrained within proper limits will the
evil disappear.   All this can be accomplished when there
shall be established a most thorough and efficient system
of State and National control over the railroad business of
the whole country.

CHAPTER X.

THE cause of the railroad manager has never been without time-servers. Not to speak of those newspaper editors who, for some consideration or another, defend every policy and every practice inaugurated or approved by railroad authorities, there has always been a school of literati who felt it their duty to enlighten, from a railroad standpoint, their fellow-men by book or pamphlet upon the transportation question, to correct what they supposed to be false impressions, and to round up with an apology or defense for the railroad manager, who is invariably represented by them as the most abused and at the same time most patriotic and most progressive man of the age.

The benefits derived from the railroad are great. It has been an important factor in the development of our country's resources and the advancement of our civilization. Its value is fully appreciated, but there is no reason why the men who have utilized the inventions of Stephenson and others, and have grown rich by doing so, should be eulogized any more than those who are ministering to the wants of the public by the use of the Hoe printing press, McCormick's reaper, Whitney's cotton gin, or any of the thousands of other modern inventions.

These authors doubtless are prompted by various motives. Some have been educated in the railroad school and are therefore blind to railroad evils. Others naturally worship plutocrats, because they hold the opinion that capital is entitled to a larger reward than brains and muscle, for the reason that the latter is more plentiful than the former.

But there is a third class of railroad authors, who, there is reason to believe, enter the literary arena in defense of railroad evils not solely for the love they bear the cause, but as the paid advocates of a class of men who feel that their cause is in need of a strong defense at the bar of public sentiment. It would be difficult to account in any other way for the extravagant statements and one-sided arguments made by this class of writers. Yet railroad literature has not confined itself to the retrospective field. Its scope has grown with the significance of its contributors. In more than one instance have men at the head of large railroad corporations, influenced by temporary interest, become the authors of documents containing assertions and prophecies highly pathetic at the time, but subsequently shown to be so replete with falsehoods and absurdities that few railroad managers would to-day be willing to father them. Thus Alexander Mitchell, the late president of the Chicago, Milwaukee and St. Paul Railroad Company, addressed on the 28th of April, 1874, shortly after the passage of the Wisconsin Granger Law, a letter to Governor Taylor, containing the following passages:

"That it [the Wisconsin law] has effectually destroyed all future railroad enterprises, no one who is aquainted with its effect in money centers will for a moment doubt. . . . . The whole amount received on the investment [Chicago, Milwaukee and St. Paul Railroad] for interest and cash and stock dividends, amounts to only six per cent. per annum of the actual cost of the property. I submit to your Excellency, and through you to the people of the

State, whether this is more than a fair and reasonable
return for the capital invested in these improvements.
Is it not far below such reasonable amount? The best and
most careful economists admit that no less than ten per
cent. per annum should be allowed on such investments.
. . . . The directors of this company have at all times had
a due regard to the interests of the public, and a desire
to furnish transportation at the lowest possible figures,
and, although not receiving a fair and reasonable return on
their investments, they have for the last four years prior
to 1873 steadily reduced their rates of freight and passengers from year to year, as will be seen from the following tables, showing the charge for freight per mile, and
the average per mile for passengers for each year, from
1868 to 1873 inclusive:

	Charges per ton per mile—cents.		Average passenger rate per mile—cents.	
1864			.04	
1868	.03	40–100	.03	86–100
1869	.03	10–100	.03	92–100
1870	.02	82–109	.03	85–100
1871	.02	54–100	.03	75–100
1872	.02	43–100	.03	54–100
1873	.02	50–100	.03	42–100

"The law in question proposes to reduce our passenger
rates twenty-five per cent. and our freight rates about the
same, thus deducting from our present tariff about twenty-
five per cent. of our gross earnings. . . . This act, as we
have seen, proposes to take from us twenty-five per cent.
of our passenger and freight earnings, and the additional
tax of one per cent. of our gross earnings, all of which is
equivalent to taking from us twenty-six per cent. of our
gross earnings. Therefore, deducting this amount, equal
to twenty-six per cent. of our entire gross earnings, from
thirty-three per cent., our average net earnings on business,would leave us only seven per cent. of our gross
earnings as the entire net earnings of the road, out of
which must be paid the interest on the bonds and the
dividends to our stockholders. It is therefore manifest
that this law will take from us over three-fourths of the
net income received under our present tariff. . . . The

board of directors have caused this act to be carefully examined and considered by their own counsel, and by some
of the most eminent jurists in the land, and after such
examination they are unanimous in their opinion that it is
unconstitutional and void. . . . The board of directors are
trustees of this property, and are bound faithfully to discharge their trust, and to the best of their ability to protect it from spoliation and ruin. They have sought the
advice of able counsel, and, after mature consideration,
believe it their duty to disregard so much of said law as
attempts arbitrarily to fix rates of compensation for freight
and passengers. . . . Being fully conscious that the enforcement of this law will ruin the property of the company,
and feeling assured of the correctness of the opinions of
the eminent counsel who have examined the question, the
directors feel compelled to disregard the provisions of the
law so far as it fixes a tariff of rates for the company,
until the courts have finally passed upon the question of
its validity."

The letter was at the time regarded by railroad men as
a very strong document, and the railroad journals were
filled with lengthy editorials in praise of the soundness of
the doctrines and arguments which it contained. The
disinterested of the enlightened portion of the community
even then realized that the "eminent jurists" whom the
company had consulted were hired attorneys and greatly
biased in their views as to the constitutional rights of corporations, and that President Mitchell on his part had
painted by far too dark a picture of the situation. It is
now quite generally admitted that many of Mr. Mitchell's
statements were as false as his counsel's interpretation of
the Constitution and the law was erroneous. From
the assertions made in this letter one is led to infer
that the then stock- and bondholders of the Milwaukee road had paid in full every dollar of the capitalized value of the road, and that they derived from their

investment an income of only about six per cent. on the
money actually invested by them.   The cost of the entire
Chicago and Milwaukee system in Wisconsin was stated
in the letter as being $38,000 per mile.   It is not likely
that this line of road ever cost to exceed $25,000 a mile,
or that those who then owned the road paid much more
than two-thirds of its actual cost for it.   The road, as the
letter itself admits, was bought at sheriff's sale, and no
mercy whatever was shown to the farmers who had mort-
gaged their farms to aid the railroad company in raising
funds for the construction of its line.

The letter contains other misstatements equally grave.
Mr. A. B. Stickney, the president of the Chicago, St.
Paul and Kansas City Railroad, in his recent excellent
work, "The Railway Problem," reviews Mr. Mitchell's
letter as follows:

"Mr. Mitchell states the average rate per mile in 1873
for passengers at 3.42 cents.   It was well understood
that this was an average rate received from those passengers who paid anything, and that, had the average rate
been obtained by using as a divisor the total number of paying passengers plus the number of those who rode free
the average would have been much below three cents, the
price fixed by the law, and consequently, if the company
would collect the legal rate from all alike and abolish the
free list, its revenues from the passenger business would
be increased rather than decreased.   If the same test is
applied to the freight rates it becomes equally evident that
this statute did not reduce the rates in Wisconsin below
the average rate of 2.50 cents per ton per mile, which,
according to Mr. Mitchell's statement, was the average for
the year 1873.   For proof, it may be stated that the law
classified freight into four general classes, to be designated
as first, second, third and fourth classes, and into seven
special classes, to be designated as D, E, F, G, H, I and
J.   The rates on the four general classes were made the

same as were 'charged for carrying freights in said four general classes on said railroads on the first day of June, 1873,' and the rate per ton per mile was fixed at certain rates for the first twenty-five miles, a less for the second twenty-five miles, and a fixed rate per mile after, as follows:

	1st 25 Miles	2nd 25 Miles:	All Over 50 Miles.
D	4 4-5 cents	3 1-5 cents	1 3-5 cents.
E	Same as class above.		
F	4 cents	2 cents	1 cent.
G	3 1-5 cents	2 cents	1 cent.
H	4 cents	2 4-5 cents	1 3-5 cents.
I	4 2-5 cents	2 2-5 cents	1 1-5 cents.
J	3 1-5 cents	2 2-5 cents	1 cent.

"When it is considered, in connection with these figures, that the four general classes were left by the legislature under the same tariffs as had been enforced by the companies, and, as a rule, first class is three times the rate of class D, and third and fourth class materially higher, the evidence seems conclusive that the rates fixed by law would produce an average materially higher than the average of the whole year, stated by Mr. Mitchell at $2\frac{1}{2}$ cents. It seems also probable that, had the rates fixed by this law been applied to the whole business of the line, the interstate as well as the State traffic, it would still have produced a larger average. The latter of course is the proper test. There are little inaccuracies in the material facts as stated by Mr. Mitchell which were pointed out at once. For example: In his tabulated statement of passenger earnings per mile, averaging the gross earnings from transportation of passengers who paid any fare, and omiting the large number who went free, the rate is stated at 3 42-100 cents per mile; then he says: 'The law in question proposes to reduce our passenger rate twenty-five per cent.,' which would have reduced the rate to 2.57 cents per mile, while the rate fixed by the law complained of was three cents per mile. Then Mr. Mitchell proceeds: 'And our freight rates about the same; thus deducting from our present tariff about twenty-five per cent. of our gross earnings.' It was immediately pointed out that the law only applied to strictly State business; that is, to traffic that originated and ended in the State of Wisconsin. All other traffic was interstate commerce, and could not be controlled by State legislation. The volume of business which would be affected by the law would therefore be comparatively small—estimated at not over ten per cent. of the total traffic of the line. Hence, if the rates fixed by the law were twenty-five per cent. less than the rates the company had been in the habit of collecting (which was denied), it could not possibly have ' deducted from its present tariff' more than two and one-half per cent., instead of twenty-five per cent. as stated by Mr. Mitchell.

" It was claimed that the facts were, that the Chicago, Milwaukee and St. Paul Company, in its efforts to bankrupt the Lake Superior and Mississippi Company, had many of its interstate rates so low that it had resulted in loss, and that its other rates had been made unreasonably high in order to recoup this loss, and that the State of Wisconsin was compelled to pay a part of the expense of the transportation of favored sections of the State of Minnesota."

All through the Granger contests the railways have weakened the force of their arguments by their misrepresentation of facts and by their extravagant predictions of ruin. The companies were continually proclaiming: 'If this or that is done, it will ruin us; it will ruin the State,' when, in fact, a road cannot be mentioned that has suffered from State legislation. Nineteen years ago no railroad manager could have written what Mr. Stickney writes to-day, and few railroad managers would write to-day what Mr. Mitchell wrote then. And yet, such is the change which public sentiment is undergoing upon these questions, that the utterances of many of our present railroad authors will appear as absurd a few years hence as Mr. Mitchell's letter of nineteen years ago appears to us now.

Many railroad attorneys have since been guilty of resorting to the sophistry employed by President Mitchell in that strange letter which he addressed to the Governor of Wisconsin. Even so distinguished a gentleman as Hon. James W. McDill, now a member of the Interstate Commerce Commission, made in 1888, as a member of a railroad lobby, the following remarkable statements before the Railroad Committee of the General Assembly of Iowa, in a speech opposing a proposed reduction of the passenger rate of first-class roads from three to two cents per mile:

" The proposition, if confined to the first-class roads of Iowa, proposes a one-third reduction of their revenues from passenger business. . . . We have earned in Iowa by first-class roads annually about $13,000,000, and a reduction of one cent, or from a rate of three cents to two, will reduce their revenues about $5,000,000 a year. . . . Thus it is seen that it is proposed to take from the revenues of a part of the railroads of Iowa, annually, almost as much as all the railroads of Iowa have paid for taxes in nine years ($6,549,505.84)."

Mr. McDill was a member of the Iowa Railroad Commission for several years. He may, therefore, be presumed to have known that the State of Iowa could not, and did not propose to, regulate interstate traffic, and that the thirteen million dollars railroad revenue to which he referred was derived both from interstate and State traffic; that the latter was only about one-fourth of the former, and that therefore the proposed reduction on the basis of schedule rates would have cut down the net revenue of the roads only about one million instead of five million dollars. But Mr. McDill himself states that the average rate earned by all the railroads of the United States was, for the year 1886, only 2.181 cents per passenger per mile. It certainly was not over $2\frac{1}{4}$ cents per mile for the first-class roads of Iowa. Thus the proposed reduction, instead of being one cent per mile, as stated by Mr. McDill, was only one-half cent per mile ; and it only applied to the local business of the first-class roads. In other words, the bili under consideration, had it been enacted into law, would have caused a reduction of 20 per cent. on about 25 per cent. of the total revenue from passenger business of the first-class roads, or of five per cent. on their total income from passenger traffic in the State of Iowa. It will be noticed that Mr. McDill in his calculation made no allowance whatever for the increase of business which would have followed such a reduction. The gain from this source would probably have greatly exceeded the loss due to this small reduction in the fare. In the same address Mr. McDill made many other equally fallacious statements.

One of the most devoted advocates of the interests of railroad managers is Marshall M. Kirkman. He is the author of a number of books and pamphlets upon railway subjects, among them a pamphlet entitled "The Relation of the Railroads of the United States to the People and the Commercial and Financial Interests of the Country."

Mr. Kirkman introduces his subject with the following rather remarkable statement:

"I shall show that while the railways of the United States are designated as monopolies, they are not so in fact. Accused of disregarding the interests of the community, I will show that they are abnormally sensitive to their obligations in this direction. While legislatures claim the right to fix rates, I shall show that the abnormal conditions under which the railway system has grown up and its chaotic nature render the exercise of such a privilege impossible. I will show that while it is assumed that rates may be fixed arbitrarily, they must, on the contrary, be based on natural causes, the competition of carriers, their necessities and the rivalries of conflicting markets and trade centers; conditions manifestly impossible to determine or regulate in advance, and therefore beyond the control of legislation. . . . While a division of business (by pooling) is thought to be contrary to the interests of the people, I shall show that it is the legitimate fruit of indiscriminate railway building and offers the only escape from the conditions such practice engenders. I shall show that, while it is assumed that rates may be based progressively or otherwise on distance, the enforcement of such a principle would restrict the source of supply, and, in so far as this was the case, render great markets or centers of industry impossible."

Speaking of the importance of the railroad, Mr. Kirkman says: "Superseding every other form of inland conveyance, it determines the location of business centers, and vitalizes by its presence, or blasts by its absence." He contends that rigid and scrutinizing supervision should be exercised by the Government over the location of railroads, and that only such lines should be permitted to be built as afford reasonable grounds for profitable enterprise. "It should be," he says, "an axiom in our day that a government that permits or encourages the construction of two railways where one would suffice is, to the extent that it does this, a public nuisance." Mr. Kirkman here makes it the duty of the Government to arbitrarily meddle with railroad affairs. He would give the Government the power to determine when and where an additional railroad is needed, and to prohibit the construction of any new road that has not the Government sanction. The interests of a thousand towns might suffer for want of adequate transportation facilities, individuals and communities might be anxious to build their own lines for the development of local resources, but all railroad enterprise is doomed to a standstill until a conservative governmental commission has been entirely satisfied that a prospected road will pay and not deprive existing roads of any part of their revenue. There can be no doubt that if such a policy were ever adopted in America, few roads would be built without having first passed the ordeal of a legal injunction, and many a prospected road, though greatly needed, would remain unbuilt because its promoters would be discouraged by the delay and cost of litigation."

But while this author is perfectly willing to trust the Government with the great responsibility of prohibiting the construction of proposed roads, he is not willing to have it exercise the power to determine what are reasonable rates. He tries to sustain his objection by the following argument: "The fixing of rates upon a railroad is as delicate a process as that of determining the pulse of a sick man. They cannot be determined abstractly, or in advance of the wants of business, but must be adjusted from hour to hour to conform to its fluctuations. Five thousand men find active employment in the United States in connection with the important duty of making rates. Each case requires particular investigation and involves, in many instances, prolonged study and research. The duty requires men of marked experience and capacity. They and men like them are the silent, unseen power that moves great enterprises of every nation. In the case of railroads we may enumerate those having official positions, but the experts from whom the official heads derive information and assistance cannot be classified. They comprise a vast army of experienced and able men familiar with railway traffic and quick to respond to its requirements. Such a body of men could not be organized by a government, or, if organized, would rapidly deteriorate under conditions so unfavorable for their support and development. Whatever authority exercises the duty of fixing rates must take up the subject in the same methodical way and, acting through skilled agents, pursue its inquiries and determine its results with the same experience, minute care and *conscientious regard* for the technical requirements of business that the railway companies observe. No government can possess the facilities for perfecting so vast and intricate an organization and at the same time render it responsive to the public good. The labor is too great and the responsibility too remote. It could not move with sufficient quickness to respond to the actual requirements of trade, and too many restrictions would necessarily govern its actions. For these and other equally important reasons governments must always be satisfied to restrict their offices in this direction."

Speaking of the men who are commonly termed railroad magnates, Mr. Kirkman says: "They alone possess the needed administrative ability that the situation demands. They not only provide largely the capital, but they discover the fields wherein it may be used most advantageously. They are the advance guard of all great enterprises, the natural leaders of men. They are an integral part of the country, a necessary and valuable element, without which its natural resources would avail little." This is a very strong statement in the face of the fact that but very few of the class of men to whom Mr. Kirkman refers ever built a line of road. They have usually found it more profitable to "gobble" roads already built than to construct new lines.

According to this author the public have no reason to complain of railroads; on the contrary, the latter have always been the victims of public persecution, and "every species of folly, every conceivable device of malice, the impossible requirements of ignorance, the selfish cunning of personal interests, the ravings of demagogues, the disappointments, envies, prejudices and jealousies of mankind have each in turn and in unison sought to injure the railway interest."

But probably the most extravagant passage in the whole treatise is the one referring to special rates, which he calls "the foundation and buttress of business," without which it could not be carried on. He expresses the opinion that without the continued and intelligent use of such rates "our cities would soon be as destitute of manufactories as one of the bridle paths of Afghanistan," and then continues: "The special rate of carriers is like the delicate fluid that anoints and lubricates the joints of the human body. It is an essential oil. Without it the wheels of commerce would cease and we should quickly revert to the period when the stage-coach and the overland teamster fixed the limits of commerce and the stature of cities."

The most recent and probably the most radical of Mr. Kirkman's books is "Railway Rates and Government Control." It would lead us too far from our subject to enter into a discussion of Mr. Kirkman's errors ; in fact, it might prove an endless task. Suffice it to say that in discussing his subject he revels in such phrases as : "Subject too vast to be comprehended." "Acts of agrarian legislation and foolish manifestations of disappointment and hate." "The rabble will avail itself of every excuse to pass laws that would, under other circumstances, be called robberies." "Ignorance and demagogism." "Government interference, the panacea of cranks and schemers." "Only understood by the few." "These people are as sincere as they are ignorant." "Governments have no commercial sense." "Those who condemn them are not so dishonest as ignorant, and not so malicious as foolish." "Silly people." "Justice and common honesty are systematically denied [the railroads]." "Legal means of plundering them." "The intelligence and facilities of Government are but one step above the barbarian." "Those who use railroads should pay for them," etc., etc. Mr. Kirkman's argument is in substance : Rate-making is a difficult subject. The people are too ignorant to understand it. Those who carry on the Government are for the most part fools and demagogues, and are utterly unfit to do justice to such a task. Railroad men are wise and just, and neither the people nor the Government should meddle with the railroad business. In order to place a true estimate upon Mr. Kirkman's utterances, one should remember that he is a railroad employe as well as the patentee and vendor of a number of railroad account forms which are extensively used by railroad companies.

The Chicago *Tribune*, in reviewing this last literary production of Mr. Kirkman, says :

"The great fault of Mr. Kirkman's statements is that they are often so general in character as to be both true and false at the same time. . . . He does not seem to comprehend the nature of the railroad, or to perceive the danger of allowing a railroad to exercise its powers uncontrolled. He denies the State's right to interfere with any discriminations which a railway corporation chooses to adopt. He would allow railways to fix whatever charges they please for long hauls and short hauls. . . . Mr. Kirkman does not adduce a single fact in support of these remarkable views. He simply says : 'Railroads cannot, if they would, maintain any inequitable local tariff.' This is not argument, it is simply assertion. Every one who has learned the alphabet of this question knows that railways have been exceedingly unjust wherever competition or the law did not restrict their powers. If this were the proper place for it we would give the author instances of this injustice by the hundred, and almost any book on the subject refers to such cases by the thousand. . . . When confronted with the facts substantiating such charges the author answers the argument by exclaiming: But how absurd! But how untrue! Our commercial morals are equal to the highest in the world.' . . . Scarcely an assertion can be taken without qualification. The author fairly revels in half-truths. . . . The book may have its merits, but they are too modest to reveal themselves."

It is a failing of mankind to take for truth without further investigation any assertion that has often been re-iterated. Most people are prone to believe that an assertion made by a thousand hearsay witnesses is true, over-looking the possibility of their drawing from a common false source. But it is surprising that an author like Prof. Arthur T. Hadley should fall into such an error. In his otherwise excellent work, "Railroad Transportation, Its History and Its Laws," Mr. Hadley bases a number of his deductions upon false premises advanced by railroad managers, and arrives at conclusions which appear strange when their source is considered. In the chapter on railroad legislation Professor Hadley says : "But a more powerful force than the authority of the courts was working against the Granger system of regulation. The laws of trade could not be violated with impunity. The effects were most sharply felt in Wisconsin. The law reducing railroad rates to the basis which competitive points enjoyed left nothing to pay fixed charges. In the second year of its operation, no Wisconsin road paid a dividend; only four paid interest on their bonds. Railroad construction had come to a standstill. Even the facilities of existing roads could not be kept up. Foreign capital

refused to invest in Wisconsin ; the development of the
State was sharply checked ; the very men who had most
favored the law found themselves heavy losers. ... By
the time the Supreme Court published the Granger decisions, the fight had been settled, not by constitutional limitations, but by industrial ones."

These statements are either utterly untrue or greatly
misleading. Mr. Hadley ought to know that the railroad
companies in the Granger States never complied with the
letter, much less with the spirit of the law. Whenever
they made an apparent effort to live up to it they only did
so to make it odious. Rates were never reduced by the
legislature to the basis previously enjoyed by competitive
points, but merely to the average charge which had
obtained before the passage of the law. As a rule the
railroad revenues increased. If any companies failed to
earn enough to pay fixed charges it was simply because
they were determined not to do so. A non-payment of
dividends did not injure the managers, but simply other
stockholders of the road. A permanent establishment of
the principle of non-discrimination, on the other hand,
would have benefited stockholders, while prejudicing the
speculative interest which managers had in the roads.
Railroad construction came, after the financial panic of
1873, to a practical standstill throughout the United
States ; and if the Granger States did not get their share
of the very small total increase during the five years following the panic, it was due solely to a conspiracy on the
part of the railroad managers to misrepresent and pervert
the legislation of these States. The laws, as has already
been stated, were finally repealed, not because the people
had tired of them or regarded them unwise or unjust, but
because it was hoped that the commissioner system would

prove more efficient. It was offered as a compromise measure and was accepted as such by the railroad managers, who, in their eagerness to rid themselves of the restrictions imposed by the Granger laws, gave every assurance of complete submission to the requirements of the proposed legislation.

Mr. Hadley even goes so far as to defend railroad pools. "Unluckily," he says, "we place these combinations outside of the protection of the law, and by giving them this precarious and almost illegal character we tempt them to seek present gain, even at the sacrifice of their own future interests. We regard them, and we let them regard themselves, as a means of momentary profit and speculation, instead of recognizing them as responsible public agencies of lasting influence and importance." We can partially account for this author's defense of pooling when we are informed that he accepts it as an axiom that "combination does not produce arbitrary results any more than competition produces beneficent ones." Referring to railroad profits, Mr. Hadley says: "The statement that corporations make too much money is scarcely borne out by the facts. The average return of the railroads of this country is only four per cent., the bondholders receiving an average of four and a half per cent., the stockholders of two and a half per cent. True, much of the stock is water, not representing any capital actually expended; but, even making allowance for this, it is hardly probable that the roads are earning more than five per cent. on the total investment. This assumes an average cost of $45,000 per mile, implying that about half of the stock and one-sixth of the bonds are water." Mr. Hadley would probably have come much nearer the truth if he had assumed three-fourths of the stock and one-fourth of the bonds to be water. Even Mr. Poor, who certainly cannot be accused by railroad men of being inimical to their interests, places the average cost of the railroads of this country no higher than at $30,000 per mile ; and this estimate, it should be remembered, includes the value of the large donations made to railroad companies by the public. With a full understanding of all the circumstances, Mr. Poor said of railroad investments several years ago that if the water were taken out of them no class of investments in this country would pay as well. In the face of this statement Mr. Hadley would do well to revise his figures.

We find, however, in Prof. Hadley's book also eminently sound views, like the following: "If the object of a railroad manager is simply to pay as large a dividend as possible for the current year, he can best do it by squeezing his local tariff, of which he is sure, and securing through traffic at the expense of other roads by specially low rates ; that is, by a policy of heavy discrimination. But the permanent effect of such a policy is to destroy the local trade, which gives a road its best and surest custom, and to build up a trade which can go by another route whenever it pleases. The permanent effect of such a policy is ruinous to the railroad as well as the local shipper." And he continues : "By securing publicity of management you do much to prevent the permanent interests of the railroads from being sacrificed to temporary ones. By protecting the permanent interests of the public you enlist the stockholders and the best class of railroad managers on the side of sound policy."

Edward Atkinson, in an essay entitled "The Railway, the Farmer and the Public," endeavors to prove that the farmers have no cause for complaining against the railroad, because rates of transportation have been greatly reduced during the past twenty years. Speaking of the reductions made in freight rates in the State of New York, he says: "Had the rate of 1870 been charged on the tariff of 1883 the sum would have been at 1.7016 cents on 9,286,216,- 628 tons, carried one mile, $158,014,262; the actual charge was $83,464,919, making a difference of $74,549,- 343 saved on one year's traffic on the lines reported in New York." It either did not occur to Mr. Atkinson, or, if it did occur to him, he failed to mention it, that these freight reductions were forced upon the railroads chiefly by water competition, and that if the railroad companies had not saved these seventy-four million dollars for the people, the canal lines, always subject to competition, would have saved a large part of it. With equal propriety might it be said that the railroads, by meeting canal competition, saved for themselves in the year mentioned a goodly share of their gross earnings. Such reasoning is absurd, and it is high time that the bubble of an argument so often used by railroad advocates be pricked. As Mr. Atkinson has introduced the farmer, let us apply his rule to him. There was a time when the farmer sold his corn for a dollar a bushel. To-day he sells it for thirty cents. He therefore saves to the people of this country, on 2,000,000,000 bushels, the enormous sum of $1,400,000,000. There is scarcely an industry in existence to which this argument does not apply with equal force. Mr. Atkinson virtually admits that railroads charge all the traffic will bear when he says : "The charge which can be put upon the wheat of Dakota or Iowa for moving it to market is fixed by the price at which East Indian wheat can be sold in Market Lane." He is opposed to the Interstate Commerce Law, which he regards as "obnoxious measures of national interference and futile attempts to control this great work." He would rely chiefly upon the publicity of accounts made by railway officers, as secured by the private publication of Poor's Railway Manual, for all needed regulation, but concedes the establishment of a figurehead commission, concluding his remarks upon the subject as follows: "A commission which may bring public opinion to bear upon railway corporations may well be established, and there the work of the legislator may well cease." When we consider the powerful agencies employed by railroads to create public sentiment in their favor we can well understand the inefficiency of such a milk-and-water method of control.

One of the most radical books ever published at the instigation of railroad managers appeared in 1888, under the title "The People and the Railways." Its author is Appleton Morgan, who attempts to "allay the animosity towards the railway interests" as shown in Mr. James F. Hudson's book, "The Railways and the Republic." The means which Mr. Morgan chooses are not well calculated to accomplish his purpose, for the masses of the people prefer in such a controversy arguments to ridicule and sarcasm, weapons of literary warfare to which this author resorts altogether too freely. Mr. Morgan s opinion as to the benefits of centralized wealth and trade combinations differs greatly from that held by the great majority of the American people. He says: "The fact, the truth is, that (however it may be in other countries) the accumulation of wealth and centralization of commerce in great combinations has never, in the United States, been a source of oppression or of poverty to the non-capitalist or wage-worker." There is scarcely an evil in railroad management which Mr. Morgan does not defend. Pools,

construction companies, rebates, discriminations and over-
capitalization all find favor in Mr. Morgan's eye. "Rebates and discriminations," he says, "are neither peculiar
to railways nor dangerous to the ' Republic.' They are as
necessary and as harmless to the farmer as is the chromo
which the seamstress or the shop girl gets with her
quarter-pound of tea from the small tea merchant, and no
more dangerous to the latter than are the aforesaid
chromos to the small recipients." Pools and combinations receive an unusually large share of Mr. Morgan's
attention. A few selections from his effusions in their
favor may be given here, viz. :

"These pools are the legitimate and necessary results
of the rechartering over and over again of railway companies to transact business between the same points by
paralleling each other. So long as the people in their
legislatures will thus charter parallel lines serving identical points—thus dividing territory they once granted
entire—it is not exactly clear how they can complain if
the lines built (by money invested, if not on the good faith
of the people, at least in reliance upon an undivided business) combine to save themselves from bankruptcy." And
again : "Against the inequality of their own rates and
the hardship of the long and short haul (in other words,
against the discrimination of nature and of physical laws)
no less than against the peril of bankruptcy and the consequent speculative tendency of their stocks (after which may
come the wrecking, the watering, and the vast individual
fortunes), the railways of this republic have endeavored,
by establishment of pool commissions, to defend both the
public and themselves. . . . The honest administration of
railways for all interests, the payment of their fixed
charges, the solvency of their securities, the faithful and

valuable performance of their duties as carriers, can be conserved in but one way—by living tariffs, such as the pools once guaranteed."

In the following passage this author denies to the State the right to regulate rates: "Granting that they [the railroads] must carry freights for the public in such a way as not to injure either the public or the freight in the carrying, most emphatically (it seems to me) it does not follow that they must add to the value of the freights they carry by charging only such rates as the public or the owners of the freight insist on."

But Mr. Morgan's indignation rises to the highest pitch in his discussion of the Interstate Commerce Act. He fears that it will cause the downfall of our liberties and sees in the background the Venetian Bridge of Sighs and the French Bastile. He asks: "Why should for any public reasons—for any reason of public safety—the Interstate Commerce Law have come to stay?" He then berates the act as follows: "To begin with, the present act abounds in punishments for and prohibitions against an industry chartered by the people, but nowhere extends to that industry a morsel of approval or protection. It bristles with penalties, legal, equitable, penal, and as for contempt, against railway companies, but nowhere alludes to any possible case in which a railway company might, by accident, be in the right, and the patron, customer, passenger or shipper in the wrong. . . . The constitutions of civilized nations, for the last few centuries at least, have provided that not even guilt should be punished except by due process of law, and have uniformly refused to set even that due process in motion except upon a complaint of grievance. But the Interstate Commerce Law denies the one and does away with the necessity for the other.

That statute provides that the commission it creates shall proceed 'in such manner and by such means as it shall deem proper,' or 'on its own motion,' and that 'no complaint shall at any time be dismissed because of the absence of direct damage to the complainant.' Even the Venetian council often provided for a certain and described hole in the wall through which the anonymous bringers of charges should thrust their accusations. Even the court of star chamber was known to dismiss inquisitions when it found that no wrong had been done. But the statute of interstate commerce appears to issue *lettres de cachet* against anything in the shape of a railway company—to scatter them broadcast, and to invite any one who happens to have leisure to fill them out, by inserting the name of a railway company. It says to the bystander: 'Drop us a postal card, or mention to any of our commissioners, or to a mutual friend, the name of any railway company of which you may have heard, and so give us jurisdiction to inquire if that company may have by chance omitted to dot an i or cross a t in its ledgers, or whether any one of its hundreds of thousands of agents—in the rush of a day's business, or in a shipper's hurry to catch a train—may have named a rate not on the schedule then being prepared at headquarters, or charged a sixpence less than some other agent 250 miles down the line may have accepted a week ago for what might turn out to be a fraction more mileage service in the same general direction. No particular form is necessary. Drop in to luncheon with our commission any day between twelve and one, and mention the name of a railway company. The railway company may have done you no damage, nor grieved you in any way; just mention the railroad, and we will take jurisdiction of its private (or quasi-public) affairs. Or, if

you don't happen to have time to mention it, we will take
jurisdiction anyhow, 'of our own motion,' of any railway
company whose name we find in the Official Gazette. It
really does not matter which; any one will do." This is
a fair example of the literature on the Interstate Commerce Law paid for by railroad men.

Mr. Stickney, although a railroad president, takes an
entirely different view of the situation. He considers the
law inadequate to bring about the reforms needed. He
says : " This enormous business is now in the control of
several hundred petty chieftains, who are practically independent sovereigns, exercising functions and prerogatives
in defiance of the laws, and practically denying their
amenability to the laws of the country. If the Government would seek to bring them to terms and compel them
to recognize and obey the laws, it must use the means
necessary to accomplish the end. It must have executive
officers sufficient in number as well as armed with an adequate power and dignity to command their respect. . . .
The power conferred upon them [the Interstate Commerce Commission] to enforce their judicial orders is the
power ' to scold.' The penalties of the law which the
courts are in power to impose are certainly severe, but the
law has been operated for about four years without any
convictions, and yet no well-informed person is ignorant
of the fact that the law has not been obeyed. The president of a large system is said to have remarked that ' if
all who had offended against the law were convicted there
would not be jails enough in the United States to hold
them.' It is evident that the Government has not provided adequate machinery for enforcing the law."

Mr. Stickney is correct in his statement that adequate
machinery for enforcement of the law has not been pro-

vided, but he does not give sufficient credit to the law or the commission. While much work remains to be done, much progress has been made.

He is of the opinion that the public welfare would be furthered if the National Government assumed the sole control of railroads. He gives his reasons for the change which he proposes, as follows:

"There are many reasons besides these in the interest of uniformity which make it desirable to transfer the entire control of this important matter to the regulation of the Nation. First, because of its constitution and more extended sessions, Congress is able to consider the subject with greater deliberation, and therefore with more intelligence, than can a legislature composed of members who, as a rule, hold their office for but one short session of about sixty days' duration. There would also be removed from local legislation a fruitful source of corruption, which is gradually sapping the foundations of public morality. . . . In the second place, the problem of regulating railway tolls and managing railways is essentially and practically indivisible, by State lines or otherwise, and therefore it is not clear but that whenever the question may come before the courts it may be held that the authority of Congress to deal with interstate traffic carries with it, as a necessary and inseparable part of the subject, to regulate the traffic which is now assumed to be controlled by the several States. The courts have held that the States have authority to regulate strictly State traffic in the absence of Congressional action, but their decisions do not preclude the doctrine that Congress may have exclusive jurisdiction whenever it may choose to exercise the authority. There is a line of reasoning which would lead to that conclusion. It may be that many will not care to follow the lead of the writer as to the measure of aggregate net revenue which railway companies are entitled to collect in tolls, but it is evident that before the tolls can be intelligently determined some measure of such aggregate revenue must be ascertained. The question

would then arise, what proportion must be levied upon
State and interstate traffic respectively? If the State
should refuse to levy its share (and how could such share
be ascertained?), then more than its share would have to
be levied on interstate traffic, and thus the State by
indirection would be able to do what the Constitution
prohibits. Of course, when the Constitution was adopted
railways and railway traffic were unknown. But it was a
similar question which brought the thirteen original States
together into one nation, under the present Constitution.
At least the first movement toward amending the original
Articles of Confederation was to give Congress enlarged
power over the subject of commerce."

In reply to this it may be said that it will be an unfor-
tunate day for the States when they surrender the power
to control their home affairs. Differences between State
and interstate rates could easily be adjusted by the
National and State commissions and by the courts. It certainly ought not to be difficult for such tribunals to see
that a rate which is made higher or lower, as it may be
for State or interstate traffic, is wrong.

Mr. Stickney has fallen into the error common to railroad men in believing that lower rates of transportation
will not prevail in the future. There are many reasons
why it is probable that they will be lower. Present rates
are highly profitable on well located lines. Labor-saving
inventions will increase, and roads will be built and operated more cheaply. Lines will be located with lower
grades, lighter curvature and more directness. Business
will increase largely, and the ratio of expenses will decrease. Steel will be improved in quality and will be sub-
stituted for iron. A heavier rail and more permanent
roadway will be used. Rates of interest will rule lower,
and there will be much more economy in superintending.
Extravagant salaries to favorites will be reduced, and sine-

cures and parasites will be cut off from the pay-rolls. Lower wages are inevitable as our population becomes more dense.

A very interesting and instructive author upon railroad subjects is Charles Francis Adams, Jr., ex-president of the Union Pacific Railroad and formerly a member of the Board of Railroad Commissioners of the State of Massachusetts. After twenty years' constant association with railroad men, Mr. Adams should certainly know the character of his quondam colleagues. In his book, "Railroads, Their Origin and Problems," he says of them : "Lawlessness and violence among themselves [*i. e.*, the various railroad systems], the continual effort of each member to protect itself and to secure the advantage over others, have, as they usually do, bred a general spirit of distrust, bad faith and cunning, until railroad officials have become hardly better than a race of horse-jockeys on a large scale. There are notable exceptions to this statement, but, taken as a whole, the tone among them is indisputably low. There is none of that steady confidence in each other, that easy good faith, that *esprit du corps*, upon which alone system and order can rest. On the contrary, the leading idea in the mind of the active railroad agent is that some one is always cheating him, or that he is never getting his share in something. If he enters into an agreement, his life is passed in watching the other parties to it, lest by some cunning device they keep it in form and break it in spirit. Peace is with him always a condition of semi-warfare, while honor for its own sake and good faith apart from self-interest are, in a business point of view, symptoms of youth and a defective education." And again, in an address delivered before the Commercial Club of Boston in

December, 1888, Mr. Adams expressed his opinion concerning the average railroad manager of to-day as follows:
'' That the general railroad situation of the country is at
present unsatisfactory is apparent. Stockholders are complaining; directors are bewildered; bankers are fright-
ened. Yet that the Interstate Commerce Act is in the
main responsible for all these results, remains to be proved.
In my opinion, the difficulty is far more deep-seated and
radical. In plain words, it does not lie in any act of legislation, State or National; and it does lie in the covet-
ousness, want of good faith and low moral tone of those
in whose hands the management of the railroad system
now is; in a word, in the absence among men of any high
standard of commercial honor. These are strong words,
and yet, as the result of a personal experience stretching
over nearly twenty years, I make bold to say they are not
so strong as the occasion would justify. The railroad
system of this country, especially of the regions west of
Chicago, is to-day managed on principles which—unless a
change of heart occurs, and that soon—must inevitably
lead to financial disaster of the most serious kind. There
is among the lines composing that system an utter disregard of those fundamental ideas of truth, fair play and
fair dealing which lies at the foundation, not only of the
Christian faith, but of civilization itself. With them
there is but one rule—that, many years ago, put by
Wordsworth into the mouth of Rob Roy:

> '' ' The simple rule, the good old plan,
> That he shall take who has the power,
> And he shall keep who can. ' ''

As regards the causes of the Granger movement, Mr.
Adams says, in the work above mentioned: '' That it [the
Granger episode] did not originate without cause has

already been pointed out. It is quite safe to go further, and to say that the movement was a necessary one, and through its results has made a solution of the railroad problem possible in this country. At the time that movement took shape the railroad corporations were in fact rapidly assuming a position which could not be tolerated. Corporations, owning and operating the highways of commerce, claimed for themselves a species of immunity from the control of the law-making power. When laws were passed with a view to their regulation they received them in a way which was at once arrogant and singularly injudicious. The officers entrusted with the execution of those laws they contemptuously ignored. Sheltering themselves behind the Dartmouth College decision, they practically undertook to set even public opinion at defiance. Indeed, there can be no doubt that those representing these corporations had at this juncture not only become fully educated up to the idea that the gross inequalities and ruinous discriminations to which in their business they were accustomed were necessary incidents to it which afforded no just ground of complaint to any one, but they also thought that any attempt to rectify them was a gross outrage on the elementary principles both of common sense and of constitutional law. In other words, they had thoroughly got it into their heads that they, as common carriers, were in no way bound to afford equal facilities to all, and, indeed, that it was in the last degree absurd and unreasonable to expect them to do so. The Granger method was probably as good a method of approaching men in this frame of mind as could have been devised."

Speaking of the educational value of railroad competition, Mr. Adams says: "Undoubtedly the fierce struggles between rival corporations which marked the history of railroad development, both here and in England, were very prominent factors in the work of forcing the systems of the two countries up to their present degree of efficiency. Railroad competition has been a great educator for railroad men. It has not only taught them how much they could do, but also how very cheaply they could do it. Under the strong stimulus of rivalry they have done not only what they declared were impossibilities, but what they really believed to be such."

Mr. Adams has, from his long association with railroad managers, imbibed one heresy which is in strange discord with the general soundness of his opinions. He holds that the railroad system was left to develop upon a false basis, inasmuch as the American people relied for protecting the community from abuses upon general laws authorizing the freest possible railroad construction everywhere and by any one. It can therefore not be surprising that Mr. Adams is an advocate of the legalized pool. He is of the opinion that secret combinations among railroads, inasmuch as they always have existed, always will exist as long as the railroad system continues as it now is. Hence he proposes to legalize a practice which the law cannot prevent, and by so doing to enable the railroads to confederate themselves in a manner which shall be at once both public and responsible. The reply might be made that there are many other conspiracies which the law cannot always prevent, but that this is no reason why conspiracies should be legalized. If pools and other railroad abuses had, since the beginning of the railroad era, been treated as crimes and misdemeanors, and punished as such by the imposition of heavy fines, few people would to-day be ready to offer apologies for them. If the time shall ever come when pools must be legalized it will be time for railroad control equivalent to Government ownership.

Among the more recent writers upon railroad subjects is W. D. Dabney, late chairman of the Committee on Railways and Internal Navigation in the Legislature of Virginia. Mr. Dabney favors State control, and is, on the whole, friendly to the Interstate Commerce Act. He sees danger in the pool, but inclines to the belief that the public benefit derived from the pooling system outweighs the danger of public detriment from its existence. The following is his chief argument for a legalized pool: "Perhaps, so long as railroad companies continue to enjoy an absolute monopoly of transportation over their own lines, so that free competition is restricted in its operation to a comparatively few favored points, it may be worthy of serious consideration whether it would not be better to legalize than to prohibit pooling, taking care to put the whole matter under strict public supervision and control. The companies would then be left comparatively free to bring their local rates into something like harmony with the long-distance rates, and should they fail to do so where the needs of the local community and their revenues make it proper to be done, then it is the function of public regulation to compel it to be done."

Of the Interstate Commerce Act Mr. Dabney says: ' The legislation recently enacted by Congress for the regulation of commerce by railway is the result of more careful and intelligent deliberation perhaps than any other measure of similar character, and it is not unlikely that the legislation of many of the States will sooner or later be conformed to it."

He speaks at some length of the drift toward railroad centralization. A few extracts from this passage may be

here given: ''That the tendency towards the unification
and consolidation of different and competitive lines has been
decidedly increased by the anti-pooling and the long and
short haul sections of the Interstate Commerce Law can
hardly be doubted. . . . The modern device of the ' trust'
as a means of unifying industrial interests and eliminating
competition had not yet been applied in the field of railroad transportation. . . . The scheme of trust here briefly
outlined would probably require for its successful operation the concurrence of the entire stockholding interest of
each company embraced in it; and herein, it seems likely,
will be found the chief difficulty in perfecting such a
scheme. Should it ever be perfected, a far more stringent
public supervision and control of the railroad transportation of the country will be demanded.''

Another author, Charles Whitney Baker, associate
editor of the *Engineering News*, suggests in his book,
'' Monopolies and the People,'' a plan for the reorganiza-
tion of our railroad system, to remedy the evils of monopoly which are at present connected with railroad
management. The following quotation from his work
outlines the system proposed : '' Let the Government acquire the title of the franchise, permanent way and real
estate of all the railway lines in the country. Let a few
corporations be organized under Government auspices,
and let each, by the terms of its charter, receive a per-
petual lease of all the railway lines built, or to be built,
within a given territory. Let the territory of each of
these corporations be so large, and so planned with regard
to its neighbors, that there shall be, so far as possible, no
competition between them. For instance, one corporation
would operate all the lines south of the Ohio and east of
the Mississippi River; another all lines east of the Hudson

and of Lake Champlain, etc. Let the terms of rental of these lines be about 3¼ per cent. on the road's actual 'present cost' (the sum of money it would cost to rebuild it entirely at present prices of material and labor), less a due allowance for depreciation. The corporations would be obliged to keep the property in as good condition as when received, and would own absolutely all their rolling-stock, machinery, etc." The proposed reform measures, it must be admitted, are very good in theory, but their practical application is unfortunately entirely out of the question under our system of government.

Mr. John M. Bonham is the author of a recent work entitled "Railway Secrecy and Trusts." This writer, upon the whole, takes advanced ground in dealing with the question of railroad reform. He deems the present interstate legislation inadequate to correct all the graver railroad evils, expressing his views upon this subject as follows:

"Railway construction continues to increase in the United States with immense rapidity. Concurrent with this increase, and notwithstanding all the efforts that have been made at restraint, the aggressions upon political and industrial rights increase also. Nor is it likely that without more rigorous control than is now exercised these aggressions will be any less active than they are to-day. It is coming to be pretty generally realized that the Interstate Commerce legislation has not fulfilled the expectation of its friends. But this is a frequent trait of tentative legislation. It is not reasonable to expect that the first efforts to solve a problem the factors of which are so hidden and complex will be followed by complete success."

Concerning the changes needed to make Government regulation in the United States more effective, he says:

" A reform which would deal with an elaborate system of evil cannot, therefore, be confined to treating consequences, the separate instances of the system. There must be a power which can go behind these and grapple with causes. There must, therefore, be something more than a court. There must be a commission, a department of government which will provide organized supervision and inspection against which the quasi-public corporation can claim no privacy as inviolable. Such a department must be clothed with the power to ascertain precisely where and how the evils of the present methods originate, and when these are ascertained it must be able to apply the remedy at the source of evil. The remedial force must be of a preventive kind."

A few grave misstatements of historical facts greatly mar Mr. Bonham's book. He makes, for instance, the following statement:

"Following this came restrictive legislation, which, in some instances, was so unreasonable as to make any railway management impossible. Some of the Granger legislation, and especially that of Iowa, was of this character, as were also some of the earlier efforts to secure Congressional legislation."

It was left to Mr. Bonham to discover that legislation ever made railroad management impossible in Iowa. The General Assembly of Iowa passed at two different times railroad laws that were greatly obnoxious to railroad managers. In 1874 it passed a maximum tariff act which, at the urgent solicitation of the railroad forces, was repealed four years later; and in 1888 it passed an act containing the principles of the Interstate Commerce Act and in addition authorizing the Board of Railroad Commissioners to fix *prima facie* rates. Strange as it may seem to Mr. Bonham and other people inclined to believe without investigation the statements of railroad men, the earnings of the Iowa roads greatly increased immediately after the enactment of the so-called Granger laws in 1874, as the following table will show:

Year.	Miles of Railroad.	Gross Receipts.
1871	2,850	$12,395,826
1872	3,642	14,534,408
1873	3,728	15,430,619
1874	3,765	15,568,907
1875	3,823	18,422,587
1876	3,938	17,221,032
1877	4,075	20,714,496
1878	4,157	21,294,275

When the Granger law was repealed in 1878, the railroads were earning $1,000 per mile more than they were earning when the law was enacted. The present railroad law, which was passed in 1888, and has also been the subject of extreme criticism on the part of railroad organs, has had the same beneficial effect. The law, owing to the obstacles thrown in its way by the railroad managers, did not become operative until 1889. From July 1st, 1889, to June 30th, 1892, the gross railroad earnings of the Iowa roads, which for three years had been at a standstill, increased and were over $7,000,000 more in 1892 than they had been any year previous to 1889, as will be seen from the table below:

Gross Railroad Earnings in Iowa.

1886–87	$37,539,730
1887–88	37,295,586
1888–89	37,469,276
1889–90	41,318,133
1890-91	43,102,399
1891–92	44,540,000

The net earnings per mile of the Iowa roads were $1,421.91 in the year 1888–89, and $1,821.37 the year following. The total net earnings of all Iowa roads during the year ending June 30th, 1891, were $14,463,106, against $11,861,310 during the year ending June 30th, 1889, and were still greater for the year ending June 30,

1892. No further vindication of the Iowa law is necessary. These figures show plainly that the lowering and
equalizing of the rates not only increased the roads' business and income, but also their net earnings. And it
must be remembered that the reports showing these facts
were made by the railroad companies and were certainly
not made with any intention of prejudicing the cause of
the railroad manager.

James F. Hudson, the author of "The Railways and
the Republic," is a very exhaustive and instructive writer
upon the subject of railroad abuses. His material is well
selected, and the subject ably presented. To the assertion
of railroad managers, that railroad regulation injuriously
affects the value of railroad property, he makes the following reply:

"Suppose that it were true, as these jurists and writers
claim, that by the assertion of the public right to regulate
the railways the value of their property is decreased, are
there no other property rights involved? Do railway
investments form the only property in the land which requires the protection of the law? Are we to understand
these judgments and their indorsers to mean that because
railroad property will depreciate if certain principles of
justice prevail, therefore justice is to be set aside for the
benefit of railway property? If the magnitude of interests
involved is to be of weight in deciding such questions, let
us put against 'the hundreds of millions' of railway
property on the one side the thousands of millions of
private property on the other. Railway regulation,
according to a writer in the *Princeton Review*, is 'confiscation of railroad property;' but this puts wholly out of
the question the idea of private property which is
rendered possible by leaving unchecked the power of the
railways over commerce and manufactures through the
manipulation of freight rates. Of the two parties in interest the shippers represent far greater property interests
than the carriers, although the latter, by their organiza-

tion, are more powerful. I have yet to hear of a single case where restrictive railway legislation has seriously damaged the honest valuation of any railway. I have yet to learn of any seriously proposed scheme of regulation that has proposed to cut down railway profits below a fair dividend on capital actually invested. But the entire Nation knows of one notorious case in which the discriminating policy of the leading railways of the country has resulted in the wholesale confiscation of private property for the benefit of a favored corporation."

Concerning the inconsistency presented by the plea of railroad managers for a legalized pool, Mr. Hudson says:

"It has been argued for years that the subject is so delicate and vast that it must not be touched by legislation in the public interest. To protect the rights of the ordinary shipper against the favorite of the railway would so hamper the operations of trade, it has been repeated times without number, as to take away the independence of the railways and destroy the freedom of competition. Yet, after years of argument that Government has no constitutional power to interfere with the railways, and of demonstration that all such interference must be ill-advised and injurious, the railway logic comes to the surprising climax of appealing to legislation for the aid of the law in upholding their efforts to prevent competition."

Mr. Hudson maintains that if the pool were legalized it would only be a means of swelling railroad earnings. He says:

"If the pool would maintain equitable rates its success might be desired, but what guarantee is there that the complete establishment of its power would make such rates? Its very character, the functions of the men who control its policy, and its avowed object of swelling the earnings of railways by artificial methods, forbid such an expectation. Make the success of the pool absolute, so that it can work without fear of competition, and its rates will be uniform, but of such a character that their uniformity will be a public grievance and burden. . . .

A grave effect of this policy, though not easily cal-
culable, is the ability it gives to railway officials to
control the prices of stocks, and the temptation to enhance their fortunes by so doing. . . . It is a heavy indict-
ment against the pooling system that it gives power to
avaricious and unscrupulous men in railway management
to enrich themselves at the cost of shareholders and
investors, both by forming combinations and by exciting
disputes or ruptures in them."

The question whether the common law does not protect the public sufficiently is well answered by Mr. Hudson as follows:

"The common law is sufficient in theory, but it has
failed in practice. . . . In practice, legal remedies against
railway injustice can be applied to the courts only by
fighting the railways at such disadvantages that the ordinary business man will never undertake it except in des-
perate cases. Every advantage of strength and position
is with the railways. . . . This [the railroad] power has
kept courts in its pay; it defies the principles of common law and nullifies the constitutional provisions of a
dozen States; it has many representatives in Congress
and unnumbered seats in the State legislatures. No
ordinary body of men can permanently resist it."

But the remedy which Mr. Hudson proposes for the
correction of railroad evils is one of doubtful efficacy. It
is this:

" Legislation should restore the character of public
highways to the railways by securing to all persons the
right to run trains over their track under proper regulations, and by defining the distinction between the proprietorship and maintenance of the railway and the business of common carriers."

While it is admitted that the opening of the railroads
to the free use of competing carriers is not necessarily
impractical from a technical point of view, it cannot be
admitted that the proposed remedy would cure the evil.

There would certainly be nothing to hinder carrying companies forming a trust which might prove more dangerous to the interests of shippers than are to-day the combinations of the railroad companies.

Mr. Hudson devotes a chapter to the railroad power in politics, and shows how corporations, through their wealth, have secured the greatest and most responsible offices in the executive, legislative and judiciary departments of the Government. Speaking of their influence in the Supreme Court of the United States, he says:

"The assertion that Jay Gould paid $100,000 to the Republican campaign fund in 1880, in return for which Judge Stanley Mathews was nominated to the Supreme Bench, is denied as a political slander; but the fact remains that this brilliant advocate of the railway theories of law has been placed in the high tribunal, and that his presence there together with Justice Field, long a judicial advocate of the corporations, is expected to protect the railways in future against such constructions of law as the Granger decisions."

An English writer, Mr. J. S. Jeans, presents, in his "Railway Problems," a great deal that is of interest to American readers. The statistical data of his work are especially interesting. We learn that the United Kingdom has nearly twenty railroad employes per mile of road operated, to less than five in the United States, and that the average number of employes per £1,000 ($4,850) of gross earnings is on the railroads of the United Kingdom 5.4 to only about half as many in the United States. We further learn that the average earnings per train mile in America are over 25 per cent. higher than they are in the United Kingdom, and exceed those of most European countries.

Of the remarkable increase in number and the profit-

ableness of the third-class passenger traffic in England
Mr. Jeans says:

"There has hitherto been a great lack of knowledge in
this country as to the extent to which the different classes
of passenger traffic yield adequate profit to the railroad
companies. English passenger traffic differs from that
of most other countries in this respect, that the chief
companies attach third-class carriages to almost every
train. The accommodation provided for third-class passengers in England is also much superior to what is found
in other countries where there is the same distinction of
classes. The effect of those two distinguishing features
of the English railway system is that third-class carriages
are much more and first-class carriages much less utilized
than in other countries. The tendency appears to be towards an increasing use of third-class, and a decreasing
use of first-class vehicles. But, all the same, the leading
English lines continue to provide a large proportion of
first-class accommodation in every train, and it is no unusual thing to find the third-class carriages of express
trains absolutely full, while first-class carriages are almost
empty. The natural result is that third-class travel is a
source of profit, while first-class travel is not. . . . So far
as passenger traffic is a source of net profit, that profit is
contributed by the third-class. The total receipts from
passenger traffic in England and Wales amounted in 1885
to £21,968,000. But if the average receipts per carriage
over the whole had been the same as in the case of the
Midland first-class vehicles, namely, £330, the total receipts from passenger traffic would only have been about
nine millions. It is not necessary to be an expert in order
to see that traffic so conducted must be attended with a
very serious loss."

Of the stock-watering of American railroad companies
Mr. Jeans says:

"It seldom happens that in the United States the cost
of a railway and its equivalent corresponds, as it ought to,
to the total capital expenditure. There is no country
in the world where the business of watering stocks is

better understood or carried out more systematically
and on so large a scale. For this reason there is liable to
be a great deal of error entertained in reference to the
natural cost of American lines."

There are many financial journals that are so closely
identified with the speculative interests of the country,
and many railway papers that depend so largely upon railway men for support, that railway managers are never
without a medium through which they can present their
views to the public. A systematic and concerted effort is
also constantly made by the railroads to pervert the press
of the country at large. The great city papers generally
yield to their influences and enlist in their service, and
yet there are notable exceptions to this.

In speaking of the extravagant sums which the railroads paid to the great dailies, ostensibly for advertising,
but in fact for their good will and other services, a railroad superintendent recently said that it was an infamous
outrage, and yet it was the best investment of money that
his company could make. The country papers have
shown more integrity in maintaining their independence,
but the railroads are not without their organs among
them. It is not unfrequent to find some of them defending railroad abuses with all the apparent zeal of a Wall
Street organ, and a glance at their columns often reminds
one of Mr. Lincoln's story of the Irishman and the pig.
Mr. Lincoln defended an Irishman against the charge of
stealing a pig. After the testimony was taken in court, Mr.
Lincoln called his client aside and told him that the testimony was so strong against him, and that the case was so
clear, that it was impossible for him to escape conviction,
and he advised him to plead guilty and throw himself on
the mercy of the court. "No, Mr. Lincoln," said Patrick, "you go back and make one of your great speeches

and swing your long arms and talk loud to the jury, and you will win the case." Mr. Lincoln, in accordance with that disposition to accommodate so strongly characteristic of him, did as he was directed by his client, and to his great surprise the jury promptly brought in a verdict of not guilty. After it was all over, Mr. Lincoln said: "Now, Patrick, tell me why that jury acquitted you. I know that you stole the pig, and my speech had nothing to do in securing your acquittal." Patrick replied: "And sure, Mr. Lincoln, every one of those jurymen ate a piece of the pig."

CHAPTER X.

RAILROAD questions have become of such general interest that their discussion has become a prominent factor of magazine literature. It is a significant fact that these contributors are usually railroad men, and under these circumstances an unbiased discussion of the questions at issue is indeed a rare occurrence. It is but too frequently the sole object of the contributor, and not unfrequently even of the publisher, to create a public sentiment in favor of the unjust demands of railroad managers.

During the last few years systematic efforts have been made by the railroad interests to influence public opinion against the Interstate Commerce Law and restrictive State legislation through the leading magazines of the country. Mr. Sidney Dillon, president of the Union Pacific Railroad, in an article which appeared in the April (1891) number of the *North American Review*, under the title "The West and the Railroads," endeavors to show that the West is indebted to the railroad managers for nearly all of the blessings which its people enjoy, and that therefore railroad legislation in the West is a symptom of rank ingratitude. He prefaces his argument with the remark that the elder portions of our commonwealth have already forgotten, and the younger portions do not comprehend or appreciate, that but for the railroads what we now style the Great West would be, except in the valley of the Mississippi, an unknown and unproductive wilderness.

He then argues that, inasmuch as the railroads carry the wheat of Dakota and Minnesota to the sea-coast, and bring those sections of our community into direct relation with hungry and opulent Liverpool, the world should "thank the railway for the opportunity to buy wheat, but none the less should the West thank the railway for the opportunity to sell wheat." It does not seem to occur to Mr. Dillon that the railway might, with equal propriety, thank the world in general, and the Great West in particular, for its opportunity to carry wheat.

We are also told that the railway has reclaimed from nature immense tracts of land that were worthless except as to their possibilities, which once seemed too vague and remote to be considered and are to-day valuable; that it has changed the character of the soil as well as the climate of the West, and we are almost given to understand that in many respects it has assumed the functions of Providence. Mr. Dillon generously admits, however, that railways have not been built from philanthropic motives and that we find among railroad promoters and contractors men of large fortunes. He then proceeds to reprimand the States west of the Mississippi for their "ungrateful" legislation, which, he says, interferes with the business of the railway, even to the minutest detail, and always to its detriment. Such legislation exasperates Mr. Dillon the more because it originated in States "which happened to be the communities that owe their birth, existence and prosperity to these very railways." Mr. Dillon then gives vent to his wrath by the use of such terms as impertinence, ignorance and demagogism. He holds that legislative enactments as to the rights and liabilities of railway corporations are useless, "because the common law has long since established these as pertaining to common carriers, and the courts are open to redress all real grievances of the citizen." Upon this theory we might as well dispense with the legislative department of the Government, for there is no relation in the community to which the principles of the common law can not be applied. Besides this, Mr. Dillon entirely ignores the fact that the railway company is not only a common carrier, but the keeper of the highway, and as such is subject to Government control as much as the turnpike toll-gate keeper or the collector of customs. "Then as to prices." Mr. Dillon continues: "These will always be taken care of by the great law of competition, which obtains wherever any human service is to be performed for a pecuniary consideration. That any railway, anywhere in a republic, should be a monopoly, is not a supposable case."

Like the rest of railway men, Mr. Dillon excels in painting dark pictures of railroad catastrophes. A sample production of his art is here presented:

"One of the greatest dangers to the community in a republic is this: that it is in the power of reckless, misguided or designing men to procure the passage of statutes that are ostensibly for the public interest and that may lead to enormous injuries. Let us imagine for a moment that all railways in the United States were at once annihilated. Such a catastrophe is not, in itself, inconceivable; the imagination can grasp it, but no imagination can picture the infinite sufferings that would at once result to every man, woman and child in the entire country. Now, every step taken to impede or cripple the business and progress of our railways is a step towards just such a catastrophe, and therefore a destructive tendency."

Mr. Dillon, losing sight of all other interests, did not think that his nonsensical mode of reasoning would apply equally well to them. Let us, for instance, imagine for a moment that all of the farms of the United States were at once annihilated. Can the imagination picture the infinite sufferings that would at once result to every man, woman and child in the whole country? Now, is not any step taken to impede or cripple the business of farming a step towards just such a catastrophe, and therefore of a destrucrive tendency? Mr. Dillon then avails himself of an opportunity to give the people of the United States some gratuitous advice when he says:

"We do not arrogate superior wisdom or intelligence to ourselves when we suggest to the people of the United States, and especially that portion of the country where railroads have been the subject of what we consider to be excessive legislation, that the rational mode of treating any form of human industry that has for its object the performance of desired and lawful service is to let it alone, and that the railway is no exception to this principle."

This is the very plea that Jefferson Davis made when he kindled the flame of treason.

In the March, 1891, number of the *Forum*, Mr. W. M. Acworth discusses, under the title "Railways under Government Control," the working of the railway systems of the different nations. He holds that the management of railroads which are the property of the State is, as a rule, greatly inferior to the management of those roads which are the property of private trading corporations ; he assigns to the railway experts of England and America the first places among the railway experts of the world, and appears to attribute all the good in the railroad management of these countries to the absence of State interference, and all the evil in the management of the railroads of other countries to the fact that such interference exists. He says of the railroads of England and the United States :

"In speed and accommodation, in the energy which pushes railways into remote districts, and in the skill which creates a traffic where no traffic existed before, they stand to-day in the front rank, as they have stood for the last half century. To say that they are very far from perfect is nothing ; it is only to say that they are worked by human agency. Their worst enemies will scarcely deny that they are at least alive; so long as there is life there may be growth, and we may hope to see them outgrow the faults of their youth. The charge made against State railway systems is that they are incapable of vigorous life. The old adage which proclaimed that ' necessity is the mother of invention ' has been re-stated of late years as the law of the survival of the fittest in the struggle for existence. If the doctrine is true, the State railway system, relieved from the necessity of struggle, must cease to be fit and will fail to survive."

While it is not intended to enter here into a defense of a State railway system, it may justly be questioned whether "the State railway system, relieved from the necessity of struggle, must cease to be fit and will fail to survive." The growth of the State system in Europe is in itself a sufficient refutation of Mr. Acworth's theory. The mail service has for several hundred years been a monopoly of the government; but, while it is far from being perfect, it remains to be demonstrated that private enterprise could give to the public a better service in the long run.

Mr. Acworth is an Englishman who in former years wrote many bitter things concerning the abuses which he then thought he saw in the management of the railroads of his native country, which, according to his own statement, are, besides those of the United States, the only roads in the world for whose regulation competition has been relied upon in the past. Mr. Acworth has become a convert to the *laissez faire* theory of dealing with railroads and now evinces an unusual, but perhaps pardonable, zeal in the defense of his new position. In the preface to his book, "The Railways of England," he says upon the subject:

"I have published before now not a few criticisms (which were meant to be scathing) on English railways anonymously. I find myself using, under my own name, the language of almost unvarying panegyric. This is partly to be explained by the plan of the book, which professes to set before the reader those points on each line which best merit description—its excellencies, therefore, rather than its defects. Much more, however, is it due to a change of opinion in the writer. . . . I have found in so many cases that a satisfactory reply existed to my former criticisms, that I have perhaps assumed that such an answer would be forthcoming in all; and if I have taken up too much the position of an apologist, where I should have been content to be merely an observer, let me plead as my excuse that I am only displaying the traditional zeal of the new-made convert."

Prof. Hadley, of whose work, "Railroad Transportation, its History and its Law," mention has been made above, contributed an article to the April, 1891, number of the *Forum,* under the title "Railway Passenger Rates." He endeavors to show that the high passenger rates of American railroads are due solely to superior service. He says:

"Continental Europe pays two-thirds as much as America or England and gets an inferior article. India pays still less and gets still less. The difference is seen both in quality and quantity of service. In India express trains rarely run at a greater speed than 25 miles an hour. In Germany and France their speed ranges from 25 to 35 miles an hour, and only in exceptional instances is more than 40 miles an hour. In the United States and in England the maximum speed rises as high as 50, or, in exceptional instances, 60 miles an hour. With regard to the comfort of the cars in different countries, there is more room for difference of opinion ; but there can be no doubt that the average traveler in the United States, or even in the English third-class car, fares better than he would in the corresponding class on continental railroads, and infinitely better than the bulk of travelers in British India."

It may be admitted that upon the whole the speed of American and English railroads is greater than that of continental roads, yet the difference is much less than Mr. Hadley would make us believe. The fast trains of the Berlin and Hamburg Railroad, according to Röll's "Railroad Encyclopedia," make the distance of 179 miles in three hours and forty-four minutes. The average speed is therefore 48 miles an hour. There are but few lines in the United States whose regular express trains run at a greater speed. The express trains of the Berlin and Brunswick line make 45½ miles an hour. Trains are run on the Vienna and Buda-Pesth Railway at the rate of 42 miles an hour and on the Paris and Calais Railway at a rate of over 40 miles an hour. Official reports give the average speed of express trains in Northern Germany as 32.2 miles per hour, which is considerably more than the average speed of our Western trains, upon which the rates charged are twice as high as those charged by German roads. The average speed of the express trains in England was 35.7 miles per hour in 1890, in the Netherlands 30.7 miles, in France 30 miles, in Denmark and Southern Germany 28.8 miles and in, Austria 27.8 miles per hour. Accurate statistics showing the average speed in America are not in existence, but it may well be questioned whether the difference between the speed of American and European trains is sufficient to justify upon that score any essential difference in the rates. Mr. Hadley's statement that the average traveler in the United States,

or even in the English third class, fares better than he
would in the corresponding class on continental railroads,
is far too sweeping to be true. It is certain that the
Belgian, German, Austrian or French second-class
coupes are much to be preferred to the smoking and emi-
grant cars which in America are made to take their
places.

To prove that much more work is demanded of American railroads than of European railroads, Mr. Hadley
presents the following table:

Countries.	Population.	Miles run by Trains annually.	Annual Train Service per head of Population.
United States......(1889)	61,000,000	724,000,000	12
Great Britain......(1889)	38,000,000	303,000,000	8
Germany (1889)...	48,000,000	181,000,000	3¾
France (1888)......	38,000,000	145,000,000	3¾
Austria-Hungary ..(1887)	40,000,000	66,000,000	1⅝
India (1889)	200,000,000	51,000,000	0¼

And he adds: "These figures are for passenger trains
and freight trains together, as some countries do not give
statistics of the two separately; but the general results
would be nearly the same if passenger trains alone could
be considered. The figures show that, for every man,
woman and child, a train is run twelve miles annually in
the United States, in Great Britain eight miles, in Germany or France a little less than four miles, in Austria
not much more than a mile and a half, and in British
India less than a quarter of a mile."

This statement, even if correct, is certainly misleading.
No allowance is made for the greater distances and the
greater average haul in America, and none for our bulky

raw products, which require more car room than the manufactured goods predominating as freight in Europe.

If Mr. Hadley's statement of miles run by trains annually is used in connection with Mr. Poor's statement showing the length, for 1889, of the railroads of the countries given in the above table, it can be shown that the average number of trains run annually per mile is considerably less here than in Europe:

Countries.	Length of Railroad in miles (1889).	Miles run by Trains annually.	Average Number of Trains per mile per annum.
United States	161,396	724,000,000	4,485
Great Britain	19,930	303,000,000	15,203
Germany	25,360	181,000,000	7,137
France	21,910	145,000,000	6,618
Austria-Hungary	15,990	66,000,000	4,127

It is seen that while the average number of trains run per mile per annum is only 4,485 in the United States, it is 6,618 in France, 7,137 in Germany, and 15,203 in Great Britain. In Austria-Hungary it is somewhat less than here. It is not claimed that this is in every respect a fair argument; but it is at least as fair as Mr. Hadley's. As has been stated before, the average earnings per train mile are larger in the United States than in most nations, and, excepting Sweden, railway capital has the highest gross earnings of any nation in the world; and when Mr. Hadley bases his argument in favor of higher rates for American railroads than for those of Europe upon the claim that the latter secure larger train loads, he simply reasons from false premises.

Mr. Hadley then continues:

"But why cannot our railroad men, with our present train service, secure larger loads by making lower rates, and give us cheap service as well as plenty of it? Why cannot we secure two good things instead of one? For two reasons: First, because it is not certain that low rates

will be followed by greatly increased travel; second, because such increased travel would not be so economical to
handle in America as it is in Europe.   It is wrong to assume that, because reductions of charges in Europe have
increased travel enormously, they would have a proportionate effect in America and a corresponding advantage
in American railroad economy.   It is a somewhat significant fact that second-class trains at reduced rates have
been extremely successful in Europe and not at all so in
America.   Other things being equal, the American public
would be glad to have its travel at lower fares; but it cares
more for comfort and speed, and for being able to travel
at its own times, than for a slight difference in charge.
The assumption so frequently made, that a reduction in
fares would cause an enormous increase in travel in this
country, is for the most part a pure assumption, not borne
out by the facts."

The great increase in business which has everywhere
followed reductions in postage rates, telegraph rates and
street-car fares, as well as railroad rates, sufficiently refutes
the assertion that it is not certain that low rates would be
followed by greatly increased travel.   If the second class
has not been as successful here as in Europe this is solely
due to the fact that the American railroad companies have
systematically discouraged second-class travel by forcing
passengers into filthy and over-crowded cars.   The statement that increased travel would not be so economical to
handle in America as in Europe scarcely needs a reply.   If,
as Prof. Hadley says, the American public demand more
frequent trains than the people of Europe, and if these
frequent trains are not at present profitable to our railroad
companies, it would seem to be plainly to their interest to
hold out every inducement to the public to increase travel
and thus fill their trains.

Mr. Hadley does not aid his argument when, referring
to the Hungarian zone system, he says: "The impor-

tance of the zone system in Austria and in Hungary lies in the fact that its adoption was accompanied by a great reduction in rates. The unit rate for slow, third-class trains, which had previously been nearly a cent and a half a mile, was reduced to less than one cent. . . . The use of railroads under the new system, though vastly greater than it was before, is vastly less than that of a well-managed American road at American rates." Mr. Hadley inadvertently presents here one of the very best reasons why our passenger rates should be reduced.

The fact is, railroad men are opposed, and always have been opposed, to reduction of rates, and to all progressive movements that require increased expenditures or threaten to temporarily reduce their revenues. When the introduction of the zone system was first advocated in Hungary it was opposed by just such men and just such arguments.

No one can contradict the following facts, viz. : That the average cost of European roads is much greater than that of American roads; that the number of railroad employes per mile is much greater there than here; that much larger sums are expended for repairing and improving the roads, and that therefore the lives of passengers are much safer in Europe than in America; and that the average speed and corresponding accommodations of European trains, and especially those of England, Germany, France and Austria-Hungary, compare quite favorably with the average speed and corresponding accommodations of our roads. It is, under these circumstances, absurd to claim that the higher prices charged by American roads are due to the greater cost of service.

Mr. Hadley's labors as a railroad author have, it seems, greatly increased his corporation bias. In an address which he delivered before the American Bankers' Association at New Orleans in November, 1891, upon the subject of "Recent Railroad Legislation and its Effects upon the Finances of the Country," he made a number of assertions which ill comport with the fairness of a public statistician or the wisdom of a Yale professor. After a few introductory remarks, Prof. Hadley made the following statement:

"Every one knows that railroad property has fallen in value since the passage of the Interstate Commerce Act four years and a half ago ; few have made any accurate estimate of the amount of that fall. Let us take the stock of the leading railroad systems centering in Chicago as a type. Here we find an aggregate shrinkage of over $60,000,000, or more than one-quarter of the par value of the stocks.

	Par Value.	Price. Apr. 4, 1887.	Nov. 4, 1891.	Shrinkage.
C., M. & St. P.	$30,904,261	93	75	$ 5,560,000
" " Preferred	21,555,900	122	119	647,000
C. & N. W.	31,365,900	121	116	1,568,000
" " Preferred	22,325,454	148	139	2,009,000
C., R. I. & P.	41,960,000	126	82	18,462,000
C., B. & Q.	77,540,500	140	98	32,567,000
Total	$225,651,000			$60,815,000

The table shows that fifty-one million of these sixty million dollars are the shrinkage of the Chicago, Rock Island and Pacific and the Chicago, Burlington and Quincy stocks. It is surprising that Prof. Hadley should be ignorant of the real causes of this depreciation, which are known to nearly every Granger in the West. In 1887 the Chicago, Rock Island and Pacific Railroad Company owned 1,121 miles of road, only 172 of which were outside of the States of Illinois and Iowa. In 1891 the same company owned 2,725 miles of road, with 1,776 miles outside of Illinois and Iowa and scattered through

Missouri, Kansas, Nebraska, Colorado, Indian Territory and Oklahoma. In Kansas alone the Rock Island system grew from two miles in 1887 to 1,059 miles in 1891. In other words, to a little over a thousand miles of *good* road the company's managers added nearly 2,000 miles of poor road and a proportionate amount of new stock, and the depreciation in the company's stock which followed was no greater than one should have expected under such circumstances. The managers of the Rock Island and the promoters of these new lines found the transactions to their advantage, while the original stockholders of the company had to bear the imposition, as hundreds of thousands of railroad stockholders had done before them. But neither the law of Congress nor that of any State was to blame for this depreciation of the Rock Island stock.

Since 1891, railroad stocks have advanced on an average at least twenty per cent., and during the last sixty days have declined about twenty-five per cent., although there has been no essential change in interstate or State legislation. It is certainly as fair to call the advance the ultimate result of restrictive railroad legislation as to attribute to that legislation the shrinkage above referred to. Extensive speculations similar to those just mentioned were, during the same period, indulged in by the managers of the C., B. & Q. Railroad Company and its protegé, the C., B. & N., who, in addition to this, greatly injured their road in 1888 by the unjust provocation of the engineers' strike. So destructive were this strike and its consequences to the company's business that it is difficult to account for the motives of those who provoked and stubbornly pro-longed it except upon the theory that it played an important role in their stock manipulations.

But the recent legislation of a considerable number of States has, in Prof. Hadley's opinion, been still more detrimental to railroad interests than that of Congress. He says:

"In the second place, the legislatures of several States, stimulated by the example of Congress, hastened to pass in imitation, of the Interstate Commerce Act, laws which, in many instances, went far beyond their model in point of stringency. Examples are furnished by the statutes of Iowa, Maryland, Minnesota and South Carolina in 1887-88; of Florida in 1888-89, and of no less than thirteen States in 1889-90, viz.: Georgia, Iowa, Kentucky, Massachusetts, Mississippi, New Hampshire, New Jersey, North Dakota, Ohio, Rhode Island, South Dakota, Virginia, Wyoming; as well as by the recently adopted Constitution of Kentucky. The legislation of 1890-91 shows a slight reaction against the movement of the three years previous.

"In two respects the State legislatures went quite beyond the scope of the Interstate Commerce Act. They tried to prescribe safety appliances to the operating department, and rates to the traffic department. Of the first of these groups little need be said, except that as a rule they have failed to accomplish any great progress toward the result in view, and have in some instances actually hindered such progress. The attempt at prescribing rates was more serious. It involved a return to the methods of the Granger legislation, fifteen years earlier, which had operated so disastrously upon the railroads and the public alike. The system of commissioners with powers to make schedules which should be at least *prima facie* evidence of reasonable rates had, during the intervening period, never been wholly abandoned; but the powers thus conferred had been sparingly exercised. It was either left unused, as was generally the case in the North from 1877 to 1887, or the schedule rates were put so high as not to interfere with good railroad economy, of which examples are seen in Georgia and other parts of the South. But from the year 1887 onward there was a pressure upon the Commissioners to make schedules, and to make them low; and lest these boards should not be able to reflect the popular feeling directly enough, they were, in some instances, no longer to be appointed by the Governor, but elected by popular vote. The law which was most severely applied and attracted most public attention was that of Iowa. . . The agitation against the railroads has many points in common with the land agitation in Ireland. Absentee ownership is at the bottom of the trouble in either case. Property is owned in one place and used in another, and the users, not satisfied with the conditions of use, insist on taking the business direction into their own hands. They claim the right to fix rates in Iowa for the same general reasons by which they claim the right to fix rents in Ireland."

It must be presumed that Mr. Hadley is ignorant of the fact that under the Iowa Commissioners' tariff the gross earnings of the Iowa railroads increased $7,000,000, or more than 17 per cent., in about three years, and their net revenue increased in proportion. Never have the railroads or the people of Iowa enjoyed a healthier prosperity than they do at present. It is true that the State of Iowa denies to the railroad companies the right to charge what they please; but this claim does not prevent them from doing justice to the absentee owner of railroad property. That absentee owners of property are disposed to take undue advantage of those who use it is illustrated in the very case which Mr. Hadley cites. So flagrant was the injustice done by the English landlord to the Irish tenant that the English Parliament was constrained to interfere and correct it.

Mr. Hadley says further:

"It is seen in Iowa to-day, where, as a result of radical legislation with regard to rates, railroad construction has almost entirely ceased, the average for the years 1888-90 being less than fifty miles."

Now Professor Hadley hails from the State of Connecticut, where railroads are permitted to make their own tariffs and where legislators are supposed not to be hostile to them. According to Poor's Manual, that State had 1,004.02 miles of railroad in 1888, and just 2.52 miles more in 1891, while Iowa had 8,364 miles in 1888, 8,436 in 1891, and 8,505 miles on January 1, 1893. Will Mr. Hadley please explain why railroad construction has ceased in Connecticut? Iowa has one mile of railroad for every 227 inhabitants, and Connecticut has one for every 741 inhabitants, although the per capita valuation is $473 in the latter, and only $273 in the former State. Nor have other Eastern States done much better than Connecticut. During the three years 1888-1891 there were built 74 miles of railroad in New Hampshire, 50 in Vermont, 23 in Massachusetts and 9 in Rhode Island. Iowa has an area of 56,000 square miles and a population of 1,911,896, an assessed valuation of $520,000,000; New England has an area of 66,400 square miles, a population of 4,700,745, and an assessed valuation of $3,500,000,000. Yet Iowa has 1,576 miles of railroad more than all the New England States together. She has a railroad net as close as that of the Empire State, having one mile of road to about 6½ miles of territory, although the population of that State is three times as dense as hers. Nevertheless, railroad construction is at present active in Iowa, several lines of road are in the process of construction at the present writing, and there is every indication of still greater activity in the near future. The *Railway Age* of March 17, 1893, in a detailed list of new lines projected or under construction in the United States, gives for Connecticut only 32 miles, while it gives for Iowa 930 miles.

Mr. Hadley continues:

"It is seen to some extent in the Northwest as a whole. At the close of the year 1887 the States included by Henry V. Poor in the Central, Northern and Northwestern groups had 25,040 miles of road, while those of the South Atlantic, Gulf and Mississippi Valley had but 24,567. To-day this relation is reversed: the Northwest has but 27,294 miles, while the South has 30,696."

Had Mr. Hadley taken the pains to look up the population of these groups he would have found that the "South" is fully three times as populous as the "Northwest," and that therefore his figures prove nothing beyond the fact that at the present rate of gain the railroad facilities of the South will in a quarter of a century be equal to those of the Northwest to-day.

But the argument is weak in another respect. The State in the Southern group that made by far the greatest gain in railroad mileage during the period mentioned by Mr. Hadley is Georgia, which gained about 1,000 miles in three years, yet that State prescribed rates for railroad companies six years before Iowa did, and has for many years exerted a more thorough control over her railroads than perhaps any other State in the Union. The smallest increase is in West Virginia, which during the period given gained an average of only .69 miles per annum ; and yet in West Virginia railroads charge their own rates and usually have their own way.

Finally Prof. Hadley says :

"Where are we to find the limit to such unwise action ? The United States Supreme Court can do something and has shown a disposition to do something. In the Minnesota cases it repudiated the doctrine of uncontrolled rights on the part of the legislature to make rates, as emphatically as it repudiated the doctrine of uncontrolled rights on the part of agents of the corporation in the Granger cases, twelve years before."

It is evident that Mr. Hadley is as much mistaken in his interpretation of the decision of the court as he has been in his other assertions, as will be seen from the following extract from Judge Blatchford's opinion in Budd vs. New York, in which he says, "The main 'question involved is whether this court will adhere to its decision in Munn vs. Illinois."

The court first quoted from the opinion of Judge Andrew of the Court of Appeals of New York, as follows : "The opinion further said that the criticism to which the case of Munn vs. Illinois had been subjected proceeded mainly upon a limited and strict construction and definition of the police power ; that there was little reason, under our system of government, for placing a close and narrow interpretation on the police power, or restricting its scope so as to hamper the legislative power in dealing with the varying necessities of society and the new circumstances as they arise calling for legislative intervention in the public interest ; and that no serious invasion of constitutional guarantees by the legislature could withstand for a long time the searching influence of public opinion, which was sure to come sooner or later to the side of law, order and justice, however it might have been swayed for a time by passion or prejudice or whatever aberrations might have marked its course."

Judge Blatchford then said: "We regard these views, which we have referred to as announced by the Court of Appeals of New York, so far as they support the validity of the statute in question, as sound and just. . . . We must regard the principle maintained in Munn vs. Illinois as firmly established."

General Horace Porter has made a contribution to the railway rate literature by an article which appeared in the

December, 1891, number of the *North American Review.*
Unfortunately many of the General's statements are either
false or misleading. Thus, in a table which he presents
for the purpose of comparing the passenger rates of
Europe with those of the United States, he gives the regular
first-class schedule rates for the United Kingdom, France
and Germany and the average earnings per passenger per
mile for this country. That this is an unfair comparison
needs no further argument, especially when it is remembered that in Europe from 85 to 90 per cent. of all passengers are carried in the third class at a regular rate
averaging about 1½ cents per mile, and that considerable
reductions are made for excursion, commutation and
return tickets.

But General Porter says concerning American rates:

"When we take into consideration the excursion and
the commutation rates, we find first-class passengers
carried as low as half a cent a mile."

Now the question arises whether American railway
companies carry passengers at such rates with or without
loss to themselves. If they are carried at a loss, an
injustice is done to the regular passengers, whose fare
must not only make up the loss, but yield a larger profit
than would otherwise be necessary. If, on the other
hand, a rate of half a cent a mile can be made remunerative, there is certainly no justice in maintaining rates
five and six times as large on well-patronized lines.
General Porter places stress upon our superior accommodations in the way of lighting, ventilation, ice-water, lava-
tories, and free carriage of baggage, etc., and then adds:

" In this connection we must also recollect that the cost
of fuel, wages and all construction materials is considerably higher here than in Europe, while the population
from which the railways derive their support is much

more sparse; the United States having 166,000 miles of railway with a population of 63,000,000, while Europe has only 135,000 miles with a population of 335,000,000."

We grant the point which the General makes on ventilation, ice-water, etc.; but, to make the comparison a fair one, he should also have referred to the much greater cost of European roads, to their much greater number of employes per mile, to the much shorter haul, to the higher price of their fuel, to the superiority of their road-bed and the greater security of their passengers. Moreover, whether the railroads of a country are profitable or not cannot be ascertained by merely comparing miles of road with square miles of territory and number of inhabitants. British India has a population of 275,000,000 and only about 16,000 miles of railroad, and yet her roads are scarcely as profitable as our own. China has 3,000,000 and Asia has about 4,000,000 people to every mile of railroad, but so far their railroads have proved no bonanza. The question is not how many people there are to each mile of railroad, but rather to what extent the railroad is used by the people. The amount of freight carried annually by the railways of the United States is about 680,000,000 tons, or 85,000,000,000 ton miles, and the number of passengers carried is about 535,000,000, representing an aggregate of travel of nearly 13,000,-000,000 miles. This shows an average of 1,300 tons of freight carried one mile, and 200 miles traveled annually for each inhabitant of the nation, and a greater use of railway facilities than that of any other country in the world. The income of the railroads per capita is $17 in the United States, $11 in the United Kingdom, $5 in Germany, $4 in France, and still less in Italy, Austria and Russia. The average freight haul is 63 miles in

Europe and 120 miles in the United States; the average passenger haul 15 miles in Europe and 24 miles in the United States. It has already been shown that the average earnings per train mile are also larger here than there. Röll's Encyclopedia of Railroads for 1892 shows that in France the average rate for all traffic for the year 1888 was for passengers 1.45 cents per mile, and for freight 1.14 cents per ton per kilometer, and that the nation had also received by way of free or reduced rates on Government business during that year benefits to the amount of $59,000,000. Large reductions have been made during the past year in passenger rates.

The General indulges in making the stereotyped railroad charge that ''the legislatures of several of the States have enacted laws to effect a reduction of rates, the literal obedience to some of which would amount to the practical confiscation of railway property.''

The General or any of his friends cannot name a road that was ever confiscated by legislation, or even seriously injured. It is a fact that the very legislation of which railroad managers so bitterly complain has had a beneficial influence on railroad earnings. Thus, in Iowa, where, according to the testimony of railroad men, Grangerism has reigned supreme during the past few years, railroad earnings increased between 1889 and 1892 from $37,000,-000 to $44,000,000, or more than 18 per cent. Still better results could have been secured if the railroad managers had been in sympathy with the law. There is no doubt that they would gladly suffer, or rather have their companies suffer, a loss of revenue, if this would lead to a repeal of the laws and restore to them the power to manipulate rates for their own purposes.

But the General comes to the main point of his article

when he complains against "the unreasonable requirements and restrictions of the Interstate Commerce Law." He says:

"Principal among these are what is known as the 'long and short haul clause,' which prohibits railway companies from receiving any greater compensation in the aggregate for a shorter than for a longer haul over the same line in the same direction, the shorter being included within the longer distance; and the anti-pooling clause, which prevents railway companies from entering into any agreement with each other for an apportionment of joint earnings."

If we carefully examine the railroad literature of the last four years, we find that it has concentrated its efforts toward the creation of public sentiment in favor of the repeal of these two clauses of the Interstate Commerce Law. Railroad men are well aware of the fact that, with these two clauses stricken out, the Interstate Commerce Law would be practically valueless, and in clamoring for their repeal they evince a persistency worthy of a better cause. The practices which these clauses aim to prohibit cannot be defended upon any consideration of justice and equity, and it is folly to expect the American people to sacrifice their convictions of right to the selfish interest of a comparatively small number of persons interested in the manipulation of railroad stocks.

The July, 1891, number of the *Forum* contains an article on the operation of the Interstate Commerce Law from the pen of Aldace F. Walker, formerly a member of the Interstate Commerce Commission, and now commissioner of the Western Traffic Association. Mr. Walker evidently belongs to the old school of railroad men, who have not yet accepted the Granger decision. Referring to it, he says:

"This decision was not unanimous, and the reasoning

presented was not so convincing as to command universal acceptance. It was at once challenged by the corporations, and has been from time to time attacked in the same tribunal; it has not yet been withdrawn, but it has been materially modified, notably in a case from Minnesota, decided in 1890, when it was established that there is a limit beyond which the State cannot go in reducing railway rates, which limit would be passed in case a State should attempt to deprive a corporation of its property, without due process of law, by fixing rates too low to permit of a fair remuneration for its use. A large debatable ground yet remains open, with a possibility that the position of the railway in Federal jurisprudence may eventually be radically modified."

The passage quoted clearly indicates that railroad men expect better things of the court in the future, but Mr. Walker is much mistaken in supposing the court materially modified the Granger decision, as will be seen by referring to the case of Budd vs. the State of New York, decided in February, 1892, by the same court.

Mr. Walker, unlike Mr. Depew, candidly admits the former universality of the evil of discrimination. He says:

"In order to secure traffic, a railway official felt called upon to underbid his rival. He gave the shipper a private rate, a rebate, a free pass—anything in the shape of a concession or a favor. The land was honeycombed with special arrangements of innumerable forms, all secret, because otherwise they would have been useless, and all forced upon the carriers by the exigencies of unbridled competition. Many shippers became wealthy from such gains. Others were envious of like success. At last the public sense of justice demanded a reform."

And Mr. Walker's candor rises to a still higher pitch when he admits that the ingenuity of railroad managers has found ways to evade the Interstate Commerce Law. The following passage from the Commissioner's article will, no doubt, be a great surprise to such law-abiding and confiding managers as Mr. Depew:

"There was nothing in the law specifically forbidding the payment of 'commissions,' and it was found that the routing of business might be secured by a slight expenditure of that nature to a shipper's friend. Other kindred devices were suggested, some new, some old ; the payment of rent, clerk hire, dock charges, elevator fees, drayage, the allowance of exaggerated claims, free transportation within some single State—a hundred ingenious forms of evading the plain requirements of the law were said to be in use. The demoralization was not by any means confined to the minor roads. Shippers were ready to give information to other lines concerning concessions which were offered them, and to state the sum required to control their patronage. A freight agent, thus appealed to, at first perhaps might let the business go, but when the matter became more serious and he saw one large shipper after another seeking a less desirable route, he was very apt to throw up his hands and fall in with the procession."

Mr. Walker is very severe on the Interstate Commerce Act, which, he says, might in its present form "well be entitled, 'An act to promote railway bankruptcies and consolidations by driving weak roads out of competitive business.'" To remedy the evil which, in his opinion, the act causes, he favors the granting of differentials by the stronger to the weaker roads. Such a device is simply a species of pool under a less offensive name. Its manifest object is to maintain rates through a conspiracy of rival railroads. Mr. Walker admits this when he says :

"It operates in practice to affect a distribution of the traffic somewhat roughly, giving rise to frequent dissensions and bickerings over the 'differentials' which are allowed ; but after all it has enabled the trunk lines usually to secure a better maintenance of tariff rates and a better observance of the provisions of the law against private rebates and discriminations than has been attainable in other sections of the country where different conditions make such an arrangement impracticable. It vividly illustrates, however, the necessity of some plan by which common business may be divided."

This problem, which apparently causes so much perplexity to railroad managers, would soon be solved if railroad abuses were done away with. So long as these abuses exist and rates are maintained by artificial means there will be bickering and strife for business which legitimately belongs to others. Mr. Walker then bewails the proscription of the pool, saying :

"It may be stated without fear of contradiction that if the carriers had been left free to make arrangements among themselves upon which each line might rely for eventually receiving in some form a fair share of competitive traffic, the temptation for secret rate-cutting would have been in great measure removed and the country would have been spared most of the traffic disturbances and illegitimate contrivances for buying business which have since been periodically rife."

This argument amounts to this, that, rather than place a law upon our statute books which reckless railroad managers might be strongly tempted to violate, they should be permitted to combine and control the highways and levy *ad libitum* upon the commerce of the country It is a most preposterous proposition.

The article especially condemns the long and short haul clause of the law. That this clause is injurious to the commerce of the country is, however, not obvious from his reasoning. Mr. Walker makes the statement that this clause of the law "has removed from many jobbing centers important advantages which they previously had, and has enabled interior communities, formerly of little apparent consequence, to deal directly with distant

markets." If he means by this that this feature
of the law has equalized shipping throughout the country,
he is doubtless right. If he wishes us to infer, however,
that it prevents the railroad companies from doing substantial justice to all, he presumes altogether too much
upon the credulity of his readers.

Another article from the same author appeared under
the title "Unregulated Competition Self-destructive," in
the December, 1891, number of the same periodical. He
commences his article with an inquiry into the pedigree
and merit of the time-bonored proverb, "Competition is
the life of trade," and arrives at the conclusion that the
phrase is fatherless and insignificant. He says:

"'Competition is the life of trade;' 'Competition is
the death of trade;' one phrase is as true as the other.
For all that appears, it was a toss-up which of the two
should become current as the expression of the general
thought."

It is its general recognition that gives a truth a
proverb's currency. Mr. Walker sneers at a disagreeable
proverb because, like the majority of his colleagues, he
holds the masses in contempt. He gives his estimate of
popular intelligence in the following words:

"Unfortunately most men do not think worthily, or do
not think at all; they are ruled by phrases, and they
catch the crude ideas of others as they fly."

Mr. Walker's whole argument is one in favor of the
legalization of the pool, though he carefully avoids the
word which grates so harshly on the American ear. He
makes the broad statement, without offering the least proof
in support of it, that measures have been everywhere
adopted "to subdue and ameliorate the evil results of
inordinate and excessive competitive strife," and then
he asks :

"Has not the time come for a reversal of the legislative attitude? Would it not be well for Congress, State legislatures and the judiciary to cease their futile attempts to maintain unqualified freedom of competition, and substitute therefore a recognition of the right of every industry to combine under proper supervision, and to make agreements for the maintenance of just and reasonable prices, the prevention of the enormous wastage consequent upon warlike conditions, and the preservation of existing institutions through the years to come?"

Mr. Walker then proceeds to make the bold prediction that revolution and anarchy will follow if the demands of the railroad corporations are not complied with, saying :

"Unless this course is adopted a social convulsion may fairly be apprehended, forced by the universal and necessary repudiation of existing laws and rules of decision, and by the general formation of combinations without their pale."

This is a strange threat indeed, and unworthy of a man who has held as great a public trust as Mr. Walker has. The article also contains the statement that combinations do not extinguish competition. "They regulate it," says Mr. Walker, "with more or less efficiency, and they often go so far as to suspend its operation in respect to one or more important features of the strife; for example, the price paid or the time consumed. But as long as the employer or the purchaser has a choice, so long there is competition." Here is a sample of Mr. Walker's irony, for the choice which the shipper has under the pool is simply Hobson's choice.

Mr. Walker has also an article in the August, 1892, number of the *Forum*, the substance of which is to show that organizations among railroad companies, like the Western Traffic Association, are necessarry for the purpose of restraining competition among them. He holds that such competition as exists in almost all other lines of business "is radically vicious to all interests, however pleasant and desirable it may seem to self-styled anti-monopolists," and that "it is a calamity not only to the owners of the roads, but to the public also."

According to his statement, the Traffic Association is simply a little innocent and inoffensive organization whose duty it is only to maintain rates, and he sees nothing wrong in allowing a few representatives of corporations to meet in secret and discuss, scheme and levy such a tax upon the commerce of this country as may suit their convenience; and he regrets that their attempts are "hampered by legislation which forbids the formation of pools." In other words, he proposes to have the case in court decided by a jury made up entirely of the parties at interest in the case. This piece of effrontery is about on a par with the average argument of this class of pleaders.

Suppose we apply the same rule to other classes. Take the farmers, for instance. Let them have an organization for the purpose of maintaining rates, with their representatives meeting in secret and fixing the price of their produce and asking the Government to enforce their orders, pools and edicts, so as to afford them relief from selling corn at ten cents per bushel, beef and pork at a dollar and a half per hundred, and hay at two dollars per ton, and their other produce at proportionate rates. Who would condemn such an organization more severely than the advocates of the Traffic Association ? They never find terms sufficiently expressive with which to condemn the Farmers' Alliance and other kindred associations, which are organized solely for the purpose of lawfully correcting existing abuses and of forming a wholesome public sentiment.

It is evident that some progress is being made upon this question, as Mr. Walker admits that " the fortunes which have been made are seen to have been the result of dealings in stocks and in titles, the consequences of which, if involving wrong, are rightly charged against the lax legislation which has made such operations possible." " Every person seeking for the services of a common carrier is entitled to know that he is charged no more than his neighbor who obtains the same service under the same conditions." " The theory that any unjust discrimination or unjust preference or advantage in respect to individuals, communities or descriptions of traffic must be suppressed by the State, has become firmly lodged in legislation." This improvement in the sentiment of railroad men is gratifying.

This gentleman, as has already been stated, was for several years a member of the Interstate Commerce Commission, a board created by Congress for the special purpose of enforcing the law which he so unreservedly condemns. No doubt Mr. Walker performed the duties of his office as he understood them; but if he held then the views which he holds now, his work must have been a hindrance rather than a help to the commission.

Among financial journals, so many of which are devoted to the support of vicious and demoralizing methods, and are ever ready to defend whatever is bad in corporation management, it is refreshing to find occasionally one that exposes abuses and favors the earning of legitimate dividends, and it is a pleasure to quote the following from the June number, 1892, of the *Banker's Magazine:*

" There are two widely differing theories concerning the

management of railroads in this country; one theory is that profits should be acquired from fluctuations in the stock, and the other is that the profits should be acquired in the old-fashioned way, by performing a useful service and receiving a reward therefor, to be divided among the stockholders in the way of a dividend.   These two theories are so different in their practical operation that they give rise to the most diverse consequences.   Of course, many railroads are not dividend-earning, and with these the profits to the managers and those who are allied with them must come from stock fluctuations and from whatever sucking arrangements can be devised whereby their vitality or sustenance can be acquired by the favored few who are in control.   Unfortunately, there are many railroads in this condition, the history of which is too well known to require description.   Once in control, the way is easy to retain it and to make money by a thousand devices which ingenious and unscrupulous managers are constantly planning and putting into operation.

" The consequences of the other theory are as different, both to the corporate property and to the public, as can be imagined.   When a railroad is properly managed and earning dividends, a policy of development is adopted, having for its end the natural expansion of the property in harmony with the growth of the country, the needs of business and the desires of the people.   The fruits of such a policy may not be apparent at once, but they inevitably come, and, when they are reaped, are enjoyed and appreciated by all.   Only by such a policy can our roads ever become great, commanding the confidence of the people, and fulfilling their highest uses; in short, only by such a policy can a railroad be brought to a high degree of perfection.

" The difference is clearly seen by contrasting a road of this character with one that is run by the Wall Street method for stock-jobbing purposes.   By this method dividends are not regarded as of so much consequence to investors as an instrument or argument for affecting the value of the stock.   In other words, if a dividend is earned and paid at all, it is chiefly as an instrument or agency for stock-jobbing purposes, and not because the road is managed primarily for this purpose. Furthermore, dividends, too often, are disregarded altogether, as well as any policy of permanent improvement or of general development. The cardinal idea always is, how can the road be maintained and manipulated so as to cause the largest variations in the stock and the most money for the managers?

"Too many managers, as is well known, have made great sums for themselves and built additions long in advance of their means, and have seriously crippled their corporations by so doing. But they have made fortunes for themselves. What the great majority of mankind consider is the immediate present, and not the future.

"It is undoubtedly a hard thing for those who are conducting their corporations in an honest and able manner, for the benefit of their owners, to keep still while their enemies are pounding them and glorifying those who are managing their corporations for personal and corrupt ends; but all cheap and false practices must finally lead to disaster. We hear a great deal of this kind of thing nowadays. One of the evil effects of speculation and newspaper reading is, that people have got in the way of not thinking much for themselves; of regarding as truth whatever is printed, and of not opening their eyes wide enough to discover the shallowness of the reasonings and falsehoods that are put forth at the behests of speculators, or of those who are managing corporations for speculative purposes. The American people have had an amazing experience in losses from following advice thus plentifully and freely given; nevertheless, there seem to be persons left who are willing to listen and fall into the old ways and be trapped, as so many others have been in the past. There is a considerable class, having means and nothing to do, who perhaps might just as well lose their money in poker, railroad or grain speculation as in any other way, for this furnishes about the only source of amusement to them; but, after all, there is no reason why railroads should be managed so exclusively for the amusement of this class. The time is coming, and probably is not far

off, when they will get enough of it; and railroad investors will conclude that dividends for themselves are better
than profits for speculators; and when they do, all stock-
jobbing managers will be consigned to the limbo which is
their proper destination."

This magazine is edited by Mr. Albert S. Bolles, author
of several excellent financial works. We are much indebted to him for the sound banking system which we now
have, and which has contributed so largely to the unex-
ampled prosperity which this country has enjoyed for the
last thirty years.

Our national banking system illustrates well how service
able the corporation may be to a people when its use is
restricted by wholesome laws to the performance of its
proper functions.

The old United States Bank was organized for practically the same purposes as our present national banks,
but for lack of proper restrictions its use was soon perverted to ignoble purposes. The bank managers showed
so much partiality in the distribution of their favors and
accommodations, and meddled in politics to such an extent, that the people became disgusted with it, and a
renewal of its charter was refused.

Mr. Clay clearly saw how dangerous a great money
power might become to our country, and, in opposing the
extension of the bank's charter, said:

"The power to charter companies is one of the most
exalted attributes of sovereignty. In the exercise of this
gigantic power we have seen an East India Company created, which is in itself a sovereignty, which has subverted
empires and set up new dynasties, and has not only made
war, but war against its legitimate sovereign! Under the
influence of this power we have seen rise a South Sea Company, and a Mississippi Company, that distracted and
convulsed all Europe, and menaced a total overthrow of
all credit and confidence, and universal bankruptcy."

Can we afford to ignore the lessons of history?

Mr. Henry Clews makes some spicy and pertinent observations on railroad men's methods in an article which recently appeared in the *Railway Age.* Mr. Clews seems to have but little confidence in the average railroad director. He advises stockholders to exercise constant vigilance and defensive conservatism, "lest they become the instruments by which unscrupulous and crafty directors work out schemes that are in reality nothing but frauds or robbery." And then he adds :

"In estimating corporate acts we must never forget that, while the best of men will bear watching as to their individual dealings with others, they need to be doubly watched when they sit around a corporation board and vote as to transactions in respect of which none of them can be called to personal account. Temptations attack with enormous force when the gains are prospectively great and the risk of penalty inappreciable or non-existent."

Mr. Clews also tells us how roads are wrecked by their boards of directors. "In one case," he says, "the stock of a leading railway, which in 1880 sold at 174, in 1884 sold at 22½, and in 1885 at 22. This vast shrinkage of value was not owing to panic or to stringency of money, nor did it arise from a diminution of traffic on the original line ; but it was because consolidation had been pushed to an extreme by the directors of the corporation, so much so that the entire system yielded no dividends ; a fleet and useful animal had been loaded down with dead wood and rubbish till he could scarcely crawl ; barren acres had been added to an originally fruitful farm until the whole estate could hardly pay taxes ; a mass of rotten apples had been thrown into the measure with sound fruit, and buyers refused the whole as a mere heap of corruption. And it was generally believed that the men who perpetrated this mischief under the names of ' construction,' ' requisite consolidation,' ' absorption of necessary branches,' etc., had made a great deal of money by it and had not made it honestly. But it was all done pursuant to legal forms and by boards of directors, so that the defrauded stockholders were without remedy."

Mr. Clews then gives us a more detailed account of the way in which branch roads are built and absorbed, viz. :

"Given a useful, well constructed, dividend-paying road, a body of people with some capital and political influence, aided by some of the directors of this prosperous line; construct a branch road to some outside point; the more important such point the better, but that is of small consequence. The road gets itself built; it is bonded for more than it cost, and it cost twice as much as it ought, since the constructors were all together in the ring and have favored each other. Then the capital stock is fixed at so much, and this is mostly distributed among the constructors. The road then, swelled to a fictitious price of three or four to one, and not worth anything to start with, is ripe for absorption and consolidation. Its directors and those of the main line meet, confer and vote the measure through. They all profit by it, more or less, but their profits are enormously in excess of the trifling losses due to the shrinkage of values of the shares of the main line. A director of the main line may perhaps lose $20,000 on a thousand shares, but what is this when compared to a gain of hundreds of thousands in his holdings of the branch road, whose liabilities are assumed by his victimized corporation? And such a director would not be equal to the demands of his covetousness if he had not sold thousands of shares short, in anticipation of the fall which the transactions of himself and his associates were inevitably bound to produce."

Mr. Clews concludes his article with the following passage:

" The profits realized on the speculative constructions are enormous and have constituted the chief source of the phenomenal fortunes piled up by our railroad millionaires within the last twenty years. It is no exaggeration to characterize these transactions as direct frauds upon the public. They may not be such in a sense recognized by the law, for legislation has strangely neglected to provide against their perpetration; but morally they are nothing less, for they are essentially deceptive and unjust, and involve an oppressive taxation of the public at large for the benefit of a few individuals who have given no equivalent for what they get. The result of this system is that, on the average, the railroads of the country are capitalized at probably fully 50 per cent. in excess of their actual cost. The managers of the roads claim the right to earn dividends upon this fictitious capital, and it is their constant effort to accomplish that object. So far as they succeed they exercise an utterly unjust taxation upon the public by exacting a compensation in excess of a fair return upon the capital actually invested. This unjust exaction amounts to a direct charge and burden on the trade of the country which limits the ability of the American producer and merchant to compete with those of foreign nations and checks the development of our vast natural resources. In a country of 'magnificent distances' like ours the cost of transportation is one of the foremost factors affecting the capacity for progress; and the artificial enhancement of freight and passenger rates due to this false capitalization has been a far more serious bar to our material development than public opinion has yet realized. The hundreds of millions of wealth so suddenly accumulated by our railroad monarchs is the measure of this iniquitous taxation, this perverted distribution of wealth. This creation of a powerful aristocracy of wealth, which originated in a diseased system of finance, must ultimately become a source of very serious social and political disorder. The descendants of the mushroom millionaires of the present generation will consolidate into a broad and almost omnipotent money power, whose sympathies and influence will conflict with our political institutions at every point of contact. They will exercise a vast control over the larger organizations and movements of capital; monopolies will seek protection under their wing, and by the ascendancy which wealth always confers they will steadily broaden their grasp upon the legislation, the banking and commerce of the nation."

These are strong words, but they come from a man whose thirty years' experience in Wall Street enables him to speak intelligently upon this subject and who certainly cannot be accused of being prejudiced against railroad men or corporate investments. In a recent number of his *Weekly Financial Review* Mr. Clews said of the railroad stock market:

"Judgment passes for little in estimating the future of many securities, for the market is almost wholly under the control of comparatively few persons, whose operations must inevitably influence the value of thousands of millions of stocks and bonds. Never in the history of Wall Street was the value of such an enormous aggregation of securities so absolutely under the control of so small a circle as at this time. Such a state of affairs cannot be considered satisfactory; hence not only is speculation likely to be unhealthily stimulated, but the future of these combinations gives birth to a variety of uncertainties which, while they may elevate prices, will certainly not add to their stability."

If the silly claim of railroad men, that Western people do not invest in railroad securities on account of their unprofitableness, needed any answer, the above words would furnish it.

The May, 1893, number of the *North American Review* contains an article entitled "A Railway Party in Politics," by Mr. H. P. Robinson, editor of the *Railway Age.* Mr. Robinson belongs to that class of reformers who can see but one side of a question, and only a short-sighted view of that. He is as zealous as a new convert, and is expert, in the ward politician's way, in defense of the worst abuses practiced by railway men. He says:

"That the right to 'regulate' the railways, which is vested in the State, has now been carried in the West to a point not only beyond the bounds of justice, but beyond its constitutional limits, and that it would soon be impossible for any railway company in the West to keep out of bankruptcy unless some vigorous and concerted action were taken to arouse public opinion, and to compel a modification of the present policy.

"It is easy to see how much strength such a party, if formed, would possess. According to the reports of the Interstate Commerce Commission there were in the immediate employ of the railways of the United States a year and a half ago 749,301 men, all or nearly all voters, which number has now, it may be assumed, been increased to about 800,000. There are, in addition, about one million and a quarter shareholders in the railway properties of the country; and in other trades and industries immediately dependent upon the railways for their support there are estimated to be engaged, as principals or employes, over one million voters more. These three classes united would give at once a massed voting strength of some three millions of voters. There are also, in the smaller towns especially, and at points where railway shops are located, all over the country, a number of persons, small tradesmen, boarding-house keepers, etc., who are dependent for their livelihood on the patronage of railway employes, and whose vote could unquestionably be cast in harmony with any concerted employes' movement. Moreover, unlike most new parties, this party would be at no loss for the sinews of war or for the means of organization. The men whom it would include form even now almost a disciplined army. With them co-operation is already a habit. While the financial backing and the commercial and physical strength of which the party would find itself possessed from its birth would be practically unlimited. . . .

"For the present it seems to them better to believe that the people—those people who are not railway men—are acting now only in ignorance, and that as soon as they see the truth they will, by their own instinctive sense of justice, re-mould their opinions and their policy without political coercion.

"At the same time there has already come into existence in some of the Western States a movement which has its significance and its practical influence.   This is what is called the Railway Employes' Club movement. It started in Minnesota, at a small meeting of railway employes held in Minneapolis in 1888.   From that meeting the movement grew, and made a certain feeble effort, not entirely unsuccessful, to influence the State election in the fall of that year.   By the State election of 1890 the movement had grown and was better organized, and the Employes' Club did exercise considerable influence in the election of certain of the State officers and certain members of the State legislature in that year.

"From Minnesota the movement spread to Iowa, and there is no contradiction of the fact that the railway employes' vote was one of the strongest forces in the State election of the fall of 1891.   It also overflowed into Kansas, Nebraska, Missouri and Texas.   Had the election of last November been normal it is probable that the effect of the Railway Employes' Club vote would have been as visible in two or three of those States then as it had been in Iowa in the preceding year.   But in the deluge which occurred all trace of the smaller streams and currents was obliterated.   Had the members of the clubs not taken the precaution to do considerable work in the local nominating conventions of both parties they would be compelled to confess that their campaign of 1892 was a failure. . . .

"So far the clubs have admitted and will admit of no negotiations with the State committees of other parties. They hold their own meetings and decide for themselves that such and such a candidate is inimical to their interests as railway employes, and such and such a man is their friend.   Then they go to the polls and vote—voting in the main their normal party ticket, scratching only a man here and a man there, their attention being chiefly centered upon members of the boards of railroad commissioners and of the State legislatures.

" In Minnesota in 1890 their weight was thrown chiefly in favor of Republicans. In Iowa in 1891 it was given to Democrats. In all States the men whom they oppose are those who have made themselves conspicuous as 'Granger' and anti-railway politicians. The keynote of the movement and the one plank in the platform of the clubs is that the extreme anti-railroad legislation of late years has reduced the earnings of the companies to a point at which they are unable any longer to keep full forces on their payrolls or to pay such wages as they should, and that by this legislation the railway employes are necessarily the immediate sufferers. . . .

" A railway party is therefore already in existence. . . . And moreover, though accidentally only, it is working forcibly in behalf of railway interests as a whole. . . .

" Meanwhile Mr. A. F. Walker, the chairman of the Joint Committee of the Trunk Line and Central Traffic Associations, prophesies that if things go on as they are going now, before long ' the managers of the railways will be chiefly receivers.' In the year 1891 receivers were appointed for twenty-six companies in the United States, representing $84,479,000 of capital, and twenty-one companies, with 3,223 miles of road, with a capitalization of $186,000,000, were sold under foreclosure.

" It is doubtful whether the result which Mr. Walker foretells would be regarded as a calamity by the ' unimformed public opinion of the West.' That Minnesota railroad commissioner was quite sure of the public applause before he made his classic declaration that he proposed to 'shake the railroads over hell ' before he had done with them, and the Governor of Iowa, who announced that he did not care if 'every d—d railroad in the State went into bankruptcy' before the expiration of his term of office, knew that the sentiment would have the sympathies of his constituents. This attitude of the Western mind is, of course, largely explained by the fact that the people of the West do not as a rule own railway securities. In two States (the only two in the West in which, so far as I am aware, the figures have been compiled) out of 27,645 stockholders in the lines within the State borders only 359 are residents of the States. If the other 27,286 were also residents of these States (that is to say, if 27,286 of the present residents were also stockholders in the railways), it is probable that the ferocity of the public opinion in these States against railways would be materially modified."

It is evident that Mr. Robinson has not been as successful in organizing small tradesmen, boarding-house keepers, employes and shareholders into a new party as he contemplated, notwithstanding "it was at no loss for the sinews of war."

He attempts to show that this movement originated with the employes, but it is too well known that the employes who organized the movement were under pay of the railroad companies and received their instructions from the railroad managers. The statement which Mr. Robinson attributes to the Governor of Iowa undoubtedly originated in the mind of one who is laboring to modify the ferocity of "the uninformed public opinion of the West." No Governor of Iowa ever made any such statement, nor ever entertained any such sentiment. It is a sheer fabrication.

There are a number of standard text-books of law which are indispensable to the student of railroad questions desiring to go back to first principles. Only a few of them can be mentioned here.

I. F. Redfield, in his "Law of Railways," says concerning the necessity for railroad supervision:

"Railways being a species of highway, and in practice monopolizing the entire traffic, both of travel and transportation, in the country, it is just and necessary and indispensable to the public security that a strict legislative control over the subject should be constantly exercised."

Regarding the original character of the railway as a common highway, Redfield says:

"The Railways Clauses Consolidation Act provides, in detail, for the use of railways by all persons who may choose to put carriages thereon, upon the payment of the tolls demandable, subject to the provisions of the statute and the regulations of the company. The view originally taken of railways in England evidently was to treat them as a common highway, open to all who might choose to put carriages thereon. But in practice it is found necessary for the safety of the traffic that it should be exclusively under the control of the company, and hence no use is, in fact, made of the railway by others."

As to the questionable financial expedients so frequently resorted to in building American railways, this author says:

"This is not the place, nor are we disposed, to read a homily upon the wisdom of legislative grants, or the moralities of moneyed speculations in stocks on the exchange or elsewhere. But it would seem that legislation upon this subject should be conducted with sufficient deliberation and firmness so as not to invest such incorporations with such unlimited powers as to operate as a net to catch the unwary, or as a gulf in which to bury out of sight the most disastrous results to private fortunes, which has justly rendered American investments, taken as a whole, a reproach wherever the name has traveled."

The opinion is expressed in this work that under certain circumstances railroad securities should be aided by State credit, and is supported by the following argument:

"Here we have no national funded stock in convenient sums for small investment, and which, being sure, is really a great blessing to the mass of those who wish to invest moderate sums as a protection against age or calamity. In those countries where such opportunities exist, it removes all temptation to invest small sums in these enterprises, which, however necessary for the public, such small owners can but poorly afford to aid in carrying forward, and which consequently should in justice either be guaranteed or owned by the State, or at all events aided by State credit, when they become indispensable for the public convenience."

Upon the subject of eminent domain Redfield says :

"That railways are but improved highways, and are of such public use as to justify the exercise of the right of eminent domain, by the sovereign, in their construction, is now almost universally conceded."

Kent says in his "Commentaries on American Law":

" The right of eminent domain, or inherent sovereign power, gives to the legislature the control of private property for public uses, *and for public uses only*. . . . So, lands adjoining New York canals were made liable to be assumed for the public use, so far as was necessary for the great object of the canals. . . . In these and other instances which might be enumerated, the interest of the public is deemed paramount to that of any private individual ; and yet, even here, the constitutions of the United States and of most of the States of the Union have imposed a great and valuable check upon the exercise of legislative power, by declaring that private property should not be taken for public use without just compensation. . . . It undoubtedly must rest, as a general rule, in the wisdom of the legislature to determine when public uses require the assumption of private property ; but if they should take it for a purpose not of a public nature, as if the legislature should take the property of A and give it to B, or if they should vacate a grant of property, or of a franchise, under the pretext of some public use or service, such cases would be gross abuses of their discretion, and fraudulent attacks on private right, and the law would clearly be unconstitutional and void."

Concerning the construction of corporate powers Kent lays down the following rule :

"The modern doctrine is to consider corporations as having such powers as are specifically granted by the act of incorporation, or as are necessary for the purpose of carrying into effect the powers expressly granted, and as having no other. The Supreme Court of the United States declared this obvious doctrine, and it has been repeated in the decisions of the State courts. No rule of law comes with a more reasonable application, considering how lavishly charter privileges have been granted. As corporations are the mere creatures of law, established for special purposes, and derive all their powers from the acts creating them, it is perfectly just and proper that they should be obliged strictly to show their authority for the business they assume, and be confined in their operations to the mode and manner and subject matter prescribed."

As to the duties of common carriers he says:

"As they hold themselves to the world as common carriers for a reasonable compensation, they assume to do and are bound to do what is required of them in the course of their employment, if they have the requisite convenience to carry and are offered a reasonable and customary price; and if they refuse without just ground, they are liable to an action."

Judge Cooley, in his very able work, "Constitutional Limitations," refers to the so-called vested rights of corporations and the abuse growing out of them as follows:

"It is under the protection of the decision in the Dartmouth College case that the most enormous and threatening powers in our country have been created, some of the great and wealthy corporations actually having greater influence in the country at large, and upon the legislation of the country, than the States to which they owe their corporate existence. Every privilege granted or right conferred—no matter by what means or on what pretense —being made inviolable by the Constitution, the Govern-

ment is frequently found stripped of its authority in very
important particulars, by unwise, careless or corrupt legislation; and a clause of the Federal Constitution whose
purpose was to preclude the repudiation of debts and just
contracts protects and perpetuates the evil."

The late President Garfield, in one of his legislative
speeches, called attention to the fact that Chief Justice
Marshall pronounced the decision in the Dartmouth College case ten years before the steam railway was born, and
then said:

"I have ventured to criticise the judicial application of
the Dartmouth College case, and I venture the further
opinion that some features of that decision, as applied to
the railway and similar corporations, must give way under
the new elements which time has added to the problem."

Charles Fisk Beach, Jr., in his recent work entitled
"Commentaries on the Law of Private Corporations,"
well defines what constitutes dedication to a public use.
He says:

"Whenever any person pursues a public calling and
sustains such relations to the public that the people must
of necessity deal with him, and are under a moral duress
to submit to his terms if he is unrestrained by law, then,
in order to prevent extortion and an abuse of his position,
the price he may charge for his services may be regulated
by law. When private property is affected with a public
interest it ceases to be *juris privati* only. This was said
by Lord Chief Justice Hale more than three hundred years
ago in his treatise *De Portibus Maris*, and has been
accepted without objection as an essential element in the
law of property ever since."

Treating of the fiduciary position of directors and officers
of corporations, the same author says:

"The directors, officers and agents of a corporation are
held to the general rule of law resting 'upon our great
moral obligation to refrain from placing ourselves in relations which ordinarily excite a conflict between self-interest

and integrity.' The directors and officers are the agents of the company, and while acting in that capacity for it cannot deal with themselves to the detriment of the corporation. All contracts of that character are voidable at the option of the corporation."

And further he says:

"A director whose personal interests are adverse to those of the corporation has no right to act as a director. As soon as he finds he has personal interests which are in conflict with those of the company he ought to resign."

T. Carl Spelling, in his treatise on "The Law of Private Corporations," says of pooling arrangements:

" Courts long ago exercised jurisdiction to regulate rates of *quasi* public corporations, and on the same principle will refuse to enforce pooling contracts between railroad and gas companies. Such contracts are void as against public policy. . . . There is substantial harmony between the English and American definitions of monopoly, the two countries agreeing that contracts entered into by and between two or more corporations, the necessary result of whose performance will crush and destroy competition, are illegal."

Upon the subject of eminent domain Mr. Spelling remarks:

" That the legislature may thus select any agency it sees fit for the exercise of eminent domain, and also that it may determine what purposes shall be deemed public, are propositions too deeply rooted in the jurisprudence of this country to admit now of doubt or discussion. Making an application of this doctrine to railway operations, conceding it to be settled that these facilities for travel and commerce are a public necessity, if the legislature, reflecting the public sentiment, decide that the general benefit is better promoted by their construction through individuals or corporations than by the State itself, it would clearly be pressing a constitutional maxim to an absurd extreme if it were to be held that the public necessity should be only provided for in the way which is least consistent with the public interest. . . . The power of eminent domain being an inherent element of sovereignty, it cannot be divested out of the State or abridged by contract or treaty so as to bind future legislatures. Nor can the right be divested by private contract."

Concerning State control of corporations the same author says:

"The subordination of all private interests to the purposes of government, subject only to the condition that the object to be accomplished shall be one in which the public has an interest, is no longer an open question. In its general bearing this principle is too well settled and uniformly recognized—underlying the adjudications by courts of all cases involving constitutional provisions—to require more than a mere statement."

And again he says:

"Nor is it longer necessary to seek a justification of the common practice of regulating the rates of charges and general management of railroads on the ground that they have received valuable franchises of a public nature and had important powers of sovereign character conferred upon them. That may be an important political consideration, and as such may strengthen the argument in favor of the right; but the right itself rests upon firmer ground, and upon other considerations than that of pecuniary consideration derived from the State. The State may regulate their business, not because they are corporations, nor yet because they are corporations of a particular kind, but because they, like the individuals of which they are composed, are subject to the laws which say that when one devotes his property to a use in which the public has an interest, he in effect grants to the public an interest in that use, and must submit to be controlled by the public for the common good to the extent of the interest he has thus created."

CHAPTER XI.

THE first survey for a railroad in the State of Iowa was made in the fall of 1852. The proposed road had its initial point at Davenport and followed a westerly course. It was practically an extension of the Chicago and Rock Island Railroad, which was then being built between Chicago and the Mississippi River. On the 22d day of December, 1852, the Mississippi and Missouri Railroad Company was formed, its object being to build, maintain and operate a railroad from Davenport to Council Bluffs. The articles of association were acknowledged before John F. Dillon, notary public, and filed for record in the office of the Recorder of Scott County, on the 26th of January, 1853, and in the office of the Secretary of State on the first day of February following. In 1853 the Mississippi and Missouri Railroad Company entered into an agreement with the Railroad Bridge Company of Illinois for the construction and maintenance of a bridge over the Mississippi at Rock Island. The work was commenced in the fall of that year, and the bridge was completed on April 21, 1856, it being then the only bridge spanning the Mississippi River. The first division of the Mississippi and Missouri Railroad, extending from Davenport to Iowa City, was completed on the first of January, 1856, and was formally opened two days later. A branch line to Muscatine was completed shortly thereafter. On the first day of July the State of Iowa had in all sixty-seven miles of railroad, bonded at $14,925 a mile, which at that time probably represented the total cost of construction. The earnings of these sixty-seven miles of road during the six months following July 1, 1856, amounted to $184,193, or $2,749 per mile, which was equal to an annual income of about $5,500 per mile.

On the 15th of May, 1856, Congress granted to the State of Iowa certain lands for the purpose of "aiding in the construction of railroads from Burlington, on the Mississippi River, to a point on the Missouri River near the mouth of the Platte River ; from the city of Davenport, Iowa, by way of Iowa City and Fort Des Moines, to Council Bluffs; from Lyons City northwesterly to a point of intersection with the main line of the Iowa Central Air Line Railroad near Maquoketa, thence on said line running as near as practical to the forty-second parallel across the State ; and from the city of Dubuque to the Missouri River near Sioux City." The grant comprised the alternate sections designated by odd numbers and lying within six miles from each of the proposed roads. Provision was also made for indemnity for all lands covered by the grant which were already sold or otherwise disposed of.

The wisdom of the land-grant policy has been questioned. When these grants were made it was believed by many that railroads would not and could not be built in the West without such aid. While others did not share this opinion, they at least supposed that land grants would greatly stimulate railroad enterprise and lead to the early construction of the lines thus favored.

The land grant of the Mississippi and Missouri Railroad was a mere donation for that part of the line which was already completed at the time the grant was made ; and the extension of this line, as well as the construction of the other lines to which the grant applied, was not made as fast as had been anticipated. The price of all Government lands lying outside of the land-grant belts was $1.25 per acre. To reimburse the public treasury for the loss resulting from these grants, the price of lands situated within the land-grant belts was advanced to $2.50 per acre, practically compelling the purchasers of the even-numbered sections of land, instead of the Government, to make the donation to the railroads, it being supposed that the benefits resulting to those regions from the immediate construction of railroads would correspondingly enhance the value of the alternate sections of land reserved by the Government. Designing men soon saw the advantages which the situation offered. They combined with their friends to organize companies for the construction of the land-grant roads, built a small portion of the proposed line, to hold the grant, and then awaited further developments, or rather the settlement of the country beyond. There are those who believe that the doubling of the price of Government land within the belt of the proposed land-grant roads greatly retarded immigration and with it the construction of roads. They hold that, had no grant whatever been made to any railroad company and had equal competition in railroad construction been permitted, the Iowa through lines, instead of following, would have led, the tide of immigration.

It has been seen that in 1856 the Mississippi and Missouri Railroad was completed as far as Iowa City. On the second day of June of that year its Board of Directors asked the Governor of the State to convene the General Assembly in extra session, to consider the disposition which should be made of the recent Congressional grant. This urgency might lead one to suppose that the company was anxious to extend its line at the earliest opportunity. The General Assembly was convened, and the land given to the State by Congress for the purpose of aiding in the construction of a railroad from Davenport to Council Bluffs was given to the Mississippi and Missouri Railroad Company. The act was approved by the Governor on July 14, 1856, and three days later the company "assented to and accepted the grant." It then executed mortgage after mortgage, and built a branch line through quite a populous territory, from Muscatine to Washington, but the main line made very slow progress. In 1865 the bonded debt of the company amounted to $6,851,754, although the line was completed only to Kellogg, in Jasper County, about forty miles east of Des Moines. In spite of the fact that the cost of operating the road had from the beginning varied but little from 60 per cent. of its gross receipts, its president, in a circular letter to the stock- and bondholders, dated October 20th, 1865, made the statement that the company was "driven to the necessity of selling the road or reorganizing." In 1866 suit was brought in the Circuit Court of the United States for the District of Iowa for the foreclosure of the company's mortgages, and a decree of foreclosure was entered on the 11th day of May of that year. The property was sold on the 9th day of July following at Davenport, and was purchased by the Chicago, Rock Island and Pacific Railroad Company, which was incorporated in this State a few weeks previous to the sale, for the purpose of acquiring the railroads built by the Mississippi and Missouri Railroad Company with all its appurtenant property, "and all the rights, privileges and franchises granted by the act of Congress of May 15th, 1856, to the State of Iowa, and by the State of Iowa granted to the said Mississippi and Missouri Railroad Company, and when so acquired to maintain and operate the said railroad." It is a significant fact that all the corporators of the new company, except one, were directors of the bankrupt company. On the 20th of August, 1866, the Chicago, Rock Island and Pacific Company of the State of Iowa consolidated with the Chicago, Rock Island and Pacific Railroad Company of Illinois, and conveyed all its property, powers and franchises to the consolidated company. The validity of the consolidation was questioned by a large number of stock- and bondholders, and the courts were appealed to to issue injunctions restraining the consolidated company from extending its line or expending any money obtained through the sale of its securities. In this predicament the company turned to the Iowa legislature for protection. Anxious to secure the early completion of the road, the Twelfth General Assembly, by an act approved February 11th, 1868, recognized the consolidated company, and resumed and granted to it "all right or interest" which the State had in the lands previously granted to the Mississippi and Missouri Railroad Company. The act expressly provided, however, that the Chicago, Rock Island and Pacific Railway Company should "at all times be subject to such rules, regulations and rates of tariff for transportation of freight and passengers as may from time to time be enacted and provided for by the General Assembly of the State of Iowa," and that if the company should neglect to comply with any of the requirements of the act, it should forfeit to the State all its franchises and corporate rights acquired by or under the laws of the State, and all lands granted to aid in the construction of its road. The line was completed to Council Bluffs in June, 1869.

The lands in aid of the construction of a railroad running across the State, as nearly as practicable along the

forty-second parallel, were granted by the General
Assembly to the Iowa Central Air Line on the 14th of
July, 1856, but as this company failed to fulfill the conditions of its grant, it was, on the 17th of March, 1860,
transferred to the Cedar Rapids and Missouri River Railroad Company. This company completed the road to
Marshalltown in 1862, to Nevada in 1864, to Boone in
1865, and to Council Bluffs in the fall of 1867.

The Burlington and Missouri River road reached the
Missouri River but a few months later. Ten years after
this company had received its grant, its line had only
been completed as far as Albia, in Monroe County. In
1867 the road was built little more than half across the
State. But it managed not to be far behind its two rivals
on the north in reaching the Missouri River.

At first sight it might seem as if these companies had
all at once become awake to their obligations. When it is
remembered, however, that in 1869 the junction of the
Union Pacific and Central Pacific railroads was effected,
and thus a continuous line across the continent formed,
the conclusion lies near that the haste with which the
three Iowa land-grant roads were completed was simply
the result of a strife for the large amount of through business which the completion of the Pacific route promised to
bring to them.

No such inducement existed for the Dubuque and Sioux
City Company, and twelve years after receiving its grant
it had not yet built half of its line. In his message to the
Twelfth General Assembly, delivered January 14, 1868,
Governor Stone said: "Under the provisions of the act
adopted by the General Assembly, at its extra session (in
July, 1856), this (the Dubuque and Sioux City) company
became the beneficiary of the grant designed to secure the

construction of a railroad leading from Dubuque to Sioux City, and this valuable donation was accepted from the State, with all the terms and conditions imposed. A large portion of this grant has already been absorbed by the company, in various ways, by pretended sales and incumbrances. This road has been constructed to Iowa Falls, a distance of 143 miles from Dubuque, but I am unable to discover any reliable evidence of earnest intention on the part of this company to construct the line to its terminal point on the Missouri River. "

The Governor further recommended that the General Assembly pass an act resuming the control over these lands. At about the same time an agreement was effected between the Iowa Falls and Sioux City Railroad Company (which was organized in the fall of 1867) and the Dubuque and Sioux City Railroad Company, by which the latter transferred to the former its land grant for the unfinished portion of the Dubuque and Sioux City road. This agreement was confirmed by the General Assembly, through an act approved April 7, 1868. The road was completed to Fort Dodge in August, 1869, and to Sioux City a year or two later. The entire line was then leased to the Illinois Central.

The land grant to this line of road embraced over 1,000,000 acres of the finest lands of the State. We can appreciate the magnitude of this donation when we consider that, had these lands been sold at only $8 per acre, the proceeds would have paid the whole expense of building and equipping the road from Dubuque to Sioux City. The lands granted to the C., R. I. & P. R. R. were sold at an average price of over $8 per acre, and those of the B. & M. at over $12 per acre.

Among the other important land grants is that made to the McGregor Western Railroad Company. This com-

pany was the successor of the McGregor, St. Peters and
Missouri River Railroad Company, which was organized
in 1857 for the purpose of constructing a railroad from
McGregor to the Missouri River. The construction of the
road was commenced in 1857 at McGregor. Large local
subscriptions were taken along the proposed line, the
writer being one of the subscribers. Work was continued the next year until much of the heavy grading
had been done, when the road was allowed to go through
the process of foreclosure, like many other roads built in
the West at that time. The old stock was completely
wiped out, and new owners came into possession of the
property, reorganizing under the name of the McGregor
Western Railway Company.   Nearly all the early investments of Iowa people were thus confiscated by the same
class of men who now cry out loudly against confiscatory
measures. By an act of Congress approved May 12,
1864, the State of Iowa was granted, for the use and
benefit of the McGregor Western Railroad Company,
every alternate section of land designated by odd numbers for ten sections in width on each side of the proposed road. The act contained the condition that in the
event of the failure of said McGregor Western Railroad
Company to build twenty miles of said road during each
and every year from the date of its acceptance of the grant
the State might resume the grant and so dispose of it as
to secure the completion of the road in question. The
McGregor Western Railroad Company failing to comply
with the conditions of the grant, the General Assembly
on the 27th day of February, 1868, resumed the lands
and on the 31st day of March of the same year regranted
them to the McGregor and Sioux City Railway Company.
The act specially provided that the company accepting

the grant "shall at all times be subject to such rules, regulations and rates of tariff for the transportation of freight and passengers as may from time to time be enacted and provided for by the General Assembly of the State of Iowa, and further subject to the conditions, limitations, restrictions and provisions contained in this act and in the acts of Congress granting said lands to the State of Iowa." It also contained the condition that at least twenty miles of road should be built by the company every year and that the whole road should be completed to the intersection of the then proposed railway from Sioux City to the Minnesota State line by the first day of December, 1875.

The McGregor and Sioux City Railway Company also failing to comply with the terms of the grant, the lands were again resumed by the General Assembly on March 15th, 1876, and regranted to the McGregor and Missouri River Railroad Company upon the condition that it complete the road to the intersection of the Sioux City and St. Paul Railroad on or before the first day of December, 1877.

But the State found itself again disappointed, and two years later the General Assembly for the third and last time resumed its grant and then conferred it upon the Chicago, Milwaukee and St. Paul Railway Company upon the express conditions that it complete the road to Spencer on or before the first day of January, 1879, and to Sheldon within a year thereafter, and that the road should at all times be subject to State control. The road was completed to Sheldon without delay; and on the 30th of November, 1878, the Governor of the State certified to the Secretary of the Interior that the Chicago, Milwaukee and St. Paul Railway Company had completed its road from Algona to Sheldon in compliance with the conditions of the original grant and the laws of the State.

It thus took over twenty years to complete this road. Ten years after its construction had commenced it had only reached Calmar in Winneshiek County. In 1869 the road was completed to Clear Lake and in 1870 to Algona. This point remained its terminus until it passed into the hands of the Chicago, Milwaukee and St. Paul Railway Company.

The State of Iowa has not derived that benefit from the large land grants made to its railroads which her people had a right to expect. In spite of these grants roads were built only when there was reason to believe that they would be immediately profitable to their owners. The land grants enriched the promoters of these enterprises much more than they did the State in whose interest the grants were presumed to be made. As a rule they enabled scheming men to hold the selected territory until a railroad through it promised to be a safe and profitable investment, and to avoid the payment of taxes on their millions of acres of land, which in the meantime became very valuable. Other roads were built at an early day without Government aid. They were pushed forward by the current of immigration until the threatened competition of roads favored by these grants checked their progress. The Chicago, Iowa and Nebraska road may be cited as a fair illustration. It was projected . on the 26th of January, 1856, in the town of Clinton, to be built from Clinton to the Missouri River via Cedar Rapids. It was opened to De Witt in 1858 and completed to Cedar Rapids the following year. The road was 82½ miles long and was built entirely with private means, receiving neither legislative aid nor local subsidy. It is more than probable that this road would at an early day have been completed to the Missouri River, had it not feared the rivalry of the subsidized Cedar Rapids and Missouri road.

The total number of acres of land granted by Congress to aid the construction of Iowa roads is 4,069,942. A fair idea of the value of these lands may be obtained from the fact that the Chicago, Rock Island and Pacific Railroad Company sold over half a million acres of its lands at an average of $8.68 per acre, and the Chicago Burlington and Quincy sold nearly 350,000 acres at an average of $12.17 per acre.

But land grants form only a small part of the public and private donations which have been made to Iowa roads. Including the railroad taxes voted by counties, townships and municipalities, the grants of rights of way and depot sites and public and private gifts in money, these roads have received subsidies amounting to more than $50,000,000, or enough to build 40 per cent. of all the roads of the State. There is no doubt that the contributions of the public toward the construction of the railroads of Iowa is several times as large as the actual contributions of their stockholders for that purpose.

The people of Iowa were from the first very favorably disposed towards railroads. Every inducement was held out to railroad builders to come here and help to multiply the tracks for the iron horse. They came and brought with them many abuses which since the first introduction of railroads had gradually been developed in other States.

The contrast between the old and the new mode of transportation was so great, and the public appreciated so highly the superior conveniences afforded by the latter, that for years the abuses practiced by the early railroads were scarcely noticed, or, if they did attract the attention of the public, they appeared more like necessary features of the new system of transportation than like abuses. The evil gradually increased, but for years no attempt was made to check its growth. The railroad managers construed this failure of the people to interfere with, or even protest against, their unjust practices as a quasi-sanction of their course, and soon claimed to do by right what they had formerly done by sufferance. The evils increased until the patience of the people finally became exhausted.

While the State thus for years dealt very leniently with the railroad companies, the laws of Iowa had from the beginning of railroad building emphasized the principle of State control. This principle was asserted in the very first railroad act ever passed in the State. Section 14 of chapter I. of the acts of the extra session of the Fifth General Assembly, regranting to the various railroad companies the lands granted to the State by Congress for railroad purposes, provides that "railroad companies accepting the provisions of this act shall at all times be subject to such rules and regulations as may from time to time be enacted and provided for by the General Assembly of Iowa. . . ." In 1866 an attempt was made in the General Assembly to regulate rates, but the Attorney-General, to whom the question of constitutionality was submitted, held in his opinion that it was not in the power of the legislature to prescribe rates for railroad companies. This opinion provoked much indignation among the people of the State, and led to the expression of a sound public opinion by legislative acts which could not be misunderstood.

When the Twelfth General Assembly (in 1868) regranted to the Chicago, Rock Island and Pacific Railroad Company the lands originally granted to the Mississippi and Missouri Company, it only did so upon the condition that "said railroad company, accepting the provisions of this act, shall at all times be subject to such rules, regulations and rates of tariff for transportation of freight and passengers as may from time to time be enacted and provided for by the General Assembly of the State of Iowa. . . ." The same restricting clause, known as the Doud Amendment, was added to all other land grant acts passed by the Twelfth and subsequent General Assemblies, and the various companies willingly and gladly accepted it.

The abuses of which the people of Iowa complained were far from being confined to their State. They were practiced throughout the Northwest, and the demand for reform was as loud in Minnesota, Wisconsin and Illinois as it was in Iowa. In 1871 laws were passed in Illinois and Minnesota fixing maximum charges for the transportation of freight and passengers and prohibiting discriminations. The railroads claimed that a State did not have the right to prescribe rates and refused to be bound by these laws. Instead of modifying their policy, they became daily more arrogant. Discriminations which had before been practiced under the veil of secrecy, or which had been defended by railroad managers as exceptions to the general rule made necessary by a peculiar combination of circumstances wholly beyond their control, were now openly and defiantly practiced by several of the larger roads. The Chicago, Milwaukee and St. Paul Railroad Company, in its effort to annihilate a rival, went so far as to openly announce to the public its intention to entirely disregard distance as a factor in rate-making. It gradually became the general rule to wage war against rivals at competitive points and to "recoup" by charging excessive rates at non-competitive points. Every encouragement was thus given by the railroads to the Granger movement, which spread in less than two years over the whole Northwest.

In the fall of 1873 Iowa elected a Granger legislature, like Minnesota, Wisconsin and Illinois. The wildest predictions were made by railroad men as to the extremes to which the Granger legislature would go, but it confined itself to enacting a law establishing an official classification and fixing maximum rates for all railroad companies. The law was approved March 23, 1874, and went into effect on the 4th of July following. This law in no case compelled companies to carry freight at a lower rate than they had voluntarily carried it in the past. Many of the rates in force at the time of the passage of the act were considerably lower than the corresponding maximum rates fixed by the legislature. The average rates fixed by the law were higher than the rates at which the railroads had previously carried a large portion of corresponding freight. The revenues of the road were not even curtailed by this law; on the contrary, by equalizing rates, *i. e.*, by leveling up the rates given to favored places and favored individuals and leveling down the exorbitant rates exacted from the public at non-competitive points, the railroad companies were enabled to effect an increase in their total revenue.

The Granger law remained in force until 1878. Its constitutionality was tested by the railroad companies in the Supreme Court of the United States, but this high tribunal held that rate-making was a legislative and not a judicial function, that it was within the province of the State legislature to prescribe rates for the transportation of passengers and freight wholly within the State, and that for protection against abuses by legislatures the people must resort to the polls, and not to the courts.

The Granger laws have been and are still severely criticised by those opposed to the principle of State control and by the ignorant. It is nevertheless true that those laws were moderate, just and reasonably well adapted to remedy the evils of which the public complained. It has been the policy of most railroad men to attack them as crude, intensely radical and socialistic. The obloquy heaped upon them was the work of designing men who desired to continue their impositions upon the people. Mr. Charles Francis Adams, however, admits that the Granger method was probably as good a method as could have been devised of approaching men who had thoroughly got it into their heads that they, as common carriers, were in no way bound to afford equal facilities to all, and, indeed, that it was in the last degree absurd and unreasonable to expect them to do so.

The Iowa law was imperfect in detail, and yet its enactment proved one of the greatest legislative achievements in the history of the State. It demonstrated to the people their ability to correct by earnestness and perseverance the most far-reaching public abuses and led to an emphatic judicial declaration of the common-law principle that railroads are highways and as such are subject to any legislative control which may be deemed necessary for the public welfare.

Defeated in the courts, the railroad managers now endeavored to make odious the new law which deprived them of the power to manipulate railroad interests to their personal advantage. By complying with only part of its letter and none of its spirit, they contrived to create hard-

ships for certain interests and localities. Instead of
charging in all cases reasonable rates, as the spirit of the
law demanded, they would frequently charge the maximum rates permitted under the law, and when they by
this practice succeeded in damaging certain interests,
they would point to the Granger law as the source of all
existing railroad evils. So, likewise, when they were
asked by their patrons to reduce a high rate, they would
plead the legislative schedule in excuse of their failure to
comply with the request. When the legislature of 1878
convened, the railroad managers appeared before it and
pleaded submissively for a repeal of the Granger law and
the establishment of a commissioner system. They
claimed that they were ready and willing to submit to all
reasonable regulation, but that a maximum tariff law was
prejudicial both to the best interests of the roads and
those of the public. They further asserted that the people had grown tired of this manner of regulating railroad
charges and earnestly desired a change of policy; that the
interference of the State with the railroad business had
injuriously affected certain industrial interests and had
greatly retarded railroad construction by driving capital
and promoters of railroad enterprises from the State.
These statements would indeed have argued strongly in
favor of a repeal of the law if they had been based on
facts. There had been, however, no expression of public
dissatisfaction during the campaign preceding the session
of the General Assembly. There were doubtless individuals and even communities to whom the law had been
made so odious that they felt they had but little to lose
by a change, but the masses of the people believed that
the law was based upon just principles and desired its
perfection rather than its repeal. As to the claim that

railroad construction had been checked by hostile legislation, statistics prove that during the five years following the great panic of 1873 Iowa fared no worse in this respect than her sister States east, west or south.

The arguments produced by the railroad managers no doubt influenced some members of the General Assembly; by far the greater number of them, however, realized that the failure of the law to bring the expected relief was not due so much to its own imperfections as to the absence of a power to enforce it. The writer, with others, was convinced that a strong and conscientious commission would be a much more potent agency to secure reasonable rates for the shipper than a maximum tariff law without proper provisions for its efficient enforcement; they, in short, preferred a commission without a tariff law to a tariff law without a commission. The question became the subject of many animated debates in both houses of the General Assembly, but the commissioner system at last prevailed. The act establishing a Board of Railroad Commissioners, and defining their duties, was approved on the 23rd of March, 1878, and went into force a few days later. The act empowered the commission to exercise a general supervision over all railroads operated in the State, to inquire into any neglect or violation of the laws of the State by any railroad corporation or its officers or employes, to examine the books and documents of any corporation, to investigate complaints of shippers that unreasonable charges had been made by railroad companies, and to modify any charge which they might deem unreasonable. It was also made the commissioners' duty to make an annual report to the Governor disclosing the working of the railroad system in the State, the officers of each company being required to make annual returns to the board for this purpose.

Though the enactment of this law was a surprise to the people, they accepted it in good cheer, and determined to give it an honest trial. The law was extensive in its scope and stringent for that time, and, if strictly enforced in letter and in spirit, promised to be, and would have been, entirely sufficient for the thorough control of railroad corporations.

Nevertheless, in the course of time it became apparent that either the law had not lodged sufficient authority in the commission or the commission did not make use of the authority which the law had given them. In spite of the commission, the railroad companies maintained pools and charged extortionate and discriminating rates, in direct violation of the law. It is true the commissioners righted many a wrong. In investigating the complaints of shippers against railroad companies they often rendered valuable services to those who had neither the means nor the inclination to prosecute their rights in the courts of law; but as they held that they could only pass upon individual charges, and did not have the power to revise the companies' tariffs, the companies were virtually in a position to become guilty of more extortions in one day than the commission could investigate in a year. Moreover, the railroad company might be ordered by the commission to return an overcharge to a certain shipper, but this did not prevent it from continuing the excessive charge. If the overcharged shipper again wanted relief it was his privilege to again apply to the commission, and to continue this tedious process until either his or the commissioners' patience became exhausted. The people soon found that the new system of control was almost as inadequate as that which it had displaced. Some attributed the weakness of the commission to its personnel, others to the law. There is no doubt that the commission might have accomplished more than it did.

It was hoped by some that as the commission gained in experience it would gain in influence, and that railroad evils would gradually diminish. But they were disappointed in their expectations. Every year seemed to add to the grievances of the public. Success greatly emboldened the railway companies. Discriminations seemed to increase in number and gravity. At many points in the western part of the State freight rates to Chicago were from 50 to 75 per cent. higher than from points in Kansas and Nebraska. A car of wheat hauled only across the State paid twice as much freight as another hauled twice the distance from its point of origin to Chicago. Minnesota flour was hauled a distance of 300 miles for a less rate than Iowa flour was carried 100 miles. Certain merchants received from the railroad companies a discount of 50 per cent. on all their freights and were thus enabled to undersell all their competitors. The rate on coal in carload lots from Cleveland, Lucas County, to Glenwood was $1.80 per ton, and from the same point to Council Bluffs only $1.25, although the latter was about thirty miles longer haul. Innumerable cases of this kind could be cited. There was not a town or interest in the State that did not feel the influence of these unjust practices. Many of the rates complained against, it is true, were beyond the direct control of the State commission, but there was an impression among well-informed shippers that if the commission had the power to fix local rates and exercised it judiciously, the railroad companies would soon find it to their interest to be as reasonable in making through rates for Iowans as they expected the commission to be in prescribing local tariffs.

The demand of the people for more equitable rates and a more thorough control of the railroad business increased from year to year. Repeated attempts were made in the General Assembly to secure the passage of an act looking to that end, but, owing to shrewd manipulations on the part of the railroad lobby, every attempt was defeated. There always was, of course, a large number of members who represented districts not well supplied with railroad facilities. These, as a rule, honestly opposed restrictive legislation, believing that such legislation would check building, and that, on the other hand, competition could be relied upon to correct abuses. Of those members who had less positive convictions many were retained as railroad attorneys and were thus made serviceable to the companies. Other members with political ambition were flattered or intimidated into subjection, and bribes in disguise, such as passes and special rates, were not unfrequently resorted to to strengthen the railroad following in both houses of the General Assembly.

Railroad corruption did not pause here. It is a notorious fact that large sums of money were paid to venal papers of both parties in consideration of an agreement on their part to defend transportation abuses and exert their influence against progressive railroad legislation. The vilest means were often resorted to by these sheets to obtain their end. Public men who had the courage to avow their opposition to existing railroad abuses or to favor a more perfect system of State control of railways were misrepresented, ridiculed, traduced and denounced as demagogues and socialists by hypocritical editors, who prostituted their political influence as long as they enjoyed railroad stipends, and who at intervals became converts to the cause of the people for the purpose of extorting

from the railroad companies a new and increased subsidy.
But truth can not long be suppressed. The masses of
the people may be imposed upon for a time, but even the
shrewdest rogue will eventually be compelled to surrender. In time even rather unsophisticated voters learned
to place a true estimate upon the motives of the editors,
whose policy, as one of them expressed it in the author's
presence, was "controlled by the counting-room."

Railroad politicians gradually lost their influence, and
the symptoms of public discontent greatly increased. In
the political campaign of 1887 State control of railroads
became one of the main issues. Both of the great political parties in their platforms had declared themselves
very emphatically in favor of such legislation as would
bring railroad corporations under complete State control,
and with very few exceptions the various legislative districts had nominated only such men as candidates for legislative offices as were known to be in thorough accord
with the masses of the people upon the railroad question.

The election resulted in an even more complete defeat
of the railroad forces than had been generally anticipated.
Yet no hasty step was taken when the General Assembly
convened. A large number of bills contemplating railroad reforms in various ways were introduced, but the
material presented was carefully sifted by the railroad
committees and a committee bill was framed which incorporated the best features of them all. The committees
listened patiently for weeks to the arguments of the representatives of both the railroads and the shippers.

Never before had so formidable a railroad lobby assem-
bled at the State Capitol. The danger signal had been
raised, and not only were the great political manipulators of
the State called into requisition, but experts from adjoining

States joined them in besieging the legislature. The dogs of war were let loose from all quarters. A legion of hirelings were zealous to show their servility and loyalty to their lords. The daily and weekly papers of the State in the service of railroad companies teemed with arguments from the pens of railroad attorneys, and their columns were profusely supplemented with editorials copied from prominent corporation papers like the New York *Tribune*, New York *Times*, New York *World*, Albany *Evening Argus*, Boston *Advertiser*, and others from various parts of the country.

These papers, attempting to disguise the motives that prompted them to come to the defense of the Wall Street interest, affected the position of disinterested and impartial observers. They condemned the proposed measures as wild and socialistic, and they painted in dark colors the disasters to railroad property, the injustice to its owners, and misfortunes to the people of Iowa, that would follow their adoption. Especially did they bewail the losses that would fall upon the widows and orphans who had confidingly invested all of their hard earnings in this property.

They never uttered a word of condemnation, but entirely ignored or defended the abuses by which the stockholders were robbed at one end of the line and the patrons were imposed on at the other.

Many of these papers were notified that their statements were altogether erroneous, but they would not admit a line to their columns in relation to the matter that indicated any other disposition than complete subserviency to the interests of Wall Street.

There were, however, an unusual number of strong men in this General Assembly, and this extraordinary display of railroad forces only tended to impress more strongly upon them the necessity of curbing the railroad power, and their best energies were concentrated upon the subject, with a firm determination to deal with it in a manner dictated by reason and experience.

So well did the bill which was finally adopted by the committee reflect the general sentiment of the members of the General Assembly that not a single vote was cast against it in either house upon its final passage. Since the adjustment of business under this law, there has been less friction between the people and the railroads than before for thirty years, and so satisfactory has it proved to all that no one, not even a railroad man, has to this day asked the legislature to repeal the law or any part of it. The act contains no new principle of railroad control. By far the greater part of its provisions were taken from the old law. Nearly every one of its features may be found either in the Interstate Commerce Act or upon the statute books of other States. It provides that charges must be reasonable and just, that no undue preference or advantage shall be given to any railroad patron, and that equal facilities for interchange of traffic shall be given to all roads; it prohibits pooling, a greater charge for a shorter than longer haul, the shorter or any portion of it being included in the longer, and discrimination against any shipping point. It requires that schedules of rates and fares shall be printed and kept for public inspection, and that no advance shall be made in rates or fares once established except after ten days' public notice; and it empowers the Board of Railroad Commissioners to make and revise schedules for railroads, the rates contained in such schedules to be received and held in all suits as *prima facie* reasonable maximum rates. The act further provides penalties and means of enforcement.

Is must not be supposed that by the passage of this act the legislature disclaimed the right to fix absolute rates; it simply chose this expedient because in the present tentative stage of rate regulation it seemed most efficient.

There has been much misunderstanding concerning the Iowa law. Many suppose that the Iowa commissioners have power to make confiscatory rates for the railroads, while in fact they can only name maximum rates which shall be deemed and taken in all courts of the State as *prima facie* evidence that they are reasonable and just maximum rates until the railroads show that they are not. They are at liberty to go into court any day and show this, if they are able.   They are, however, careful not to undertake it, for no one knows better than they do that the rates fixed by the commissioners are liberal for the railroads.

There are nine States, besides Iowa, in which the power to fix rates has been conferred upon railroad commissioners.   This feature of the law was therefore far from being a novel one, yet noprovision of the act was, previous to its passage, so furiously opposed, or subsequent to it so stubbornly resisted as this.   Railroad managers realized that a surrender of the right to make their own rates was virtually a surrender of the power to practice abuses.

Soon after the passage of the law the commissioners commenced the work of preparing schedules of the rates for the roads.   They endeavored to do justice to both the railroad companies and their patrons by affording a fair compensation to the former and at the same time giving

relief to the depressed interests represented by the latter
Their rates were not as low as the special rates that
had at various times been granted to favorite shippers,
but were a fair average of the various rates in vogue at
the time. While the schedule was under consideration,
the railroad managers were given frequent hearings, in
which they endeavored to impress their views upon the
commissioners and to obtain many important concessions,
which they urged as essential to the welfare of the railroad interests. Their views guided the commission to
such an extent that it was generally supposed that the
schedule as finally adopted would be accepted by the railroad companies without protest.

The schedule of the Iowa commission has been sharply
criticised by Mr. Stickney in his '' Railway Problem.'' He
finds in it inconsistencies and confusion, due, as he
charges, to faulty mathematics. But it is claimed by the
commission, and Mr. Stickney should know, that whenever
mathematics were ignored in the construction of the schedule it was done at the earnest and persistent solicitation
of the railroad managers, who, it seems, were more interested in maintaining their interstate rates than in the con-
sistency of the Iowa schedule.

The rates were published, as required by law, and June
28, 1888, was fixed as the day on which they were to take
effect. A few days previous to this date the companies
asked that the taking effect of the new tariff be postponed
a week. When this request was granted by the chairman
of the commission, the railroad managers took advantage
of the courtesy by enjoining the commissioners in the
Federal court from enforcing it.

Several months later the commissioners modified their
schedule by the adoption of the Western Classification.

Again the railroad managers asked the court for an injunction, but this time met with a refusal.

After many suits for penalties had been instituted against them, and many more threatened, they adopted the new schedule, but endeavored to inaugurate a policy of retaliation by reducing their train service and discharging a large number of employes, and in many ingenious ways continued their seditious course with a determination characteristic of a band of insurrectionists. But the impetus which railroad traffic received under the operation of the commissioners' schedule was such that they soon found it necessary to restore to the service its former efficiency.

The Railroad Commissioners' report shows that while the number of employes was 24,642, and their yearly compensation was $14,212,500 in 1889, in 1892 there were 30,492 employes, and their yearly compensation $18,070,915.

The increase in both the gross and net earnings of Iowa lines has been remarkable, as shown in the following table gathered from the commissioners' reports:

Year.	Gross Earnings, Total.	Net Earnings, Total.	Per Mile.
1888–89	$37,369,276	$11,861,310	$1,421
1889–90	41,318,133	12,798,430	1,522
1890–91	43,102,399	14,463,106	1,720
1891–92	44,540,000	14,945,000	1,777

It was claimed by railroad men that the effect of Iowa legislation would be particularly disastrous to her local roads, which had no opportunity to make up on through business the losses incurred in the local traffic. The Burlington, Cedar Rapids and Northern was particularly cited as a line which would have to go into bankruptcy under the new law. Its earnings commenced to increase, however, immediately after the adoption of the commissioners' schedule, and at the end of the first year they were large enough to change this line from a Class "C" to a Class "B" road. They continued to increase, and in 1891 its gross earnings on substantially the same mileage were 36 per cent. and its net earnings 64 per cent. larger than they had been in 1888. The increase continued and enabled the company to make a dividend to its stockholders February 1, 1893, it being the first dividend ever made by the company. It is a good illustration of what the Iowa law has done for weak railroads. It has again changed class and is now a Class "A" road.

It is seen that the fears, or rather the pretended fears of the railroad managers, that the legislature of Iowa would bankrupt her railroads, were entirely groundless. As a result of the law railroads have been able to increase their gross earnings as well as their profits. They have been enabled to give employment to a larger number of men, and there has been no occasion for them to carry out the dishonest threat to decrease the wages of their employes. Had it not been for their increased earnings in Iowa, the losses recently sustained in other States by several of the through lines would have made it impossible for them to declare the dividends which they did.

Under her beneficial railroad policy Iowa has prospered wonderfully, and her railroads have been more prosperous than when they were allowed to have their own way. The commissioners' tariff has made jobbing and manufacturing profitable where it was unprofitable before. It has added to our industries and our commerce, and has made new business for the people as well as the railroads. It has contributed to the increase in the value of our farms and factories and their products, and the time will come when wise railroad managers, like the majority of former slaveholders of the South, would not resurrect the past if they could. In fact, honorable managers now acknowledge that they would not if they could.

The railroad companies are at present making a systematic effort to weaken the Iowa commission, but if they should succeed in doing so, the people, under our system of electing the commissioners, can readily correct the evil.

Other States have much experience similar to that of Iowa. Nebraska has just adopted a maximum tariff law for the control of her roads. It will, of course, be resisted by the railroad managers of that State.

The State of Texas is not so productive in proportion, but is much greater in extent than Iowa, and upon the whole resembles it much in its prominent characteristics. Both are thrifty, progressive States, with no large commercial or manufacturing centers where their people can easily organize to protect their financial interests.

The people of Texas endured patiently the abuses so prevalent in railroad management until a few years since they enacted a railroad law similar to that of Iowa. The Wall Street managers of the Texas railroads are at the present time using all of their familiar methods to influence the people of that State to repeal their law. The following letter serves to show the spirit with which they are approached:

"23 BROAD STREET,
"NEW YORK, November 30, 1891.
"James B. Simpson, Esq., Dallas, Tex.

"DEAR SIR: Yours of the 26th is received and contents carefully noted. Very likely you have valuable franchises, or what would be valuable in almost any other State than Texas; but while their are many places in Texas where we would like to build some railroads—mostly short ones —we cannot do anything so long as the disposition exists that now seems to in Texas; that is, to do all the harm they can do this kind of property, and I think my views are shared by all people who have money to invest. No one is disposed to create property which, after being created, is not to be controlled by its ownership. Of course, we all expect to be subject to the police regulations and to pay the taxes of any State even as other property, but whenever anything is done beyond that it checks this kind of improvement, and where it approaches so near confiscation as the sentiment of Texas tends it entirely prevents capital from being invested.

"I think there is no road in Texas that is to-day earning its operating and fixed charges. Every road, I think, has been or is in the hands of a receiver, excepting our great east and west line, which is supported by business going entirely through the State, which business could also be sent another way, and would be so sent, excepting that we believe the people of Texas will some time take a sober second thought and treat the railroads as they do other kinds of property. When that time comes I shall be ready to talk to you about your franchises, if it comes in my day, and I believe it will, as I think no other people are suffering from an unwise policy persistently pursued as are the people of your State.

"Yours truly,
"C. P. HUNTINGTON."

"Now, in the name of all the gods at once,
Upon what meat doth this our Cæsar feed,
That he hath grown so great?"

It was but a few years ago when this Mr. Huntington was keeping a small retail store in the city of Sacramento, and he exhibited then no greater ability, except perhaps that he was a little more venturesome, than thousands of others engaged in the same occupation; subsequently he engaged, with several others, in the Central Pacific Railroad scheme, and received from the bounties of our generous Government as his share of the profits in that enter-prise several million dollars, which sum has ever since been continually swelled by the exercise of a power scarcely inferior to the power of taxing the property of the Pacific Coast. He has been so successful for years in manipulating Congressmen and State legislatures and shaping the policies of States that he now considers it impertinent and short-sighted for a people to take steps to limit his levies upon them. It is to be hoped that the boycotting and intimidating methods resorted to will have no more effect upon the people of that State than they had on the people of Iowa.

Iowa is the queen among the States of the Union. No other State has so little waste land or is so productive. Her annual output of staple products amounts to hundreds of millions of dollars in value. Her people are intelligent, progressive and just. None are governed more by the precepts of the golden rule, or are more disposed to render unto Cæsar the things that are Cæsar's. She can well be proud of the progress she has made in State control of railroads. Let no backward step be taken.

CHAPTER XII.

THE INTERSTATE COMMERCE ACT.

THE Constitution of the United States was adopted nearly fifty years before the locomotive made its appearance. Had the steam railroad been in existence in 1787 and been as important an agency of commerce as it is to-day. there is every reason to believe that the railroad question would have received the special attention of the framers of that instrument. It is a well-known fact that the "new and more perfect government" had its origin in the necessities of commerce, and while the future exigencies of trade were beyond the reach of the most speculative mind, the provisions of the Constitution relating to the subject of interstate commerce were made broad and far-reaching. Section 8 of Article I. of the Constitution provides that "the Congress shall have power .... to regulate commerce with foreign nations, and among the several States, and with the Indian tribes .... and to make all laws which shall be necessary and proper for carrying into execution the foregoing powers and all other powers vested by this Constitution in the Government of the United States, or in any department or officer thereof."

If any doubt ever existed as to the import of the phrase "to regulate commerce," it has been entirely removed by the decisions of the Supreme Court. In the Passenger cases, 7 Howard, 416, the court said:

"Commerce consists in selling the superfluity; in purchasing articles of necessity, as well productions as manufactures; in buying from one nation and selling to another, or *in transporting the merchandise* from the seller to the buyer to gain the freight."

And again, in the Philadelphia and Reading Railroad vs. Pennsylvania, the Supreme Court said:

" Beyond all question the transportation of freights or of the subjects of commerce for the purpose of exchange or sale is a constituent of commerce itself. This has never been doubted, and probably the transportation of articles of trade from one State to another was the prominent idea in the minds of the framers of the Constitution when to Congress was committed the power to regulate cammerce among the several States. . . . It would be absurd to suppose that the transmission of the subjects of trade from the seller to the buyer, or from the place of production to market, was not contemplated, for without that there could be no consummated trade with foreign nations or among the States."

Chief Justice Marshall, in Gibbons vs. Ogden, 9 Wheaten, 196, construed the words "power to regulate" as follows:

" This power, like all others vested in Congress, is complete in itself, may be exercised to its utmost extent, and acknowledges no limitations other than are prescribed in the Constitution."

It is a strange fact that during the first eighty years of the Government's existence Congress did not exert its power to regulate the conduct of common carriers engaged in interstate transportation. The first act regulating such carriers was passed in July, 1866. It authorized railroad companies chartered by the States to carry passengers, freights, etc., "on their way from any State to another State, and to receive compensation therefor, and to connect with roads of other States so as to form continuous lines for transportation of the same to the place of destination." The passage of this act, it should be remembered, was urged by the railroad companies themselves.

Seven years later an act was passed providing that "no railway within the United States, whose road forms any part of a line or road over which cattle, sheep, swine or other animals shall be conveyed from one State to another, or the owners or masters of steam, sailing or other vessels carrying or transporting cattle, sheep or swine or other animals from one State to another, shall confine the same in cars, boats or vessels of any description for a longer period than twenty-eight consecutive hours, without unloading the same for water, rest and feeding, for a period of at least five consecutive hours, unless prevented from so unloading by storm or accidental causes."

Every violation of this act was made punishable by a penalty of from $100 to $500.

Though Congress had asserted the right to regulate commerce among the States, it had made previous to 1873 very limited use of that power. In the midst of the Granger movement the Senate of the United States passed on the 26th day of March, 1873, the following resolution:

"*Resolved*, That the Select Committee on Transportation Routes to the Seaboard be authorized to sit at such places as they may designate during the recess, and to investigate and report upon the subject of transportation between the interior and the seaboard; that they have power to employ a clerk and stenographer, and to send for persons and papers. . . ."

The committee, under the chairmanship of Mr. Windom, discharged their duty with great fidelity, and submitted their report to the Senate during its next regular session. They declared that the defects and abuses of the then existing systems of transportation were insufficient facilities, unfair discrimination and extortionate charges. As the principal causes of such excessive rates they assigned stock watering, capitalization of surplus earnings, construction rings, general extravagance and corruption in railway management, and combinations and consolidations of railway companies. The committee were of the opinion that the promotion of competition would not permanently remedy the existing evils, and laid it down as a general rule that competition among railways ends in combination and in enhanced rates. As expedient and practical remedies for the existing evils they recommended the following measures:

1. Direct Congressional regulation of railway transportation, under the power to regulate commerce among the several States.

2. Indirect regulation and promotion of competition, through the agency of one or more lines of railway, to be owned and controlled by the Government.

3. The improvement of natural water-ways and the construction of artificial channels of water communication.

The report was accepted and considered, but there the matter rested, so far as the practical results were concerned.

In 1878 Mr. John H. Reagan, of Texas, introduced in the House of Representatives a bill for an act to regulate railroad companies engaged in interstate commerce. This may be said to have been the first real interstate commerce bill before Congress. It was a progressive, thorough and well-planned measure, but failed to receive the approval of Congress because a majority of its members considered it too radical a measure. The bill contained many of the provisions of the present Interstate Commerce Act, including the anti-pooling and the long and short haul clauses; but instead of creating a commission it lodged in the courts, both State and Federal, the power to enforce the law.

Other bills were introduced from year to year, but during a period of nine years none of them drew sufficient votes to make it a law. Congress may be said to have been divided into three camps upon the railroad question, viz. : those who favored the system of regulation proposed by Mr. Reagan, those who favored the commissioner system and those who were opposed to every mode of Federal regulation of interstate commerce. In the meantime, the inactivity of Congress caused considerable restlessness among the people, and the demand for action became louder every year. The issue entered into politics, and a number of Western Congressmen owed their failure to be re-elected to their indifference or enmity to Federal railroad legislation.

On March 21st, 1885, under authority of a resolution adopted by the Senate of the United States, the President of the Senate appointed a select committee to investigate and report upon the subject of the regulation of the transportation of freight and passengers between the several States by railroad and water routes. Senator Cullom, of Illinois, became its chairman. The committee examined a large number of witnesses, including railroad managers and shippers, addressed letters to the railroad commissioners of the several States, to boards of trade, chambers of commerce, State boards of agriculture, Patrons of Husbandry, Farmers' Alliances, etc., and made every effort to obtain the opinions of those who had given special attention to the transportation problem.

The report of the committee was submitted to the Senate on January 18, 1886. Concerning the abuses of railroad transportation it differed but little from that of the Windom committee. The report declared publicity to be the best remedy for unjust discrimination and recom-

mended that the posting of rates and public notice of all
changes in tariffs be required. It also recommended that
a greater charge for a shorter than a longer haul be made
presumptive evidence of an unjust discrimination, and
that a national commission be established for the enforcement of any laws that might be passed for the regulation
of interstate commerce. Upon the question of pooling
the report stated:

"The committee does not deem it prudent to recom-
mend the prohibition of pooling, which has been urged
by many shippers, or the legalization of pooling compacts,
as has been suggested by many railroad officials and by
others who have studied the question. . . . The
majority of the committee are not disposed to endanger
the success of the methods of regulation proposed for the
prevention of unjust discrimination by recommending the
prohibition of pooling, but prefer to leave that subject for
investigation by a commission when the effects of the
legislation herein suggested shall have been developed and
made apparent."

The report was accompanied by a bill representing
"the substantially unanimous judgment of the committee
as to the regulations which are believed to be expedient
and necessary for the government and control of the
carriers engaged in interstate traffic."

The bill was before Congress for more than a year,
receiving several important amendments before its final
passage in both houses. It was approved by the President on the 4th day of February, 1887, and took effect
sixty days after its passage, except as to the provisions
relating to the appointment and organization of an Interstate Commerce Commission, which took effect at once.

The act contains twenty-four sections, but is by no
means cumbersome. It is, in many respects, the most
important piece of legislation that has been had in Con-

gress for the past twenty years. It applies to common carriers engaged in the transportation of passengers or property wholly by railroad, or partly by railroad and partly by water, when both are used, under a common control, management or arrangement, for a continuous carriage or shipment from one State or Territory of the United States, or the District of Columbia, to any other State or Territory in the United States or the District of Columbia, or from any place in the United States to an adjacent foreign country, or from any place in the United States through a foreign country to any other place in the United States. It prohibits unjust and unreasonable charges, special rates, rebates, drawbacks, undue or unreasonable preferences, advantages, prejudices and disadvantages, as well as all discriminations between connecting lines. It makes unlawful a less charge for a longer than for a shorter haul over the same line, in the same direction, the shorter being included within the longer distance, except when specially authorized by the Interstate Commerce Commission. It prohibits pools, requires schedules of freight rates and passenger fares to be kept in all depots and stations, permits no advance in the rates, fares and charges once established, except after ten days' public notice, and makes it unlawful for common carriers to charge either more or less than schedule rates.

It also requires them to file copies of all schedules, traffic contracts and joint schedules with the Interstate Commerce Commission, as well as to make them public when directed by the commission, and prohibits combinations to prevent the carriage of freight from being continuous from the place of shipment to the place of destination. It makes common carriers liable for all damages

to persons injured by violations of the act, and specially
provides that any court before which such a damage suit
may be pending may compel any director, officer, receiver, trustee or agent of the defendant company to
appear and testify in the case, and that the claim that
any such testimony or evidence may tend to criminate the
person giving such evidence shall not excuse such witness
from testifying, but that such evidence or testimony shall
not be used against such person on the trial of any criminal proceeding. It likewise subjects such officers and
employes of a railroad company as may be guilty of aiding or abetting in violations of the act to fines not exceeding $5,000 for each offense.

These provisions are covered by the first ten sections
of the act. Section 11 establishes the Interstate Commerce Commission, to be composed of five commissioners
appointed by the President by and with the advice and
consent of the Senate. It provides that the commissioners
first appointed shall continue in office for the term of two,
three, four, five and six years, respectively, from the first
of January, 1887, the term of each to be designated by
the President, and that their successors shall be appointed
for terms of six years, except that any person chosen to
fill a vacancy shall be appointed only for the unexpired
term of the commissioner whom he shall succeed. No
more than three commissioners may be appointed from
the same political party, and the President has the power
to remove any commissioner for inefficiency, neglect of
duty or malfeasance in office. Authority is given to the
commission to inquire into the management of the business of all common carriers subject to the provisions of
the act and to require the attendance of witnesses and to
invoke the aid of any court of the United States for that
purpose.

Section 13 authorizes any person, firm, corporation or association, any mercantile, agricultural or manufacturing society, any body politic or municipal organization to file complaints against any common carrier subject to the provisions of the act, with the commission, whose duty it is made to forward a statement of the charges to such common carrier and call upon him to satisfy the complaint or answer the same in writing, and to investigate the matters complained of, if the complaint is not satisfied. The commission is also charged with the duty of making such investigations at the request of State or territorial railroad commissions and may even institute them at its own motion. Section 14 requires the commission to make a report in writing of any investigation it may make and to enter it of record and furnish copies of it to the complainant and the common carrier complained of. Section 15 makes it the commissioners' duty, when it is found that any law cognizable by it has been violated by a common carrier, to serve notice on such carrier to desist from such violation and to make reparation for an injury found to have been done. If any lawful order or requirement of the commission is disobeyed by a common carrier, it becomes their duty and is lawful for any company or person interested in such order to apply by petition to the Circuit Court of the United States sitting in equity in the judicial district in which the common carrier complained of has its principal office, and the court has power to hear and determine the matter speedily and without the formal pleadings and proceedings applicable to ordinary suits, and to restrain the common carrier from continuing such violation or disobedience. It is further provided by this section that on such hearings the report of the commission shall be accepted as *prima facie* evidence.

Section 17 regulates the proceedings of the commission. A majority constitute a quorum for the transaction of business. The commission may from time to time make or amend rules for the regulation of proceedings before it. Any party may appear before it and be heard in person or by attorney, and every vote or official act of the commission must be entered of record and its proceedings made public upon the request of either party interested.

Section 19 provides that the principal office of the commission shall be in Washington, but that for the convenience of the public it may hold special sessions in any part of the United States.

Section 20 authorizes the commission to require annual reports from all common carriers subject to the provisions of the act, to fix the time and prescribe the manner in which such reports shall be made, and to require from such carriers specific answers to all questions upon which the commission may need information.

Section 21 excepts from the operation of the act the carriage of property for the United States, State or municipal governments, or for charitable purposes, or for fairs and expositions; also the issuance of mileage, excursion and commutation tickets, the giving of reduced rates to ministers of religion, the free carriage by a railroad company of its own officers and employes, and the exchanging of passes or tickets among the principal officers of railroad companies.

The sections not noticed are of minor importance, relating to annual reports, salaries, appropriations of funds, etc.

The act was amended on March 2, 1889, but the amendments made did not materially affect its principal provisions.

When the law was passed its friends well realized that its success would greatly depend on the character of the commissioners whom it was incumbent upon the President to appoint. It was feared that if the railroad influence should control these appointments, the power to suspend the long and short haul clause would be the chief and perhaps the only power exercised by the commission. There was great danger that the office of Interstate Commerce Commissioner might become a sinecure for servile railroad lawyers, as similar State officers had been before, and that a public trust might be turned into an additional corporation agency for evil. The selection of the commissioners, and especially that of Judge T. M. Cooley, of Michigan, was greatly to the credit of President Cleveland. A man of unquestionable integrity, an eminent jurist and close student of railroad affairs, Judge Cooley was particuliarly well qualified for the office of chairman of the Interstate Commerce Commission, which he occupied for nearly five years with signal fitness, and from which he only retired to the sincere regret of the American people. Under Judge Cooley's leadership the commission has been more than a purely executive board. It was under the Constitution not in the power of Congress to clothe the Interstate Commerce Commission with full judicial authority without giving its members, like other Federal judges, tenure for life, instead of a term of years. The inherent force of the commission's decisions in its interpretation of the law made them in many cases virtually the equivalent of judicial rulings.

A few of the most important decisions of the commission may be mentioned here. Construing the long and short haul clause, they held that, in case of complaint for violating this section of the act, "the burden of proof is on the carrier to justify any departure from the general rule described by the statute, by showing that the circumstances and conditions are substantially dissimilar." They also decided that "when a greater charge in the aggregate is made for the transportation of passengers or the like kind of property for a shorter than a longer distance over the same line in the same direction, the shorter being included in the longer distance, it is not sufficient justification therefor that the traffic which is subjected to such greater charge is way or local traffic and that which is given the more favorable rates is not; and that it is not "sufficient justification for such greater charge that the short-haul traffic is more expensive to the carrier, unless when the circumstances are such as to make it exceptionally excessive, or the long-haul traffic exceptionally inexpensive, the difference being extraordinary and susceptible of definite proof; nor that the lesser charge on the longer haul has for its motive the encouragement of manufactures or some other branch of industry, nor that it is designed to build up business or trade centers."

Upon the question of publicity of the railroad business the commission held that, as the books of the defendant carriers, as to rates charged, facilities furnished and general movements of freight, are in the nature of semi-public records, the officers and agents of defendant carriers ought to give promptly to a complainant any statement of facts called for, if such statement may probably have importance on the hearing.

Judge Brewer's opinion as to what constitutes a reasonable rate was evidently not shared by Judge Cooley and his colleagues, for in the case of the New Orleans Cotton Exchange vs. the Cincinnati, New Orleans and Pacific Railway Company the commission decided that the fact that a road earns but little more than operating expenses cannot be made to justify grossly excessive rates, and that "wherever there are more roads than the business at fair rates will remunerate, they must rely upon future earnings for the return of investments and profits." In another case the commission hold that "in fixing reasonable rates the requirements of operating expenses, bonded debt, fixed charges and dividend on capital stock from the total traffic are all to be considered, but the claim that any particular rate is to be measured by these as a fixed standard, below which the rate may not lawfully be reduced, is one rightly subject to some qualifications, one of which is that the obligations must be actual and in good faith."

The rules governing the proper construction of classification sheets which the commission has laid down are founded upan common sense and justice. They say:

"A classification sheet is put before the public for general information; it is supposed to be expressed in plain terms so that the ordinary business man can understand it and, in connection with the rate sheets, determine for himself what he can be lawfully charged for transportation. The persons who prepare the classification have no more authority to construe it than anybody else, and they must leave it to speak for itself."

In defining what is legitimate traffic the commission made the following decision:

"The transportation of traffic under circumstances and conditions that force a low rate for its carriage or an abandonment of the business, but which affords some revenue above the cost of its movement, and works no material injustice to other patrons of a carrier, is to be deemed legitimate competition. When, however, its carriage is at a loss and imposes a burden on like traffic at other points and on other traffic, it is to be deemed destructive and illegitimate competition."

It has been shown in a former chapter that the weaker oil refiners have been discriminated against by the railroads, which permitted the Standard Oil Company to use their own tank cars in the shipment of oil and charge its competitors excessive rates for like shipments in barrels. Complaint being made of this discrimination, the commission held that it is properly the business of a carrier by railroad to supply rolling stock for the freight he offers or proposes to carry, and that "if the diversities and peculiarities of traffic are such that this is not always practical, and the consignor is allowed to supply it for himself, the carrier must not allow its own deficiencies in this particular to be made the means of putting at unreasonable disadvantage those who may use in the same traffic all the facilities which it supplies."

A most important ruling of the commission is that relating to the pass abuse. Complaint was made that the Boston and Maine Railroad Company issued in the States of Maine, New Hampshire, Vermont and Massachusetts free passes to certain classes of persons, among them "gentlemen long eminent in the public service, higher officials of the States, prominent officials of the United States, members of the legislative railroad committees of the above named States, and persons whose good will was claimed to be important to the defendant." The commission decided that such a discrimination is unwarranted, that a carrier is bound to charge equally to all persons, regardless of their relative individual standing in the community, and that the words "under substantially similar circumstances and · conditions" relate to the nature and character of the service rendered by the carrier, and not to the official, social or business position of the passenger.

It is a notorious fact that the practice of issuing free passes to public officials and other influential persons has been more or less indulged in by nearly every railroad in the country up to the present time. It is to be hoped that this ruling of the commission will be enforced in such a manner as to put an end to this intolerable abuse.

The Interstate Commerce Commission has been equally efficient in its administrative capacity. From the very first it called attention to the great advantage of having one classification of freight throughout the country, and it has since labored diligently to unify the various classifications in use. As the commission in this undertaking is only armed with the armor of moral suasion, it is a difficult task; but there is little doubt that the accomplishment of this great reform is only a question of a few years. Iniquities in classifications and rates are constantly pointed out by the commission and corrected by the companies. Moreover, the annual reports of the commission, not to mention its very excellent statistical data, diffuse much useful information and dispel many delusions. Thus the fourth annual report of the commission says:

" A stranger to the law might infer, from some public addresses and pamphlets which have assumed to discuss this subject, that the railroad companies were prohibited from carrying the necessities of life over long distances at very low rates, unless their rates on other subjects of transportation for shorter distances were made to correspond. Indeed, instances have been pointed out in which it was said that certain articles of commerce could not now be transported for long distances, because, by reason of this provision, they would not bear the charges that must under compulsion of law be imposed upon them. Among such instances has been mentioned the granite industry of New England, as to which it has been said that valuable manufactories have ceased to be profitable because it has now become impossible for the proprietors to obtain from the railroad companies the nominal rates for the transportation of their products which they formerly enjoyed, since it is now, by the long and short haul clause, made criminal for the companies to give such rates.

" A complaint of this nature is not to be met by argument, because it is baseless in point of fact. The instance mentioned may safely be assumed to be chosen rather from regard to the need of an attack upon the law than from any belief in the justice of its application. The prohibition of the fourth section, so far as concerns this article of commerce, or any other that can be named, will have no application whatever until it is made to appear that elsewhere upon the lines of the road conveying it there is property of the same kind, for transportation by the same carriers in the same direction, upon which the carriers are disposed to making greater charges in the aggregate for the shorter hauls.

"The wheat of the extreme West, it is also said, can no longer have the nominal rates which were formerly made for transportation to the seaboard, but this assertion is also without point or applicability, unless it is shown that the carriers are not only disposed to give such rates, but propose to make up for the consequent losses to themselves by the imposition of greater charges in the aggregate for the carriage of the like grain when offered for carriage by growers in the States nearer the seaboard. Nominal rates impartially made as between shippers of like articles in the same direction and under like circumstances and conditions are as admissible now as they ever were."

The same report contains a rather pointed reply to Judge Brewer's ruling in the Iowa rate cases, viz., that, " where the rates prescribed will not pay some compensation to the owners, then it is the duty of the courts to interfere and protect the companies from such rates," and that compensation implies three things: "Payment of cost of service, interest on bonds and then some dividends." The commission reviews this stupid rule as follows:

"The effort has sometimes been made to indicate a rule which must constitute the minimum of reduction in all cases, and it has been said that rates must not be made so low that the carriers would be left unable to pay interest on their obligations and something by way of dividend to stockholders, after maintaining the road in proper condition and paying all running expenses. This comes nearer to a suggestion of a rule of law for these cases than any other that has come to the knowledge of the commission. But it is so far from being a rule of law, that it is not even a rule of policy, or a practical rule to which any name can be given, and to which the carriers themselves or the public authorities can conform their action. In the first place, when we take into consideration the question of the condition of roads and of equipment, the proper improvements to be made, the new conveniences and appliances to be considered and made use of, if deemed desirable, and the innumerable questions that are involved in the matter of running expenses, it is very obvious that there can be no standard of expenses which the court can act upon and apply, but that the whole field is one of judgment in the exercise of a reasonable discretion by the managing powers or by the public authorities in reviewing their action. It is to be borne in mind that there are many roads in the country that never have been and in all probability never will be able to pay their obligations and to pay dividends, even the slightest, to their stockholders. . . If the rule suggested is a correct one, and must be adhered to by the public authorities, then it is entirely impossible that those who operate these roads can prescribe excessive charges, since it is impossible to fix any rates that would bring their revenues up to the point of enabling them to pay any dividends . . . . But the rule suggested would also be one under which those roads would be entitled to charge the most which, instead of being built with the money of the stockholders themselves, had been constructed with money borrowed; the larger the debt the higher being the rates that would be legal. If a road were out of debt so that it had no bonds to provide for, it must content itself with such rates as would pay some dividend to its stockholders. If the road were in debt, though it perhaps served the same communities, it might be entitled to charge rates 50, or possibly 100 per cent higher. . . . But over and beyond all this the attempt to apply the rule suggested would be absolutely futile for the reason that the rates prescribed for one road would necessarily affect all others that either directly or indirectly came in competition with it."

It is no exaggeration to say that the annual reports of the commission stand unexcelled as dauntless, clear, concise and instructive public documents. It may also be asserted that whatever success has so far attended the Interstate Commerce Law, that success is in a great measure due to the tact, courage and ability of the men who, in the past, have been the guiding spirits of the commission.

Efforts will be made by railroad managers in the future, as they have been made in the past, to weaken the commission by securing the appointment of men servile to the railroad interest as members of that body.

Mr. Depew says that "all railroad men are politicians, and active ones." This is true as to manipulating managers and will continue to be so just as long as we allow such extraordinary powers to be exercised by them. The saloon men are politicians, and active ones. There is not a city or town in this broad land that is not in danger of falling under their sway unless their offensive efforts are resisted. The old United States Bank managers were politicians, and active ones. They perverted the trust reposed in their hands to such an extent that the indignation of the people was aroused, and under the lead of a stern old patriot the bank was swept out of existence. Shall we restrain corporation management within proper limits and make corporations serve the public welfare, or shall we let the abuses go on until the people, under the lead of another Jackson, demand emphatically the application of some remedy, for better or for worse? Perhaps Government ownership, perhaps something else. Nations, like individuals, should profit by the experience of the past.

The Interstate Commerce Commission, in their sixth annual report, say, concerning the Interstate Commerce Law:

" It was scarcely possible that it should be so complete and comprehensive at the outset as to require no alteration or amendment. Those who are familiar with the practices which obtained prior to the passage of this law, and contrast them with the methods and conditions now existing, will accord to the present statute great influence in the direction of necessary reforms and a high degree of usefulness in promoting the public interest.

" Whoever will candidly examine the reports of the commission from year to year, and thus become acquainted with the work which has been done and is now going on, will have no doubt of the potential value of this enactment in correcting public sentiment, restraining public injustice and enforcing the principle of reasonable charges and equal treatment. Imperfections and weaknesses which could not be anticipated at the time of its passage have since been disclosed by the effort to give it effective administration. The test of experience, so far from condemning the policy of public regulation, has established its importance and intensified its necessity. The very respects in which the existing law has failed to meet public expectation point out the advantages and demonstrate the utility of Government supervision. . . .

"Of this much we are convinced: The public demand for Government regulation and the necessity for legal protection against the encroachments of railroad corporations have not been diminished by the experience of the last six years. The act to regulate commerce was not framed to meet a temporary emergency, nor in obedience to a transient and spasmodic sentiment. The people will not tolerate a return to the injustice and wrong-doing which inevitably occurs when no correction is undertaken and no regulation attempted. The evils of unrestricted management will not be permanently endured, and legal remedies will continue to be sought until they are amply provided. The present statute, however crude and inadequate in many respects, was the constitutional exercise of most important powers and the legislative expression of a great and wholesome principle. Its fundamental and pervading purpose is to secure equality of treatment. It assumes that the railroads are engaged in a public service, and requires that service to be impartially performed. It asserts the right of every citizen to use the agencies which the carrier provides on equal terms with all his fellows, and finds an invasion of that right in every unauthorized exemption from charges commonly imposed.

"The railroad is justly regarded as a public facility which every person may enjoy at pleasure, a common right to which all are admitted and from which none are excluded. The essence of this right is equality, and its enjoyment can be complete only when it is secured on like conditions by all who desire its benefits. The railroad exists by virtue of authority proceeding from the State, and thus differs in its essential nature from every form of private enterprise. The carrier is invested with extraordinary powers, which are delegated by the sovereign, and thereby performs a governmental function. The favoritism, partiality and exactions which the law was designed to prevent resulted, in large measure, from a general misapprehension of the nature of transportation and its vital relation to commercial and industrial progress. So far from being a private possession, it differs from every species of property, and is in no sense a commodity. Its office is peculiar, for it is essentially public. The railroad, therefore, can rightfully do nothing which the State itself might not do if it performed this public service through its own agents instead of delegating it to corporations which it has created. The large shipper is entitled to no advantage over his smaller rival in respect of rates or accommodations, for the compensation exacted in every case should be measured by the same standard. To allow any exceptions to this fundamental rule is to subvert the principle upon which free institutions depend and substitute arbitrary caprice for equality of right.

" The spirit of the law is opposed to usages so long continued and so familiar that their unjust and demoralizing character has not been clearly perceived, but it is a long step towards such regulation of the agencies of transportation as will make them equally available to all without discrimination between individuals or communities. It can hardly be the fault of those who are charged with its administration if the beneficial aims of this statute have not been fully attained and compliance with its provisions not completely secured. A better understanding of its purpose and an educated public sentiment, aided by the needful amendments which experience suggests, will fully vindicate the policy of Congress in undertaking to bring the great transportation interests of the country into general harmony with its requirements.

" It affords us gratification to add that many railroad managers of the highest standing now concede the necessity for Government regulation, and avow themselves in favor of such further enactments as will make that regulation effective. "

CHAPTER XIII.

RAILROAD managers frequently make the assertion that the average freight rates charged in the United States are lower than those usually charged in European countries and that this fact is in itself sufficient proof that they are too low. A comparison of the transportation problem of Europe with our own will show this argument to be fallacious.

While from $25,000 to $30,000 a mile is a very liberal estimate of the average cost of American roads, the average cost of European railroads, owing to their expensive rights of way, substantial road-beds and heavy grades, is probably not less than $75,000 per mile. British railway companies have laid out for the purchase of land, for right of way and depot accommodations an amount about equal to the entire average cost of American roads for the same number of miles.

For instance, the Southeastern Company paid $20,000; the Manchester and Leeds Company, $30,750, and the London, Birmingham and Great Western, $31,500 per mile. The first Eastern Counties line paid even $60,000 per mile for land through an agricultural district. As nearly as can be ascertained, the average cost of the right of way of railroads was over $20,000 for the United Kingdom. In Belgium the average cost of the right of way was $11,000. It was lower, however, in the other countries of the European continent.

The topography of the country through which the

English railways are built is such as necessitated enormous expenses for heavy embankments, cuttings, viaducts, tunnels and bridges, and in some cases increased the cost of the roads to fabulous sums. The Lancashire and Yorkshire Railway actually cost $260,000 per mile for the whole of its 403 miles. European roads have been built in a much more permanent manner and have terminal facilities whose cost is far beyond any sum paid for such purposes in this country. In Great Britain, moreover, the expenses of contests and of procuring charters have been very great and have probably averaged $3,000 per mile.

English railway men charge Americans with having indulged in stock-watering to a greater extent than any other people in the world. This is probably true, yet the English have not been dull students of this art, and they are far from free of having indulged in this luxury. Much of their railroad stock was issued in a wasteful manner and represents no actual investment, and it is safe to say that from 30 to 40 per cent. of their present railroad capitalization is water.

If upon the above basis both European and American railroads are to yield an interest of $4\frac{1}{2}$ per cent. on the actual investment, the former will have to earn at least $2,250 per mile more than the latter, and this difference equals about 50 per cent. of the average operating expenses of American roads per mile. Labor is cheaper across the Atlantic, but this difference is more than equalized by the employment of a much larger number of men per mile, as the following table will show:

Countries.	No. of men employed per mile.	Average wages per annum.	Wages paid per mile.
United Kingdom	18	$335	$6,000
Belgium	22	210	4,620
Russia	15	240	3,600
Germany	14	250	3,500
France	14	220	3,080
United States	5	555	2,625

The London and Northwestern Railway is 1,793 miles
long and has over 55,000 employes, or over 30 per mile.
The Lancashire and Yorkshire Company employs over
42 per mile.

The train men of Europe work less hours and earn less
per capita for their employers than do the train men of
this country.   The average annual gross earnings per
employe on sixteen of the leading lines of Great Britain,
as shown by Mr. Jeans, appear to be $975 against $1,600
on fifteen leading lines of the United States, while the
average net earnings per employe are $465 on the British
lines against $720 on the American lines; making a
difference in favor of this country of 70 per cent. in gross
earnings and 53 per cent. in net earnings.   If American
labor is more expensive, it is also more efficient than
labor is elsewhere.

It must also be considered that the average haul in
Europe is much less than the average haul in the United
States.   It has always been maintained by the railroad
companies, and very justly, too, that the terminal charges
are as important a factor of freight rates as is the cost of
carriage.   The terminal charges are the same for a
twenty-five-mile haul as for a thousand-mile haul; they
form a comparatively large part of the total charges for
the former and a very small part of the total charges for
the latter.   It is therefore manifestly unjust to compare
the rates per ton per mile of Europe with those of the
United States without making due allowance for the
difference in the length of their average hauls.   All other
things being equal, a fair comparison between the freight
rates of different countries should be based upon hauls of
equal length.

There is another consideration which should not be lost
sight of.   The commodities in the United States which

contribute principally to the long haul are raw products. The universally low rates of these commodities greatly lower the general average. In Europe, on the other hand, manufactured goods predominate as long-haul freight, and based upon increased risk and increased cost of carriage, considerably swell the general average of freight charges. The railroads of the United States also do more business per train mile than those of any other country excepting perhaps Austria, Russia and India. This should certainly enable them to do business for less than it is done by transatlantic lines.

In addition to all this, a number of European countries, particularly France, require their railroads to perform large services, such as the carrying of the mails and the transportation of the officers and employes of the Government, gratuitously, and to carry soldiers at reduced rates.

Another factor in the equation should be considered. Eurpean roads are built, equipped and all permanent improvements wholly made at the expense of the stock- and bondholders, while in this country they are partially constructed at the expense of the patrons of the road. In the former case the capitalization of the road represents what has been paid by the stock-and bondholders, and in the latter, not only what they have paid, but large contributions paid from the income of the road and from public and private donations.

It will thus be seen that railroad rates ought to be lower, and even much lower, here than in Europe. If it *is* true that the average rate per ton per mile is lower in America than across the Atlantic, this is chiefly due to the fact that water transportation has forced down through (or long-haul) rates and has thus lowered the general average.

This reduction was by no means made voluntarily by the railway companies, but was forced upon them. Where in the United States water does not exist, as in local traffic, rates are usually much higher than in Europe.

The reduction in freight rates was brought about by a number of inventions which greatly lowered the cost of both the construction and the operation of railways. Through the introduction of the steam shovel, of the wheel-scraper, of improved rock-drills, and of other labor-saving machines, as well as by a general improvement in the methods of grading, the cost of grading has been reduced from 25 to 50 per cent., and railroad bridges are now built at one-third of their former cost. Owing to Bessemer's great invention, steel rails can at the present time be bought for one-half of what iron rails cost ten or fifteen years ago, and about one-third of the cost twenty years ago. According to David A. Wells, the author of "Recent Economic Changes," the annual producing capacity of a Bessemer converter was increased fourfold between 1873 and 1886, and four men can now make a given product of steel in the same time and with less cost of material than it took ten men ten years ago to accomplish. A ton of steel can now be made with 5,000 pounds of coal, while it required twice that quantity in 1868. When it is considered that rails and tires made of steel last three times as long as those made of iron, permit greater speed, carry a much larger weight, and require less repairs, the importance to the railroad interests of the improvements made in the manufacture of steel can hardly be overestimated. Similar reductions have been made in the car and machine shops. An average train to-day probably costs no more than one-half as much as it did twenty years ago. Mr. Wells, in the work just mentioned, says:

"In 1870–'71 one of the leading railroads of the Northwestern United States built 126 miles, which, with some tunneling, was bonded for about $40,000 per mile. The same road could now (1889) be constructed, with the payment of higher wages to laborers of all classes, for about $20,000 per mile."

A great saving has also been made in the consumption of coal. Under favorable circumstances a loaded freight car can now be propelled a mile with one pound of coal. A similar economy of fuel has, through the improvement of their engines, been effected in ocean steamers. The invention of the compound engine has reduced the expense of running about one-half, while it has doubled the room left for the cargo. The statement has recently been made that a piece of coal half as large as a walnut, when burned in the compound engine of a modern steamboat, drives a ton of food and its proportion of the ship one mile on its way to a foreign port.

Furthermore, the invention of the air-brake has materially reduced the number of train men formerly necessary to safely manage a train, just as the introduction of steam-hoisting and other machines, both upon docks and vessels, has greatly decreased the number of men employed upon the mercantile marine.

There is certainly much similarity between the railroad and the steamboat as agencies of transportation. Whatever fuel and labor-saving causes operate on one must necessarily operate upon the other. When we, therefore, find that the ocean rates are only from one-third to one-fourth of what they were thirty years ago, we are justly surprised to see railroad rates maintained as high as they are. Operating expenses have been greatly reduced and passenger travel has largely increased during the past twenty years, but reductions corresponding in the passenger rates of the United States have not been made.

It is, nevertheless, no easy matter always to determine what are reasonable rates. It is easier to tell what rates are unreasonable. Rates are unreasonable that bring an income in excess of sufficient to keep the road in proper condition, to pay operating expenses, including taxes and a fair rate of interest on the amount, not including donations, actually invested in the road. The patrons of a road should not be taxed to pay interest on their own donations, or on public donations, to the road, as the donations were made for the benefit of the public, and not for the benefit of private individuals. A rate which may appear reasonable to the carrier is apt to be regarded as too high by the shipper; and, again, one that seems reasonable to the shipper is denounced as too low by the railroad man. Each is tempted to consult only his own interests and to disregard the just claims of the other side. Thus, while the shipper will claim that his rates ought to be low enough to enable him to compete with other shippers more advantageously located than he is, the railroad manager will demand a rate which would enable him to declare high dividends on largely fictitious values. The owners of roads which were built merely for purposes of speculation or blackmailing insist on being permitted to charge exorbitant rates to bring up their earnings to the level of those roads for whose construction there was a legitimate demand.

It is a settled principle of common law that all rates must be reasonable, but no uniform rule has as yet been adopted by which the question of reasonableness is to be determined. The doctrine laid down by Judge Brewer, that ''where the rates prescribed will not pay some compensation to the owners, then it is the duty of the courts to interfere and protect the companies from such rates,'' and that "compensation implies three things: cost of service, interest on bonds, and then some dividends," is absurd. A question is never settled until it is settled right, and this rule is certainly open to very serious objections. A road may be bonded for several times its cost or its real value, it may be managed with such recklessness or extravagance that its operating expenses may be twice what they would be under a careful and economical management, yet under this rule the shipper must pay the premium which bond-watering and bad management command. The general enforcement of such a rule would place the public at the mercy of scheming railroad manipulators. No matter to what extent the business of a road may increase, a reduction of rates can always be prevented by the issue of new bonds and the doubling of the already lordly salaries of its managers. Again, under the operation of this rule a road which entirely suffices to do the business between two points may be paralleled by another and the public be compelled to pay excessive rates to maintain both. It might be said that the public cannot be forced to patronize any road, that if it would not withdraw its patronage from the old line, the new line would soon become bankrupt, and that in such an event its owners, and not the public, would be the sufferers. This argument may be met by the statement that, aside from the fact that concerted action among a large number of people can never be secured, few roads rely for their support solely upon local business, and that any loss which the older road sustains from encroachments by its rival upon its through traffic it is compelled to make up by raising its rates upon its local business. It is the almost inevitable consequence when one road is paralleled by another that the business which was previously done by one road will be nearly equally divided between the two, and under the rule laid down by Judge Brewer the public will be called upon to pay the operating expenses and the interest on the bonds of both, together with such dividends on the stock as the financiering ability of their managers may secure. The better judgment seems to be that to determine what are reasonable rates is not a question for judicial adjudication.

The Interstate Commerce Commission, in their fourth annual report, assert that "there can be no standard of expense which the courts can act upon and apply, but that the whole field is one of judgment in the exercise of a reasonable discretion by the managing powers, or by the public authorities in reviewing their action." Their views upon this subject are still more definitely stated in the following words contained in the same report:

"An attempt is made to give authority to the courts to interfere by the suggestion that property or charter contract rights, or both, are involved in the matter of fixing rates, and therefore that it is not possible the conclusions of administrative boards should be final. This is an endeavor, by the mere use of words, to confer jurisdiction upon the courts where the substance is altogether wanting. Property or contract rights are involved in these cases precisely as they are in numerous other cases of the exercise of power under the police authority of the State, either by the State itself or by its municipalities."

These views cannot fail to commend themselves to any unprejudiced mind. It is a well-established fact that all officials will, if permitted, extend their jurisdiction, and judges are no exception to the rule. It was therefore but natural that the courts should attempt to solve the problem of railroad rates.

The attempt so far has been fruitless, nor will it be otherwise as long as the courts persist in approaching with abstract legal maxims a question which, above all things, requires the light of experience and the exercise of sound discretion. The question of railroad rates will never be satisfactorily settled until it is definitely referred to expert administrative State and National boards empowered and prepared to meet the many contingencies that will always arise in the transportation business.

It is not difficult to account for the inability of the courts to properly adjudicate the question of reasonable rates. The legislature, or a board to which it has delegated its power, prescribes for a railroad company a classification and tariff. The company claims that the rates so fixed are unreasonably low and applies to the courts for redress.

Now, if the rates were based upon the cost of service only, it might, perhaps, be possible for a court to determine whether the prescribed rates are adequate or not. But even in such a case the question would arise whether the capitalization and the operating expenses of the road are not excessive, and its determination would require expert knowledge and sound discretion rather than legal lore. However, since the cost of service is not the only, and with railroad men not even an essential, factor in rate-making, it is evident that the rates upon single commodities can not be reviewed upon their individual merits, but the tariff must, in the judicial determination of the question whether it is reasonable or not, be viewed as a whole. But as it is impossible to foretell what effect a readjusted tariff would have on the revenues of a road, even courts are forced to admit that an actual trial of the tariff is necessary to establish its merits or demerits.

If the complaining company were as anxious to give the new tariff a fair trial as it usually is to demonstrate to the satisfaction of the court that it is devoid of every principle of justice, such a test might be accepted by the public as a reliable basis of judicial procedure. But railroad managers are not only striving to perpetuate their own high rates, but to show to the public that freight tariffs not emanating from a railroad company's office are of necessity crude and unjust to the carrier. They know that if they should succeed in convincing the public that administrative boards are incapable of dealing with that question, they might for years to come be left in undisputed possession of the power to make their own rates. This is certainly for the railroad manager a prize worth contending for, and no sacrifice is too great for him to make when there is any hope of ultimate victory. Being absolutely uncontrolled in his action, he finds it an easy matter, by temporarily diverting business from his line, by the increase of operating expenses and by repressing growing industries, and in many other ways, to curtail the business of his road and diminish its revenues. He can court losses in a thousand different ways discernible neither to the courts nor the general public. In short, it is in the power of any railroad manager to manipulate such a trial in his own interest, and, if determined, to obtain a verdict against any tariff not of his own making. This policy was pursued by several Iowa roads subsequent to Judge Brewer's decision that the alleged unreasonableness of the Iowa commissioners' tariff must be established by an actual trial, and was persevered in until the suit was withdrawn.

But even if the competency of the courts to properly determine such questions were admitted, there would still exist one serious objection to their jurisdiction. Courts necessarily move slowly, while all differences arising between the public and the railways, and especially those concerning rates of transportation, require prompt and decisive action. There are no fixed conditions in commerce. It is a kaleidoscope constantly presenting new phases. Competition at home and abroad, tariff duties, the condition of the crops and a thousand other influences affect it and may require a prompt readjustment of the tariff. So long as railroad companies are permitted to resort to injunctions and effect other delays rendered possible through the machinery of the courts, to prevent for years the enforcement of tariffs prescribed by administrative authorities, so long will the public be at their mercy. So long as they have nothing to lose and everything to gain by a judicial contest, it will be their policy to delay through the courts the enforcement of any tariff, whether prescribed by legislature or by an authorized commission, that falls below their standard. It is not to be understood that the acts of railroad commissioners should never be subject to a judicial view. If such boards clearly exceed their authority or are otherwise guilty of maladministration, if they violate constitutional rights, then railroad companies, if injured by their acts, should be permitted to seek redress in the courts; but they should not be permitted to nullify an official tariff by legal maneuvers. It is clearly not within the province of the courts to make rates or to lay down rules to be followed by those to whom the law has delegated the power to make them, nor should the courts aid the railroads in any attempt to nullify an official tariff that has been legally promulgated. A tariff prepared by sworn and disinterested officials is more likely to be just than one prepared by interested railroad men, and railroad companies should be compelled to adopt it and continue

it in use until it is amended or revoked by legal
authority.

Individual shippers are powerless as against strong
corporations. Railroads apply to the courts for what
they are pleased to term redress, and in the meantime
refuse with impunity to accept an official tariff; but the
shipper has no protection: he must pay their rates or go
out of business. What reason can be assigned why the
weaker should thus be discriminated against? A promulgation of a tariff prepared by a commission is equivalent
to a declaration on the part of these officials that the rates
or some of the rates charged by the railroads are unreasonably high. The railroad, in applying to the courts
for protection, claims that the tariff prescribed by the
commission is unreasonably low. Both tariffs are therefore impeached, one being that of an interested private
company, the other that of a disinterested public board.
It is evident that, even if the people should see fit to give
the courts jurisdiction in such controversies, one of these
tariffs must temporarily prevail pending the decision of
the court, and sound public policy and justice to the
patrons of the road certainly require that the official
tariff be recognized by the courts and made to be respected by the railroad company until it is proved to be
unreasonable and is set aside by lawful authority.

It is claimed by railroad men that they should be
allowed to make their own tariffs because rate-making is
so intricate a subject that none but railroad experts can do
it justice. If this were so the courts would be even less
competent to review a schedule of rates than a State or
National commission would be to make one. Courts cannot be expected to have expert knowledge in all matters
that are likely to be brought before them. They must

rely upon the testimony of expert witnesses whenever technical questions are involved in the determination of cases. The identical sources of information from which courts draw are accessible, or may be made accessible, to a commission, which has the additional advantage that its members may be selected with special reference to their fitness for the duties which they will be called upon to perform and are expected to devote their whole time to the settlement of questions arising in the transportation business. Such a commission can practically be made a court with jurisdiction over all matters connected with railroad business. The railroad manager, no doubt, is thoroughly familiar with the wants and desires of his company; but it may fairly be presumed that he is less familiar with the needs of the public than a railroad commission whose members are in constant communication with the people, patiently listen to the complaints of shippers, court and receive suggestions as to needed changes in classification and rates, and study the relative advantages of the different sections and different interests of the State or the country as regards transportation. A railroad freight agent, on the contrary, is disposed to think that shippers ought to be satisfied with any rate lower than those charged fifty years ago for carting or other crude methods of transportation. He regards their views and suggestions as chimerical and not worthy of any notice, and does not even hesitate to inform them that rate-making is a branch of the railroad business wholly beyond their comprehension, and ought not to be meddled with or even inquired into by the public. The general freight agent is the employe of a company which rates his usefulness solely by his ability to constantly increase its revenues, and he invariably proceeds upon the theory that the best tariff is that which comes nearest imposing upon each commodity offered for carriage the maximum transportation tax that it will bear. A man who entertains such opinions cannot be supposed to be able to do justice to the shipper, and should not be permitted to act as arbitrator in rate controversies between the public and the company whose employe and advocate he is. Nor have we any reason to hope for a change in the present tariff policy of railroads. History has sufficiently demonstrated the fact that reforms must come from without. As long as human nature remains as it is, railroad officials will, if permitted, arrange tariffs in the interest of the men who give them employment, for if they did otherwise their services would soon be dispensed with. A freight tariff should be in the nature of a contract between the carrier and the shipper, and the assent of both parties ought to be essential to its validity. But as it is impracticable for all the parties interested to meet for the purpose of effecting an agreement, the power to make rates has in several States wisely been conferred upon railroad commissioners, and there is a strong tendency in others to adopt the same policy. Such boards have every opportunity to obtain any information needed for the efficient and faithful discharge of their duties. They can hear the representatives of the railroads as well as those of the shippers, investigate carefully disputed points, summon experts and witnesses, and obtain official information relating to classifications and rates from every State in the Union, and, if necessary, from every quarter of the civilized world. The assertion may safely be made that, with experience, a commission acquires more expert knowledge relating to the business of rate-making than a railroad manager. If there is any mystery connected with the business of rate-making which has so far been in the sole possession of railroad men, it is to their interest to initiate the commissioners into their profound secrets. It will be their privilege to enlighten the commissioners as to the actual cost of their respective lines, the cost of every branch of the railway service, and as to a thousand other matters which the public has both a desire and a right to know. If, after a schedule of rates has been prepared, and before it is promulgated, railroad men can suggest any improvement in it, they should have the privilege to do so; or if, after giving it a fair trial, they should be prepared to show that any rate is unreasonably low and injurious to them, their complaint should be carefully investigated, and, if found well grounded, the wrong should at once be righted.

But the same privileges should be extended to shippers. Their rights and their welfare should be guarded as sacredly as those of the railroad companies. They should have the same opportunity to examine a proposed schedule before its promulgation and protest against any feature of it which they may regard prejudicial to their interests, and their statements should receive the same consideration as is accorded to those of representatives of the railroad companies. So, likewise, when shippers prove to the satisfaction of the commission that a rate has outlived its reasonableness, their complaints should at once be investigated, and if their cause is found to be a just one, the tariff should be so amended as to give them relief.

The labors of a board of railroad commissioners are onerous, and their responsibility is great. No uniform rule can be laid down for their guidance in the fixing of rates, yet there are a few fundamental principles which should always be adhered to. The cost of service should invariably be an important factor of a rate. Railroads should not be compelled to carry any commodity for less than the actual cost of moving it, nor should rates be fixed greatly in excess of such cost of service. The carload should be the unit of wholesale shipments. Since it costs the railroad company as much to move ten carloads of freight which belong to one shipper as it costs to move ten carloads belonging to ten shippers, no advantage beyond the general car load rate should be given to the large shipper. The difference in the rates between shipments in less than carload lots ought to be determined solely by the difference in the cost of carriage and handling. Where shipments are made in carload lots, the loading and unloading is usually done by the shipper and consignee, cars are loaded to their full capacity, and no loading or unloading of shipments at intermediate points is necessary. It is therefore but just that the consignor and consignee should have the benefit of the reduced cost of such shipments. Raw materials, and especially coal and lumber and kindred articles, the transportation of which requires neither an expensive rolling stock nor warehouse accommodations nor speedy movement, and in which the risk of loss or damage is insignificant, should be carried at the lowest rate possible. Such a policy will tend to foster other interests, which will develop business for the road and will build up remote sections of the country, and will often enable railroads to carry large quantities of these commodities at times when they would otherwise be nearly idle. There should be a uniform classification throughout the country, based upon considerations of justice and equity instead of railroad tradition. Such articles should be classed together as resemble each other as concerns bulk, weight and risk, or what is virtually the same, cost of carrying and handling. It may be safely assumed that a rate which has been made and used by railroad companies is remunerative. If it is claimed by railroad men that it is not, the burden of proof should rest upon them. A rate may also be considered remunerative to a road if other lines similarly situated have voluntarily adopted it. A schedule finally must be considered reasonable if it enables the company for which it is prescribed to earn under efficient and economical management sufficient to maintain its road in proper condition and a fair rate of interest upon a fair valuation of its road. Property is never worth more than what it can be duplicated for, and railroad property is no exception to the rule. If there has been a depreciation in the property of a company, it should not demand dividends upon values which no longer exist. Nor can the same returns be conceded to railroad property as to private capital. Its investment is permanent and well secured, if it is honestly and intelligently made; and its dividends are net returns after the payment of all expenses, including taxes, cost of management and maintenance. The three per cent. bonds of the United States Government find a ready sale at prices above par. Were there less speculation and more honesty and stability in railroad management, railroad securities yielding a revenue of from $2\frac{1}{2}$ to 4 per cent. on the actual investment would be eagerly sought after by conservative capitalists.

Rate-making requires honesty of purpose, intelligence and discretion, qualities as likely to be found among the servants of the people as among those of corporations. A commission may err, but its errors are not likely to prove

as detrimental to the railroad companies as the extortionate and discriminating rates imposed by railroad managers have proved to the interests of the public. Railroad managers acknowledge no obligation except that of
earning dividends for their companies, while the members
of a railroad commission, on the contrary, are responsible
for their acts to the people, with us the source of all government and all power. To question the justice and sincerity of the people, or to deny the efficacy of such a
control, is to deny the wisdom of popular government.

Railroads might be permitted to reduce their rates
below the official tariff, but they should be required to
give at least thirty days' notice of such a change, to enable
shippers to prepare for it. The companies should not be
permitted, however, to raise rates again without obtaining the commissioners' consent and giving at least two
months' notice of the proposed advance. Sudden fluctuations in rates are a fruitful source of disaster in those
branches of business in which the cost of transportation
forms an important factor in the price of commodities,
and are as unjust and unwarrantable as would be fluctuations in import duties. As long as they are tolerated there
can be no reliable basis for business calculations or contracts. There is little doubt that, were such regulations
enforced, railroad wars, so demoralizing to the business
of the country, would soon belong to the things of the
past, and a far-reaching assurance of future welfare
would be given to the commercial, manufacturing and all
other legitimate interests of the country. It should
always be kept in view by the rate-making power that the
railroad company, like the gas company, the water company and the street car company, is acting in the capacity
of a public agent, and the rate of compensation should be
fixed by public authority.

CHAPTER XIV.

REMEDIES.

THE railroad in America is still in its infancy, both as regards extent of mileage and methods of operation. In 1860 the United States had in round numbers 30,000 miles of road; in 1870 this number had increased to 53,000; in 1880 to 93,000, and in 1890 to 167,000. It will thus be seen that the average increase during each of those three decades was nearly 80 per cent. Should this rate of increase continue during the next three decades there would be in the present territory of the United States a little over three hundred thousand miles in 1900, 550,000 miles in 1910 and close to one million miles in 1920, or about one mile of road for every three miles of territory. It is not likely that the rate of increase of the past will continue in the future; but even if this should be reduced from 80 to 40 per cent. it would be less than fifty-five years when the railroad mileage of the United States would reach the million point.

Even this might seem an extravagant estimate, but it must be remembered that there are already a number of States in the Union with a railroad mileage closely approaching this proportion. The District of Columbia has one mile of road for every 3.39 square miles of territory, New Jersey for every 3.79, Massachusetts for every 3.96, and Connecticut for every 4.96 square miles. Ohio, Pennsylvania, Rhode Island and Illinois follow with one mile of railroad for every 5.14, 5.20, 5.57 and 5.59 square miles of territory, respectively, and Indiana, New York, Delaware and Iowa are not far behind them.

It should also be borne in mind that many of the through lines have double, some triple, and some even quadruple tracks, which, if taken into the account, would increase the mileage much more; and still railroad construction in most of these States is far from being at a standstill. The United States will eventually be able to sustain a closer net of railways than any country in Europe, and we may rest assured that the time will come when the fertile prairie States of the Northwest will have a mile of railroad for every square mile of territory.

In view of the future magnitude of the transportation interest the importance of placing its control and management early upon sound principles should not be underestimated. Abuses crept into railroad management in the past, not because the men who controlled it were necessarily worse than men engaged in other pursuits, but because the States failed to provide adequate legislation for the control of this new social and commercial force, and the license enjoyed by railroad men gradually turned into serious evils what seemed at first only harmless practices. It cannot be denied, however, that the absence of restraint in time attracted to the business unscrupulous men whose sharp practices frequently forced their colleagues of better conscience to do what their sense of honor and justice condemned. These evils and abuses have increased with the growth of the railroad system, and nothing short of the sovereign power can now correct them. It is incumbent upon the state not only to correct the evils of the past, but to base legislative control of railroads upon principles so wise and so broad as to endure for ages, permitting the unlimited growth of the system and at the same time insuring commercial liberty and prosperity to the generations to come.

As it is always easier to tear down than to build up, so it is likewise easier to point out evils than it is to provide proper remedies for their cure. Almost any one can criticise existing conditions, but it requires wise and constructive statesmanship to propose practical measures which will bring about desired improvement. The apparent magnitude of the work of correcting the evils and abuses connected with the transportation business, many of which have been in vogue for more than a generation, has discouraged many from seriously undertaking it. And yet we shall find the problem by no means a difficult one, if we properly analyze it and go to the root of the evil. Prof. Bryce, in his work "The American Commonwealth," refers to the fact that the people of this country have been equal to the task of solving the gravest problems which have been presented to them, and we need have no doubt of their ability to solve the railroad problem. Railroad regulation does not require the adoption of any new principle of law. If the common law is rightly applied and provision is made for its strict and systematic enforcement, it will meet every condition that is likely to arise in the transportation business. It should always be remembered that the railroad is an improved highway, and the principal reason for which it is built is to accommodate the people and promote their welfare, and not to serve the selfish ends of a few individuals, and that private companies were permitted to build and operate it only because the State believed that the public interests could best be served in this way.

It is one of the duties of the State to facilitate transportation by establishing highways. These highways may be built by the State directly or through municipalities or even private corporations. Thus, under authority derived from the State, cities lay out, construct and maintain streets within their limits. But these streets become public and are always subject to State control. The same rule applies to turnpikes and ferries. Although the State transfers to an individual or a company its right to maintain a ferry or to build and maintain a turnpike, and to compensate itself for its outlay by the collection of tolls, the ferry and turnpike nevertheless remain highways, subject to the control of the State.

The railroad partakes of two natures, that of a highway and that of a common carrier. Railroad companies therefore enjoy the privileges and assume the duties of both. The State justly exercises in behalf of such companies the right of eminent domain, *i. e.*, the right of the sovereign to apply private property to public use; but it cannot rightfully appropriate private property for private use, even if legal compensation were to be made for it. It is only upon the theory that railroads are highways, constructed for the public good and subject to public control, that the State has authorized railroad companies to take private property for their own use by paying for it a reasonable compensation. A railroad may even take possession of and intersect a public road for the purpose of carrying on its functions. But while the sovereign may exercise the right of eminent domain, it cannot delegate it to any individual or number of individuals, except to its agents, performing its functions and being bound to comply with any rule which may be prescribed for the public good. Under the common law the individual is entitled to as full use of the railroad as he is of the common highway. If he is not allowed to put on his own vehicle, this restriction is simply due to the fact that the people believe that the business can be done most safely, most economically and most efficiently by one company or a limited number of companies operating the road for a reasonable compensation. Nor does this restriction differ materially from that which the law has placed upon the use of the common road. Without legislative sanction no one has a right to put upon it a team of elephants or a locomotive and train of cars, or other strange motors, and thereby obstruct the public travel. These restrictions might be removed by the legislative power, and there is also no doubt that under the common law the State has the right to permit the independent use of the railroad track by any person having motive power and cars adapted to it. The persons and freight transported on the railroad are taxed to maintain it, while in the case of the common road this tax is placed upon the people and the adjoining property. How to collect the tax necessary to sustain the road is simply a question of public policy, and it cannot be collected in any case except with the expressed permission of the State. If a company is permitted by the State to operate a railroad it should only be permitted to collect such tolls as are just and reasonable, and what is just and reasonable should be determined by the sovereign State, and not by the operating company. The railroads of the United States collect from our people in round numbers a transportation tax of eleven hundred million dollars annually. This tax is equal to a levy of $17 per head, or $85 per family; it is about as large as all our other taxes combined. In the State of Iowa it amounts to about $22 per head, or $110 per family, and is two and one-half times as large as all the State, county, school and municipal taxes collected within her borders.

When we consider how thoroughly other public charges are hedged about, by careful restrictions and limitations,

and with what caution the amount to be collected is fixed
after thorough public discussion, by agents of the people
selected by them to serve only for short periods, and that
those who collect and disburse the funds are under oath
and bonds for a faithful performance of their duty, is it
not preposterous to permit agents appointed by a few
interested persons, and often serving for a long term of
years, without any responsibility to the public, to fix the
rate of this tax, and to collect and disburse the immense
sums levied for the support of these highways without
any supervision or restraint?

The Government might as well lease the post-office,
waterways and the collection of import duties to
the highest bidder and permit the lessees to reimburse
themselves by the collection of such tolls as they
might see fit, without any governmental restraint whatever, their franchises enabling the operating companies to
tax each individual, each locality and each letter, parcel
or article as they saw fit.   How long would the people of
this country endure such a condition of things?   The
collection of taxes has been farmed out, but not by any
civilized nation in modern times.   History shows that this
system of taxation has always been productive of the
gravest abuses, and prejudicial to the public welfare.   As
has already been shown, the railroad is an improved highway, and the railroad company in operating it is doing a
public business and not a private business, and therefore it should be governed by rules applicable to public
business, and not such as are applicable to private business.   It is admitted by all that for the services which it
performs the operating company should receive a reasonable compensation; but to say what a reasonable compensation is, how it shall be collected, and to prescribe rules

regulating the business of the public carrier, is solely the right and the duty of the State. The people have never permitted the rate of any other public charge to be fixed by the beneficiary. Why, then, should privileges be conceded to one beneficiary which are denied to all others?

The assertion is often made by railroad managers that railroad transportation is a private business as much as any other branch of commerce. It is not likely that these same managers would wish to have their argument carried to its logical conclusion, for, should the courts at any time take their view, they would be under the necessity of declaring null and void all their charters, which were granted to them upon the assumption that the railroad was a highway operated under the authority and control of the State by private companies for the public good. If, on the other hand, railroad managers are, for their own protection, forced to recognize the public character of railroads, they can no longer question the right of the State to so control their business as the public good may demand. And this shows the absurdity of the claim often made by railroad managers, that, as long as the rates charged by them are reasonable, the State has no right to interfere with their business, or, in other words, that they may discriminate between individuals and localities, and that they may legally practice a thousand other abuses as long as individual shippers find it beyond their power to prove that they have been charged exorbitant rates.

Charles Fisk Beach, Jr., in his "Commentaries on the Law of Private Corporations," lays it down as a general principle of law that " whenever any person pursues a public calling and sustains such relations to the public that the people must of necessity deal with him, and are under a moral duress to submit to his terms if he is unrestrained by law, then, in order to prevent extortion and an abuse of his position, the price he may charge for his services may be regulated by law." And applying this principle to common carriers, and especially railroads, this author says:

"The sovereign has always assumed peculiar control over common carriers as conducting a business in which the public has an interest, and in the case of railway carriers an additional basis of governmental control is grounded in the extraordinary franchise of eminent domain conferred upon these companies. For corporations engaged in carrying goods for hire as common carriers have no right to discriminate in freight rates in favor of one shipper, even when necessary to secure his custom, if the discriminating rate will tend to create a monopoly by excluding from their proper markets the products of the competitors of the favored shipper."

If railroads had no obligations or advantages beyond those of other common carriers, such as stage lines and steamship companies, their discriminations might be less objectionable, but, as keepers of the toll-gates of the public highways, they are no more at liberty to regulate their own business regardless of the public welfare than were their predecessors, the toll-collectors stationed along the public turnpikes and canals. As such public tax-collectors they are bound to give equal treatment to all persons and places.

Although the business of constructing and keeping in repair the turnpike roads was, as a rule, left to private persons, and the promoters of such enterprises were permitted to reimburse themselves for their outlay by the collection of tolls, their schedules of tolls were prescribed by the State and their business was placed under the supervision of public officers, whose duty it was to see that neither extortion nor discrimination was practiced in the collection of these tolls, and that the private management of a public business did not become the source of abuse. The State thus insisted upon exercising a restraining influence over the business of turnpike companies because it realized the danger of entrusting the management of a semi-public business to companies organized solely for private gain, with officers responsible only to their stockholders, who, under ordinary circumstances, could be relied upon to measure the usefulness of an employe by his ability to contribute to the increase of the annual dividends. It will scarcely be claimed, even by railroad men, that since the days of turnpikes and stage-coaches corporations have become more unselfish and their officers less servile. The temptations have increased, while human frailty remains the same.

Of course, if we consult the railroad managers as to the best policy to be adopted for the future control of railroad companies, we shall be informed that we have already gone too far in railroad legislation, that nearly all the present evils of transportation of which the public and the railroad companies complain may be traced to legislative restrictions, and especially to certain features of the Interstate Commerce Act. They reluctantly admit that this act has been instrumental for good inasmuch as it has corrected some of the abuses that formerly existed, but they insist that several of its provisions are too radical and do infinitely more harm than good, both to the railroad companies and the people; that these obnoxious provisions ought to be repealed, and that under such restrictions as would still remain railroad companies ought to be permitted to manage their own business. If we inquire what modification of the Interstate Commerce Act the railroads desire, we find that if the act were amended in conformity with their wishes there would be little of it left that is of value. But the features which are specially obnoxious to them are the long and short haul and the anti-pooling clauses. They even go so far as to demand that the Government should not only permit pooling, but should use its strong arm to enforce all pooling contracts which railroad companies might see fit to enter into. This means, in other words, that the Government should enforce an agreement to restrict competition, which is made in direct violation of the common law, and aid the companies in maintaining such rates as they see fit to establish. If the railroad manager is cross-examined and forced to confess the truth, he will have to admit that what he really desires is freedom from all restraint, or, if public opinion will not tolerate this, then only law enough in letter to satisfy a public clamor and permit him to violate its spirit, and to then trust to him and the future to bring it into disrepute and cause its repeal.

Some shrewd managers have recently expressed a willingness to submit their pooling arrangements to a public commission for approval, before they should go into effect. This is objectionable on the ground that they would then, more even than before, endeavor to control the making of the commission. It is far safer to absolutely prohibit pooling and all devices used as a substitute for it. No necessity for pooling exists, and no good reason can be given why it should be permitted unless complete government control is established.

State control of railroad transportation is as essential to the welfare of the companies as it is to that of the public. The history of the past twenty years has shown that railroad companies are utterly unable to regulate their relations with each other. They either cannot arrive at an understanding, and then the stronger companies resort to hostilities to bring the weaker ones to their terms; or, when an agreement has been reached among them, they find themselves unable to enforce it. Anarchy then reigns supreme, until finally a truce is patched up, to be again followed by evasions, defiance and " war." The nature of the railroad business is in fact such that, in the absence of strict State control, it is impossible for a conscientious manager to retain the business to which his road is naturally entitled, and do full justice to both the patrons and the stockholders of his road. Efforts have been made again and again by railroad companies to regulate their affairs and adjust their difficulties by resorting to pools, agreements, associations and combinations, formed with all the ingenuity of which men are capable, and supported by penalties and fines; but the unscrupulous railroad manager has always found a way to violate or subvert the agreement. There is a disposition among railroad companies to arrogate all the powers of sovereignty. They want to make their own laws, impose fines and declare war, and often go even so far as to openly defy the power of the State that has given them their existence.

When railroad managers are shorn of the power to practice abuses, they are at the same time deprived of the many advantages they now have to speculate in railroad securities and enrich themselves at the expense of the public and of other railroad stockholders. The great fortunes of this country have been amassed within a few years, and chiefly from manipulations of railroad property. If the people permit these practices to go on without restraint but a few years more, the property of the nation will be largely under the control of a few bold adventurers. The great fortunes of Europe which it has required centuries to accumulate are already outstripped by the "self-made" millionaires of this country. However persistently railroad managers may assure the people that abuses in the transportation business have been reduced to a minimum and that more stringent legislation will be an evil, it is a fact that many of the graver railroad abuses are still practiced and that much more reformation is needed in railroad management, or in railroad supervision, or in both, to make the railroad what it was designed to be, a highway operated for the public and open to all upon equal and equitable terms.

The virtual ruler of the United States is public opinion. It is the power that controls the legislative as well as the executive and judicial departments of the Government. Enactments of legislatures and of Congress and decisions of the courts, even of the Supreme Court of the United States, not in harmony with an intelligent and determined public opinion, cannot endure, and executives not in accord with the masses of the people cannot long retain public confidence or official authority.

Under these circumstances no reform movement has any prospect of success unless it is supported by public opinion. It should therefore be the principal endeavor of all advocates of railroad reform to create public opinion in favor of the measures proposed by them. With an intelligent public on the alert, the Government may be relied upon to pursue a healthy and progressive railroad policy. Unfortunately, there are times when public opinion upon great questions is dormant, while pecuniary interests, like the force of gravity, never suspend their action. To arouse the masses at such times, we must rely largely upon an honest, independent and courageous press, not influenced by gift or patronage.

Many plans have been proposed for a better control of railroads. Some of these are merely theoretical; others have been tried in part, and a few have been tried in their entirety, but under circumstances radically different from those surrounding us. A system which may be well adapted to a monarchy with a centralization of governmental powers would probably prove a failure here, when brought in contact with the principles of dual sovereignty and local rule. Unless a revolution should change our system of government, a dual system of railroad control will always be necessary in the United States; for it is not at all likely that the individual States will ever voluntarily give up their right to regulate commerce carried on within their respective borders. On the other hand, the common welfare requires that the commerce which is carried on between the States should not be hampered by local interference, but should be regulated only by Congress. Our experience as a nation has shown that such a quality of sovereignty is not inconsistent with strength or efficiency, nor need it be productive of rivalry or friction. The fact that a certain mode of railroad management has been successful elsewhere is not sufficient proof that it would be successful here, nor is the fact that it has not been successful elsewhere sufficient proof that it would not be successful here. The more the conditions which exist here resemble those under which it was tested, the greater is the probability that it can be adapted to our circumstances. Independent thought and action is an essential element of progress, yet it is the part of wisdom to profit by the speculation and experience of others.

The following are the principal methods that have been tried or proposed for the control and management of railroads:

1. Publicity of the railroad business.

It is held by some that the secrecy with which railroad business is at present transacted is the source of all evils. It is contended that if railroads were required to report to the public every item of income and expenditure, discrimination and extortion, as well as bribery and corrupt subsidizing, would soon cease. If the companies were compelled to render an account of all receipts, special rates and drawbacks could not safely be granted by railroad managers, or, if granted, would soon lose their charm for recipients, for it would be but a short time until others would demand and even exact the same privileges. An attorney would, as a member of the legislature, be slow to accept a retaining fee if the amount of such fee were made known to his constituents. Publishers would hesitate to apply for railroad subsidies if the companies were compelled to render periodically an itemized account of such expenditures, and railroad companies would, under similar circumstances, hesitate to pay subsidies, for the subsidized journal would soon be without patrons. If the items annually expended upon railroad lobbies were reported, these lobbies would soon be frowned, or even hissed, out of legislative halls. There can be no doubt that full and complete publicity in railroad business would correct a large number of existing abuses, and it should therefore be insisted upon as one of the first and essential features of railroad reform. It is questionable, however, whether railroad managers are so sensitive to public opinion that publicity could be relied upon as a cure for all railroad evils. To what extent it is desirable to supplement publicity by other measures of State control will be considered hereafter.

It will, of course, be urged by railroad managers that the State has no right to pry into the privacy of their business and that they should be guaranteed the same protection against intrusion that is enjoyed by other branches of business. To this we must reply that not even banks or insurance companies are permitted to conduct their business as private, and that controlling the highway and levying a transportation tax upon every article of commerce passing over it is essentially public business and unquestionably subject to public control. Every citizen is as much interested in it as he is in the transactions of the custom-house, or of the public treasury, and any transaction of a railroad manager that shuns public inspection can be set down as a public evil and should be suppressed. It may safely be laid down as a general rule that the refusal of a railroad company to give publicity to its transactions is presumptive evidence of wrong. The people are not alone interested in such publicity. Stockholders have likewise a right to be protected against the sinister manipulations of dishonest managers, and publicity furnishes them the best guarantee of honest management.

Stockholders should attend the meetings of their companies and should obtain full knowledge of the management of their affairs. If they will make thorough examination and get at bottom facts the chances are that contracts will be found with owners of patents, white lines, blue lines, refrigerator car lines, coal companies, ferry companies, manufacturing companies, packing companies and other kindred organizations, by which hundreds of millions of dollars are diverted from the treasuries of the railroad companies to the pockets of influential persons connected with the management of the roads.

It has recently come to light that the officers of a Pennsylvania railroad company, during fifteen years, by some means of secret rebates and other allowances, have taken about $100,000,000 out of the treasury of the company and distributed it as largesses to about half a dozen iron and steel establishments.

This is a method of getting wealthy at the expense of others not unknown to many another great fortune accumulated in the last twenty years. Railroad discriminations have been a fruitful source of those gross inequalities in wealth distribution which now agitate society and call people's parties and the like into existence. The modern millionaire appears to be an entirely natural creation. Perhaps this money taken in special rates from the Pennsylvania railroad's treasury, or, rather, from the pockets of the road's other patrons, and of the men who may have sought, without special rates, to compete with the favored ones in their business, only to be crushed in financial ruin, will be spent in a praiseworthy way, in accord with the principles of ''the gospel of wealth.'' What we need now is the gospel of distribution of facilities for the accumulation of wealth, as well as the gospel of distribution of great fortunes.

Whether inspired by a bull or a bear interest or neither, all will concede the ability of Mr. Henry Clews to picture the evils of railroad management; and his lack of generosity in accrediting ability or honesty to legislators who are called upon to provide remedies for the wrongs that he so well depicts will not deter me from indorsing the following statement made by him in a magazine article which is pertinent to this discussion:

" One great difficulty that present railroad legislators have to contend with is the evil methods of railroad building and extension. A great deal of the mileage of the last two years has been premature, and doubtless for speculative purposes. Most of it has been constructed, however, by old companies who had good credit to float bonds and could raise all the money required. Hence there has been but little financial embarrassment arising from the too rapid construction. But people are beginning to find out that a great deal of this building has been in the interest of speculative directors and their friends, who, for a mere song, had bought up barren lands considered worthless because there was no means of transportation. But these lands soon become immensely valuable for sites of villages, towns and cities. The construction companies, by which these roads were generally built, raised the cost to the highest possible figures, in order, I fear, to make dividends for the construction stockholders. It is noteworthy that the directors connected with these construction schemes have been exceedingly prosperous, while the stockholders of the roads have grown poor in an inverse ratio. The dividends of the latter have disappeared. The new mileage, much of which, I apprehend, has been made on this principle, was about twenty-one thousand miles, which is greater than the entire mileage of Great Britain. There should be additions to the Interstate Law, or a special law regulating the methods of construction companies, which are probably doing more to demoralize the railroad system—and doing it very insidiously, too—than any other factor connected with these great arteries of the country's prosperity.

" Legislative reform is greatly needed in the matter of railroad reports, especially for the safety of investors, and to prevent speculative abuses among railroad officials and their friends and favorites. There should be statements issued annually, or perhaps more frequently, upon the truth of which everybody might rely. These should be sworn statements, and should bear the signatures of at least three of the directors. These directors should be required to call to their aid expert accountants, and should have placed at their disposal all the books of the company or corporation and all the other papers necessary to verify the accuracy of their report. The correctness of the statement, when issued, would then be a foregone conclusion, and an investor in London, Paris or Berlin could buy or sell on his own judgment, an experiment which, under existing arrangements, might prove very costly. It is proverbial that a railroad statement now is defective in the most essential particulars, and, to put it mildly, usually covers a multitude of sins. According to one plan approved by railroad companies, the statement published to-day, for instance, is made to show a surplus of many millions, but there is nothing said about an open construction account to which the surplus is debtor. On this favorable showing (with this *suppressio veri*) the stock goes up and the insiders quickly unload upon the investment public. The following statement, which comes out six months later, shows that the surplus has been used to settle the construction indebtedness.   The surplus has disappeared; consequently the stock suffers a serious decline.   Those who bought on the strength of the large surplus sell out, on being informed of its distribution.   Then the inside sharks come forward again and purchase at reduced prices, probably at a depreciation of from ten to fifteen points or more, and keep their stock until the next periodical appearance of the bogus surplus. Thus the insiders grow rich, while the outsiders become poor.   The only remedy for this abuse is a sworn statement at regular intervals, and if the directors should commit perjury they would render themselves liable to State prison. If a few of them should be tempted to fall into the trap, and be made examples of in this way, nothing would do more to work a speedy reform in this contemptible method of book-keeping.

"I would also suggest a change in the character of the directors. Those usually chosen for this office now are men who have vast interests of their own, more than sufficient to absorb their entire time and thoughts. They are selected mainly on account of their high-sounding names, to give tone to the corporation and solidify its credit, in order that the lambs of speculation may have proper objects in whom confidence can be reposed and no questions asked. The management of the affairs of the corporation is frequently intrusted to one man, who runs the business to suit his own individual interests."

We can appreciate the force of the above remarks when we consider that last year seventy-five companies realized a gross income of $846,888,000, which is equal to about 80 per cent. of the total income received by all of the railroads of the United States.

2. *Free competition upon all railroads.*

Mr. Hudson, in his excellent work, "The Railways and the Republic," recommends the following remedy:

"Legislation should restore the character of public highways to the railways, by securing to all persons the right to run trains over their tracks upon proper regulations, and by defining the distinction between the proprietorship and maintenance of the railway and the business of common carriers."

Mr. Hudson proposes to leave the track in the possession of its present owners, but to permit any individual or company to run, upon the payment of a fixed toll, trains and cars over it, under the control of a train-despatcher stationed at a central point. This train-despatcher is to be notified by telegraph of the movement of each train, and is to give his orders to the officers in charge of each train, as to what points they are to go, where to pass one train and where to wait for another. Each transportation company is to own, load and forward its own trains; it is to be required to run its regular train on schedule time or to have it follow another train as an extra. They are to be liable to their shippers as well as to the railway company for all damages caused by their neglect, while the railroad company is to be held responsible for the condi-

tion of its track.   It will not be necessary to go into the
details of Mr. Hudson's plan.   Suffice it to say that he
proposes to establish free competition in the railway
business by making the use of the railway track as free
as that of the turnpike or canal, subject only to such
control on the part of the public train-despatcher as the
paramount considerations of speed and safety may require.

The adoption of Mr. Hudson's plan would simply be a
return to the first principle of railroad transportation.   It
has already been shown that the first English charters
permitted the public to use their own vehicles and motive
power upon the railroad track, but that shippers and
independent carriers could not avail themselves of these
provisions of the early charters because it was in the
power of the railroad companies to make their tolls prohibitory.   There is but little question as to the practicability of Mr. Hudson's plan from a purely technical standpoint, and its adoption might be advisable if it should be
demonstrated that a monopoly of the track is inconsistent
with the operation of the railways for the public good.   It
is seriously doubted, however, whether such ideal competition as Mr. Hudson desires to bring about could be secured except at the expense of true economy.   Concen-
tration, or, rather, consolidation in the railroad business
has, under proper legal restriction, always resulted in a
saving of operating expenses, and usually in a reduction
of rates.   Any step in the opposite direction, whatever
other merits it may possess, is in the end not likely to
give lower rates.   If it is a settled principle that railroads
are only entitled to a fair compensation for their services,
it must be evident that what would be a fair compensation for the same or similar services to a large, well-
organized, well-regulated and well-managed company

cannot be sufficient compensation to an individual carrier or a small company, whose expenses will always be comparatively larger than those of its better-equipped rival. Monopoly and extortion need not necessarily be synonymous. In fact, States and municipalities in their public works often prefer monopoly to competition as the cheaper of the two. Nevertheless, should it ever be found that monopolies cannot be reconciled with justice and economy, a return to the first principles of railroading may become advisable.

3. *State ownership and management.*

A number of European states, notably Prussia, France and Belgium, as well as Australia, British India and the British colonies in Southern Africa, have adopted government ownership of railroads. The motives which led to this step in the various countries differ greatly. While in Europe military and political considerations predominated, in Africa and Australia it was more the want of private capital and energy which led the government to engage in railroad enterprises. There has in most of these states been a desire to avoid the evils usually connected with private management. The experiment of state ownership and management of railroads has been longest tried in Belgium, and with the best results. With an excellent service the rates of the Belgian state roads are the lowest in Europe. Their first-class passenger tariffs are, next to the zone tariff recently adopted on the state roads of Hungary, the lowest in the world, and are, for the same distance, lower than those of American roads. In Prussia the state service, upon the whole, is also superior to that of private companies, and is probably equal to the public demand. In France the government only owns and operates less important lines, but furnishes upon these a more efficient and cheaper service than private companies would either be able or disposed to furnish. The oft-repeated statement of those opposed to government regulation to the contrary notwithstanding, government ownership and management of railroads is a decided success in Europe, Mr. Jeans says of state railroads:

" Notwithstanding the superior financial result, the lines worked by the state are those kept in the best order, and the working of which gives the greatest satisfaction to the commercial world and the public in general as regards regularity of conveyance, cheapness of transit and the comfort of travelers."

It is difficult to see how any unbiased person can travel on any of the state roads of Europe without coming to the same conclusion. State management offers certainly some decided advantages to the public. Above all, the business of the roads is not conducted for the pecuniary advantage of a few, but for the common good. Commerce is not arbitrarily disturbed to aid unscrupulous managers in their stock speculations. New lines are not built for speculative purposes, but for the development of the country. Rates are based more upon the cost of service than upon what the traffic will bear, and the ultimate object of the state's policy is not high profits, but a healthy growth of the country's commerce, while the sole aim of a private company is to get the largest revenue possible. The permanent way of the state road is kept in better condition, the public safety and convenience being paramount considerations. Rates are stable and uniform, instead of being changeable and discriminating, and all persons and places are as equal before the railroad tax collector as before the law. It may be laid down as a general rule that under private management of railroads efforts will be made to secure the highest rates possible, while it is the aim of the Government to grant the lowest rates possible. Mr. Jeans proves by statistics that the cost of maintenance of way is generally higher on the state lines, and that traffic expenses are higher on the lines of private companies. In commenting upon this difference he says:

"It might easily be contended, and even proved beyond all doubt, that the first characteristic is a result of the better condition in which the state keeps the permanent way; and, so far as this is the case, the public convenience, safety and general advantage are promoted.

"The highest range of traffic expenses on companies' lines undoubtedly argues greater laxity of management, since, as we have already shown, this is one of the most elastic of items, and may be either very high or very low, according as economy or extravagance is the prevailing system. . . . The experience of Continental Europe points unmistakably to the exercise of greater economy in state management."

Judge Dillon, of the United States Court, in his order appointing Hon. J. B. Grinnell receiver for the Central Railroad of Iowa, in 1876, said:

"The railroads in the hands of the court—and in the circuit there are eight or ten—have all been run with less expense, and have made more money, than when they were operated by the companies; and we hope and believe under your supervision that this road will prove no exception, and that the property will be worth more at the end of the litigation."

Upon Mr. Grinnell's resignation, after nearly three years of service, Judge Grant said, in asking for the discharge of his bondsmen:

"I concur entirely in the opinion of the State commissioners that he has very much improved the condition of the road, and he left it in far superior condition to that in which he received it."

Yet Government ownership and management of railroads also has its drawbacks. It is claimed by some that such management is more expensive than that of lines owned by private companies. It has already been shown that the permanent way is kept in better condition by the state than by private corporations. In Russia, Germany, Austria-Hungary, France and Italy the state expends from 15 to 30 per cent. more for the maintenance of the permanent way than the private companies. It is perhaps also true that the rank and file of railroad employes fare, on an average, better under government than they do under private management; but, as an offset to this, it should be remembered that quite a saving is effected by the state in the salary account of general officers. The people will not consent to pay the manager of a railroad line a salary six times as large as that of a cabinet officer, and provide at the same time sinecures for his sons, brothers, nephews and cousins.

It is furthermore claimed that, as government is organized, it cannot, all other things being equal, respond to the demands of commerce as promptly as private companies. This feature, however, may be an advantage to the country at large rather than a detriment. But the strongest argument that can be produced against state ownership of railroads is that under a democratic form of government it might exert a demoralizing influence in politics. The 1,700 railroad companies of the United States have at present an army of about 800,000 employes. This number is constantly increasing, and it is more than probable that before the end of the present century it will have reached a million. When it is considered what importance is at present attached to the political influence of a hundred thousand Federal officers, it is not surprising that conservative citizens should hesitate to add to the ranks of these officeholders a six or seven times larger force. Dangerous as the railroad influence now is in politics, it would be ten times more dangerous if under a system of Government management considerations of self-interest should induce a million railroad employes to act as a political unit and political parties should vie with each other in bidding for the railroad vote. Could our civil service ever be so organized as to divest it entirely of political power, state management of railroads might still offer the best solution of the railroad problem.

Mr. T. B. Blackstone, president of the Chicago and Alton Railroad Company, has recently created somewhat of a surprise by declaring in favor of Government ownership of railroads. That Mr. Blackstone's programme will eventually receive the approval of a large number of his colleagues there can be but little doubt. With the people wide-awake upon this subject, the opportunities for railroad speculation are lessening, and the scheme to early unload the railroads of the country on the Government at a highly inflated value speaks well for the financial farsightedness of its author. Mr. Blackstone proposes to have railroad stockholders do here what the former owners of the telegraph did in Great Britain, *i. e.*, dispose of their property to the Government, at a price representing several times its original cost or even several times the cost of duplication.

Mr. C. Wood Davis, formerly general freight and passenger agent of one of the leading roads east from Chicago, is one of the best informed and clearest-headed writers upon the railroad question. He has, after much experience and long study, been converted to the advocacy

of national ownership as a solution of the railroad prob
lem. In a recent article published by the Arena Publish-
ing Company, entitled "Should the Nation own the
Railways?" he presents the objections and advantages of
national ownership. He says:

"The objections to national ownership are many, that
most frequently advanced, and having the most force,
being the possibility that, by reason of its control of a
vastly increased number of civil servants, the party in
possession of the Federal administration at the time such
ownership was assumed would be able to perpetuate its
power indefinitely. . . . This objection would seem to be
well taken, and indicates serious and far-reaching results
unless some way can be devised to neutralize the political
power of such a vast addition to the official army. . . .
In the military service we have a body of men that exerts
little or no political power, as the moment a citizen enters
the army he divests himself of political functions; and it
is not hazardous to say that 700,000 capable and efficient
men can be found who, for the sake of employment, to be
continued so long as they are capable and well behaved,
will forego the right to take part in political affairs. If
a sufficient number of such men can be found, this objection would, by proper legislation, be divested of all its
force. . . .

"2. That there would be constant political pressure to
make places for the strikers of the party in power, thus
adding a vast number of useless men to the force, and
rendering it progressively more difficult to effect a change
in the political complexion of the administration.

"That this objection has much less force than is
claimed is clear from the conduct of the postal department, which is unquestionably a political adjunct of the
administration; yet but few useless men are employed,
while its conduct of the mail service is a model of
efficiency after which the corporate-managed railways
might well pattern. Moreover, if the railways are put
under non-partisan control, this objection will lose nearly,
if not quite, all its force.

"3. That the service would be less efficient and cost more than with continued corporate ownership. This appears to be bare assertion, as from the very nature of the case there can be no data outside those furnished by the government-owned railways of the British colonies, and such data negative these assertions; and the advocates of national ownership are justified in asserting that such ownership would materially lessen the cost, as any expert can readily point out many ways in which the enormous costs of corporate management would be lessened. With those familiar with present methods, and not interested in their perpetuation, this objection has no force whatever.

"4. That with constant political pressure unnecessary lines would be built for political ends. This is also bare assertion, although it is not impossible that such results would follow; yet such has not been the case in the British colonies where the governments have had control of construction. . . .

"5. That, with the amount of red tape that will be in use, it will be impossible to secure the building of needed lines. While such objection is inconsistent with the fourth, it may have some force, but as the greater part of the country is already provided with all the railways that will be needed for a generation, it is not a very serious objection even if it is as difficult as asserted to procure the building of the new lines. It is not probable, however, that the Government would refuse to build any line that would clearly subserve public convenience, the conduct of the postal service negativing such a supposition. . . .

"6. That lines built by the Government would cost much more than if built by corporations. Possibly this would be true, but they would be much better built and cost far less for maintenance and betterments, and would represent no more than actual cost; and such lines as the Kansas Midland, costing but $10,200 per mile, would not, as now, be capitalized at $53,024 per mile, nor would the president of the Union Pacific (as does Sidney Dillon, in the *North American Review* for April) say that "a citizen, simply as a citizen, commits an impertinence when he questions the right of a corporation to capitalize its properties at any sum whatever," as then there would be no Sidney Dillons who would be presidents of corporations, pretending to own railways built wholly from Government moneys and lands, and who have never invested a dollar in the construction of a property which they have now capitalized at the modest sum of $106,000 per mile. . . .

"7. That they are incapable of as progressive improvement as are corporate-owned ones, and will not keep pace with the progress of the nation in other respects; and in his *Forum* article Mr. Acworth lays great stress upon this phase of the question and argues that as a result the service would be far less satisfactory.

"There may be force in this objection, but the evidence points to an opposite conclusion. When the nation owns the railways trains will run into union depots, the equipment will become uniform and of the best character, and so sufficient that the traffic in no part of the country would have to wait while the worthless locomotives of some bankrupt corporation were being patched up, nor would there be the present difficulties in obtaining freight cars growing out of the poverty of corporations which have been plundered by the manipulators, and improvements would not be hindered by the diverse ideas of the managers of various lines in relation to the adoption of devices intended to render life more secure or to add to the public convenience. . . . Existing evidence all negatives Mr. Acworth's postulate that "state railway systems are incapable of vigorous life."

"8. An objection to national ownership which the writer has not seen advanced is that States, counties, cities, townships and school districts would lose some $27,000,000 of revenue derived from taxes upon railways. While this would be a serious loss to some communities, there would be compensating advantages for the public, as the cost of transportation could be lessened in like measure.

"Many believe stringent laws, enforced by commissions having judicial power, will serve the desired end, and the writer was long hopeful of the efficacy of regulation by State and National commissions; but close observation of their endeavors and of the constant efforts—too often successful—of the corporations to place their tools on such commissions, and to evade all laws and regulations, have convinced him that such control is and must continue to be ineffective and that the only hope of just and impartial treatment for railway users is to exercise the 'right of eminent domain,' condemn the railways, and pay their owners what it would cost to duplicate them; and in this connection it may be well to state what valuations some of the corporations place upon their properties.

"Some years since the Sante Fe filed in the counties on its line a statement showing that at the then price of labor and materials—rails were double the present price— their road could be duplicated for $9,685 per mile, and, the materials being much worn, the actual cash value of the road did not exceed $7,725 per mile.

" In 1885 the superintendent of the St. Louis and Iron Mountain Railway, before the Arkansas State Board of Assessors, swore that he could duplicate such a railway for $11,000 per mile, and yet Mr. Gould has managed to float its securities, notwithstanding a capitalization of five times that amount."

Among the advantages to be derived from Government ownership he names the following:

"First would be the stability and practical uniformity of rates, now impossible, as they are subject to change by hundreds of officials, and are often made for the purpose of enriching such officials. . . .

" It would place the rate-making power in one body, with no inducement to act otherwise than fairly and impartially, and this would simplify the whole business and relegate an army of traffic managers, general freight agents, soliciting agents, brokers, scalpers and hordes of traffic association officials to more useful callings, while relieving the honest user of the railway of intolerable burdens.

" Under corporate control, railways and their officials have taken possession of the majority of mines which furnish the fuel so necessary to domestic and industrial life, and there are few coal fields where they do not fix the price at which so essential an article shall be sold, and the whole nation is thus forced to pay undue tribute.

" Controlling rates and the distribution of cars, railway. officials have driven nearly all the mine owners, who have not railways or railway officials for partners, to the wall.

"With the Government operating the railways, discriminations would cease, as would individual and local oppression; and we may be sure that an instant and absolute divorce would be decreed between railways and their officials on one side, and commercial enterprises of every name and kind on the other.

" The failure to furnish equipment to do the business of the tributary country promptly is one of the greater evils of corporate administration, enabling officials to practice most injurious and oppressive forms of discrimination, and is one that neither Federal nor State commission pays much attention to. With national ownership a sufficiency of cars would be provided. On many roads the funds that should have been devoted to furnishing the needed equipment, and which the corporations contracted to provide when they accepted their charters, have been divided as construction profits, or, as in the case of the Santa Fe, Union Pacific, and many others, diverted to the payment of unearned dividends, while the public suffers from this failure to comply with charter obligations.

" There would be such an adjustment of rates that traffic would take the natural short route, and not, as under corporate management, be sent around by the way of Robin Hood's barn, when it might reach its destination by a route but two-thirds as long, and thus save the unnecessary tax to which the industries of the country are subjected. That traffic can be sent by these roundabout routes at the same or less rates than is charged by the shorter ones is *prima facie* evidence that rates are too high.

" There would be a great reduction in the number of

men employed in towns entered by more than one line. For instance, take a town where there are three or more railways, and we find three or more full-fledged staffs, three or more expensive up-town freight and ticket offices, three or more separate sets of all kinds of officials and employes, and three or more separate depots and yards to be maintained. Under Government control these staffs—except in very large cities—would be reduced to one, and all trains would run into one centrally located depot; freight and passengers be transferred without present cost, annoyance and friction, and public convenience and comfort subserved, and added to in manner and degree almost inconceivable.

"The great number of expensive attorneys now employed, with all the attendant corruption with the fountains of justice, could be dispensed with, and there would be no corporations to take from the bench the best legal minds, by offering three or four times the Federal salary. . . .

"Every citizen riding would pay fare, adding immensely to the revenues. Few have any conception of the proportion who travel free, and half a century's experience renders it doubtful if the evil—so much greater than ever was the franking privilege—can be eliminated otherwise than by national ownership. From the experience of the writer, as an auditor of railway accounts, and as an executive officer issuing passes, he is able to say that fully ten per cent. travel free, the result being that the great mass of railway users are yearly mulcted some thirty millions of dollars for the benefit of the favored minority; hence it is evident that if all were required to pay for railway services as they are for mail services, the rates might be reduced ten per cent. or more, and the corporate revenues be no less, and the operating expenses no more. In no other country—unless it be under the same system in Canada—are nine-tenths of the people taxed to pay the traveling expenses of the other tenth. By what right do the corporations tax the public that members of Congress, legislators, judges and other court officials and their families may ride free? Why is it that when a legislature is in session passes are as plentiful as leaves in the forest in autumn? . . .

"The corporations have ineffectually wrestled with the commission evil, and any number of agreements have been entered into to do away with it; but it is so thoroughly entrenched, and so many officials have an interest in its perpetuation, that they are utterly powerless in the presence of a system which imposes great and needless burdens upon their patrons, but which will die the day the Government takes possession of the railways, as then there will be no corporations ready to pay for the diversion of traffic.

"As a rule, American railways pay the highest salaries in the world for those engaged in directing business operations, but such salaries are not paid because transcendent talents are necessary to conduct the ordinary operations of railway administration, but for the purpose of checkmating the chicanery of corporate competitors. In other words, these exceptionally high salaries are paid for the purpose, and because their recipients are believed to have the ability to hold up their end in unscrupulous corporate warfare where, as one railway president expressed it, 'the greatest liar comes out ahead.' . . .

"Government control will enable railway users to dispense with the services of such high-priced umpires as Mr. Aldace F. Walker, as well as of all the other officials of sixty-eight traffic associations, fruitlessly laboring to prevent each of five hundred corporations from getting the start of its fellows, and trying to prevent each of the five hundred from absorbing an undue share of the traffic. It appears that each of these costly peace-making attachments has an average of seven corporations to watch. . . .

"With National ownership the expenditures involved in the maintenance of traffic associations would be saved and railway users relieved of a tax that, judging from the reports of a limited number of corporations of their contribution towards the support of such organizations, must annually amount to between $4,000,000 and $5,000,000.

"Of the six hundred corporations operating railways, probably five hundred maintain costly general offices, where president, secretary and treasurer pass the time surrounded by an expensive staff. The majority of such offices are off the lines of the respective corporations, in the larger cities, where high rents are paid and great expenses entailed, that proper attention may be given to bolstering or depressing the price of the corporation's shares, as the management may be long or short of the market. So far as the utility of the railways is concerned, as instruments of anything but speculation such offices and officers might as well be located in the moon, and their cost saved to the public. . . .

"Railways spend enormous sums in advertising, the most of which National ownership would save, as it would be no more necessary to advertise the advantages of any particular line than it is to advertise the advantages of any given mail route. . . . A still greater expense is involved in the maintenance of freight and passenger offices off the respective lines, for the purpose of securing a portion of competitive traffic. In this way vast sums are expended in the payment of rents and the salaries of hordes of agents, solicitors, clerks, etc., etc. . . .

"Under Government control discriminations against localities would cease, whereas now localities are discriminated against because managers are interested in real estate elsewhere, or are interested in diverting traffic in certain directions. . . .

"Another, and an incalculable benefit, which would result from National ownership, would be the relief of State and National legislation from the pressure and corrupting practices of railway corporations, which constitute one of the greatest dangers to which republican institutions can be subjected. This alone renders the nationalization of the railways most desirable, and at the same time would have the effect of emancipating a large part of the press from a galling thraldom to the corporations. . . .

"Estimated net annual saving to the public which would result from Government control:

From consolidation of depots and staffs..........$20,000,000
From exclusive use of shortest routes............ 25,000,000
In attorneys' fees and legal expenses............ 12,000,000
From the abrogation of the pass evil............. 30,000,000
From the abrogation of the commission evil...... 20,000,000
By dispensing with high-priced managers and
    staffs.. 4,000,000
By disbanding traffic associations............... 4,000,000
By dispensing with presidents, etc............... 25,000,000
By abolishing all but local offices, solicitors, etc.. 15,000,009
Of five-sevenths of the advertising account...... 5,000,000

Total savings by reason of better administration $160,000,000

" It would appear that, after yearly setting aside $50-000,000 as a sinking fund, there are the best reasons for believing that the cost of the railway service would be some $310,000,000 less than under corporate management.

" That $6,000,000,000 is much more than it would cost to duplicate existing railways will not be questioned by the disinterested familiar with late reductions in the cost of construction, and that such a valuation is excessive is manifest from the fact that it is much more than the market value of all the railway bonds and shares in existence."

The above quotations from Mr. Davis' article hardly do it justice, and it should be read in full to appreciate its full force. Many of the predictions and estimates are undoubtedly in the main correct, yet upon the whole it must be admitted that it is a rather rosy and too hopeful view to take of Government ownership of our railroads.

4. *State ownership with private management.*

This is a compromise between a public and a private system of railway ownership and management. It is claimed by the advocates of this system that if the Government would aquire by purchase or through condemnation proceedings all of the railroads of the country, pay for them by issuing its bonds, and then lease the various lines to the highest responsible bidders, prescribing a schedule and rules of management, most of the benefits resulting from state ownership of railroads could be secured while nearly all its disadvantages would be avoided. It is proposed to purchase railroads at their actual value and to issue in payment bonds bearing the same rate of interest as other Government securities. This would deprive managers of every opportunity to manipulate the railroad business for purposes of stock speculation. It would also reduce the fixed charges of our railroads at least 50 per cent., the benefits of which reduction the public would chiefly share. The acquisition of the railroads by the Government would, moreover, afford the conservative capitalist a safe and permanent investment, which, with the gradual disappearance of our war debt, might become a national desideratum.

It is proposed by the advocates of this system that the Government fix rates of transportation for a certain period, to be reviewed at the end of that period upon an agreed basis. The operating companies would be required to keep their roads in repair and give sufficient bonds for the faithful performance of their contracts. If found guilty of persistent violations of the terms of their leases or of such laws as Congress might enact for their control, their bonds and leases might be declared forfeited. A new Government department or bureau would have to be established and charged with the duty of exercising the same control over railroads which the Government now exercises over national banks, and in addition to this complete publicity of the service would have to be relied upon to prevent the introduction of abuses.

There are at least two valid objections that can be urged against the adoption of such a system. Responsible companies could not be induced to lease a line for a valid consideration unless their rates were definitely fixed for a

series of years. Such a course might, however, in time
result in great hardship to the commerce of the country,
as the great and unavoidable difference in the rates of the
various railroad lines of the country would give to the
commercial interests of some sections decided advantages
over those of others. Besides this it would be very
difficult to compel the different companies to keep the
lines leased by them in repair. Controversies would constantly arise between the officers charged with the supervision of the roads and the operating companies, which
could be ultimately determined only by the courts, causing
to the Government loss, or at least delay in the adjust-
ments.

5. *National control.*

Mr. A. B. Stickney, in his work, "The Railway
Problem," holds that in the interest of uniformity it is
desirable to transfer the entire control of railroads to the
National Government. He assigns two reasons for the
proposed change; one being that Congress would consider the subject of railroad control with more intelligence
and greater deliberation; the other, that "the problem of
regulating railway tolls and of managing railways is
essentially and practically indivisible by the State lines or
otherwise," and that the authority of Congress to deal
with interstate traffic carries with it the right to regulate
the traffic which is now assumed to be controlled by the
several States.

It must be admitted that it is a difficult matter to draw
the line of demarcation between National and State control,
and that Congressional regulation of railways would
remedy many evils which now affect our transportation
system; yet there is reason to believe that the proposed
change would in the end be productive of more evil than

good. It is an essentially American maxim that the home government only should be trusted with the administration of home affairs. The people of each State know best their local needs, and it is safe to say that for a generation or two no serious effort will be made to amend the Federal Constitution in this respect or to secure from the courts an interpretation of the interstate commerce clause greatly differing from that which now obtains.

It is thus seen that nearly all the methods of railroad management which we have discussed are, at the present time at least, more or less impracticable on account of the radical changes which they would necessitate. It is not likely that for many years to come the American people could be induced to try any extensive experiments in state ownership of railroads; nor is it any more likely that the present generation will undertake the difficult task of separating the ownership of railroads from their operation.

A nation is, like the individual, inclined to follow beaten tracks. It finds it, as a rule, easier to improve these tracks than to abandon them and mark out a new course. Any proposition made for the improvement of our system of railroad transportation is in the same proportion likely to receive the approval of the masses in which it makes use of existing conditions. It will, therefore, be my aim, in making suggestions as to a more efficient control of this modern highway, to retain whatever good features the present system possesses, and to only propose such changes as may seem essential to restore to the railroad the character of a highway.

As has been indicated above, any system of railway regulation, to be applicable to our circumstances, must recognize the dual sovereignty of Nation and State. **The** great majority of our railroad corporations were originally created by the State, and are only responsible to the State as long as they do not engage in interstate commerce. Even foreign corporations must submit to all police regulations of the State in which they may do business, and as long as the American Constitution remains intact the individual States will, and should, assert their right to regulate local traffic and to exercise police supervision over all railroads crossing their boundaries.

All power should be kept as closely to the people as is consistent with efficiency in the public service. It may even be questioned whether entire transfer to the Federal Government of the supervisory powers now exercised by the States in railroad affairs would tend to correct existing railroad evils more speedily or more effectually than they can be corrected through the agency of local rule. The conditions, and therefore the wants, of the different States differ so greatly that general legislation must always fail when it attempts to regulate matters of merely local concern.

The means employed by the State for the regulation of the roads under its jurisdiction should be such as are least likely to lead to a conflict with Federal authority, and experience has shown that the authority of the General Government and that of an individual State over a railroad company, which is incorporated under the laws of the latter, but is engaged in interstate commerce, may be so harmonized as to avoid conflicts between the two sovereignties without any great sacrifice of power on the part of either. Judge Cooley said recently in reference to regulation by National and State commissions:

"There is no good reason in the nature of things why the conformity should not be complete and perfect. It is

remarkable that up to this time there has been so little—
I will not say of conflict, but even of diversity of action
between the National and State commissions. Indeed, I
recall no instance at this time when anything done by the
one has seemed to me to afford just ground for complaint
by the other. This may justly be attributed to the fact
that there has been no purpose on the part of either to do
any act that could afford ground for just complaint on the
part of managers of the business regulated and no desire
to do anything else than to apply rules of right and equality for the protection of the general public. The aim of
all regulation ought to be justice, and when it is apparent
that this is the purpose of the several commissions, the
railroad managers of the country may more reasonably be
expected to coöperate with them much more generally
than they do now. If these managers were to come generally and heartily into more full and complete recognition of the rules of right and justice that the law under-
takes to lay down for the performance of their duties in
their management of the great interests they represent,
there cannot be the least doubt that the general result
would be, not only that their service to the public would
be more useful than it is now, but that the revenues derived from their business would be materially increased
through the cutting off of many of the drains upon them,
which now, while affecting injuriously the returns they
can make to their stockholders, at the same time have
the effect of prejudicing the mind of the general public
against railroad management to an extent quite beyond
what is generally understood by those who suffer from it.
The prejudice is inevitable, and not at all unreasonable
when it is seen, as it very often is, that these drains
result from an unjust discrimination against the public or
some portion thereof, that they are of a character that
ought to need no law and no criminal or other penalties to
put them under the ban of condemnation in every office
of railroad management.

"I take the liberty of adding one more thought: that
the more perfect is railroad legislation, the less we shall
hear of transportation by rail being made a Government

function, the General Government making purchase of all the roads and entering upon a course which will lead we know not where or into what disasters."

There has been during the past twenty years a tendency in a majority of the States to place the local control of railroads in the hands of executive boards, usually styled "railroad commissioners." Previous to this period the various States relied solely upon legislation for the regulation of the transportation business, but in time they became convinced that such laws were inoperative for the want of an enforcing power. It was found that the individual shipper was unable to cope with a powerful company and usually would rather suffer wrong than to enter into a contest which nearly always resulted in great pecuniary loss to him. On the other hand, it was apparent that if the claim of the individual were pressed by a railroad commission, even though such a body had but limited powers, it would, under ordinary circumstances, be honored, provided it was meritorious; and if the commission was compelled to enforce a demand through the courts, it would have the support of the State to poise the wealth and power of the corporation.

The term "railroad commissioner" in the United States is nearly as old as the railroad itself; but the first officials bearing that title were merely successors to the turnpike commissioners of yore; their duties consisted chiefly in supervising, passing or reporting upon the construction and condition of the highway.

The first railroad commission, in the present acceptation of the term, was created in the State of Massachusetts, in 1869. The commission consisted of three persons, whose principal duty was to "make an annual report to the General Court, including such statements, facts and explanations as will disclose the actual working of the system of railroad transportation in its bearing upon the business and prosperity of the commonwealth, and such suggestions as to its general railroad policy, or any part thereof, or the condition, affairs or conduct of any railroad corporation, as may seem to it appropriate." This board also had the general supervision of all railroads and power to examine the same. It was required to give notice in writing to any railroad corporation which, in its judgment, was guilty of any violation of the railroad laws of the State; and if such company continued the violation, after such notice, it became the duty of the commission to present the facts to the Attorney-General. It was further made the duty of the board to examine, from time to time, the books and accounts of all railroads, to see that they were kept in a uniform manner, and upon the system prescribed by the board. It was also required to investigate the cause of any accident on a railroad resulting in loss of life. These being the principal duties of the board, its powers were very limited; but its personnel supplied the power which the law had withheld. The success of this commission exceeded even the expectations of the advocates of the system, who, in view of the limited powers of the commission, had anticipated but meager results.

To quiet the Granger movement the railroads favored and finally secured the adoption of the commissioner system in the West and South, in which sections it attained its highest development. It was soon found that a commission after the Massachusetts model, when composed of men less competent or less disposed to do their duty, was liable to dwindle into a statistical board or even become a pliant tool in the hands of the railroads. Furthermore,

the conditions in Massachusetts, where railroad owners
and railroad patrons lived side by side and were in many
instances even identical, differed materially from those
found in the West and South, where railroad patrons were
made to pay excessive rates, to produce liberal dividends
on fictitious stocks for non-resident stockholders.   Here a
conflict between the railroads and such commissions as
were determined to do their duty became often unavoidable.   Railroad companies were as a rule disposed to disregard the recommendation of a commission to reduce exorbitant rates.   This led in those States which suffered
most from unjust tariffs to a popular demand to endow
the commission with the power to fix *prima facie* rates.
While the number of States which have taken this step is
at present still limited, public opinion in its favor is growing throughout the nation, and a general adoption of this
policy is probably only a question of time.   There is every
reason for believing that a commission vested with the
right to fix local rates, to require full and complete reports
from railroad companies, and to make proper regulations
for their control, aided by penal legislation to compel compliance with their orders, will be a sufficient aid to the
State in exercising such control over the companies operating lines within its borders as its dignity and the welfare of its people demand.

   Viewing the question from a national point of view, we
find that, owing to the great and constantly increasing
importance of interstate traffic, improved Federal agencies
for railroad control are a pressing need.   While much has
been accomplished by the Interstate Commerce Act, much
yet remains to be done.   Violations of the act are still far
too frequent, and they have been encouraged by unfriendly
decisions by some of the inferior Federal courts.

It must be admitted that nearly all the evils connected with interstate transportation could soon be remedied were it not for the difficulties which the Interstate Commerce Commission encounters in the enforcement of the law. On the one hand it is not possible with the machinery at present provided to detect and prove a considerable part of the violations of which railroad managers are daily guilty; and on the other hand, if these violations are brought to light, there would not, according to the testimony of a prominent railroad man, be courts enough in the country to try the violators. Besides this, such is the artfulness of railroad managers that in a majority of cases it would be impossible to reach the guilty party, and subordinates would have to answer for the transgressions of their superiors.

To provide adequate machinery for the supervision of the transportation business, a national bureau of commerce and transportation should be established. As its chief a director-general of railroads should be appointed by the President, on the recommendation of the Secretary of the Interior, by and with the advice and consent of the Senate. This officer should hold his office for a term of at least six years, unless sooner removed by the President, upon reasons to be communicated by him to the Senate. He should not be interested either directly or indirectly in railroad securities. The Interstate Commerce Commission should be continued as an advisory board. It should upon the whole retain its present functions and should be consulted by the director-general in all matters requiring expert investigation. A number of divisions or sub-bureaus should be established, and each should be entrusted, under the supervision of the director-general, with such duties as may be deemed necessary to secure the greatest efficiency.

There should be a division charged with the duty of carefully examining and compiling the detailed reports which the various companies should by law be required to make to the bureau. An inspection service should also be established, similar to that now maintained by the Treasury and Post-office Departments. Its officers should be empowered to enter all railroad offices and examine the companies' books, board trains and employ other legal means to detect violations of the railroad law and report them to the chief of the bureau.

Railroad companies might be permitted to make interstate rates, but all schedules should be submitted to the bureau for approval or revision. Legal provision should be made against every sort of speculation in railroad stocks on the part of railroad officers, who should, in addition, be prohibited from sharing in the profits of favorite rates, as at present. All executive officers and directors of railroad companies should, like officers of national banks, be required to qualify by taking an oath of office, and should be held to strict accountability for their official acts. Officers of railroad companies should not be allowed to receive and use proxies at stockholders' meetings.

The director-general should have the power, when he has proof that a railroad manager is persistently violating the law, to remove him and to appoint a receiver to take charge of the road until its owners can make provision and furnish sufficient guarantee for a more responsible management. Such a procedure would not be without analogy in the sphere of Federal authority. The Comptroller of the Currency is authorized by law to remove the derelict officials of a national bank and place its business in charge of a receiver. The beneficial effect of this provision is evinced in the extreme rareness of such a step. When railroad managers are held responsible for their own official acts, as well as for those of their subordinates, and when all railroad transgressions are visited upon their source in such a manner as to be remembered by the stings of disgrace and of a blighted career, unfaithful railroad managers will be extremely rare.

The plan here outlined is of course capable of being greatly improved. Experience only is a reliable guide as to the merits of the various details of such a system of control. What is needed above all things is a beginning, the establishment of the principle of complete control of railroad transportation by the State and the Nation. When this step is once taken, the friends of railroad reform may safely trust to time for the solution of the subordinate questions of this important problem.

By thorough State and Federal supervision of the railroad business many of the present abuses can be prevented. But the temptations of railroad managers to violate the law will continue to exist as long as the speculative element is permitted to remain in railroad securities. To remove the fountain-head of the evil eventually, the way should gradually be paved for a change in railroad organization and ownership which would also greatly increase the responsibility and efficiency of railroad management. In the beginning of the railroad era, nearly all, and not unfrequently all the capital needed for the construction of a new line was supposed to be furnished by the company's stockholders. But as it often happened that the cost of construction considerably exceeded the original estimate, the State authorized railroad companies to mortgage their property for the purpose of raising the money necessary to complete the road.

In time this provision of the law was taken advantage of by speculative stockholders to such an extent that roads were often bonded for the full amount necessary to construct them, and even for more, while the stock was issued simply as a bonus to the promoters and the bondholders of the road. But as the bonds and shares scarcely ever remain in the same hands, such a condition was eventually brought about that roads were controlled by those who had little or nothing invested in the enterprise, and their real owners were deprived of all influence in their management, retaining only the right to foreclose their mortgages when things came to the worst. It is evident that men who have only a speculative interest in property cannot have the same concern for its permanent value and prosperity as those who hold it as a permanent investment. Many of the railroad abuses of the past had their origin in the law permitting the bonding of railroad property. Were it desirable to make a property for the sole use and convenience of speculators and gamblers, a better scheme could hardly be devised than the present system of our railroad organizations. Were railroad companies organized like national banks, were each shareholder required to pay the full amount of the face value of his shares, and were mortgaging railroad property entirely prohibited, it is not likely that the proportion of bankrupted railroads would be any larger than that of bankrupted banks. Few, if any, railroads would be built for purely speculative or blackmailing purposes.

Capital is naturally conservative, and speculation is only invited where the chances of gain are greatly out of proportion to the capital invested. Were the principle of ownership which applies to national banks and other well regulated corporations also applied to the railroads, and

were bonds entirely abolished, only such persons would
by the shareholders be placed in charge of their property
as could give to them the best assurance of honest and
conservative management. Such a change would greatly
increase public confidence in, and the value of, railroad
securities, and would eventually place them above bank
stock as desirable investments. With the great fluctuations which under present circumstances obtain in railroad
stocks, these securities are regarded as unsafe and unsatisfactory investments by conservative people. During a
period of less than twelve months in 1891 and 1892 the
stock of the Atchison, Topeka and Santa Fe fluctuated
from 28½ to 43½, or 53 per cent. ; that of the Chesapeake
and Ohio from 15¼ to 25⅞, or 70 per cent. ; of the Chicago
and Northwestern from 101 to 118, or 17 per cent. ; of
the Chicago, Saint Paul, Minneapolis and Omaha from 20½
to 38½, or 88 per cent. ; of the Chicago, Milwaukee and
St. Paul fron 48¾ to 78½, or 61 per cent. ; of the Iowa
Central from 6½ to 13, or 100 per cent.

If we look over the stock quotations of the past ten
or twelve years we find still greater fluctuations. The
following table, taken from the *United States Investor*,
shows the range of prices of a few of the principal stocks
during this period :

Name.	Lowest.	Highest.
Central Pacific..	26½ (1888)	102⅞ (1881)
Chesapeake and Ohio	1 (1888)	33⅞ (1881)
Erie.	9¼ (1885)	52⅞ (1881)
Illinois Central	79¼ (1879)	150½ (1882)
Lake Erie and Western	1⅜ (1885)	65¾ (1881)
Michigan Central.	46½ (1885)	130⅛ (1880)
New Jersey Central	31 (1885)	131 (1889)
New York Central	81¾ (1885)	155⅜ (1880)
Northern Pacific	14 (1884)	54⅜ (1882)
Rock Island	63⅜ (1891)	204 (1880)

Name	Lowest.	Highest
C., M. & St. P	34⅜ (1879)	129¼ (1881)
Texas and Pacific	5½ (1884)	73⅝ (1881)
Wabash	2 (1885)	60 (1881)
Atchison and Topeka	23¾ (1890)	152½ (1880)
Chicago, Burlington and Quincy	75⅝ (1891)	182½ (1881)
N. Y. & N. E	9 (1884)	86 (1881)
Wisconsin Central	2 (1880)	39 (1881)
Union Pacific	28 (1884)	131 (1881)

And such fluctuations have always been rather the rule than the exception. It is a gross outrage upon the investing public to let this state of affairs continue. It should be corrected without delay.

How many high officials in charge of railroad property will under these circumstances resist the temptation to speculate in the stock of their companies, and, so long as it is permitted, how many will resist the temptation to adopt such policies in the government of their roads as will cause such fluctuations? It is a common report that it is not an unfrequent occurrence for Senators and members of Congress to receive information from railway officials that enables them to raise their campaign funds by speculation in Wall Street.

Mr. Henry C. Adams, statistician of the Interstate Commerce Commission, says in his third annual report:

" It certainly appears . . . that the motive for ownership in railroad stock is quite different from the ordinary motives which lead men to invest in corporate enterprises, thus presenting an additional proof that railways are a business not subject to ordinary business rules. "

There is no safer business in the world than railroad transportation; there is none that has less elements of uncertainty; none whose returns in the aggregate are less varying. Every other business in the country, whether prospering or struggling, pays tribute to it. It rests on a cash basis, and suffers probably less from hard times than any business of its magnitude. Both the merchant and the manufacturer run large risks in doing business largely on a credit basis. The farmer sows in the spring, harvests in the fall, and often cannot realize on his products until winter; but the railroad company always receives its pay as soon as its work is done, and not unfrequently even before it is done. Statistics show that railroad revenues are, in the aggregate, remarkably uniform, and there is no reason why railroad securities should be less stable than bank or insurance stocks. Mr. Jeans says:

"It is observable, in respect to the net profits from railway working, that they have not fluctuated from year to year in the same way as nearly all other profits have done. . . . It comes, then, to this, that, next after land and house property, the railway interest is the largest and most important in the country. But it is superior to both of these rival interests in its profit-earning capabilities, yielding, as it does, more than 4 per cent. on the capital expended, against a possible average of $2\frac{1}{2}$ to 3 per cent. in respect to the others."

There may be some arguments in favor of bonding railroads, but this practice is, upon the whole, productive of infinitely more evil than good. The State should, therefore, compel railroad companies to liquidate all of their bonded indebtedness without unnecessary delay. In the proportion in which this is accomplished railroad shares will gain in stability and value.

Railroad men complain that the small savings of the poor invested in railroad securities do not yield adequate returns and are often lost in consequence of the foreclosing of the roads in which these investments have been made. Others complain that railroads are bankrupted in the interest of designing bondholders. Still others charge

that rich and powerful roads contrive to obtain a controlling interest in the depreciated stock of weaker roads and
then manage these roads in their own interest and greatly
to the detriment of other stockholders. All these evils
would disappear if the law required the identity of actual
and virtual ownership.   "Freezing-out" processes could
no longer be resorted to by expert directors to obtain
without compensation the property of their less sophisti-
cated fellow stockholders. One railroad could no longer
obtain control of another by acquiring an insignificant
part of the sum total of its securities. There would be
no longer any clashing between the interests of bondholders and stockholders, and railroads would no longer
be managed in the interest of a small minority of their
owners.

In addition to the cancellation of all railroad mortgages
the State should require that all railroad stocks should, in
the future, be paid in full. Furthermore, roads should
be built only from the proceeds of the capital stock, and
the expense of repairs should be defrayed from the revenues of the road. Dividends should only be paid from
surplus earnings and should in no case exceed a fair rate
of interest on the actual present value of the road. The
statistician to the Interstate Commerce Commission suggests the creation of a special commission charged with
the duty of converting the actual capitalization of railroad
lines into a just value of their property. To do justice to
both the railroads and their patrons in the fixing of rates,
it is important that the just value of railroad property be
ascertained, but the work could probably be done with
less friction by a coöperation of National and State commissions. A number of reforms are needed within the
province of railroad management. Passenger rates are,
as a rule, too high, and out of all proportion to freight

rates. Many passenger tariffs still recognize the old
stage-coach principle of fixing the fare in an exact proportion to the distance traveled. Thus a passenger who
takes the train for a five-mile trip pays only fifteen cents
for his own transportation and that of one hundred
pounds of baggage, while the passenger who buys a
ticket for a journey of one hundred miles pays, on most
American lines, exactly twenty times the amount paid by
the five-mile passenger. Here the principle of collecting
terminal charges is entirely ignored. Sufficient inducements are not held out to the passenger to prolong his
journey, and as a consequence of this short-sighted policy
of the railroad companies the average distance traveled
in the United States by each passenger, instead of having
gradually increased, has gradually decreased of late years
until it is now only 24.18 miles. The average freight
haul in the United States is 120 miles, or about five times
as long as the average journey per passenger. How can
such a difference be accounted for except by the dis-
similarity in the principles which govern the computation
of passenger and freight charges? The same rule should
be adopted in fixing passenger rates that is recognized by
railroad men in fixing freight rates: the rate per mile
should decrease with the increase of the number of miles
traveled.

The principle of arranging passenger tariffs on a sliding
scale has found recognition in Europe. In Denmark
first-class passenger fare is 3.13 cents for each of the
first 47 miles, 2.67 cents for each of the next 47 miles,
and only 2.22 cents for every additional mile. The practical application of this principle is, in fact, only limited
by the extent of the kingdom. In nearly all European
countries a uniform reduction, ranging from 20 to 30 per
cent., is made from regular rates for return trip tickets,

and coupon tickets are issued to tourists almost everywhere at largely reduced rates.

Hungary recently adopted a new method of making passenger and freight tariffs for its state lines. This is now generally called the zone system. There are two classes of tickets sold, one for short trips on suburban or branch lines, the other for longer journeys on the main lines. The distances that can be traveled on short or suburban lines are divided into two zones of stations, and those on main lines into fourteen zones. The division of the kingdom into zones is made with Buda-Pesth as the center. A ticket purchased for a particular zone carries the passenger to the end of that zone or any nearer station.

The following table will show the extent of each zone and the fares paid:

Zone.	Distance.	Local Trains.			Fast Trains.		
		First Class.	Second Class.	Third Class.	First Class.	Second Class.	Third Class.
Short Lines.		Fl.	Fl	Fl.	Fl.	Fl.	Fl.
	First Station	0.30	0.15	.10	....	....	....
	Second Station	.40	.22	.15	....	....	....
Main Lines.							
1	1– 25 km.	.50	.40	.25	0.60	0.50	0.30
2	26– 40 "	1.00	.80	.50	1.20	1.00	.60
3	41– 55 "	1.50	1.20	.75	1.80	1.50	.90
4	56– 70 "	2.00	1.60	1.00	2.40	2.00	1.20
5	71– 85 "	2.50	2.00	1.25	3.00	2.50	1.50
6	86–100 "	3.00	2.40	1.50	3.60	3.00	1.80
7	101–115 "	3.50	2.80	1.75	4.20	3.50	2.10
8	116–130 "	4.00	3.20	2.00	4.80	4.00	2.40
9	131–145 "	4.50	3.60	2.25	5.40	4.50	2.70
10	146–160 "	5.00	4.00	2.50	6.00	5.00	3.00
11	161–175 "	5.50	4.40	2.75	6.60	5.50	3.30
12	176–200 "	6.00	4.80	3.00	7.20	6.00	3.60
13	201–225 "	7.00	5.30	3.50	8.40	6.50	4.20
14	225 km. and over	8.00	5.80	4.00	9.60	7.00	4.80

(The florin is a little more than one-third of a dollar.)

A ride from a city to the first suburban station costs from 3 to 10 cents, according to class of car, and to the second station 5 to 13.6 cents. On through trains a person may travel 15 miles at a cost of from 8½ to 20 cents, according to kind of train and class of car, a hundred miles for from 85 cents to $2.00 ; 140 miles for from $1.15 to $2.80 and any distance above 140 miles for from $1.35 to $3.25. A person may thus travel from Buda-Pesth to Predeal, a distance of 472 miles, with a third-class ticket for zone 14, purchased at a cost of $1.35, or 28-100 of a cent per mile.

Our railroad men with much complacency point to the fact that these rates do not cover the forwarding of passengers' baggage and that this service must be paid for separately. These charges, however, are very moderate, being on 120 pounds of baggage 8⅓ cents a distance of 34 miles or less, about 17 cents for a distance of more than 34 and less than 62 miles, and about 34 cents for any distance over 62 miles. The additional charge for carrying 120 pounds of baggage from Buda-Pesth to Predeal is therefore about one-fourteenth of one cent per mile. It must be admitted that this system of charging separately for passenger and baggage is eminently just, for there is no good reason why the passenger without baggage should be taxed to pay for the carriage of that of his fellow-traveler.

The zone tariff was introduced on the state railways of Hungary by M. Barosz, the Hungarian Minister of Commerce, on the 1st of August, 1889. The adoption of the new tariff was ridiculed and condemned as visionary by road experts, who even went so far as to prove to the satisfaction of practical railroad men that the innovation was destined to be a failure. For a month or two it almost seemed as if their prediction might be fulfilled, the number of passengers carried remaining behind the number carried during the corresponding period of previous years. But soon the reaction set in. The month of November, 1889, already witnessed an increase in the number of passengers as well as in receipts over the same month of the year previous. The result of the first year's trial demonstrated the wisdom of the "innovation." The number of passengers carried, which had been only 5,186,227 in 1888–89, rose to 13,060,751 in 1889–90, and the total receipts for passengers and baggage rose from 9,138,715 florins to 11,186,321 florins, a gain of 2,047,606 florins, or 22 per cent., during the first year. There is a continued increase both in the number of passengers and in receipts, and the success of the system must be pronounced phenomenal. The railroad experts of Europe, who had predicted the signal failure of the zone system, now that the unexpected has happened, are trying to discover the particular favorable conditions which made the success of the system possible in Hungary. It will probably be a decade, or even two, before the railroad experts of both hemispheres will be entirely reconciled to this new application of the old principle that a reduction in the price of a commodity increases the demand for it.

It is strange, indeed, that intelligent men should be so slow in recognizing an economic principle for which both history and daily experience furnish an unlimited number of illustrations. The post-office receipts everywhere have increased with a reduction in postage. The Government telegraph in England did not become self-supporting until Parliament made a sweeping reduction in its rates. The revenue from the Brooklyn bridge never paid a fair interest on the capital expended in its construction until its tolls were cut down. Were it necessary, hundreds of other examples could be added to these.

Hungary has also applied the zone system to its freight traffic. Three zones are fixed for the carrying of goods, viz.: Zone I, for distances less than 200 kilometers (124 miles); Zone II, for distances over 200 and less than 400 kilometers, and Zone III, for distances over 400 kilometers. A uniform tariff is established for each zone, which is one-third less than the average freight rates for equal distances formerly in force. American railroads should profit by the wisdom and experience of the Hungarian Government, and adopt at an early day such features of its system as upon our soil and under our institutions may be made practicable. The Hungarian system, with some modifications, is now being tried by Austria and a few of the German states, and is increasing railroad revenues wherever adopted.

There is a growing demand for lower fares. This demand increases in the same proportion in which the desire and the necessity for travel increase. European states have not been slow to meet it. Reductions are made everywhere, and chiefly favor the lower classes. Thus, when France, within the last year, changed her passenger tariff, she reduced first-class fare 9 per cent., second-class fare 18 per cent., and third-class 27 per cent.

The European passenger reports show the numbers of first and second-class passengers are continually falling off, while those of the third-class passengers are fast increasing. In England and Wales the number of first-class passengers fell between 1875 and 1889 from 37,000,000 to 24,000,000 while the number of third-class passengers increased during that same period from 350,000,000 to 601,000,000, and this increase still continues. In the

United Kingdom the number of third-class passengers for 1891 was over 750,000,000. Furthermore, passenger revenue comes chiefly from the third class. In the United Kingdom the receipts from first-class passengers were in 1889 £3,188,000; from second-class passengers, £2,705,000; and from third-class passengers, £19,-785,000. It is thus seen that receipts from third-class passengers are nearly 3½ times as large as those from the first and second-class passengers combined. A similar proportion is found in nearly every country on the continent. European roads discovered some years ago that first and second-class passengers were carried at a loss, and all the passenger earnings were derived from third-class passengers. The profits from this source show a considerable increase every year.

The average fare per mile is 2.15 cents in the United States, and only 1.17 cents in Germany, 1.67 cents in Austria, 1.18 cents in Belgium, 1.29 cents in Denmark, 1.45 cents in France, 1.64 cents in Italy, and 1.45 cents in Russia. It is often claimed by railroad men that we travel more luxuriously than the people of any other country in the world, but it should not be forgotten that traveling in the United States is also more expensive than anywhere else. It is contended that class distinctions are odious in America, and that second and third-class cars would not be patronized. The same argument might be applied to theaters, hotels, clothiers, grocers, etc. It is difficult to see why distinction here should be less odious than on the railroad train. The truth is, Americans are just like other people and will avail themselves of accommodations in keeping with their means if they have the opportunity. Many passengers who will not travel in an uncouth smoking-car would, if clean second-class cars were provided, gladly dispense with the luxury of an upholstered seat if by doing so they could save from $5 to $10 a day.

A common laborer in this country earns from a dollar to a dollar and a half a day, and in the performance of his labor as a rule suffers greater inconvenience than does the traveler who travels the country in a second-class car. Is it under these circumstances at all likely that the American would hesitate to travel for a day in a plain but clean car, if by doing so he could save a week's earnings? We may even go further and say that it is a very reasonable assumption that the man who earns his bread by the sweat of his brow would choose the cheaper car if the difference in one day's fare were equal to one day's wages. It is a common saying in Europe that the first-class passengers consist of lords and fools, and few of the hundreds of thousands of American tourists traveling abroad give the natives occasion to class them with either. The first-class car has almost fallen into disuse in Europe, and even the patronage of the second-class is less than ten per cent. of that of the third.

Reduced rates for return tickets should be provided under rules and regulations of commissioners.

The Massachusetts legislature recently passed a law requiring the railways of that State to sell interchangeable thousand-mile tickets for $20. The State commission is given power to except any company from its requirements if the public welfare or the financial condition require or demand it. This is a step in the right direction and should be followed by other States. Michigan also requires certain roads to carry first-class passengers at two cents per mile.

Railroad companies should be compelled to discard the

pass as a courtesy as well as a consideration. The giving
of passes under the guise of mileage books, or tickets for
pretended or unnecessary services, is very pernicious and
should be prohibited. Such a reform would soon enable
them to offer low fares to all. An employe may be furnished free transportation while actually engaged in the
business of his company, and it should be made the duty
of the State and National commissions to make proper
regulations governing such free transportation of employes.
Half-fare tickets for adults should also be abolished. The
pauper ticket is given to the minister of the gospel to
secure for the railroads the influence of the pulpit, though
offered under the pretense of charity or support of
the church. The State should not permit the railroad
companies to practice this or any other kind of charity at
the expense of the general public. The railroad is a highway, and the company operating it is entitled to rates
sufficient to pay operating expenses and a fair interest on
the value of the property. It can therefore easily be seen
that the so-called gifts show no liberality on the part of
the railroad company, but are made at the expense of
other people. Donations made by railroad companies
should be made from the pockets of their stockholders
and not from the pockets of their patrons.

All perquisites of railroad officers should be abolished.
When a railway official has become so pompous and conse-
quential that he requires a special car, it is about time to
look about for his successor. If we are to have a special-
car aristocracy in this country let it be supported at the
expense of some other interest.

Another railroad reform is needed on this side of the
Atlantic. While the great majority of railroad officials
are courteous and considerate, and perform their duties in

the most agreeable and acceptable manner, there are a few who do not properly appreciate the relation which they sustain to the patrons of their companies. They are inclined to forget that they are quasi-public servants, and that the public has a right to demand courteous treatment at their hands. All railroad employes should realize that their first duty is to administer to the welfare and the convenience of the public, and each one should have the full protection of the law in his efforts to do so. The American public objects much less to an inferior car than to rude treatment by the companies' agents. Railroad superintendents may justly be blamed for the incivilities of their subordinates. It is their duty to know the character of those whom they employ, and not to retain in their employ those who are derelict in their duty to the public. Nothing offends the feelings of a true American more than the display of a bureaucratic spirit on the part of public servants. Nothing more commends a line of railroad to the public than uniform painstaking kindness and courteous treatment on the part of its employes. It is made the duty of railroad employes of France " to so treat the public as if they were eager to oblige it," and the very first paragraph of the official instructions to the railroad employes of Germany enjoins them "to assume a modest and polite demeanor in their intercourse with the public." In this connection it might be stated that the second paragraph of those instructions positively forbids the acceptance of any gratuity by a railroad employe. If our American sleeping and dining-car companies would give their employes adequate compensation and then adopt and enforce the German rule concerning "tipping," their service would gain popularity and their employes self-respect.

Entrance into the railway service should be by agreement for a definite time, and dismissals and resignations should be governed by rules agreed upon by boards of commissioners and the companies.

The use of the corporation has done so much to secure for capital so large a share of the profits of industrial enterprises, and large salaries also for the officers who manage them, that laborers have been led to organize themselves into associations for like purposes, and ambitious men have not been slow in availing themselves of the advantages afforded them in this new field.

It is right and proper for laborers to organize such associations when they can do so under wise and economical management, for the purpose of securing greater intelligence, better education, higher culture, higher wages, a shorter work-day, and a general ameliorating of their condition, all of which will tend to make them more efficient workmen and also better enable them to resist the aggression of centralized wealth; for, in the absence of organization, the single-handed employe of the great modern employer is comparatively helpless. But if these organizations are allowed to be controlled by ignorant, unreasonable or designing men, who will, at trifling provocations, resort to violent and unlawful measures, they are sure to prove harmful, and a great detriment, instead of a help, to their members, and the sooner they are abandoned the better for all.

Great conflicts are sure to arise between organized capital and organized labor, and they must be settled in a reasonable way, or anarchy will prevail. They cannot be left for headstrong or inconsiderate men representing either side to determine, but the line must be drawn by the public authorities.

Remedies. 449

Each year affords accumulated evidence of the necessity of extending legal restrictions over the management of the railway business, and the law, as laid down by Judge Ricks to the Ann Arbor strikers last March, in the United States Circuit Court, at Toledo, is undoubtedly correct and will meet with general approval from the public.

He says:

"You are engaged in a service of a public character, and the public are interested not only in the way in which you perform your duties while you continue in that service, but are quite as much interested in the time and circumstances under which you quit that employment. You cannot always choose your own time and place for terminating these relations. If you are permitted to do so you might quit your work at a time and place and under circumstances which would involve irreparable damage to your employers and jeopardize the lives of the traveling public."

Mr. Powderly, in commenting upon the above decision, does not complain of it, but says:

"The decision shows, as I have said before, that the principle of Government ownership of the railroads is being recognized by the courts. While the decision is apparently against the men, it emphasizes our position that the Government has the right to supervise the railroads. Now it is a poor rule that won't work both ways.

"The Interstate Commerce Law was passed for the purpose of controlling the railroads, but up to date no railroad has paid any attention to the law. Anarchy of the worst kind has prevailed. By that I mean a total disregard of the law, and that is what the corporations charge against the anarchists. The courts hold themselves in readiness to obey the will of the corporations when a charge is made against the workmen, but no effort is made to carry out the mandates of the law when the provokers of strikes, the corporations, violate the law."

There is but little doubt, if the judges of the Federal courts would show the same zeal in holding railroad managers amenable to the law as Judge Ricks has displayed in this case with the employes, they would secure increased confidence from the people in the tribunals over which they preside.

All fair-minded persons will agree that labor as well as capital must be subjected to proper restraints, and that the public will demand nothing unreasonable from either.

Accidents are too frequent upon American railroads. The reports of the Interstate Commerce Commission give the following as the numbers killed and injured during the years named:

| | 1888 | | 1889 | | 1890 | | 1891 | |
	Killed.	Injured.	Killed.	Injured.	Killed.	Injured.	Killed.	Injured.
Employes.	2,070	20,148	1,972	20,028	2,451	22,396	2,660	26,140
Passeng's..	315	2,138	310	2,146	286	2,425	293	2,972
Others......	2,897	3,602	3,541	4,135	3,598	4,206	......	......
Total......	5,282	25,888	5,823	26,309	6,335	29,027	.....	.. ...

For the year ending June 30, 1890, the total number of employes was 749,301. There was, therefore, one death for every 306 men employed and one injury for every 33 men employed. For the previous year one was killed for every 357 men employed, and one was injured for every 35 men employed. While trainmen represent but 20 per cent. of the total number of employes, the casualties among them represent 58 per cent. of the total number of casualties.

For the year 1888, one passenger was killed in every 1,523,133 passengers carried, and one injured in every 220,024 carried.

The corresponding rate in England for the year 1888 is one passenger killed for every 6,942,336 carried, and one injured for every 527,577 carried.

Railroads doing a large business should be compelled to adopt the most improved appliances for avoidance of accidents.

The occupation of trainmen is especially hazardous, and too long continued service should not be required, but proper intervals of rest should be allowed. It is to the want of this, undoubtedly, that a great many of the serious accidents are owing.

No more Sunday trains should be run than are absolutely necessary. Provision should be made by law to enable trainmen to procure insurance at the lowest rate possible, for indemnity against loss of health, life or limb.

It was only a few days before the great disaster occurred on the Hudson River Railroad at Hastings, over a year ago, that an announcement had been made to the public of the extreme prosperity of the road during the year. The great slaughter that occurred there is another illustration of the disregard of public duty, and another instance of the sacrifice of life and limbs of passengers and employes by a railway corporation in order to secure large dividends on watered stock. It is not only gross, but criminal neglect for a company with such an immense income not to provide greater safety appliances, and the coroner's jury in this case was too modest when it decided that the management of the road was morally responsible for the disaster.

Parliament has compelled the British railways to adopt, in the interest of the public safety, the block system and continuous brake, and great lines like the New York Central and Hudson River companies should be compelled to adopt such improvements.

The traveling public has another grievous cause for complaint. There are but few companies that make any efforts to have their trains connect with those of rival roads. On the contrary, a good deal of scheming is often done by railroad companies to so arrange their time-tables with reference to those of their rivals as to inconvenience passengers as much as possible by delays at competing points. To remedy this evil the State should require that every time-table should have the approval of proper authorities, and no change should be permitted without their approval.

Railroad companies are chartered for the purpose of promoting the public welfare, and every violation of their charter should be punished.

It should be the main object of railroad legislation to compel companies to fulfill their public obligations without depriving them of their efficiency. Above all things these companies should be stripped of the power to use their great wealth for the purposes of corruption or the attainment of political influence. Our railroads to-day probably represent no less than one-fourth of the personal property of the country, and this vast wealth is controlled by a comparatively small number of men, many of whom have in the course of time become so arrogant and despotic that they have little regard for popular rights or the expressed will of a free people.

It is reported that when, a few years ago, a representative of the press directed Mr. Vanderbilt's attention to the fact that the public disapproved of his railroad policy, the latter gave vent to his contempt for public opinion by the no less profane than laconic reply: "The public be damned." Ex-Railroad Commissioner Coffin called on one of the Goulds to urge the adoption of the automatic car-coupler and other safety appliances for the roads controlled by them. He was very curtly told that not a cent would be expended by the Gould roads for such a purpose until the West had repealed its obnoxious railroad laws. The Gould dynasty thus intends to accomplish the repeal of these laws by coercion. Railroad magnates and their lieutenants often show still greater arrogance in dealing directly with their employes.

It may be difficult for railroad managers of the present school to adapt themselves to new conditions; it may be impossible for them to understand how any other practices than those which have long been established can succeed; yet in spite of them both the law and public sentiment have already undergone great changes, and still greater changes will follow. It may take years to accomplish this work; to bring about any great reform requires time and a determined purpose on the part of its advocates. Yet I believe the era is not far off when railroads will be limited to their legitimate sphere as common carriers, when they will treat all persons and all places as impartially as does the Government in the mail service, when their chief factor in rate-making will be the cost of service, when they will respect the rights of the public and those of their stockholders, insuring perfect service to the former and fair profits upon the actual value of the lines operated to the latter.

The fact should, finally, not be overlooked that it is in the power of the General Government to prevent many railroad abuses, and especially excessive freight charges, by the improvement of our rivers and harbors. That our water-courses act as levelers of interstate rates is apparent from the fact that railroad rates invariably rise with the freezing of the water-ways and fall with the opening of river and lake navigation. By connecting, wherever feasible, our large Western rivers with the great lakes, the Government could greatly extend the reign of competition in transportation, and thereby keep freight rates within reasonable bounds. Lake transportation even now plays an important role. In 1892 it was not less than 20,000,000,-

000 ton miles during the season of eight months' duration, and it is almost equal to one-fourth of the total ton mileage of all the railroads in the country for the entire year. The average rate of lake transportation has been reduced to 1.3 mills per ton per mile, which is only about one-seventh of the average railroad freight rate in the United States

Where the masses hold the sovereign power, there, if anywhere, the welfare of the people should be the supreme law. Violent political commotions never disturb the government whose policy is to secure the greatest good to the greatest number. Thorold Rogers justly remarks that the strength of communism lies in the misconduct of administrations, the sustentation of odious and unjust privileges and the support of what are called vested interests. Lord Coleridge, in a remarkable article published not long ago, recommended a revision of the laws relating to property and contract, in order to facilitate the inevitable transition from feudalism to democracy, and laid down the rule that the laws of property should be made for the benefit of all, and not for the benefit of a class.

During the middle ages, and even up to the beginning of the present century, nearly all the laws on the statute books looked towards the protection of the rights of the feudal lord. Provision was made for the expeditious collection of his dues and a severe punishment of his delinquent debtor. The peasant was forced to labor fifteen hours per day and three hundred and sixty-five days in the year to pay the baron's rentals and sustain life. The law permitted him to be flogged for failing to courtesy the feudal lord, and to be executed for injury to the lord's person, while to kill a peasant was no worse a misdemeanor than to kill his lordship's favorite dog or falcon. In short, all laws were made to protect and perpetuate the wealth and power of the few by impoverishing, humbling and enslaving the masses.

The age of feudalism has given way to an age of democratic liberty, but there is many a feudal feature left in our statutes and many a feudal doctrine is enunciated by our judges and learned expounders of modern jurisprudence. In his decision in the Iowa tariff case Judge Brewer said:

"I read also in the first section of the Bill of Rights of this State [Iowa] that 'all men are by nature free and equal and have certain inalienable rights, among which are those of enjoying and defending life and liberty, acquiring, possessing and protecting property and pursuing and obtaining safety and happiness,' and I know that while that remains as the supreme law of the State, no legislature can, directly or indirectly, lay its withering or destroying hand on a single dollar invested in the legitimate business of transportation."

Had Judge Brewer taken the pains to read on, he would have found in section 2 of the Bill of Rights the following:

"All political power is inherent in the people; government is instituted for the protection, security and benefit of the people."

It is strange that the learned Judge failed to see the difference between "men," the creatures of God, "by nature free and equal," and "possessing certain inalienable rights," and corporations, the creatures of man, having no rights except those which the State sees fit to give them. Had the learned Judge perused the whole of the document to which he refers, he would have found in article VIII, section 12, the following provision:

"The General Assembly shall have power to amend or

repeal all laws for the organization or creation of corporations, or granting of special or exclusive privileges or immunities, by a vote of two-thirds of each branch of the General Assembly."

It should thus have been plain to the learned Judge that in Iowa corporations have not human or inalienable rights, and government was not instituted for their special protection, but for the protection, security and benefit of her people. Nor should it be otherwise.

The corporation for pecuniary gain has neither body nor soul. Its corporeal existence is mythical and ethereal. It suffers neither from cold nor from hunger, has neither fear of future punishment nor hope of future reward. It takes no interest in schools or in churches. It knows neither charity nor love, neither pity nor sympathy, neither justice nor patriotism. It is deaf and blind to human woe and human happiness. Its only aim is pecuniary gain, to which it subordinates all else.

Should the State sacrifice the welfare of all her people rather than lay its "withering or destroying" hand on a single dollar of corporate wealth? Are there no human rights, for the protection of which government was established, more sacred than the rights of a wealthy corporation's dollar? Have the people made the judiciary a coördinate branch of the Government in order that it may protect the vested or rather usurped rights of corporations against legislative attempts to curtail them? If the courts so interpret the power which has been delegated to them, they will awake one day to the painful reality that popular convictions of right are more potent than judicial decrees.

It is the duty of the State not so much to defend the so-called vested rights of corporations as to make such just and beneficial laws as will temper inequality, mitigate poverty, protect the weak against the strong, preserve life and health, and, in short, promote the welfare and the happiness of the masses. Constitutions have been made to accomplish these ends, to protect the lives, the liberty and the conscience of human beings, while laws have been sufficient to protect the dollars of corporations. It is a short-sighted policy on the part of the latter to take unfair advantage of their wealth and influence, for "As ye sow, so shall ye reap," is the inexorable law of Providence. There is no dynasty so mighty, no class so privileged, no interest so influential or wealthy as to obtain immunity from its operation.

APPENDIX.

TABLE No. 1.

COMPILED FROM THE SIXTH ANNUAL REPORT OF THE INTER-
STATE COMMERCE COMMISSION.

Mileage in the United States June 30, 1891.....	168,402.74
Number of men employed.................... .	784,285
Number of employes per 100 miles............	486
Number of locomotives per 100 miles..........	19
Number of passenger cars per 100 miles.......	17
Number of cars per 100 miles.................	721
Capital......................................	$9,829,475,015
Capital per mile..............................	60,942
Gross earnings...............................	1,096,761,395
Gross earnings per mile......................	6,801
Operating expenses	731,887,893
Operating expenses per mile..................	4,538
Net income from operation...................	364,873,502
Net income per mile..........................	2,263

Of gross income 67.17 per cent. was earned on freight.

Of gross income 25.64 per cent. was earned on passengers.

Received for carrying mails	$ 24,870,015
Received rentals from express companies......	21,594,349
Received from investments....................	133,911,126
No. of passengers carried.....................	531,183,988
No. of tons freight carried....................	675,608,323
Average journey per passenger................	24.18 miles
Average haul per ton of freight	120 miles
Average number passengers per train	42
Average number tons freight per train	181.67
Average revenue per passenger per mile.......	2.142 cents
Average revenue per ton per mile of freight. ..	.895 cents
Average revenue per train mile, passenger	$1.06
Average revenue per train mile, freight	1.64

i

TABLE No. 2.

STATISTICS OF THE RAILWAYS OF THE UNITED KINGDOM FOR
THE YEAR ENDING DEC. 31, 1891.

From the English Reform Almanac for 1893 and from the
Report of Commissioners R. Giffen and Courtenay
Boyle to the Board of Trade.

Mileage	20,191 miles
Double, triple or quadruple	10,853 miles
Capital per mile	£45,536
Gross income per mile	3,873
Net income per mile	1,818
Income from passenger traffic	35,130,916
Income from goods traffic	43,230,717
Income from miscellaneous	3,498,974
Income, total	£81,860,607
Operating expenses, 55 per cent	£45,144,778
Rates and taxes	2,246,430
Government duty	321,260
Paid for persons injured	165,219
Paid for damage and loss of goods	257,804
Number of first-class passengers	30,423,776
Number of second-class passengers	63,378,397
Number of third-class passengers	751,661,495

Number of third-class passengers over 88 per cent. of all.

Number of employes	346,426
Number of employes per 100 miles	1,750
Number of locomotives per 100 miles	80
Number of passenger cars per 100 miles	249
Number of freight and other cars	2,595
Revenue per train mile	58.37d
Expense per train mile	30.54d
Per cent. of earnings on capital	4.21

TABLE No. 3.

SHOWING SALARIES AND WAGES PAID TO OFFICIALS AND EMPLOYES OF STATE RAILWAYS IN EUROPE.

Compiled from Röll's Encyclopädie des Eisenbahnwesens.

POSITION.	AUSTRIA. Fl., equal to about 33⅓ cents.	HUNGARY. Fl., equal to about 33⅓ cents.	PRUSSIA. Mark, equal to about 24 cents.	BELGIUM. Fr., equal to about 20 cents.
President	7,000	....	10,500	9,000
Directors and Superintendents	4,000—5,500	4,000—4,800	4,200—6,000	7,000—8,000
Chief Engineer	1,600—2,000	1,900—2,500	3,600—4,800	2,700—5,500
Clerks	500—1,200	640—1,000	1,000—2,700	900—3,100
Station Agents in Cities, Division Superintendents	2,200—2,600	2,600—3,400	....	....
Station Agents in Towns	500— 850	520— 880	1,500—3,200	1,600—4,000
Locomotive Engineers	500— 850	520— 780	1,200—2,000	....
Firemen	300— 350	380— 480	1,000—1,500	....
Conductors	450— 550	520— 850	1,100—1,500	2,000—2,400
Brakemen	300— 350	380— 480	800—1,200	1,200—2,000
Section Men	288— 336	270— 370	700— 900	....

TABLE No. 4.

Compiled from Röll's Encyclopädie des Eisenbahnwesens.

FREIGHT TARIFFS.--BELGIUM.

All freight is divided into three general classes:

1. *Express Freight,* which is delivered by special messengers. Parcels weighing 5 kg. (11 lbs.) and less, if prepaid, are carried for .80 fr. (16c.) for all distances. Parcels not prepaid and such as weigh from 6 to 10 kg. pay .90 fr. for a distance of from 1 to 25 km,; 1 fr. for 26 to 75 km.; 1.10 fr. for greater distances.
2. *Fast Freight,* which may be made use of for consignments weighing up to 200 kg. (440 lbs.) Parcels weighing up to 5 kg. pay .50 fr. for all distances. Parcels not prepaid and such as weigh from 5 to 10 kg. pay .50 fr. for from 1 to 25 km.; .60 fr. for distances ranging from 26 to 75 km., and .70 fr. over 75 km.
3. *Common Freight,* which is again sub-divided into four classes: In Class I 400 kg., in Classes II and III 5,000 kg., and in Class IV 10,000 kg. is recognized as the minimum weight.

TARIFF FOR THE FOUR DIFFERENT CLASSES OF COMMON FREIGHT.

Terminal Charges—Franc 1.00.

I Class—For 1,000 kg. (2,250 lbs.)

From 1 to 5 km .... Fr. 1.00	
From 6 to 75 km, per km ..... .10	
From 76 to 150 km. .... .08	(per km. above 75)
From 151 to 200 km .... .06	(per km. above 150)
Above 200 km .... .06	(per km. above 200)

BELGIUM—*Continued.*

II Class—For 1,000 kg.
 From 1 to 5 km...........Fr. 0.40
 From 6 to 75 km., per km.... .08
 From 76 to 125 km........... .04 (per km. above 75)
 Above 125 km................ .02 (per km. above 125)

III Class—For 1,000 kg.
 From 1 to 5 km.............................Fr. 0.30
 From 6 to 75 km., per km........................ .06
 From 76 to 100 km.............................. .03
 From 101 to 125 km .... .02
 Above 125 km................................. .01

IV Class—For 1,000 kg.
 From 1 to 24 km., per km.................... Fr. 0.06
 From 25 to 75 km., per km....................... .04
 From 76 to 100 km.............................. .02
 From 101 to 350 km............................. .01
 Above 350 km .... .02
For distances from 1 to 24 km. the terminal charges are only
 .5 fr. for Class IV.

TABLE No. 5.

GERMANY.

The tariff recognizes the following distinctions:
1. Fast parcel freight.
2. Fast carload freight.
3. Parcel freight.
4. General carload Class A1, for shipments of at least 5,000 kg.
5. General carload Class B, for shipments of at least 10,000 kg.
6. Special tariffs.

GERMANY—*Continued.*

Distance charges per ton per kilometer: (*Pfennig,* ¼ *c.*)

1. For parcel........................ 11.0 pfennige
2. For carload Class A1 .... 6.7   "
3. For carload Class B................ 6.0   ".
4. For Special Tariff A2.............. 5.0   "
5. For Special Tariff I ..:........... 4.5   "
6. For Special Tariff II .... 3.5   "
7. For Special Tariff III:
       For distances up to 100 km....... 2.6   ".
       For distances above 100 km ...... 2.2   "
8. For fast parcel freight .... 22.0   "
9. For fast carload freight, twice the rate of Classes A1 and B.

Terminal Charges.

1. For parcels and carload Class A1:

       Up to 10 km............................10 pfennige
       From 11 to 20 km.......................11   "
       From 21 to 30 km ... .12   "
       From 31 to 40 km 13   "
       From 41 to 50 km 14   "
       From 51 to 60 km 15   "
       From 61 to 70 km 16   "
       From 71 to 80 km 17   "
       From 81 to 90 km 18   "
       From 91 to 100 km 19   "
       Above 100 km...........................20   "

2. For carload Class B:

       Up to 10 km............................ 8 pfennige
       From 11 to 20 km....................... 9   "
       From 21 to 30 km 10   ".
       From 31 to 40 km 11   "
       Above 40 km...........................12   "

GERMANY—*Continued.*

3. For Special Tariffs A2, I, II and III:
   Up to 10 km .... 8 **pfennige**
   From 11 to 100 km 9   "
   Above 100 km 12   "

Charges for Live Stock.

(a) Horses. Terminal charge per head, 1 m. (24c.)
   Distance charge per kl. for one head........0.30 **mark**
   Charge per kl. for 2 head................... .40   "
   Charge for each additional head........... .10   "

(b) Cattle.
   Terminal charge, per head.................0.60 **mark**
   Distance charge per kl., for one head....... .10   "
   Distance charge for each additional head... .03   "

(c) Sheep, Hogs, Calves, etc.:
   Terminal charge, per head ....0.20 **mark**
   Distance charge, per kl., for each of the first
     10 heads.... .... .02   "
   Distance charge, per kl., for each additional
     head............................... .01   "

If shipped in carloads the charges for live stock are .03 m.
per square meter per kilometer.

TABLE No. 6.

FRANCE.

The French railroads divide all freight into six different classes. The following is the tariff adopted by a majority of the principal roads:

Common Freight.

Classes.	1	2	3	4	5	6
Up to 25 km.	16	14	12	10	8	8
From 26 to 100 km	16	14	12	10	8	4
From 101 to 150 km	15	13	11	9	8	3.5
From 151 to 200 km	15	13	11	9	7	3.5
From 201 to 300 km	15	13	11	9	4	3.5
From 301 to 500 km	14	12	10	8	4	3
From 501 to 600 km.	13	11	9	7	4	3
From 601 to 70) km	12	10	8	6	4	2.5
From 701 to 800 km	11	9	7	5	4	2 5
From 801 to 900 km	10	8	6	4	4	2.5
From 901 to 1000 km	9	7	5	4	4	2
Above 1,000 km..	8	6	5	4	4	2

Centimes per Ton—Kilometer.

The rates for fast parcel freight are, on all roads, for less than 40 kg., per ton, km.:

Up to 200 km.	35	centimes
From 201 to 300 km.	32	"
From 301 to 400 km.	31	"
From 401 to 800 km.	30	"
From 801 to 1,000 km.	28	"
Above 1,000 km	25	"

For more than 40 kg.:

Up to 100 km.	32	centimes
From 101 to 300 km.	30	"
From 301 to 500 km.	28	"
From 501 to 600 km.	26	"
From 601 to 700 km.	24	"
From 701 to 800 km.	22	"
From 801 to 900 km.	20	"
From 901 to 1,000 km.	18	"
Above 1,000 km.	16	"

Express parcels weighing up to 3 kg. (6 3-5 lbs.), pay 1 fr. for all distances, and parcels weighing from 3 to 5 kg. pay fr. 1.20. Delivery to the house, 25 centimes (5c.) additional.

Live Stock, per piece, per km.:

Horses and cattle	16	centimes
Calves and hogs	6	"
Sheep, etc.	3	"

TABLE No. 7.

ITALY.—*Freight Tariff.*

RATES.	GENERAL CLASSES.							
	1	2	3	4	5	6	7	8
For the ton—km	0.1632	0.1428	0.1224	0.1020	0.0816	0.0714	0.612	0.0510
Terminal charges, per ton.	2.04	2.04	2.04	2.04	2.04	1.224	1.224	1.224

The rate on merchandise sent as fast freight is .452 lire (9c.) per ton kilometer.

Live Stock—(5 Classes.)

FIRST-CLASS.	Horses.	Cattle, Swine and Sheep.
1 head, per km	0.1530	0.136
2 heads, per km	.0918	.0765
3 heads, per km	.0816	.0714
4 heads, per km	.0765	.0663
5 heads, per km	.0714	.0612
6 heads or more, per km	.0663	.0561

SECOND-CLASS.	Horses.	Cattle, Swine and Sheep.
1 head, per km	0.1530	0.1326
2 heads, per km	.0816	.0714
3 heads, per km	.0663	.0612
4 heads, per km	.0612	.0561
5 heads, per km	.0561	.0510
6 heads or more, per km	.0510	.0459
III Class		.02244
IV Class		.01224
V Class		.00612

TABLE No. 8.

Austrian Tariff (in florins, about 33⅓ cents).—July 1, 1891.

	Fast Freight.		Parcel Rate.		Carload Rate.			Special Tariff Rate.			Exceptional Rate.
	Ordinary Rate.	Reduced Rate.	I	II	A	B	C	1	2	3	
From 1 to 50 km......	1.20	0.60	0.60	0.50	0.34	0.24	0.18	0.26	0.18	0.15	0.12
From 50 to 150 km.....	1.16	.58	.58	.46	.29	.22	.15	.23	.15	.13	.10
From 150 to 300 km...	1.12	.56	.56	.42	.25	.18	.12	.19	.12	.10	.09
For every addit'n'l km	1.00	.50	.50	.30	.20	.12	.10	.15	.10	.08	.08

Terminal Charges.

From 1 to 30 km......	6.0	3.0	3.0	3.0	3.0	2.0	2.0	2.0	2.0	2.0	2.0
From 31 to 80 km......	6	3	3	3	3	3	3	3	3	3	2
Above 80 km..........	8	4	4	4	4	4	4	4	4	4	2

Horses and *mules* are placed in Class II, with a minimum weight of 1,400 kg. for one head and 700 kg. for every additional head.

Cattle are placed in Class II, and are billed at actual weight.

Potatoes, hay, straw, wood, coal and coke enjoy the "exceptional rate" when shipped in carload lots.

TABLE No. 9.

Hungarian Tariff (in florins).—January 1, 1891.

	Fast Freight		Parcel Rate		"Sperrgüter,"	Carload Rate			Special Tariff			Except'n'l Tariff	
	Ordinary Rate.	Reduced Rate.	I	II		A	B	C (Lumber)	I	II	III	I	II
From 1 to 200 km	1.3	0.6	0.72	0.52	0.9	0.32	0.21	0.16	0.27	0.16	0.13	0.13	0.11
From 201 to 400 km	1.	.5	.52	.42	.8	.24	.17	.13	.15	.13	.10	.10	.09
Above 400 km	1.	.5	.52	.42	.8	.16	.10	.09	.10	.09	.07	.07	.06
Terminal Charges for 100 kg.	.10	.10	.10	.10	.10	.06	.06	.04	.05	.04	.03	.03	.03

Exceptional Tariff I comprises coal, wood, potatoes, stone, hay and straw.
Exceptional Tariff II comprises manure, earth and Hungarian ores.

TABLE No. 10.

STATE OF IOWA.

SCHEDULE

OF

REASONABLE MAXIMUM RATES OF CHARGES

In Effect March 1, 1893,

FOR THE TRANSPORTATION OF

*Freight and Cars on each of the Railroads in the State of Iowa, together
with a Classification of Freights, prepared by the Railroad
Commissioners, in accordance with the Laws
of the State of Iowa.*

Superseding all former schedules on the said railroads,
including all bridges and ferries used or operated in connection with any railroad; and, also, all the roads in use
by any corporation, receiver, trustee or other person
operating a railroad, whether owned or operated under
contract, agreement, lease or otherwise, or which may
hereafter be purchased, leased, acquired or operated
within the State of Iowa.

The classification of freights applies to all the lines,
regardless of class. The schedule of maximum rates
applies to all Class "A" roads. The rates on Class "B"
roads will be FIFTEEN per cent. higher, and the rates on
Class "C" roads THIRTY per cent. higher than the rates
named for Class "A" roads. The respective roads have

been classified by the Executive Council of the State as follows, which classification is adopted by the Railroad Commissioners, and made part of this schedule:

CLASSIFICATION OF ROADS.

CLASS " A."

Where gross annual earnings, per mile, shall be $4,000 or more.—Burlington, Cedar Rapids and Northern Railway; Chicago and Northwestern Railway; Chicago, Burlington and Quincy Railroad; Chicago, Milwaukee and St. Paul Railway; Chicago, Rock Island and Pacific Railway; Chicago and Great Western Railway (operating the Chicago, St. Paul and Kansas City Railway); Dubuque and Sioux City Railroad; Chicago, St. Paul, Minneapolis and Omaha Railway; Sioux City and Northern Railway; Chicago, Santa Fe and California Railway; Sioux City and Pacific Railroad; Toledo, Peoria and Western Railway; Union Pacific Railway

CLASS "B."

Where gross earnings are $3,000 or over and less than $4,000 per mile.—Iowa Central Railway; Kansas City, St. Joseph and Council Bluffs Railroad; Omaha and St. Louis Railway.

CLASS " C."

Where annual earnings are less than $3,000 per mile.— Chicago, Burlington and Kansas City Railway; Chicago, Ft. Madison and Des Moines Railway; Chicago, Iowa and Dakota Railway; Crooked Creek Railroad and Coal Company; Des Moines and Kansas City Railway; Des Moines, Northern and Western Railway; Humeston and Shenandoah Railroad; Iowa Northern Railway; Mason City and Fort Dodge Railroad; Minneapolis and St. Louis Railway; St. Louis, Keokuk and Northwestern Railroad; Tabor and Northern Railway; Wabash Railroad; Winona and Southwestern Railway; Keokuk and Western Railway.

Burlington and Western ; Burlington and Northwestern ; Ames and College; Albia and Centerville.

Appendix.

MILES.	MERCHANDISE IN CENTS PER 100 LBS.					SPECIAL CARLOAD CLASSES IN CENTS PER 100 LBS.				
	First Class.	Second Class.	Third Class.	Fourth Class.	Fifth Class.	Class A.	Class B.	Class C.	Class D.	Class E.
5	14	11.9	9.34	7	4.9	5	4.9	4.2	3.5	2.8
10	14.8	12.58	10.1	7.4	5.18	5.3	5.18	4.44	3.7	2.96
15	15.6	13.26	10.4	7.8	5.46	5 6	5.46	4.68	3.9	3.12
20	16.4	13.94	10 94	8.2	5.74	5.8	5.74	4.92	4.1	3.25
25	17	14.45	11.34	8.5	5.95	6	5.95	5.1	4.25	3.4
30	17.6	14.96	11.73	8.8	6.16	6.2	6.16	5.28	4.4	3.52
35	18.2	15.47	12.1	9.1	6.37	6.4	6.37	5.46	4 55	3.64
40	18.8	15 98	12.5	9.4	6.58	6.6	6.58	5.64	4.7	3.76
45	19.4	16.49	13	9.7	6.79	6.8	6.79	5.82	4 85	3.88
50	20.	17	13.34	10	7	7.05	7	6	5	4
55	20 4	17.34	13.6	10.2	7.14	7.2	7.14	6.12	5.1	4.08
60	20.8	17.68	13.87	10.4	7.28	7.4	7.28	6.24	5.2	4 16
65	21.2	18.02	14.14	10.6	7.42	7 6	7.42	6.36	5.3	4.25
70	21.6	18.36	14.4	10.8	7.56	7.8	7 56	6.48	5.4	4.32
75	22	18.7	14.67	11	7.7	8	7.7	6.6	5.5	4.4
80	22.4	19.04	14.94	11.2	7.84	8.2	7.84	6.72	5 6	4.48
85	22 8	19 38	15.2	11.4	7.98	8.4	7.98	6.84	5.7	4.56
90	23 2	19 72	15.47	11.6	8.12	8 6	8.12	6.96	5.8	4.64
95	23.6	20.06	15.73	11.8	8.26	8.8	8.26	7.08	5.9	4.72
100	24	20.4	16	12	8.4	9	8.4	7.2	6	4.8
105	24 8	20.89	16.35	12.33	8.69	9.35	8.63	7.4	6.17	4.96
110	25.6	21.38	16 7	12.66	8.98	9.7	8.86	7.6	6.34	5.12
115	26 4	21 87	17.05	12 99	9.27	10.05	9.09	7.8	6.51	5.28
120	27.2	22.36	17.4	13.32	9.56	10.4	9.32	8	6 68	5.44
125	28	22.85	17.75	13.65	9.85	10.75	9.55	8.2	6.85	5.6
130	28.8	23.34	18.1	13.98	10.14	11.1	9.78	8.4	7.02	5.76
135	29.6	23.83	18.45	14.31	10 43	11.45	10.01	8.6	7.19	5.92
140	30.4	24.32	18.8	14.64	10.72	11 8	10 24	8.8	7.36	6.08
145	31.2	24.81	19.15	14.97	11.01	12.15	10.47	9	7.53	6.24
150	32	25.3	19.5	15.3	11.3	12.5	10.7	9.2	7.7	6.4
155	32.8	25 79	19.85	15.63	11.59	12 84	10.93	9.39	7.87	6.56
160	33.6	26.28	20 2	15 96	11.88	13.18	11 16	9.58	8.04	6.72
165	34.4	26.77	20 55	16.29	12.17	13.52	11.39	9.77	8.21	6 88
170	35.2	27.26	20.9	16 62	12.46	13.86	11.62	9.96	8.38	7.04
175	36	27.75	21.25	16.95	12.75	14.2	11.85	10.15	8.55	7.2
180	36.8	28.24	21.6	17.28	13.04	14.54	12 08	10.34	8.72	7.36
185	37.6	28 73	21.95	17.61	13.33	14.88	12.31	10 53	8 89	7.52
190	38.4	29.22	22.3	17.94	13.62	15.22	12.45	10.72	9.06	7.68
195	39.2	29.71	22.65	18.27	13 91	15 56	12.77	10.91	9.23	7.84
200	40	30.2	23	18.6	14.2	15.9	13	11.1	9.39	8
210	41.6	31.18	23.7	19 24	14.78	16.56	13.45	11.49	9.71	8.3
220	43.2	32.16	24.4	19.88	15.36	17.22	13.9	11.88	10.03	8.6
230	44.8	33.14	25.1	20.52	15.94	17.88	14.35	12.27	10.35	8.9
240	46.4	34.12	25 8	21..6	16.52	18 54	14.8	12.66	10.67	9.2
250	48	35.1	26.5	21.8	17.1	19.2	15.25	13.05	10.99	9.5

MILES.	MERCHANDISE IN CENTS PER 100 LBS.				SPECIAL CARLOAD CLASSES IN CENTS PER 100 LBS.					
	First Class.	Second Class.	Third Class.	Fourth Class.	Fifth Class.	Class A.	Class B.	Class C.	Class D.	Class E.
260.	49.6	36.08	27.2	22.44	17.68	19.86	15.7	13.44	11.31	9.8
270........	51.2	37.06	27.9	23 08	18.26	20.52	16.15	13.83	11.63	10..
280.	52.8	38.4	28.6	23.72	18 84	21.18	16 6	14.22	11 95	10 4
290.	54.4	39.02	29.3	24.36	19.42	21.84	17.05	14.61	12.27	10.7
300.	56	40	30	25	20	22.5	17.5	15	12.5	11
310........	56.5	40.5	30.5	25.5	20.5	23	18	15.5	13	11.5
320.	57.	41	31	26	21	23.5	18.5	16	13.5	12
330.	57.5	41.5	31.5	26.5	21.5	24	19	16.5	14	12.5
340.	58.	42	32	27	22	24.5	19.5	17	14.5	13
350........	58.5	42.5	32.5	27.5	22.5	25	20	17.5	15	13.5
360.	59	43	33	28	23	25.5	20.5	18	15.5	14
370.	59.5	43.5	33.5	28 5	23.5	26	21	18.5	16	14.5
380.	60	44	.4	29	24	26.5	21.5	19	16.5	15
390.	60.5	44.5	34.5	29.5	24.5	27	22	19 5	17	15.5
400.	61	45	35	30	25	27.5	22.5	20	17.5	16
410.	61.5	45.5	35.5	30.5	25.5	28	23	20.5	18	16.5
420.	62	46	36	31	26	28.5	23.5	21	18.5	17
430........	62.5	46.5	36.5	31.5	26.5	29	24	21.5	19	17.5
440.	63	47	37	32	27	29.5	24.5	22	19.5	18
450.	63.5	47.5	37.5	32.5	27.5	30	25	22.5	20	18.5
460.	64	48	38	33	28	30.5	25.5	23	20.5	19
470.	64.5	48.5	38.5	33.5	28.5	31	26	23.5	21	19 5
480.	65	49	39	34	29	31.5	26.5	24	21.5	20
490.....	65 5	49.5	39 5	34.5	29.5	32	27	24.5	22	20.5
500........	66	50	40	35	30	32.5	27.5	25	22.5	21

NOTE.—When rates are not shown in this table for the exact distance, the rates given for the next greater distance will prevail. When these rates and the classification conflict, these rates will govern.

MILES	Wheat, flour, millet, flaxseed.	Corn, oats, barley, other grain and mill-stuffs.	Hard and soft lumber, lath, shingles, sash, doors and blinds.	Salt, lime, cement, plaster, stucco.	Horses and Mules in carloads—minimum weight 20,000 lbs., 31-foot cars, inside measurement.	Fat cattle in carloads—minimum weight 19,000 lbs., 31-foot cars, inside measurement.	Hogs (single deck) in carloads—minimum weight 15,000 lbs., 31-foot cars, inside measurement.	Sheep (single deck) in carloads—minimum weight 15,000 lbs., 31-foot cars, inside measurement	Hard coal.	Soft coal, lump and nut.	Soft coal, pea and slack.
5...	4.5	3.75	3.5	3.25	5 37	5.13	5.67	8.4	.60	.30	.25
10...	4.7	3 92	3.66	3 39	5 75	5 53	6	8 8	.64	.34	.28
15...	4.9	4.09	3.82	3.53	6 12	5.92	6 33	9 2	.68	.38	.31
20...	5.1	4.26	3.98	3.67	6 5	6.32	6.67	9.6	.72	.42	.34
25...	5.3	4.43	4.14	3.81	6.87	6.71	7	10	.76	.46	.37
30...	5.5	4.6	4.3	3.95	7.25	7.11	7.33	10 4	.80	.50	.40
35...	5.7	4.77	4.45	4.09	7.62	7.5	7.67	10 8	.84	·54	.43
40...	5.9	4.93	4.6	4.23	8	7.89	8	11.2	.88	.58	.46
45...	6.1	5.09	4.75	4.37	8.37	8.29	8.33	11.6	.92	·62	.49
50...	6.3	5.25	4.9	4.51	8.75	8.68	8.67	12	.96	.66	.52
55...	6.5	5.4	5 04	4.65	9.12	8 95	9	12.4	1.00	.70	.55
60...	6.7	5.55	5.18	4.79	9.5	9.21	9.33	12 8	1.04	.74	.58
65...	6.9	5.7	5 32	4.93	9.87	9.47	9.67	13.2	1.08	.78	.60
70...	7.1	5.85	5 46	5 07	10 25	9.74	10	13.6	1.12	.82	.62
75...	7.3	6	5.6	5.2	10.62	10	10.16	14	1.16	.85	.64
80...	7.5	6.15	5.74	5.33	11	10 26	10.32	14.4	1.20	.88	.66
85...	7.7	6 3	5.88	5.46	11.37	10 53	10.48	14.8	1.24	.91	.68
90...	7.9	6.45	6.02	5.59	11.75	10 79	10 64	15 2	1.28	.94	.70
95...	8	6.6	6.16	5.72	12 12	11.05	10.8	15.6	1.32	.97	.72
100...	8.1	6.75	6.3	5.85	12.5	11.32	10 96	16	1.36	1.00	.74
105...	8.24	6.87	6 41	5.95	12.75	11.53	11.12	16.3	1.40	1.015	.755
110...	8.38	6.99	6.52	6.05	13	11.74	11.28	16.6	1.44	1.03	.77
115...	8.52	7.11	6.63	6.15	13.25	11.95	11.44	16.9	1.48	1.045	.785
120...	8.66	7.23	6.74	6.25	13.5	12.16	11.6	17.2	1.52	1.06	.80
125..·	8.8	7.35	6.85	6.35	13.75	12.37	11.8	17.5	1.55	1.075	.815
130...	8.94	7.46	6.96	6.45	14	12.58	12	17.8	1.58	1.09	.83
135...	9 08	7.57	7.07	6 55	14.25	12.79	12.2	18.1	1.61	1.105	.845
140...	9.22	7.69	7.18	6 65	14 5	13	12.4	18.4	1.64	1.12	.86
145...	9.36	7.79	7.29	6.75	14.75	13 21	12.6	18.7	1.67	1.135	.875
150...	9.5	7.9	7.4	6.85	15	13.42	12.8	19	1.70	1.15	.89
155...	9.63	8.01	7.5	6 95	15.25	13.63	13	19.3	1.73	1.165	.905
160...	9.79	8.12	7.6	7.05	15 5	13.84	13.2	19 6	1.76	1.18	.92
165...	9.89	8.23	7.7	7.15	15.75	14 05	13.4	19 9	1.79	1.195	.935
170...	10.02	8.34	7.8	7.25	16	14.26	13.6	20.2	1.82	1.21	.95
175..·	10.15	8.45	7.9	7.35	16.25	14.47	13.8	20.5	1.85	1.225	.965

MILES.	CARLOAD CLASSES IN CENTS PER 100 LBS.				LIVE STOCK IN CENTS PER 100 LBS.				COAL IN CENTS PER TON OF 2,000 LBS.		
	Wheat, flour, millet, flaxseed.	Corn, oats, barley, other grain and mill-stuffs.	Hard and soft lumber, lath, shingles, sash, doors and blinds.	Salt, lime, cement, plaster, stucco.	Horses and mules in carloads—minimum weight 20,000 lbs., 31-foot cars, inside measurement.	Fat cattle in carloads—minimum weight 19,000 lbs, 31-foot ca..., inside measurement.	Hogs (single deck) in carloads—minimum weight 15,000 lbs., 31-foot cars, inside measurement.	Sheep (single deck) in carloads—minimum weight 10,000 lbs., 31. foot cars, inside measurement.	Hard coal.	Soft coal, lump and nut.	Soft coal, pea and slack.
180...	10 28	8.56	8	7.44	16 5	14.68	14	20.8	1.88	1.24	.98
185...	10.41	8.67	8.1	7.53	16.75	14.89	14.2	21.1	1.91	1.255	.995
190...	10.54	8.78	8.2	7.62	17	15.11	14.4	21.4	1.94	1.27	1.01
195...	10 67	8.89	8.3	7.71	17.25	15.32	14.6	21.7	1.97	1.285	1.025
200...	10.8	9	8.4	7.8	17.5	15.53	14.8	22	2.00	1.30	1.04
210...	11.07	9.23	8.61	8	17.87	16	15.22	22.3	2.04	1.32	1.06
220...	11.34	9.46	8.82	8.2	18.25	16.47	15 64	22.7	2.08	1.34	1.08
230...	11.61	9 69	9.03	8.4	18.62	16.95	16.06	23.1	2.12	1.36	1.10
240...	11.88	9.92	9.24	8.6	19	17.42	16.48	23.5	2.16	1.38	1.12
250...	12.15	10.15	9.45	8.8	19.37	17.89	16.9	23.9	2.20	1.40	1.14
260...	12.42	10.37	9 66	8.99	19.75	18.37	17.32	24.3	2.24	1.42	1.16
270...	12.69	10.59	9 87	9.18	20.12	18.84	17.74	24.7	2.28	1.44	1.18
280...	12 96	10.81	10 08	9 37	20 5	19.32	18.16	25.1	2.32	1.46	1.20
290·..	13.26	11.03	10 29	9.56	20.87	19.79	18.58	25.5	2.36	1.48	1.22
300...	13.53	11.25	10.5	9.75	21.25	20.26	19	25.9	2.40	1.50	1.24
310...	13.8	11.48	10.71	9.95	21.6	20.53	19.13	26.7	2.44	1.52	1.25
320...	14 07	11.71	10.92	10.15	21.95	20.79	19.25	27.1	2.48	1.54	1.26
330...	14.34	11.94	11.13	10.35	23 3	21.05	19.37	27.5	2.52	1.56	1.27
340...	14.61	12.17	11.34	10.55	22.65	21.32	19.5	27.9	2 56	1.58	1.28
350...	14.88	12.4	11.55	10.75	23	21.58	19.62	28.3	2.60	1.60	1.29
360...	15.15	12.62	11.76	10.94	23.35	21.84	19.75	28.7	2.64	1.62	1.30
370...	15.42	12.84	11.97	11.13	23 7	22.11	19.87	29.1	2.68	1.64	1.31
380...	15.68	13.06	12.18	11.32	24 05	22.37	20	29.5	2.72	1 66	1.32
390...	15.94	13.28	12.39	11.51	24 4	22.63	20.5	29.9	2.76	1.68	1.33
400...	16.2	13.5	12.6	11.7	24.75	22.89	21	30.3	2.80	1.70	1.34
410...	16.47	13.72	12.81	11.89	25.1	23.15	21.12	30.7	....	....	..
420...	16.73	13.94	13.02	12.08	25.45	23.41	21.25	31.1	2.88	1.74	1.36
430...	17	14.16	13.23	12.22	25.80	23.67	21.37	31.5	....	....	..
440...	17.27	14.38	13.44	12.46	26.15	23.93	21.5	31.9	2.96	1.78	1.38
450...	17.54	14.60	13.65	12.65	26.5	24.19	21.62	32.3	....	..	..
460...	17.80	14.82	13.86	12.84	26.85	24.45	21.75	32.7	3.04	1.82	1.40
470...	18 06	15.04	14.07	13.03	27 2	24 71	21.87	33.1	....	....	..
430...	18 33	15.26	14.28	13.22	27.55	24 97	22	33.5	3.12	1.86	1.42
490...	18.60	15.48	14.49	13.41	27.9	25.23	22.12	33.9	....	..	..
500...	18.87	15.70	14.70	13.60	28.15	25.49	22.25	34.3	3.20	1.90	1.44

*Stock cattle or feeders and calves take 75 per cent. of fat cattle rate; 31-foot car (internal measurement) is adopted as the standard for minimum weight, as per heading in table; 28-foot cars, 90 per cent. of above; 33-foot 6-inch cars, 108 per cent. of above; other lengths of cars to take same proportion as above.

INDEX.